May 29–31, 2014
Singapore, Singapore

Association for Computing Machinery

Advancing Computing as a Science & Profession

I0041870

SIGMIS-CPR'14

Proceedings of the 2014 Conference on
Computers and People Research

Sponsored by:
ACM SIGMIS

Supported by:
Nanyang Technological University and Information Management Research Center

Association for
Computing Machinery

Advancing Computing as a Science & Profession

The Association for Computing Machinery
2 Penn Plaza, Suite 701
New York, New York 10121-0701

Copyright © 2014 by the Association for Computing Machinery, Inc. (ACM). Permission to make digital or hard copies of portions of this work for personal or classroom use is granted without fee provided that copies are not made or distributed for profit or commercial advantage and that copies bear this notice and the full citation on the first page. Copyright for components of this work owned by others than ACM must be honored. Abstracting with credit is permitted. To copy otherwise, to republish, to post on servers or to redistribute to lists, requires prior specific permission and/or a fee. Request permission to republish from: permissions@acm.org or Fax +1 (212) 869-0481.

For other copying of articles that carry a code at the bottom of the first or last page, copying is permitted provided that the per-copy fee indicated in the code is paid through www.copyright.com.

Notice to Past Authors of ACM-Published Articles

ACM intends to create a complete electronic archive of all articles and/or other material previously published by ACM. If you have written a work that has been previously published by ACM in any journal or conference proceedings prior to 1978, or any SIG Newsletter at any time, and you do NOT want this work to appear in the ACM Digital Library, please inform permissions@acm.org, stating the title of the work, the author(s), and where and when published.

ISBN: 978-1-4503-2625-4 (Digital)

ISBN: 978-1-4503-3080-0 (Print)

Additional copies may be ordered prepaid from:

ACM Order Department
PO Box 30777
New York, NY 10087-0777, USA

Phone: 1-800-342-6626 (USA and Canada)
+1-212-626-0500 (Global)
Fax: +1-212-944-1318
E-mail: acmhelp@acm.org
Hours of Operation: 8:30 am – 4:30 pm ET

Printed in the USA

Foreword

It is our great pleasure to welcome you to the 52nd Association of Computing Machinery Annual Computers and People Research Conference - *ACM SIGMIS CPR 2014*. In the past 51 years, ACM SIGMIS CPR has engaged the academic and practitioner communities towards understanding issues at the intersection of society, organizations, individuals and information technology (IT). This year's conference is the third, in its long history to take place outside North America. This edition of the conference is the first to be held in Asia, specifically in Singapore. Singapore is known for its nation-level IT implementation and as a hub for IT service delivery. It is timely, therefore, that we explore – "The Globalization of IT Work"; this year's theme.

The globalization of IT work that began with the "offshoring" of IT work to Asia has now matured and transformed into a globalized phenomenon. The nature of IT work now routinely requires access to centers of knowledge and expertise that are dispersed across the globe. The globalization of IT work has benefited the Asian IT workforce; as it does in Latin America and Africa. But, global and globalized IT work has also raised a number of challenges and issues. IT professionals now face problems of collaboration, coordination, control, and knowledge transfer due to the geographical and cultural distances between them.

Towards this end, the papers and panels within this proceedings address topics ranging from the development of cultural competencies to the development of an IT workforce that meets the current work demands. This edition of the proceedings also includes studies in enduring topics such as stress and IT education. We hope the papers in these proceedings serve as a valuable reference for computer and people researchers and practitioners in the coming years.

Putting together the ACM SIGMIS CPR 2014 conference was made possible by the work of many dedicated individuals. We thank the authors for providing content for the program. We are grateful to the program committee, led by Indira Guzman and Rajiv Kishore, who worked diligently to develop the conference program; the many academics who reviewed papers and provided constructive feedback for authors. In addition, we are indebted to Mike Gallivan for organizing this year's doctoral consortium; and to Susan Yager for her role as Treasurer. Finally, we appreciate the work of our publicity team comprising Nita Brooks, Shirish C. Srivastava, Liisa Von Hellens and Mike Dixon. Special thanks go to Lisa Tolles and her team at Sheridan Communications for their work in processing this proceedings in a timely manner.

Finally, we thank our sponsors - SIGMIS, the Nanyang Business School (Nanyang Technological University) and the Information Management Research Centre (Nanyang Business School) - for their support of this conference.

We hope that you will find these proceedings beneficial and that the conference will provide you with a valuable opportunity to share ideas with other researchers and practitioners from institutions around the world.

Damien Joseph
Nanyang Technological University
Conference Co-Chair

Conrad Shayo
California State University, San Bernardino
Conference Co-Chair

Table of Contents

Journal Editors Panel
Canning Room I & II

Industry Panel: Globalization of IT Work
Canning Room I & II

Session I: Behavioral Issues
Grand Ballroom I

Session I: IT Workforce Development
Grand Ballroom I

Session II: Knowledge Sharing and Research Design
Grand Ballroom I

Session II: Innovation and Strategy
Grand Ballroom I

Keynote
Grand Ballroom I

Session III: Women in IT
Grand Ballroom I

Session III: Children and IT
Grand Ballroom I

Panel: Active Learning Approaches in Information Technology (IT)
Grand Ballroom I

Panel: Corporate Psychopaths: Implications for the IS Workforce
Grand Ballroom I

Session IV: Methodological Developments
Canning Room I & II

Session IV: IT Workforce Behavioral Issues
Canning Room I & II

Session V: Future Development for IS Personnel
Canning Room I & II

Session V: Globally Distributed Teams
Canning Room I & II

ACM SIGMIS CPR 2014 Conference Organization

Conference Chairs: Damien Joseph, Nanyang Technological University
Conrad Shayo, California State University, San Bernardino

Program Chairs: Indira R. Guzman, Trident University International
Rajiv Kishore, SUNY at Buffalo

Doctoral Consortium Chair: Michael J. Gallivan, Georgia State University

Doctoral Consortium Mentors: Deb Armstrong, Florida State University
Genevieve Bassellier, McGill University
Maung K. Sein, Agder University
Cindy Riemenschneider, Baylor University

Treasurer & Registration Chair: Susan Yager, Southern Illinois University Edwardsville

Local Arrangements Chairs: Damien Joseph, Nanyang Technological University
Lai-Tee Cheok, Singapore Management University

Publicity Committee: Nita Brooks, Middle Tennessee State University
Shirish C. Srivastava, HEC Paris, France
Liisa Von Hellens, Griffith University
Mike Dixon, Murdoch University

Program Committee Members: Monica Adya, Marquette University
Vangel Ajanovski, Saints Cyril and Methodius University
Jorn Altmann, Seoul National University
Deb Armstrong, Florida State University
Nita Brooks, Middle Tennessee State University
Darlinton Carvalho, Federal University of São João Del-Rei!
Stipe Celar, University of Split
Dan Daniels, Oakwood University
Tom Dillon, James Madison University
Thomas Ferratt, University of Dayton
Sven Laumer, University of Bamberg
Diane Lending, James Madison University
Gaetan Mourmant, IESEG School of Management
Robert Muehlbacher, Focus Solutions
Makoto Nakayama, Depaul University
Sandra Newton, Sonoma State University
Shari Plantz-Masters, Regis University
James Pomykalski, Susquehanna University
Norah Power, University of Limerick

Program Committee Members:

(continued)   Jeria Quesenberry, Carnegie Mellon University

Malu Roldan, San Jose State University

Ilias Santouridis, Technological Educational Institute of Thessaly

Tenace Setor, Nanyang Technological University

Jun Shen, University of Wollongong

Ven Yu Sien, HELP University

M. Rita Thissen, RTI International

James Tollerson, West Georgia Technical College

Greg Tutunjian, scrum doc

Karthikeyan Umapathy, University of North Florida

Faith-Michael Uzoka, Mount Royal University

Gianluigi Viscusi, University of Milano-Bicocca

Kevin White, University of Maryland, Baltimore County

Manuel Wiesche, Technische Universität München

Elaine Yakura, Michigan State University

Fani Zlatarova, Elizabethtown College

ACM SIGMIS CPR 2014 Sponsor & Supporters

Sponsor:  **sigmis**

Supporters: NANYANG TECHNOLOGICAL UNIVERSITY

Nanyang Business School

IMARC
Information Management Research Centre
Nanyang Technological University

Editors Panel

Deborah J. Armstrong
Florida State University
600 W. College Avenue
Tallahassee, Florida 32306 USA
+1-850-644-8228
djarmstrong@cob.fsu.edu

Genevieve Bassellier
McGill University
1001 rue Sherbrooke Ouest
Montreal, Quebec, Canada H3A 1G5
+1-514-398-4221
genevieve.bassellier@mcgill.ca

Thomas W. Ferratt
University of Dayton
300 College Park
Dayton, Ohio 45469 USA
+1-937-229-2728
tferratt1@udayton.edu

Rajiv Kishore
State University of New York at Buffalo
325N Jacobs Management Center
Buffalo, New York 14260-4000 USA
+1-716-645-3507
rkishore@buffalo.edu

Fay Cobb Payton
North Carolina State University
Campus Box 7229
Raleigh, North Carolina 27695 USA
+1-919-513-2744
fay_payton@ncsu.edu

Maung K. Sein
University of Agder
Servis Boks 422
4604 Kristiansand, Norway
+47 38141617
maung.k.sein@uia.no

Janice C. Sipior
Villanova University
800 Lancaster Avenue
Villanova, PA 19073 USA
+1-610-519-4347
janice.sipior@villanova.edu

ABSTRACT

The purpose of the Editors Panel session is to provide attendees with an opportunity to meet and interact with journal editors from leading international IS journals.

Categories and Subject Descriptors

A.0 GENERAL.

General Terms

Human Factors.

Keywords

IS journals; publishing; submission requirements; peer review.

1. PANEL OVERVIEW

This panel targets scholars seeking to gain insights into successfully publishing in leading international IS journals. Editors will discuss what they expect from submissions and their experiences in the editorial process. Attendees will benefit by gaining insights from the perspective of editors. Attendees may further benefit by asking questions about manuscript preparation, submission requirements, the review process, responding to peer reviewers' comments, and preparing the final article. After the session, interested attendees can talk with the editors and collect information about the journals, such as flyers or calls for papers.

2. PANELISTS

The panel is comprised of faculty who hold editorial positions with the following leading international IS journals:

- Deborah J. Armstrong, Managing Editor of Information Technology and People
- Genevieve Bassellier, Associate Editor of MIS Quarterly
- Thomas W. Ferratt, Senior Editor of Journal of the AIS
- Rajiv Kishore, Associate Editor of Information & Management
- Fay Cobb Payton, Editor-in-Chief of Health Systems and Associate Editor of Information Technology and People
- Maung K. Sein, Senior Editor of Journal of the AIS
- Janice C. Sipior, Editor-in-Chief of Information Systems Management

Permission to make digital or hard copies of part or all of this work for personal or classroom use is granted without fee provided that copies are not made or distributed for profit or commercial advantage and that copies bear this notice and the full citation on the first page. Copyrights for third-party components of this work must be honored. For all other uses, contact the Owner/Author.Copyright is held by the owner/author(s).

SIGMIS-CPR '14, May 29-31 2014, Singapore, Singapore
ACM 978-1-4503-2625-4/14/05.
http://dx.doi.org/10.1145/2599990.2602233

Industry Panel: Globalization of IT Work

Rajiv Kishore
SUNY at Buffalo, USA
rkishore@buffalo.edu
(Moderator)

Shveta Arora
Infosys
Singapore
shveta@infosys.com

Ramakrishna (Ramki) Desiraju
IBM Global Business Services
Singapore
ramki@sg.ibm.com

K. Ravi Kumar
Nanyang Technological University
Singapore
rkumar@ntu.edu.sg

Sudhakar Nibhanupudi
Standard Chartered Bank
Singapore
nibhanupudi.sudhakar@sc.com

Balu Thyagarajan
Hewlett-Packard
Singapore
balu_t@yahoo.com

ABSTRACT
The purpose of the Industry Panel session is to provide attendees with an opportunity to hear the views of a distinguished group of panelists on the theme of the conference, particularly as they relate to the future opportunities and challenges that organizations and individuals may face in the arena of globalization of IT work.

1. PANEL OVERVIEW
The globalization of IT work that began modestly with "offshoring" of software maintenance work in the early 1990s has now matured and transformed into a true globalization phenomenon. Companies of all stripes and sizes now routinely distribute their IT and IT-enabled business processes to various countries around the globe, thus gaining access to knowledge and diverse talent pools. While IT-enabled globalization has the potential to create benefits for companies, realizing those benefits requires the development of new capabilities to overcome the several challenges that are often associated with global projects and processes due to geographic, time zone, cultural, language, and legal system distances and differences. Some of these challenges include cross-cultural collaboration, distributed coordination and control, and knowledge transfer in virtual team settings, leveraging the global workforce for innovation, managing contracts and relationships with alliance partners and providers of IT services, and dealing with work-life balance issues for the IT workforce.

This industry panel will include a distinguished group of industry executives from global IT services firms and firms in industry verticals as well as distinguished academics. The panel discussion will focus on the challenges of global IT and IT-enabled work from an industry perspective, highlighted above, and the best practices to overcome these challenges and create measurable organizational value from globalization of IT and IT-enabled business processes. The intent is to provide insights from real world examples of global IT projects that highlight the importance of these challenges and the practices that have given positive results. The panelists have a wide variety of experiences, approaches, and practices. This session is designed to provide a rich, multi-faceted view on the benefits, challenges, and lessons learned from real-world examples of globalization of IT and IT-enabled work.

2. PROFILE OF PANELISTS
Ms. Shveta Arora: Ms. Arora is a global business leader with Infosys having worked across the US, India, Japan and other APAC geographies in various capacities. She has over 20 years of experience in the field of business consulting, business development and account management. Ms. Arora is currently based in Singapore and is responsible for growing Infosys' Retail, CPG & logistics business for the APAC region. Prior to this she was leading strategic client relationships for Infosys based out of US. Before Infosys, Ms. Arora worked for A.T. Kearney and ST Microelectronics. She holds an MBA from IIM, Bangalore and B.E from Delhi University in India.

Dr. Ramakrishna (Ramki) Desiraju: Dr. Desiraju is a Partner and Vice President in IBM Global Business Services. He serves as the Global Lead Account Partner to the IBM CIO. He represents Global Business Services on the CIO's global leadership team and manages application development and software delivery for IBM worldwide. He leads a global team operating out of 40 countries, leveraging key innovations and capabilities in software engineering, business modeling, talent management and project delivery. Previously, Dr. Desiraju served as the leader responsible for Application Management Services and Global Delivery in North America. He oversaw a practice that creates and delivers a complete set of solutions for application maintenance services with a portfolio exceeding $2.5B with 20,000 practitioners. He oversaw global delivery to offer the best value proposition to the customers, leveraging IBM's vast network of global delivery centers in India, Philippines, China and Brazil, serving customers in US and Canada. He was one of the six services leaders expatriated to India to improve the competitive edge of its India Global Delivery which he accomplished by establishing the global delivery supply chain service line and subsequently transforming the global delivery center operating model. Previously, Dr. Desiraju served as the lead account partner on select global electronics customers. Dr. Desiraju has a broad background in global operations, practice management, business transformation, operations integration, analysis, design, planning and management of supply chains, service organizations, manufacturing, and distribution systems. He has over 19 years of extensive knowledge in supply chain management, decision support systems, mathematical modeling, analysis and design. He has managed client relationships and portfolios of client projects for large enterprises. Dr. Desiraju is the recipient of several awards including the 2011 Asian American Executive of the Year. In

Permission to make digital or hard copies of part or all of this work for personal or classroom use is granted without fee provided that copies are not made or distributed for profit or commercial advantage, and that copies bear this notice and the full citation on the first page. Copyrights for third-party components of this work must be honored. For all other uses, contact the owner/author(s). Copyright is held by the author/owner(s).

SIGMIS-CPR'14, May 29–31, 2014, Singapore, Singapore.
ACM 978-1-4503-2625-4/14/05.
http://dx.doi.org/10.1145/2599990.2602232

addition to publishing in leading journals, Dr. Desiraju is the Principal Investigator on three patents.

Dr. Rajiv Kishore: Dr. Kishore's research interests are in global IT outsourcing, IT innovation, knowledge management, social media/social web, and health IT management. He predominantly uses quantitative empirical research methods with primary field surveys and secondary data, but has also used qualitative methods including in-depth case studies, interviews, and the grounded theory methodology. His research on IT outsourcing was funded by the National Science Foundation as a Co-PI with a large, multi-year grant. Dr. Kishore's research papers have been published in premier journals including MIS Quarterly, Journal of Management Information Systems, Information & Management, Decision Support Systems, and IEEE Transactions on Engineering Management. He has also presented numerous research papers at international, national, and regional conferences, and has also participated in panels at conferences. He currently serves as an Associate Editor for Information & Management, a premier journal in the IS field. Earlier, he served as a guest Co-Editor of a special issue of the Journal of the Association for Information Systems, the flagship journal of the Association for Information Systems (AIS), and as the Co-Editor-in-Chief of the Journal of Information Technology Theory and Application, a journal of the AIS. He also continues to speak with industry and professional groups on topics of his research interests. Before joining the academia, Dr. Kishore worked in the industry for more than 12 years in the IT services and strategic consulting arenas. He has consulted with several large companies including Blue Cross Blue Shield of Minnesota, BellSouth, Dun and Bradstreet Software, Pioneer Standard Electronics, and IBM, and continues to leverage his rich industry and consulting experience in both the classroom as well as his research activities.

Dr. K. Ravi Kumar: Dr. Kumar is the Shaw Chair Professor and Dean of Nanyang Business School at Nanyang Technological University (NTU). He joined NTU in June 2013 from the Marshall School of Business in the University of Southern California (USC), where he was a professor in the Department of Information and Operations Management. Dr. Kumar has held many key leadership roles in several academic institutions. He was chairman of Marshall's information and operations management department from 1989 to 1994, Vice-Dean for International Programs from 2003 to 2006, and Vice-Dean for Graduate Programs from 2004 to 2006. From 2009 to 2011, he served as Distinguished Professor and Dean of the College of Business at Korea Advanced Institute of Science and Technology (KAIST), on a leave of absence from USC. During his term at KAIST, Dr. Kumar implemented reforms to create a world-class business school. The institute broke into the Financial Times Global MBA Rankings in 2011, the first Korean business school to be ranked among the top 100 listing. In his 27 years at USC Marshall, Dr. Kumar had responsibilities in several key initiatives. He was Executive Director for the school's experiential learning courses for MBA and undergraduate students. These involve faculty across a diverse range of disciplines and over 150 companies in Asia-Pacific and Latin American countries every year. He was also a long-standing champion for USC Marshall's globalisation. In 2004, he launched in Shanghai, a global EMBA degree programme in collaboration with Shanghai Jiao Tong University. And in 2013, he was set to launch a Master of Science degree programme in global supply chain management across India, China, South Korea and the US, which employed a hybrid model of online and face-to-face teaching. Before joining USC in 1986, Dr. Kumar taught at the University of Illinois at Urbana-Champaign. He has received several teaching excellence awards from both the University of Illinois (Outstanding Educator Award) and USC (Golden Apple Award). Dr. Kumar received his Bachelor of Technology degree in Mechanical Engineering from the Indian Institute of Technology in Madras, India. He holds a Master of Science degree in Industrial Engineering from the University of Texas, and a PhD from the Industrial Engineering and Management Sciences Department at Northwestern University. Dr. Kumar's research interests include management issues in continuous quality improvement, including environmental aspects; flexible and cellular manufacturing systems; economic modeling of functional integration between marketing and manufacturing; as well as the development of sustainable information technology industries in developing countries (such as IT hardware in Taiwan and software in India). His research has been funded by major corporations and organisations such as Nike, TRW, Fidelity Investments, Caterpillar, Bourns Instrument, Southern California Edison as well as the National Science Foundation. He has extensive international consulting experience, including projects with Nike, Rolls Royce, BMW, Daimler Benz Aerospace, ABB, Ericsson, BAX Global, Motorola, Reuters, Du Pont, Korean Air, Infosys, Acer, and Shell Hong Kong. He has authored and co-authored more than 60 articles, which have been published in top academic journals such as Management Science, Marketing Science, Journal of Economic Theory, Production and Operations Management, Journal of Operations Management and Journal of Management Information Systems. Dr. Kumar serves on the board of several companies, including Korea Exchange Bank in South Korea. He was a former board member of Goodwill Industries in Southern California. From 2000 to 2001, he served as a member of a special interest group advising the Indian Ministry for Information Technology on IT hardware and software policies.

Mr. Sudhakar Nibhanupudi: Mr. Nibhanupudi has over 20 years of experience in banking technology. He has worked in application design & development, program management, support, and M&A areas covering financial markets, core banking, finance, customer experience, statements, data warehousing, business intelligence, and application integration services. He has worked in various capacities with Standard Chartered Bank in India, UK, and Singapore. He has vast experience in successfully setting up, building, and delivering large programs of work in offshore model. He currently heads up the technology delivery function globally for information management and application integration, with teams based in Singapore, India, Malaysia, and Philippines.

Mr. Balu Thyagarajan: Mr. Thyagarajan has built and delivered IT services over the past 30 years in multiple client engagements with P&L responsibility. His experience spans the entire spectrum of IT in multiple domains -Telecom, Infrastructure, and Financial Services industries cutting across applications, BPO, networks, operating systems and hardware. He has engaged in strategic planning, sales, portfolio consolidation, solution development, service delivery, project management, and operations management. He was instrumental in winning and setting up the Facilities Management Business in Wipro. He has international experience – Asia Pacific and Americas - building strong client relationships and teams working in multiple locations including setting up offshore development centers in India. He is currently working for HP as a program manager and has worked for Satyam, Wipro, Tata Burroughs in the past.

Stars Matter – How FLOSS Developers' Reputation Affects the Attraction of New Developers

Andreas Schilling
Centre of Human Resources Information Systems
University of Bamberg, Germany
+49 951 8632873

andreas.schilling@uni-bamberg.de

Sven Laumer
Centre of Human Resources Information Systems
University of Bamberg, Germany
+49 951 8632873

sven.laumer@uni-bamberg.de

Tim Weitzel
Centre of Human Resources Information Systems
University of Bamberg, Germany
+49 951 8632871

tim.weitzel@uni-bamberg.de

ABSTRACT

The attraction of new developers is a key challenge for initiatives developing Free Libre Open Source Software (FLOSS). While previous evaluations consider status gains and competence evaluations to be key drivers for novices' joining behavior, it is unclear how FLOSS developers' relationships with others affect the attraction of new developers. In this research, we look at FLOSS developers' relationships in terms of positive evaluations given by others. Using this perspective, we examine how FLOSS developers' reputation among members within and beyond the project community affects their projects' ability to attract new developers. We draw on Social Resource Theory (SRT) and hypothesize that developers with a high reputation among others enjoy high visibility and credibility, which in turn helps their projects to attract new members. Finally, we propose an evaluation approach for our research model that examines the reputation and project behavior of more than 1,000 FLOSS developers on a longitudinal base.

Categories and Subject Descriptors

K.6.1 [**Management of Computing and Information Systems**]: Project and People Management - Staffing

General Terms

Management, Measurement, Human Factors,

Keywords

Free Libre Open Source Software, Open Source Software Development, Attraction, Reputation, Social Resource Theory

1. INTRODUCTION

Initiatives developing Free Libre Open Source Software (FLOSS) are an important element in our daily life. Today, more than every

Permission to make digital or hard copies of all or part of this work for personal or classroom use is granted without fee provided that copies are not made or distributed for profit or commercial advantage and that copies bear this notice and the full citation on the first page. Copyrights for components of this work owned by others than the author(s) must be honored. Abstracting with credit is permitted. To copy otherwise, or republish, to post on servers or to redistribute to lists, requires prior specific permission and/or a fee. Request permissions from permissions@acm.org.

SIGMIS-CPR'14, May 29–31, 2014, Singapore, Singapore.
Copyright is held by the owner/author(s). Publication rights licensed to ACM.
ACM 978-1-4503-2625-4/14/05...$15.00.
http://dx.doi.org/10.1145/2599990.2599991

second firm relies on FLOSS for its mission critical tasks [8]. In addition, most private households use FLOSS for browsing the Internet [25]. However, despite these broad adoption rates, many study results suggest that the majority of all FLOSS projects fails; most commonly, due to a lack of contributors [7]. Hence, the attraction of new developers becomes a key challenge for FLOSS initiatives to succeed. Existing FLOSS research examined this aspect from either an individual-centric or a group-centric perspective. Individual-centric studies commonly analyze the motives which make developers to become active in a FLOSS project. Many of these studies come to the conclusion that novices are commonly driven by status gains and competence evaluations to join FLOSS projects [14]. In contrast, evaluations with a group-centric research perspective examine the role of novices' relationships to the developers of a FLOSS project. These studies similarly stress that novices have to perceive a competent and supportive project atmosphere to become active in the project. However, there is a general dissent if and to which degree FLOSS relationships with others actually stimulate the attraction of new developers. While Grewal et al. provide evidence that project members' connectedness to other developers does not necessarily lead to a higher attraction rate [10] other evaluations support the positive role of project members' relationships to other developers [11]. With respect to this dissent, managers of FLOSS projects find themselves in a situation where they are aware of the importance to attract new developers, while not knowing how to act practically.

This research examines how FLOSS projects can attract newcomers by satisfying their needs for status and competence. To do so, we take a differentiated perspective on FLOSS developers' interactions. In contrast to existing literature which commonly infers personal ties between FLOSS developers based on overlaps in their contribution or mailing-list behavior, we look at the evaluations of FLOSS developers given by others. This perspective allows us to distinguish between FLOSS developers who are appreciated by others from those who are considered confounders. Building on this new perspective, this research examines how FLOSS developers' reputation among users and developers of related projects (the project community) and beyond affects their projects' attraction of new developers. As the theoretical foundation for our research, we draw on Social Resource Theory (SRT) [16]. According to SRT, individuals have access to various beneficial resources (e.g. power, authority, etc.)

based on their position in the social hierarchy. As a result, SRT considers the connectedness to high status individuals essential to achieve beneficial economic outcomes. With respect to the similarities between the social-hierarchy described in SRT and FLOSS projects' meritocracy, we draw on SRT to understand how FLOSS developers' reputation among others can help their projects in attracting new members. Therefore, we examine the research question:

Does FLOSS developers' reputation within and beyond the project community help their projects to attract new developers?

By examining this question, our research contributes to literature and practice. On the one hand, we add to FLOSS literature by looking at interpersonal relationships in a completely new way. By doing so our research can help to bring together the different results of previous evaluations. On the other hand, our research provides practical advice for project managers on how to foster the attraction of new members. Beyond the FLOSS context, our research contributes to the organizational domain as researchers recommend considering knowledge workers as volunteers [6]. In particular, our research complements literature which evaluates the consequences of employees' activities in Social Network Sites (SNS). Moreover, our research may help organizations to attract new talent by showcasing the competence and reputation of their current employees.

For the purpose of presenting our research model and proposing an evaluation strategy, this paper is structured as follows: In the next sections, we present the current status quo on literature regarding the attraction of FLOSS developers and SRT. Hereafter, we provide theoretical arguments and develop our research model. For evaluating our research hypotheses we propose a measurement model which is based on a longitudinal analysis of more than 1,000 FLOSS developers. Finally, we discuss the expected implications of our research.

2. FLOSS RESEARCH

Existing FLOSS literature commonly examines the attraction of developers either from an individual- or a group-centric research perspective. Prior FLOSS studies using an individual-centric research approach examined the motives which drive new developers to join a particular FLOSS project. These studies commonly highlight the role of extrinsic motives for newcomers to become active in a FLOSS project. According to Fang and Neufeld, new developers need to perceive their project participation as instrumental in order to become active in a FLOSS project [7]. Such a concrete need may be either to add certain functionality to the FLOSS project or to achieve a personal goal, such as learning [23]. Moreover, Raymond considers status gains as a key driver for newcomers' project commitment [18]. In a similar vein, Roberts et al. [19] and Ke and Zhang [14] highlight status gains as an important driver for FLOSS developers' project commitment.

In contrast, FLOSS literature with a group-centric research perspective used either a structural or a relational approach to examine the effects of developers' relationships on the attraction of new developers. Studies taking a relational approach on the role of FLOSS developers' relationships stress the importance of trust. According to Stewart and Gosain, there are two inherent different forms of trust which are relevant to FLOSS developers [26]. On the one hand, cognitive trust, which stems from individuals' positive competence evaluations of one another. This form of trust describes the degree to which a developer is confident that another developer's contributions are useful and

helpful to the FLOSS project. On the other hand, affective trust between individuals describes FLOSS developers' emotional attachment to each other. This form of trust arises between FLOSS developers when there is a supportive atmosphere amongst them [26]. But high levels of cognitive and affective trust do not only foster FLOSS developers' teamwork but also their projects' ability to attract new developers. In the case of cognitive trust, outsiders to the project are more likely to evaluate the competence of the involved developers positively, which in turn makes them believe that their participation efforts are well invested. In contrast, affective trust stimulates newcomers to join as it ensures them that the project provides a supportive climate for their contribution. The development of these two forms of trust is not distinct but rather intertwined. For example, Stewart and Gosain point out that cognitive trust between team members leads to affective trust, which in turn positively affects a project's team size [26]. Xu and Jones support the important role of cognitive trust for FLOSS developers [27].

Research using a structural approach for examining the effects of group-level aspects on the attraction of new developers examines the role of the overall interaction network. Hahn et al. provide evidence that FLOSS developers' connectedness to others has a strong effect on their projects' inflow of new developers [11]. In contrast, Grewal et al. show in their evaluation that a project manager's connectedness to other projects has *per se* no direct effects on the attraction of new project members [10]. Despite this disagreement on the role of personal ties, many studies provide evidence for the existence of preferential attachment among FLOSS developers [13]. This phenomenon is also known as 'the rich get richer' and describes FLOSS developers' tendency to join those projects where experienced and well-known developers are involved. However, this means at the same time that projects with developers who are less known among others have difficulties in attracting new members.

This research seeks to bring together existing individual-centric and group-centric approaches to derive a comprehensive understanding for the attraction of FLOSS developers. With respect to prior motivational research, we assume that FLOSS projects need to offer newcomers the perspective of status gains and a competent and supportive team atmosphere. In contrast to existing structural studies, we do not expect that there needs to be a direct personal relationship between the involved developers and novices to stimulate them to join the project. Instead, we suppose that novices' joining behavior is largely influenced by the reputation of the involved developers. With this theory, we build on prior study results by Schilling et al. which indicate that developers with a high reputation in the particular project community foster considerably the working motivation of the project members they have worked with [21]. With respect to these evaluation results, we propose that the reputation of the developers involved in a FLOSS project exerts a similar stimulating effect on the attraction of new project members. In order to derive a nuanced understanding for these effects, we look not only at FLOSS developers' reputation within but also beyond the project community. In the following section we detail SRT, which provides the theoretic foundation for our evaluation.

3. SOCIAL RESOURCE THEORY (SRT)

In contrast to social-network theories which consider the benefits of members' personal relationships in terms of the heterogeneity of their interaction partners [9] or based on characteristics in the overall interaction topology [2], Social Resource Theory (SRT) focuses on individuals' social status [16]. The basic tenet of SRT is that individuals' status is defined by a social hierarchy, e.g. by individuals' level of education, their previous job position or the prestige of their current job [16]. Individuals with a high position in this social hierarchy have accesses to various tangible (e.g. financial resources) and intangible (e.g. high visibility, reachability, power, etc.) resources. With respect to this resource allocation, individuals in high status positions are more successful in achieving economic outcomes by utilizing their resources and connections to others [16]. Although individuals in low status positions may also have social relations to each other, SRT suggests that these relationships are less helpful for achieving favorable economic outcomes. Hence, people with low social status need to seek relations to persons with a high status position in order to gain beneficial outcomes. Moreover, because of their existing power and social contacts, it is much easier for high status individuals to gain additional resources than it is for low status individuals.

Evaluations within the organizational context support the validity of SRT. For example, study results by Casey suggest that entrepreneurs with a low status generally receive less funding than their high status counterparts [3]. Further, Seibert et al. provide evidence that relationships to employees in high positions within the organization are especially relevant for employees to advance their career [22]. In a similar vein, research by Cross and Cummings suggests that consultants achieve better performance ratings if they have contact to individuals in high status positions [5]. In the following section, we will draw on SRT to develop our research hypotheses regarding the influence of FLOSS developers' reputation on the attraction of new developers.

4. HYPOTHESES DEVELOPMENT

With respect to previous evaluations within the organizational domain, we build on SRT to understand how FLOSS developers' reputation can enhance their projects' ability to attract new members. We suppose that those FLOSS developers who have a high reputation in the project community are more closely observed by others than developers with a low reputation. In particular, we consider the high visibility and credibility to be key resources for attracting newcomers from the project community and beyond. Moreover, we suppose that not only a FLOSS developer's reputation within but also beyond the project community can catalyst the influx of new developers. Figure 1 visualizes our research model.

FLOSS projects generally follow a meritocracy; this means that a developer's status within a FLOSS project is determined by the recognition and appreciation of his or her code contributions. Because of this, top contributors are observed more closely and are considered more competent than regular developers. With regard to SRT, we consider both of these characteristics important for attracting new developers. On the one hand, top contributors' high visibility ensures that the projects to which they contribute enjoy high publicity in the corresponding project community, which encompasses users and developers of related projects. On the other hand, because of the meritocracy in FLOSS projects, top contributors are also associated with a higher level of competence. This satisfies the wish of many novices that the FLOSS project, they contribute to, succeeds [23]. Hence, in line with SRT, we suppose that those FLOSS projects with developers who have a high reputation amongst members of the project community are better in attracting new members. Previous evaluations within the FLOSS context support this assumption. According to Roberts et al., developers' project participation is strongly driven by their wish to improve their community status [19]. In a similar vein, Ke

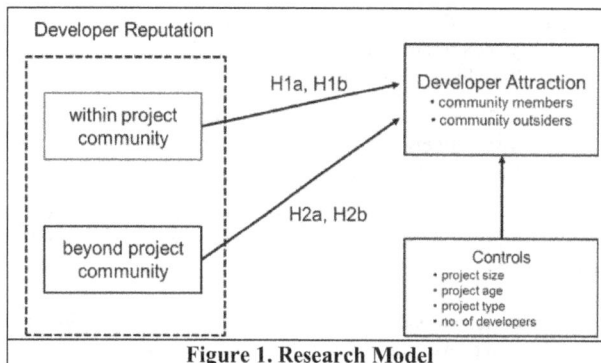

Figure 1. Research Model

and Zhang provide evidence that developers' task efforts are strongly dependent on the level of recognition within the project community [15]. In line with these results, we suppose that FLOSS developers choose projects in which developers with a high reputation within the project community are active, as they give them a higher visibility and better changes to improve their standing within the project community. With respect to the common engagement of FLOSS developers in multiple projects [12] we suppose further that those developers with a high reputation among members of the project community are well known beyond community boarders. As a result, we expect that contributors with a high reputation among community members also enjoy a high level of visibility and appreciation outside the project community. Hence, we suppose that the reputation of the involved developers within the project community increases their FLOSS projects' attraction of both community members and community outsiders.

Hypothesis 1a: FLOSS developers' reputation within the project community positively affects their project's ability to attract members from the project community.

Hypothesis 1b: FLOSS developers' reputation within the project community positively affects their project's ability to attract members from outside the project community.

Further, we suppose that FLOSS developers' reputation among outsiders of the project community, has a stimulating effect on the attraction of new developers. This is because FLOSS communities are commonly not isolated from each other. Both developers and users are often committed to multiple FLOSS projects [12]. Therefore, it seems likely that contributors with a high reputation among community members are also known beyond the project community. As a result, it is possible that, FLOSS developers who gained a high reputation outside their current project community could also enjoy high appreciation among members of their current project community, for example, if they are known for expertise which is currently lacking in the project. In such situations project members' external reputation is much more relevant than their reputation within the project community. Moreover, FLOSS developers who gained a high reputation outside their current project community may still be watched by their former colleagues, which in turn stimulates the attraction of community outsiders. Hence, with respect to FLOSS projects' interrelatedness, we suppose that developers with a high external reputation increase the influx of new developers from within and outside the project community to their projects. Therefore, we hypothesize that:

Hypothesis 2a: FLOSS developers' reputation beyond the project community positively affects their project's ability to attract members from the project community.

Hypothesis 2b: FLOSS developers' reputation beyond the project community positively affects their project's ability to attract members from outside the project community.

In addition to FLOSS developers' reputation, we consider several control variables in our research model. First we control for the **project size**. In line with Colazo and Fang [4] we expect that larger FLOSS projects can offer new developers much more possibilities to add or modify functionality than small projects can. Moreover, we control for FLOSS **projects' age**. This is because older projects are generally more mature in terms of functionality and documentation, which makes it easier for new developers to join. Another characteristic which we control for is the **project type**, as it can be a key factor regarding the interest and the amount of potential new developers [20]. Finally, we consider a FLOSS project's **number of developers.** Following research results by Oh and Jeon we suppose that a higher developer count makes a FLOSS project not only more visible but also more attractive for potential novices [17].

5. RESEARCH METHODOLOGY

In order to evaluate our research hypotheses, we rely on a diverse set of secondary data sources. The use of secondary data provides several key advantages for our evaluation. First, the recorded data enables us to derive objective measures to analyze FLOSS developers' project participation and determine precisely the point in time when they joined a FLOSS project. In comparison, subjective measures depend essentially on individuals' accurate memories. Moreover, the use of archival data gives us the possibility to derive a comprehensive picture of how developers' reputation affects both novices from within and beyond the project community, without having to achieve a certain response rate. Finally, the use of archival data enables us to study the effects of FLOSS developers' reputation on a longitudinal base without having to survey developers multiple times.

By bringing together a rich developer community and a broad project spectrum, the K Desktop Environment (KDE) provides an appropriate research setting for our evaluation. KDE is a popular desktop environment for UNIX systems. With more than 1,000 registered developers, it is one of the largest FLOSS communities worldwide. In particular, KDE encompasses more than 300 different FLOSS projects. Another advantage for our research is that KDE has a popular portal (*http://kde-look.org/*) where users and developers of the KDE community can register and share their desktop settings. In the following, we describe how we will measure FLOSS developers' reputation (within and beyond the project community) and their projects' attraction of new developers.

For examining **FLOSS developers' reputation** on a longitudinal base, we will use archival data from the SNS Ohloh.com. Ohloh is an online community for FLOSS projects. It allows users and developers of FLOSS projects to register and send each other 'Kudos'. Kudos resemble a form of appreciation for the work or assistance that the receiver provided to the sender [13]. Ohloh provides access to these Kudo relationships including their exchange date through its public Application Programming Interface (API). Using this API, we wrote programming routines which extract the received Kudos for all KDE developers and recursively the Kudos received by the senders. Overall, this collection routine will collect approximately 34,000 Kudo records

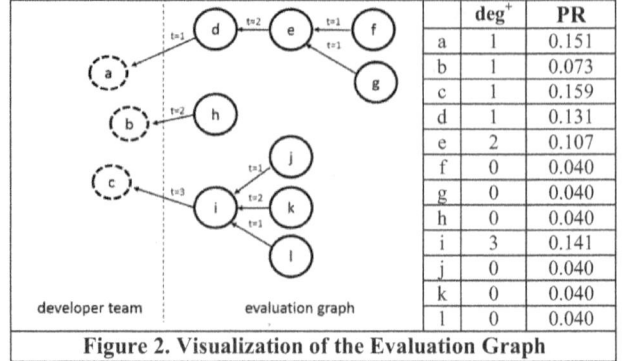

	deg$^+$	PR
a	1	0.151
b	1	0.073
c	1	0.159
d	1	0.131
e	2	0.107
f	0	0.040
g	0	0.040
h	0	0.040
i	3	0.141
j	0	0.040
k	0	0.040
l	0	0.040

Figure 2. Visualization of the Evaluation Graph

from over 8,000 Ohloh accounts (n). In a second step, we use this data to construct a directed graph. In this graph, nodes represent KDE developers respectively their evaluators and edges between these nodes positive evaluations. Further, we include the inception date of the Kudo relationships which allows us to study the evolution of this graph over time. Using this graph, we derive each developer's reputation. To do so, we use a ranking algorithm. Compared to a degree based measure we think that a ranking algorithm is more accurate, as we illustrate in Figure 2. If we were to use, for example, the in-degree (deg$^+$) for assessing a developer's reputation, the three developers a, b, and c in our example would have at time $t = 3$ the same reputation. However, this measurement approach disregards the reputation of the evaluators. In order to account for this aspect, we will use a rank based measure to assess developers' reputation. A suitable ranking algorithm for our context is the PageRank (PR) algorithm by Brin and Page [1]. This algorithm recursively ranks nodes based on the number and rank of their incoming links and the damping factor $d = 0.85$. In our example, developer 'c' has the highest PageRank (0.159), followed by developer 'a' (0.151) and 'b' (0.073). To adopt the PageRank algorithm for our evaluation context, we need to modify the original version so that it does not consider the set of all developers but instead distinguish between community internal and external evaluations. To do so, we calculate two reputation scores, one representing a developer's reputation within the project community ($int\_rep^t_i$) and one for his or her reputation outside the project community ($ext\_rep^t_i$) at time t. To categorize a Kudo sender into one of these two categories we check if he or she registered at the KDE-Look portal.

To measure the **number of new developers** on a longitudinal base, we will reconstruct the complete contribution history of each KDE project. Based on this contribution history, we iteratively identify the number of new developers by examining for each active developer if he or she has already contributed to the project in the past. Hence, we can precisely determine for each KDE project the influx of new developers at any point in time. Finally, we differentiate between newcomers from the project community and external ones. To do so, we combine the contributor data with data from the KDE-Look portal. This allows us to derive distinct measures for the attraction of community members (int_nov^t) and community outsiders (ext_nov^t) at time t.

As for our dependent and independent variables we draw on existing FLOSS evaluations for measuring our control variables. In line with previous evaluations by Colazo and Fang we quantify the **project size** ($proj\_size_t$) by the amount of lines of code in t (LoC_t) [4]. For measuring **project age** ($proj\_age_t$), we follow Singh et al. and count the number of months between its inception and t (NoM_t) [24]. To account for the **project type** ($proj\_type$) we follow Santos et al. and classify the FLOSS project into one of their 18 different software classes [20]. Finally, we quantify the **number of developers** (no_devs_t), by assessing the cardinality of the set of active developers in t.

For the testing of our research hypotheses, we take a project-centric evaluation approach. This means that, we will identify, in a first step, those KDE projects where most developers registered at Ohloh.com. Then, we calculate for each project in this sample the average reputation of the involved developers within the KDE community (int_rep^t) and beyond (ext_rep^t) and the numbers of novices from within (int_nov^t) and from outside (ext_nov^t) KDE. Finally, we apply a rolling regression analysis on these time series. This regression technique allows us to assess if and how strong changes in one time-series (i.e. external and internal reputation) lead to changes in another time-series (i.e. number of internal and external project newcomers).

6. EXPECTED RESULTS

With respect to organizational literature, we expect that FLOSS developers' reputation plays a key role in attracting newcomers to FLOSS projects. A particular aspect, which will be interesting to observe, is how strong this effect will be and if it poses only a temporary or instead a sustainable stimulus for the influx of new developers. Further, it will be interesting to see if we find in our data the existence of a herding effect, as Oh and Jeon suggested [17]. To the best of our knowledge, this is the first study which differentiates between FLOSS developers' reputation (community vs. external) and FLOSS novices' background (community member vs. community outsider). It seems plausible to assume that community members are more affected by the evaluations from the FLOSS community than from outsiders. However, this does not have to be the case. Just as well, it could be that FLOSS developers follow closely the contribution behavior of external top contributors which in turn exerts a strong influence on the selection of the projects they commit next to. Finally, our evaluation has implications for FLOSS practice. In particular, our research provides practical advice for FLOSS managers on how they can stimulate the influx of new project members. Apart from the FLOSS context, our research provides value to the organizational domain, considering the advice to treat knowledge workers as volunteers [6]. In particular, our research complements organizational literature which examines how companies can attract more talent by showcasing the competencies of their current personnel.

7. REFERENCES

[1] Brin, S. and Page, L. 1998. The anatomy of a large-scale hypertextual Web search engine. *Computer Networks and ISDN Systems* 30, 1-7, 107–117.

[2] Burt, R. S. 1995. *Structural holes. The social structure of competition*. Harvard Univ. Press, Cambridge.

[3] Casey, C. 2012. Low-Wealth Minority Enterprises and Access to Financial Resources for Start-Up Activities: Do Connections Matter? *Economic Development Quarterly* 26, 3, 252–266.

[4] Colazo, J. A. and Fang, Y. 2010. Following the Sun: Temporal Dispersion and Performance in Open Source Software Project Teams. *Journal of the Association for Information Systems* 11, 12, 684–707.

Table 1: Measurement

Variable Definition	
$proj\_dev_t$	Set of active developers at the FLOSS project in t
$comm\_mem_t$	Set of community members (developers & users) in t
$kudo_{i,j}$	Positive evaluation given by i to j
$kudos_i$	Number of positive evaluations received by i

Developer Attraction

(a) Community members

$$int\_nov^t = \left| \{ i \mid i \notin \bigcup_{j=1}^{t-1} proj\_dev_j \wedge i \in comm\_mem \} \right|$$

(b) Community outsiders

$$ext\_nov^t = \left| \{ i \mid i \notin \bigcup_{t=1}^{t-1} proj\_dev_t \wedge i \notin comm\_mem \} \right|$$

Developer Reputation

(a) Within project community

$$int\_rep^t = \sum_{\forall i \in proj\_dev_t} int\_rep_i^t$$

$$int\_rep_i^t = \frac{1-d}{|\, comm\_mem\,|} + d \times \sum_{\forall j \ni kudo_{j,i} \wedge j \in comm\_mem} \frac{int\_rep_j^t}{kudos_j}$$

(b) Beyond project community

$$ext\_rep^t = \sum_{\forall i \in proj\_dev_t} ext\_rep_i^t$$

$$ext\_rep_i^t = \frac{1-d}{|\, comm\_mem\,|} + d \times \sum_{\forall j \ni kudo_{j,i} \wedge j \notin comm\_mem} \frac{ext\_rep_j^t}{kudos_j}$$

Developer Reputation

$$proj\_size_t = LoC_t$$

$$proj\_age_t = NoM_t$$

$$proj\_type = \{ \text{'Text Editor', 'Education', 'Games', ... } \}$$

$$no\_devs_t = |\, project\_dev_t\,|$$

[5] Cross, R. and Cummings, J. N. 2004. Tie and Network Correlates of Individual Performance in Knowledge-Intensive Work. *Academy of Management Journal* 47, 6, 928–937.

[6] Drucker, P. F. 2002. They're not Employees, They're People. *Harvard Business Review* 80, 2, 70–77.

[7] Fang, Y. and Neufeld, D. 2009. Understanding Sustained Participation in Open Source Software Projects. *Journal of Management Information Systems* 25, 4, 9–50.

[8] Gold, A. 2007. *Open Source Solutions: Seek Value Beyond Cost*. Accessed 1 May 2011.

[9] Granovetter, M. 1983. The Strength of Weak Ties: A Network Theory Revisited. *Sociological Theory* 1, 201.

[10] Grewal, R., Lilien, G. L., and Mallapragada, G. 2006. Location, Location, Location: How Network Embeddedness Affects Project Success in Open Source Systems. *Management Science* 52, 7, 1043–1056.

[11] Hahn, J., Moon, J. Y., and Zhang, C. 2008. Emergence of New Project Teams from Open Source Software Developer Networks: Impact of Prior Collaboration Ties. *Information Systems Research* 19, 3, 369–391.

[12] Hahn, J. and Zhang, C. 2005. An Exploratory Study of Open Source Projects from a Project Management Perspective. In *MIS Research Workshop 2005*, 1–27.

[13] Hu, D., Zhao, J. L., and Chen Jiesi. 2012. Reputation Management in an Open Source Developer Social Network: An Empirical Study on Determinants of Positive Evaluations. *Decision Support Systems* 53, 3, 526–533.

[14] Ke, W. and Zhang, P. 2010. The Effects of Extrinsic Motivations and Satisfaction in Open Source Software Development. *Journal of the Association for Information Systems* 11, 12, 785–808.

[15] Ke, W. and Zhang, P. 2011. Effects of Empowerment on Performance in Open-Source Software Projects. *IEEE Transactions on Engineering Management* 58, 2, 334–346.

[16] Lin, N., Vaughn, J. C., and Ensel, W. M. 1981. Social Resources and Occupational Status Attainment. *Social Forces* 59, 4, 1163–1181.

[17] Oh, W. and Jeon, S. 2007. Membership Herding and Network Stability in the Open Source Community: The Ising Perspective. *Management Science* 53, 7, 1086–1101.

[18] Raymond, E. S. 1999. *The cathedral and the bazaar. Musings on Linux and open source by an accidental revolutionary*. O'Reilly, Sebastopol.

[19] Roberts, J. A., Hann, I.-H., and Slaughter, S. A. 2006. Understanding the Motivations, Participation, and Performance of Open Source Software Developers: A Longitudinal Study of the Apache Projects. *Management Science* 52, 7, 984–999.

[20] Santos, C., Kuk, G., Kon, F., and Pearson, J. 2012. The attraction of contributors in free and open source software projects. *The Journal of Strategic Information Systems*.

[21] Schilling, A., Laumer, S., and Weitzel, T. 2013. In the spotlight - evaluating how celebrities affect floss developers' participation motivation. In *Proceedings of the 21th European Conference on Information System (ECIS)*.

[22] Seibert, S. E., Kraimer, M. L., and Liden, R. C. 2001. A Social Capital Theory of Career Success. *Academy of Management Journal* 44, 2, 219–237.

[23] Shah, S. K. 2006. Motivation, Governance, and the Viability of Hybrid Forms in Open Source Software Development. *Management Science* 52, 7, 1000–1014.

[24] Singh, P. V., Tan, Y., and Mookerjee, V. 2011. Network Effects: The Influence of Structural Social Capital on Open Source Project Success. *MIS Quarterly* 35, 4, 813–829.

[25] Statcounter Inc. 2011. *Firefox overtakes Internet Explorer in Europe in browser wars*. http://gs.statcounter.com/press/firefox-overtakes-internet-explorer-in-europe-in-browser-wars. Accessed 14 March 2011.

[26] Stewart, K. J. and Gosain, S. 2006. The Impact of Ideology on Effectiveness in Open Source Software Development Teams. *MIS Quarterly* 30, 2, 291–314.

[27] Xu, B. and Jones, D. R. 2010. Volunteers' Participation in Open Source Software Development: A Study from the Social-Relational Perspective. *Database for Advances in Information Systems* 41, 3.

The Influence of Labelling and Social Exchange on Group Cohesion of IT-Contract Employees

Rajendra K Bandi
Indian Institute of Management
Bangalore
+91-80-26993095
rbandi@iimb.ernet.in

Ravikumar Narasimhamurthy
Indian Institute of Management
Bangalore
+91-9986459869
ravikumarn@iimb.ernet.in

Rajiv Kishore
State University of New York at Buffalo
Buffalo, NY
+1- 716-645-3507
rkishore@buffalo.edu

ABSTRACT

Employee turnover in IT sector remains one of the most persistent challenges facing organizations. IT services organizations have been contracting their employees to support the global client requirements. There is an increasing trend in using IT contract employees in organizations, both at the service provider side and in the client organizations. With the increasing presence of contract employees, their interaction with employee co-workers could have impact on the group performance and turnover intentions. In this article, drawing on the categorization and labelling theories, we argue that the practices followed in client organizations to identify the contract employees by using distinct signifiers, such as different badging, Email ID prefixes, work location assigned to contract employees etc., will evoke a set of cognitions, which can have a negative influence on the group cohesion. We also propose that the quality of social exchange between the employee co-workers and contractors, and the quality of social exchange between the line manager and contract employee can attenuate the negative influence on group cohesiveness. The proposed conceptual framework is important in terms of understanding the relationship between contractors and employee co-workers from a managerial perspective.

Categories and Subject Descriptors

K.6.1 People and Project Management - Staffing.

General Terms

Management, Human Factors,

Keywords

Labelling, contract employee, social exchange, IT, Organization, employee co-worker, Group cohesion, employee turnover

1. INTRODUCTION

Employee turnover in information technology (IT) sector remains one of the most persistent challenges facing organizations. From the 1970s into the 1990s, IT turnover rates ranged from 15 to 33 percent in the United States [19]. In the 21st century,

Permission to make digital or hard copies of all or part of this work for personal or classroom use is granted without fee provided that copies are not made or distributed for profit or commercial advantage and that copies bear this notice and the full citation on the first page. Copyrights for components of this work owned by others than the author(s) must be honored. Abstracting with credit is permitted. To copy otherwise, or republish, to post on servers or to redistribute to lists, requires prior specific permission and/or a fee. Request permissions from Permissions@acm.org.
SIGMIS-CPR '14, May 29 - 31 2014, Singapore, Singapore
Copyright is held by the owner/author(s). Publication rights licensed to ACM.
ACM978-1-4503-2625-4/14/05...$15.00.
http://dx.doi.org/10.1145/2599990.2599992

notwithstanding the recent trend of relocating IT jobs offshore, IT turnover remains a chronic problem [1]. In India, the turnover has been as high as 80% in the IT services sector [17]. Turnover of information technology professionals is one of the most persistent challenges facing organizations [29]. Considering the above studies, employee turnover is a major issue in the IT services sector.

IT service sector has been providing contract employees to client organizations to support their business IT needs. Organizations hire employees on contract basis, to buffer uncertainties and to quickly ramp up the teams to meet business needs. However high turnover can be a deterrent in meeting the business needs. The increasing presence of contract employees in organizations and their interaction with the employee co-workers is of interest as this could have a bearing on the performance of the group and employee turnover intentions.

Given the uncertain economic situation, organizations have been adapting various flexible models to fulfil the human resource needs. Organizations look at four different employment modes [20]: Internal development, Acquisition, Contracting, and Alliance. In case of internal development, firms have both financial and strategic incentive to internally develop this particular form of human capital. Acquisition mode enables the firms to reap the benefits of valuable skills that have been developed elsewhere while holding them internally. Contracting human capital contains human capital that is generic and of limited strategic value. Apart from full time employee hiring, organizations are looking at contract employees to buffer the uncertainties. Researchers have noted that, internal hiring provides, greater stability, better control & coordination, and lower transaction costs thereby leading to organizational flexibility [20].

The 'job-for-life' scenario of the old employment relationship has been mostly replaced by 'the contract' – a shorter-term, more tenuous arrangement, wherein the contract employee being treated little more than a 'temporary resident' in the organization [22]. Research indicates that there is a rapid growth in the number of firms that provide the temporary staffing services and it is estimated that such firms have doubled in size over the period 1994–1999 and again in the years 1999–2006 – reaching a level of US$341 bn in 2007 [8]. As the number of firms that provide temporary staffing increases and the risk inherent in contractual arrangements decreases, organizations are able to contract work without the risk of losing their competitive position [20]. The contractual terms stipulate the location of the work execution, which could be done off the company premises or performed on site. It is increasingly common that contractual work is performed on-site to safe guard intellectual property, better management and control. Contract employees are a growing presence in many organizations, taking many forms: agency nurses work in hospitals, job shop engineers bring special technical expertise to design teams, consultants provide a variety of services, and clerical temporary employees are ubiquitous in many organizations [25]. The presence of IT contract employees is growing significantly in organizations. Some companies (in IT sector) have reported that up to 30% of their employees belong to contract category [10].

The organizations in IT sector fall into one of the following categories- IT product companies, that produce software products, IT services companies, and ITES (IT Enabled services) companies that provide commercial services using IT. It is the IT services / ITES companies that mostly provide contract employees to other organizations to meet their IT business needs. These organizations depute their employees globally on contract basis. The fluctuating business cycles are adding to the need of more contract positions.

"The more there will be uncertainty, the more flexi staffing industry will grow. We see almost 14% rise in number of organized flexi staff across India and 18% jump in business volume for the industry this year. So there is a huge market waiting to be tapped,"—Pandia Rajan, president, Indian Staffing Federation (ISF), an apex body of flexi-staffing industry" [28].

Given that IT is not the core business area for the non-IT organizations, these organizations consider that their IT needs can be better served by external vendors. Organizations may have a few key positions held by their own employees and the rest are mostly filled by contract employees. The ratio of regular employees to contract employees may vary across the organizations. IT professionals have been identified as knowledge workers – as most are university educated, and the dynamic nature of the domain needs them to keep updated with the technological trends. Turnover of these professionals remains one of the most persistent challenges facing organizations [19].

The focus of this article is on collocated teams, where in the contract employee working at the client organization facility works along with the client organization's regular employees. The contract can be of long duration, extending to a couple of years or can be of short duration for a few months. The IT contract employees, we refer to in this article are specialists involved in providing a range of services such as, supporting IT infrastructure (Servers, databases, network etc.), software applications etc., who work at the client organization supporting the IT requirements. Once the contract employees join the contracting organization, they may sometimes go through a limited level of induction program to align with the organization. They are typically identified with a different kind of name badge, email ID and sometimes even a different desk location etc. which clearly distinguishes them from the regular employees. They may be addressed as "associates" or as employees of the respective organizations they are employed with. We argue that these symbolic identifications evoke certain expectations leading to altered interpersonal interaction thereby influencing the group cohesion, which in turn could influence the contract employee's job commitment, job satisfaction, intention to leave etc.

2. LITERATURE REVIEW

There have been contrasting arguments on hiring employees versus using contract employees. One factor in the decision to hire employees rather than retain contract employees is that, regular employees tend to have greater quasi-moral involvement, or greater commitment and a stronger sense of moral obligation to the organization, than contract employees, whose involvement tends to be more calculated [31]. Countering this argument, in a study that investigated the psychological contract of organizational identification, social (corporate) attraction, team spirit and intention to leave, it has been noted that contract employees are not inevitably 'emotionally' detached from their place of work, and in some cases investing in it as much as direct company employees [22]. This study included employees from various industries including IT contract employees.

Research in organizational identification builds upon social identity theory whereby individuals classify themselves and others into various social categories such as organizational membership, gender, race, age cohort, or religious affiliation and view their membership in particular groups based on social roles and role relationships [18]. The more qualified workers (with university education, IT-based degrees) are less likely to possess a strong organizational identity as they are less reliant on the organization for their occupational identity or feelings of self-worth [21].

A study conducted on the IT contract employees indicates that, IT contract workers identify with both employing and client organizations based on perceived characteristics of the organization (organizational prestige, distinctiveness and congruence in values) as well as on social relations (level of trust in management and their attraction to their colleagues) within the organization [13]. The literature review reveals that there is not much research done looking at IT contract employees and their relationship with regular employees.

2.1 Influence of labelling
Labelling theory focuses primarily on how institutions and social control agents define social objects, principally individuals, and their acts. As a sociological theory, it is largely concerned with the role that authority, status, and power play in the assignment of social identities to individuals.

Ashforth &Humphrey, 1997 [3] argue that, a label is a signifier of a given object, and typically activates a set of cognitions (and related affects) about the object and continuing the same line of argument, they contend that the labels have a profound effect on how organizational members conceive of social objects and on how they act toward those objects.Individuals come to view their labels and schemas as a reliable and valid mirror of reality, as simply reflecting what is "out there." Thus, labels become *institutionalized* in the sense meant by Zucker, 1977 [32], that is, as objective and exterior accounts of reality that are resistant to change. Labels are often used to justify shunting of individuals into occupational ghettos or gilded cages [2].

IT Contract employees are often provided with different badges, different e-mail ID's, work location etc. Thus all these labels signify that the person is a "contract employee", evoke expectations about how the person will behave and how one should respond to him or her [3]. We contend that this labelling effect, can lead to a pernicious form of altered interaction [2] between contract employees and employee co-workers.

2.2 Social exchange theory
One of the basic tenets of social exchange theory (SET) is that relationships evolve over time into trusting, loyal, and mutual

commitments. For this to happen, parties must abide by certain 'rules' of exchange. Rules of exchange form a 'normative definition of the situation that forms among or is adopted by the participants in an exchange relation [11]. Though there are a number of social exchange rules outlined in SET, most of the management research focuses on expectations of reciprocity. Reciprocity or repayment in kind is probably the best known exchange rule. Research indicates that employees form various kinds of social exchange relationships. The interaction could be, with their immediate supervisor, co-workers, employing organizations, customers and suppliers [9]. These relationships have implications on their social behavior. Specifically, because individuals return the benefits they receive, they are likely to match the goodwill and helpfulness toward the person with whom they have a social exchange relationship [9].

There are several views of social exchange and theorists agree that social exchange involves a series of interactions that generate obligations [11]. Within social exchange theories, these interactions are usually seen as interdependent and contingent on the actions of another person [5]. Researchers who study employee exchange behavior note one form of exchange or another such as organizational citizenship behavior, leader-member exchange, bargaining and identity based orientations etc. Social exchange relationships evolve when employers or employees take care of one another, which thereby engender beneficial consequences.

Blau's contribution to social exchange theory was his comparison of economic and social exchanges [9]. He maintained that 'the basic and most crucial distinction is that social exchange entails unspecified obligations' (1964: p. 93). He argued that only social exchange 'involves favours that create diffuse future obligations . . . and the nature of the return cannot be bargained' (1964: p. 93) and 'only social exchange tends to engender feelings of personal obligations, gratitude, and trust; purely economic exchange as such does not' (p. 94). Thus social exchange between contractors and rest of the related employee co-workers engenders relationships which don't get established purely by economic exchange.

2.3 Group Cohesiveness
Group cohesiveness has been defined as an essential component of the group's overall social integration, as well as an individual's perceived attraction to the group, satisfaction with other members of the group, and view of social interaction among the group members [24]. Group cohesiveness has been viewed as an important determinant of team performance [4] [12] [23]. In this article we argue that the signifiers used to identify the contract employees evokes the labels, and this can lead to a pernicious form of altered interaction [2] between contract employees and employee co-workers, thus negatively impacting the group cohesion. Research indicates group cohesion leads to team performance cohesive groups are typically described as having strong morale or group spirit [7], and positive influence of group cohesion on employee turnover [24].

2.4 LMX theory
The leader–member exchange (LMX) theory, which evolved from what was originally called the vertical-dyad linkage provided a different view about the leadership style theories by proposing

that leaders do not treat all followers same but, they develop different quality of relationships with followers [6].

Leader-member exchange (LMX) has been viewed as the exchange relationship that takes place between an employee and the supervisor [27] [30].

Graen & Scandura, 1987 [15] described a three-stage process for the development of LMX, role-taking, role-making and role routinizing. In the role-taking stage, the leader attempts to evaluate the member; exchanges are purely contractual. In the role-making stage, the leader assigns unstructured tasks to the member, and trust develops in the dyad. Finally, in the role routinization stage, leader–member relationships reach a mature stage; exchanges are based on respect, trust, and the fulfilment of mutual obligations. Thus the quality of social exchange can be considered to be at the highest level in the role routinizing stage. Researchers have assessed the quality of the relationship based on the confidence of the member in leader, support that the member gets from the leader etc. [16] [15].

We argue that, the quality of this relationship will have an influence on the labelling effect. The studies done on LMX indicate that, LMX has been positively related to job attitudes and performance evaluation [30], and that LMX predicts performance evaluations and organization citizenship behavior (OCB) [27].

3. CONCEPTUAL MODEL
As noted in the previous section, different labels are used by organizations to differentiate contractor s from regular employees. These labels refer to an occupational group performing a certain function [3]. These labels can evoke expectations about how the person will behave and how one should respond to him or her [4]. Labels such as different badges, e-mail ID's, and work location, could lead to a pernicious form of altered interaction [2] between contract employees and employee co-workers. We argue that this active discrimination due to labelling influence can lead to lower group cohesion. We suggest that social exchange between contract employee and employee co-workers, and the quality of social exchange between Line manager and contractor can moderate the influence of labelling and might have a positive influence on group cohesion as shown in figure-1. Considering these relationships we formulate some propositions which will be discussed later. Refer Table-2 for construct details.

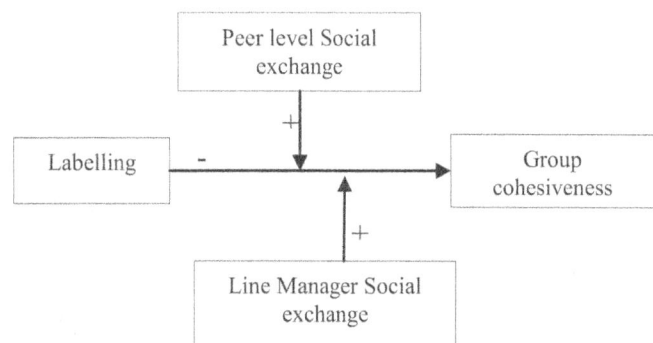

Figure-1 Conceptual Model

Construct	Definition used	Reference
Labelling	A salient label, as a master status, largely defines a person and thus can drastically affect the tone and content of interpersonal interaction	[2]
Peer level social exchange	The relationships that evolve over time into trusting, loyal, and mutual commitments	[11]
Line manager social exchange	Leader-member exchange (LMX) has been viewed as the exchange relationship that takes place between an employee and the supervisor	[27]
Group cohesion	Group cohesiveness has been defined as an essential component of the group's overall social integration, as well as an individual's perceived attraction to the group, satisfaction with other members of the group, and view of social interaction among the group members	[24]

Table - 1

3.1 Influence of labelling

Contract employees' main work-related interactions occur within the client organization, though contract employees are not members of the client organization and could by law be required to be treated differently from other employees [13] depending on country specific labor laws. They may have to wear a badge, their e-mail ID's are usually prefixed with the word "contractor", their work desk could be located in an identifiable location etc. Though it may be a legal requirement, these labels will have influence on how others perceive these labels and thereby influences communicating experience of the contract employee within the organization. These labels activate a set of cognitions about the person who is identified with the label [4], for example, a different colored badge (label) refers to a person who is a contract employee performing a certain function.

Employee co-workers associate contract employees with these labels thus categorizing them as much different from themselves. Contract employees perceive these labelling as indicator of out-group, which impacts their social exchange with the employee co-workers thus having negative influence on the group cohesion. Thus we make the below proposition:

P1: The influence of labelling leads to lower group cohesion

3.2 Contract employee-Line manager relationship

Contract employees' main work-related interactions occur within the client organization. They have very limited or no interaction with their employers. They may not even be able to access their official emails as well due to client policy and restrictions. While, a contract employee is likely to engage in social exchange at several levels, we are focusing here on the exchange relationship with the client manager as, for all practical purposes the manager of the client organization will be the line manager for all work related and hygiene related issues at work place. Thus for the contract employee, the client manager would be a key support in establishing good social interaction with the employee co-workers. We explore this relationship through Leader member exchange (LMX) theory. LMX reflects the

quality of the social exchange relationship between an employee and his or her line manager [14]. We argue that if this relationship quality is high, employees will socialize more with the contract employees. Managers at the client organization play an important role in providing contract workers with adequate work facilities and facilitating their social inclusion at the client site. Further, these managers make or implement decisions that affect the way the colleagues at the client site deal with the contract workers [13].

The quality of the interactions between the contract workers and the line manager is reflected in part in their level of trust in the management of the employing and client organizations. We argue that the quality of relationship with the line manager, can enhance the inside status of the contractor with the employees, thus reducing the negative labelling influence. This leads to the following proposition:

P2: The quality of line manager social exchange with contract employee would moderate the labelling influence-group cohesion relation

3.3 Employee co-worker and contract employee social exchange

In this article we look at the relationship between employee co-worker and contractor employee from Blau's, 1964, social exchange theory perspective. Blau defines the social exchange frame as "Social exchanges as here conceived is limited to actions that are contingent on rewarding reactions from others."

Social exchange relationships evolve when employees "take care of employees," which thereby engenders beneficial consequences. Advantageous and fair transactions between strong relationships and these relationships produce effective work behavior and positive employee attitudes [9]. This theory proposes that an exchange relationship develops between two parties when one party provides a benefit to the other, thereby causing an obligation to respond by providing something beneficial in return. Exchange processes evolve because individuals are interested in balancing between inputs and outputs and having positive balance in their transactions [5].

Many contract workers are normally not allowed to participate in the social activities formally organized at their client site. Their distance from their employer could also prevent their participation in the formally organized social events at their employer. Thus their dependency on the client organization is more. The essential goal of the contract employees is to support the business needs of the client organization, thus the employee co-workers are their customers. It is not unusual to see contract employees supporting the client requirements beyond the contractual obligations, thus creating a positive social exchange. Within social exchange theory, these interactions are usually seen as interdependent and contingent on the actions of another person [5].

It is argued that the employee co-workers don't perceive the contract employees as one among them due to labelling effect. The social exchange process between them develops the relationship between them. Thus we make the final proposition:

P3: The quality of social exchange process between employee co-worker and contract employee would moderate the labelling influence- group cohesion relation

4. DISCUSSION

The purpose of this conceptual article is to examine the impact of the labelling on contract employees and their relationship with employee co-workers by applying social exchange and LMX theories. The contract employees suffer because of the dual association with organizations. The labelling processes, clearly sends the message that they are not part of the employee co-workers. Thus their interaction with the employee co-workers will be limited to the task related interaction. Employee co-workers perceive that the contract employees are much different from them in associating their emotional attachment to the organization. This gets reified due to the labeling and the signifiers used to differentiate send out different signals. For example, E-mails sent out by contract employees may not be taken seriously by employee co-workers as they perceive that they are not part of their organization and have little say. The action taken by employees may depend upon if the mail is sent by contractor or a co-worker. The prefix "Contractor" associated with the email makes all the difference in the response. The content of the email loses the significance, because of the labelling effect. Employee co-workers may not like to have contract employees in some important decision making meetings, which are of importance to the organization or group. Thus the quality of social exchange between contract and employee co-workers will not be good.

"As a contractor now, I have to stop at the desk every single day and sign in and sign out. I have to sign out every time I leave the building, even if it is only going to the car. In the holiday season, there are parties and everyone is invited ... except the contractors." (Comment by contract IT employee in Ranganathan & Outlay, 2009 [26])

Managers can play a pivotal role in reducing the effect of labelling by making or implementing decisions that affect the way colleagues deal with the contract workers. Contract workers would depend on managers at the client site to take care of hygiene factors such as providing them with decent work facilities and involving them in the social life of the organization [15].

Managers can support the contract workers inclusion into the group in various ways, thus sending equally powerful signals to counter the labelling effect. This enhances the relation between the employee co-workers and contract employees to a greater extent by enhancing the social exchange between them. The perceived quality of social exchange with line manager and contract employees reduces the impact of the labelling by enhancing the inclusion process. Managers can include contract employees in some of the decision making activities, idea proposal initiatives, etc., signaling inclusion to the employee co-workers. Many contract workers are not allowed to participate in the social activities formally organized at work place. Involving contract employees in such events where ever it is feasible enhances the social exchange with the employee co-workers. Thus the enhanced social exchange between the employees and contract employees will reduce the labelling effect.

In summary, the impact of the labelling can be reduced by quality of line manger exchange and employee co-worker social exchange. Thus this research would be of practical significance from managerial implications. Management has to provide enough time and guidance for the line manager to play this role of influencing the social exchange process for the contract employee to settle down in the role.

5. CONCLUSION AND FUTURE WORK

The conceptual analysis supports the idea that labelling can negatively influence the group cohesion. Prior research has established the impact of group cohesion on important parameters like job satisfaction, commitment etc. In particular, the conceptual model highlights moderating influence of the quality of social exchange of contractor with the line manager and employee co-workers in attenuating the labelling effect. Empirical studies are planned to assess the conceptual model. The severity of impact of different types of signifiers used to identify the contract employees such as badging, work location within the organization, Email ID prefixing etc., on the affiliation of employee co-workers with contractor can also be of future interest to researchers and managers.

6. REFERENCES

[1] Adams, C., Clark, L. M., Goldman, M., Jester, R., Lee, M., Noseworthy, D. & Thompson, E. 2006. Skills shortages are emerging in the CSI service market. Publication G00140837, Gartner Inc., Stamford, CT

[2] Ashforth, B. E., & Humphrey, R. H. 1995. Labeling Processes in Organization-Constructing the Individual. Research in organizational behavior: An annual series of analytical essays and critical reviews, 17, 413-461.

[3] Ashforth, B. E., & Humphrey, R. H. 1997. The ubiquity and potency of labeling in organizations. Organization Science, 8(1), 43-58.

[4] Beal, D. J., Cohen, R. R., Burke, M. J., & McLendon, C. L. 2003. Cohesion and performance in groups: a meta-analytic clarification of construct relations. Journal of Applied Psychology, 88(6), 989.

[5] Blau, P. M. 1964. Exchange and power in social life, New York: John Wiley.

[6] Boies, K., & Howell, J. M. 2006. Leader–member exchange in teams: An examination of the interaction between relationship differentiation and mean LMX in explaining team-level outcomes. The Leadership Quarterly, 17(3), 246-257.

[7] Bollen, K. A., & Hoyle, R. H. 1990. Perceived cohesion: A conceptual and empirical examination. Social Forces, 69(2), 479-504.

[8] Coe, N. M., Jones, K., & Ward, K. 2010. The business of temporary staffing: a developing research agenda. Geography Compass, 4(8), 1055-1068.

[9] Cropanzano, R., & Mitchell, M. S. 2005. Social exchange theory: An interdisciplinary review. Journal of Management, 31(6), 874-900.

[10] Editorial - Employment in Indian IT industry, some concerns Issue 5 November 2012 http://www.itecentre.co.in/node/166 : Accessed on November 3, 2013

[11] Emerson, R. M. 1976. Social exchange theory. Annual review of sociology, 2(1), 335-362.

[12] Evans, C. R., & Dion, K. L. 1991. Group cohesion and performance a meta-analysis. Small group research, 22(2), 175-186.

[13] George, E., & Chattopadhyay, P. 2005. One foot in each camp: The dual identification of contract workers. Administrative Science Quarterly, 50(1), 68-99.

[14] Gerstner, C. R., & Day, D. V. 1997. Meta-Analytic review of leader–member exchange theory: Correlates and construct issues. Journal of applied psychology, 82(6), 827.

[15] Graen, G. B., & Scandura, T. A. 1987. Toward a psychology of dyadic organizing. Research in organizational behavior, 9(1), 175-208.

[16] Graen, G. B., & Uhl-Bien, M. 1995. Relationship-based approach to leadership: Development of leader–member exchange (LMX) theory of leadership over 25 years: Applying a multi-level multi-domain perspective. Leadership Quarterly, 6(2), 219–247

[17] Gupta, P. 2001. Scenario of IT Industries in. Communications of the ACM, 44(7), 41.

[18] Hogg, M. A., Terry, D., & White, K. 1995. A Tale of Two Theories. Social psychology quarterly, 58(4), 255-269.

[19] Joseph, D., Ng, K. Y., Koh, C., & Ang, S. 2007. Turnover of information technology professionals: a narrative review, meta-analytic structural equation modeling, and model development. MIS Quarterly, 31(3), 547-577.

[20] Lepak, D. P., & Snell, S. A. 1999. The human resource architecture: Toward a theory of human capital allocation and development. Academy of management review, 24(1), 31-48.

[21] Marks, A., & Scholarios, D. 2007. Revisiting technical workers: professional and organisational identities in the software industry. New Technology, Work and Employment, 22(2), 98-117.

[22] Millward, L. J., & Brewerton, P. M. 1999. Contractors and their psychological contracts. British Journal of Management, 10(3), 253-274.

[23] Mullen, B., & Copper, C. 1994. The relation between group cohesiveness and performance: An integration. Psychological bulletin, 115(2), 210.

[24] O'Reilly Ill, C. A., Caldwell, D. F., & Barnett, W. P. (1989). Work Group Demography, Social integration, and Turnover. Administrative Science Quarterly, 34(1), 21-37.

[25] Pearce, J. L. 1993. Toward an organizational behavior of contract labourers: Their psychological involvement and effects on employee co-workers. Academy of Management Journal, 36(5), 1082-1096.

[26] Ranganathan, C., & Outlay, C. N. 2009. Life After IT Outsourcing: Lessons Learned from Resizing the IT Workforce. MIS Quarterly Executive, 8(4), 161-173.

[27] Settoon, R. P., Bennett, N., & Liden, R. C. 1996. Social exchange in organizations: Perceived organizational support, leader–member exchange, and employee reciprocity. Journal of applied psychology, 81(3), 219-227

[28] Sovon Manna, TNN, OCT 17, 2013 Flexi-staff eases pressure on India Inc., Times of India http://timesofindia.indiatimes.com/business/india-business/Flexi-staff-eases-pressure-on-India-Inc/articleshow/24277107.cms : Accessed on October 18, 2013

[29] Valerie F. Ford and Diana L. Burley. 2012. Once you click 'done': Investigating the relationship between disengagement, exhaustion and turnover intentions among university IT professionals. In Proceedings of the 50th annual conference on Computers and People Research (SIGMIS-CPR '12).ACM, New York, NY, USA, 61-68.

[30] Wayne, S. J., Shore, L. M., & Liden, R. C. 1997. Perceived organizational support and leader-member exchange: A social exchange perspective. Academy of Management journal, 40(1), 82-111.

[31] Williamson, O. E. 1981. The economics of organization: the transaction cost approach. American journal of sociology, 87(3), 548-577.

[32] Zucker, L. G. 1977. The role of institutionalization in cultural persistence. American sociological review, 42(5), 726-743.

The Effect of Job Stress on Job Performance amongst IT Professionals: The Moderating Role of Proactive Work Behaviours

Tenace Kwaku Setor
Nanyang Technological University
tenacekw001@e.ntu.edu.sg

ABSTRACT

The heavy dependence of modern businesses on information technologies and systems has expanded the job roles and increased the work demands and pressures of Information Technology practitioners. IT professionals who cannot cope with the ever increasing demands of their work experience high levels of occupational stress. Occupational stress has a negative income on work-related outcomes such as job performance. Extant research on stress-related studies have focused on passive or reactive strategies of coping. I propose a proactive approach by arguing that proactive work behaviours moderate negative relationship between job stress and job performance. I draw on Hobfoll's Conversation of Resources theory (1989) and the proactive coping literature (Aspinwall and Taylor, 1997) in the present proposal. A quantitative methodology is proposed for the study. Theoretical and practical contributions are discussed.

Keywords

Proactive Work Behaviour; Proactive Coping; Job Performance; Job Stress

1. INTRODUCTION

Despite the demanding workload of jobs today, and the expanding job tasks in terms of complexities, businesses must still meet deadlines to stay in competition. Wide job scopes (range of job-related activities performed by the employee, Xie and Gary, 1995) may not be exclusive to the IT profession. However, Messersmith (2007) provides evidence that suggests that workers in the Information Technology/Systems discipline experience higher rates of burnouts, work-life conflicts, longer work duration than their co-workers. Wide job scopes will exert strain on the cognitive, physical and even affective life of workers which may ultimately affect their performance.

IT professionals more often than not have tighter deadlines to meet to solve complex IT issues. Tighter deadlines are largely due to the reliance of business processes on IT, and a delay in providing timely IT services halt business activities. Meeting deadlines to solve complex IT problems translates into working for longer hours, sometimes on weekends, which is characteristic of IT work (Trauth, 2006).

Permission to make digital or hard copies of all or part of this work for personal or classroom use is granted without fee provided that copies are not made or distributed for profit or commercial advantage and that copies bear this notice and the full citation on the first page. Copyrights for components of this work owned by others than ACM must be honored. Abstracting with credit is permitted. To copy otherwise, or republish, to post on servers or to redistribute to lists, requires prior specific permission and/or a fee. Request permissions from permissions@acm.org.
SIGMIS-CPR'14, May 29–31, 2014, Singapore, Singapore.
Copyright © 2014 ACM 978-1-4503-2625-4/14/05...$15.00.
http://dx.doi.org/10.1145/2599990.2599993

Tight deadlines, complex work problems, long working hours and frequent updating of skills (Mok and Berry, 2011) have been argued as stressors of IT work (McGee, 1996). Stressors are external stimuli that evoke psychological and/or physiological responses. Stressors found at workplaces activate stress in workers that may ultimately affect their performance when they cannot cope.

Employee performance is a critical subject to managers. Perhaps, today's competitive business environment accounts for the managerial attention given to the subject of employee performance. It is not surprising that organizations are investing a great deal of resources in recruiting, training and building employee capacity, and ultimately looking to improve employee performance. Employee performance has also received scholarly attention in employment relations, job satisfaction and other human capital related studies.

Many studies have found a negative relationship between employee or job performance and stress at the workplace (job stress) Jex (1998) Mohsan et al. (2011) Khalid et al. (2012). The symptoms (such as fatigue, anxiety, tension) associated with stress distracts the employee from performing well. Effort and time that should have gone into performing tasks are spent countervailing the negative symptoms (Hunter and Thatcher, 2007; Hon and Chan, 2013).

The strength of the effect of job stress on job performance is moderated by "coping variables" such social support and self-efficacy (Cobb, 1976; Khalid et al 2012). Cognitive and behavioral efforts to manage stress (coping variables) (Lactack and Havlovic, 1992) are consequential responses to stress, perhaps to alleviate the uncomfortable strain associated with stress. The moderating role of such variables explains reactive ways of coping with job stress. By reactive, I mean that these forms of coping (presented as moderators) are intended to alleviate the cognitive, physical and affective strain visited on workers after the stress event has occurred or whiles it is still ongoing (Schwarzer, 2001). In alleviating job stress, individual IT professionals are motivated to develop new but effective ways of going about their work, to help reduce the complexities of tasks they perform, beat deadlines and gain control (job autonomy) of the demands of their work.

Extant research have overemphasized and paid more scholarly attention to reactive coping strategies that moderate the effects of job stress on organizational and individual work-related outcomes. This study incorporates a proactive dimension in a stress model in search of empirical evidence of an action-focused moderator rather than the belaboured passive-oriented coping variables. I suggest proactive work behavior as a moderating factor in explaining how job stress impacts on the performance of a knowledge worker such as the IT professional.

Aspinwall and Taylor's (1997) conceptual framework on proactive coping process, inspired by Hobfoll's Conservation of Resources theory (1989), provides the theoretical foundation upon which I argue that proactive work behaviours (Parker & Collins, 2010) moderate the relationship between work stress and work-related outcomes. Proactive coping as delineated by Aspinwall and Taylor, starts by accumulating and reserving resources. In anticipation of a potentially stressful event, a "proactive coper" taps into this resource reservoir to palliate the impact of stressors or prevent the stress event from occurring.

This study seeks to bridge the gap between the occupational stress and proactive behaviour literatures by shifting the focus of scholarly attention from reactive approach of coping with stress, to a proactive-oriented paradigm of dealing with stress. As pointed out by Aspinwall and Taylor, a proactive approach in stress management literature is largely understudied. Examining the theoretical bridge that connects proactive work behaviours, stress and coping bodies of literature provides insight on "coping behaviours" prior to a stress event. Such proactive behaviours might be overlooked in reactive coping models, and individuals who exhibit such behaviours might even be excluded from stress-coping studies (Aspinwall and Taylor). Also, Crant (2000) in his paper on "Proactive Behaviour in Organizations" acknowledged the construal ambivalence of proactive behavior, and called for studies examining the moderating role of the construct in other streams of research. Extending the functional roles of proactive behaviours to moderating models, from the much researched main-effects models, will enable scholars and managers gain a deeper insight of the complexities surrounding the construct..

2. JOB PERFORMANCE

Job Performance is a multidimensional construct based on a two-factor model – Task Performance and Contextual Performance. Task performance encompasses all those activities performed by the employee that are defined by the job requirements/description which are contractually binding, and the employee receives compensations for performing them. These activities are directed at the organization's technical core in achieving specific organizational goals. (Borman & Motowildo, 1997). The technical core refers to the overall processes and activities that transform raw inputs into goods and services. Task performance measures will therefore differ across jobs since different jobs require different activities and processes to transform raw inputs into goods and services. Framing task performance as actions specified by job descriptions is narrow and somehow problematic. Pulakos et al. (2000) and Rotundo (2002) argue that modern-day jobs are not static. The incorporation of technology into work processes and the emphasis on skills upgrade by employers account for the dynamism in jobs. There are no consequential changes in job descriptions despite the dynamism. Hence, evaluating task performance based on tasks outlined as part of the formal job descriptions is inaccurate. Thus, Rotundo conceptualizes task performance as a combination of activities that contribute directly and indirectly to the transformation of raw inputs into goods and services.

Contextual Performance on the other hand does not contribute to the organization's technical core. Contextual performance behaviors maintain the broader organizational, social, and psychological environment within which the technical core and processes function (Motowildo et al. 1997). Contextual performance behaviors provide room for task performance to thrive well. Other researchers have discussed a similar construct

of contextual performance behaviors-Organizational Citizenship Behavior (OCB). Smith et al (1983) describes OCB as extra-role discretionary behaviors such as helping behaviors (altruism) or demonstrating conscientiousness. Dekas et al (2013) however have proposed a modern approach to viewing OCB at the workplace. Their re-conceptualization of OCB is hinged on the premise that modern workforce has shifted to a knowledge-based industry rather than the traditional industries present at the early days of OCB research. As such, foundational scales measuring OCB may have items that may no longer be relevant to knowledge organizations.

3. JOB STRESS

Job Stress occurs when the employee can no longer cope with the demands and pressures of his or how work and as such experiences negative psychological or physiological reactions (Montgomery et al. 1996, Westman, 2005). Stressors influence stress at the workplace. Schaubroeck and Ganster (1993) identified mental demands and people complexity as stressors at the workplace. Mental demands encompass job characteristics aspects of problem solving, concentration and attention to information from the environment. Jobs characterized by a high demand of the employee's cognitive attention to information and concentration to solve problems will trigger stress. People complexity involves the relationship conflicts that arise when employees' interact with one another to function. Jobs designed in a way that demand a lot of interaction between individual employees may trigger stress. Maintaining interactions and relationships with teammates, co-workers, or other employees on a job task requires good people skills. Managing these interactions and relationships (people skills) depletes the employee's cognitive attention and concentration, and this may lead to stress.

The IT profession requires much mental and cognitive effort to solve complex problems. For example, software engineers, systems analysts and architects are burdened with the task of finding new but efficient ways of building and optimizing applications for clients. In IT intensive businesses, IT workers are either expending cognitive resources in troubleshooting systems or brainstorming to solve niggling IT problems in organizations. The recent dependence of business processes on IT puts time and workload pressures on IT workers. Without timely IT services, businesses will be crippled and become dysfunctional. IT workers, thus, spend longer hours at work (Messersmith, 2007) to keep systems up and provide IT services for the business to function. IT professionals must also keep up to date with the ever-changing technologies. Frequent updating of skills to match changing technologies puts pressure on the mental and cognitive resources of IT workers. IT work is characterized by working in teams to solve problems. Team player interactions and relationships may also lead to stress. Mental demands, people complexities (Shaubroeck and Ganster, 1993), demanding workloads, deadline pressures and frequent skills updating which characterize the IT profession deplete cognitive, affective and physical resources.

Past studies have found ruinous impact of a wide variety of stressors on the speed, accuracy and performance of individuals on verbal tasks such as sentence formation and verbal reasoning. (Lazarus et al., 1952; Wilkinson, 1969; Motowildo et al. 1986).

The deleterious impact of stress on performance is due to the drain of the individual's energy or resources. Aside focusing on the task, the individual pays additional attention to stressors, which creates conditions of cognitive information overload (Cohen, 1980). Information overload results in cognitive fatigue, which drains energy needed for task performance (Motowildo et al. 1986).

Based on the job characteristics and associated stressors of IT and IS work, I expect job stress to decrease the task performance of the IT professional. Hence, aside psychological and physiological strain experienced by IT workers due to stress (Weiss, 1983) I posit that,

H 1 (a) Job Stress will be negatively related to Task Performance.

Job stress impacts strain on the affective state of employees, that leads to anxiety, hostility and depression (Motowildo et al, 1980). These negative emotions evoked by stress "incline people toward more aggressive and less altruistic behavior" (Motowildo et al, 1980 p619). Individuals under stress become less sensitive to others (or more hostile) and thus disengage themselves from helping behaviors.

The IT professional will not only have limited cognitive, affective and physical resources to perform his or her task but he or she may not exhibit organizational citizenship behaviors. That is, the IT professional experiencing job stress may not offer help to co-workers or comply with organizational rules and regulations. Hence, I also posit that

H 1 (b) Job Stress will be negatively related to Contextual Performance.

4. PROACTIVE WORK BEHAVIOUR

Proactive Work Behaviors are set of actions or behaviors that are purposely initiated to change a situation or environment (Bindl and Parker, 2010).

The oxford online dictionary (2013) defines proactive as "creating or controlling a situation rather than just responding to it after it has happened:"

(http://www.oxforddictionaries.com/definition/english/proactive).

By the definition, proactive work behaviors are set of future-oriented behaviors or actions self-initiated by an employee to change the working environment positively (Crant, 2000). Prior studies in proactive work behaviors have identified personal initiative (Frese et al 1996) and taking charge (Morrison and Phelps 1999) as the main components of proactive work behavior. Personal initiative is a form of proactive work behavior that involves going beyond assigned roles and tasks in an attempt to solve anticipated problems. Taking charge is defined as "constructive effort by employees to effect functional change with respect to how work is executed" (Crant, 2000). Taking charge focuses on bringing about effective change in the way employees approach their work duties.

4.1 Proactive Work Behaviour and Job Stress

Employees with high personal initiative change the complexity of their jobs and gain control over job demands Frese, Garst & Fray (2007). Taking charge involves developing constructive approaches to work methods. As proactive work behavior is a construal composition of *taking charge* and *personal initiative,* a proactive worker is one high in personal initiative and taking charge.

Proactive work behaviours are resourceful. Proactive employees build resource reservoirs to be used later (Aspinwall and Taylor, 1997). According to Hobfoll's Conversation of Resource theory (1989), when a person's resources come under the threat of depletion or even threatened, stress occurs. Proactive employee's whose resources come under threat due to work demands and pressures can then tap from these resource reservoirs to replenish the depleting resources. The psychological preparedness a proactive employer may have enables him to deal with the stress event ahead well. The proactive employee being aware of his pool of extra resources will experience less anxiety and more confidence going into a stressful event.

Proactive work behaviours should minimize the impact of demanding workload and long working durations (stressors) because a proactive employee wields "anticipatory behaviors" (resources) to counteract them.

The IT job market is that of a fast paced, dynamic environment set apart by continuous and pervasive innovation. Organizations and IT managers, therefore, are in the market looking to hire talented individuals with specific core skills, competencies and matching behaviours to keep up with the dynamism and spirit of competitive innovation. Mok and Berry suggest that the dynamism in IT work demands "a set of new behaviours". As rightly suggested by Salanova and Schaufeli (2008) in their study, proactive behaviours are one of such specific behaviours an IT professional must wield in order to keep up with rapidly changing technologies and the dynamism characterizing such a knowledge-based profession.

In the case of the IT professional whose job is characterized by high mental demands, long working hours, problem solving and high work complexities, we argue that proactive work behaviors is critical for such work.

A proactive IT worker will thus reduce the effect of job stressors through proactive work behaviors such as personal initiative and taking charge. The reducing effect of job stressors is expected to mitigate job stress. The proactive approach to mitigating job stress suggests that the IT professional will have enough resources (mental, time and effort) to cope with job demands.

Hence, I posit that

H (3a-b) Proactive Work Behavior moderates the effect of job stress on job(task and contextual) performance.

5. METHODOLOGY

Data collection : An web survey is proposed is proposed for the collection of the data. Target participants, sampled from IT workers in an organization will be e-mailed questionnaires addressing the study objectives. Surveys are used by researchers to assess attitudes, characteristics and behaviours of subjects. A web survey enables the researcher to reach a larger sample of the participants and thus enhances the generalizability of the study's conclusions. Objective data on performance of subjects will be obtained from, in addition to the self-reported measures of performance. Objective data reduces response bias problems associated with self-reported measures on work performance, and also common method bias.

Data Analysis : An hierarchical regression analysis technique will be used to analyze and evaluate the proposed model. The technique provides the researcher with the flexibility of testing for the proposed hypotheses of the study.

6. CONTRIBUTIONS

First, from a theoretical perspective, this study seeks to extend the coping literature on job stress by shifting the focus of scholarly attention from the reactive approach of coping with stress, to an action-oriented paradigm of dealing with stress by providing empirical evidence. As pointed out by Aspinwall and Taylor (1997), a proactive approach in stress management literature is largely understudied. Examining the theoretical bridge that connects proactive work behaviours, stress and coping bodies of literature provides insight on "coping behaviours" prior to a stress event. Such proactive behaviours might be overlooked in reactive coping models, and individuals who exhibit such behaviours might even be excluded from stress-coping studies (Aspinwall and Taylor, 1997).

Secondly, Crant (2000) acknowledged the construal ambivalence of proactive behavior, and called for studies examining the moderating role of the construct in other streams of research. Extending the functional roles of proactive behaviours to moderating-effect models, from the much researched main-effects models, will enable scholars gain a deeper insight of the complexities surrounding the construct.

The study contributes to Information Technology and Systems management and practice by providing Information Technology and System Managers useful coping insights which could be incorporated into the stress management programme of the IT staff. A proactive stress management programme may not only be beneficial to the employee's health and general wellbeing but could potentially drive down the financial costs associated with reactive coping programmes in an organization.

REFERENCES

1) Aspinwall, L. G., & Taylor, S. E. (1997). A stitch in time: Self-regulation and proactive coping. Psychological Bulletin, 121(3), 417-436.

2) Bindl, U. K., & Parker, S. K. (2010). Proactive work behavior: Forward-thinking and change-oriented action in organizations. APA handbook of industrial and organizational psychology, 2, 567-598.

3) Borman, W. C., & Motowidlo, S. J. (1997). Task performance and contextual performance: The meaning for personnel selection research. Human Performance, 10(2), 99-109.

4) Cobb, S. (1976). Presidential Address-1976. Social support as a moderator of life stress. Psychosomatic medicine, 38(5), 300-314.

5) Crant, J. M. (2000). Proactive behavior in organizations. Journal of management, 26(3), 435-462.

6) Dekas, K. H., Bauer, T. N., Welle, B., Kurkoski, J., & Sullivan, S. (2013). Organizational Citizenship Behavior, Version 2.0: A review and Qualitative Investigation of OCBs for Knowledge Workers at Google and beyond. The Academy of Management Perspectives, 27(3), 219-237.

7) Frese, M., Garst, H., & Fay, D. (2007). Making things happen: Reciprocal relationships between work characteristics and personal initiative in a four-wave longitudinal structural equation model. Journal of applied psychology, 92(4), 1084.

8) Frese, M., Kring, W., Soose, A., & Zempel, J. (1996). Personal initiative at work: Differences between East and West Germany. Academy of Management Journal, 39(1), 37-63.

9) Hobfoll, S. E. (1989). Conservation of resources: A new attempt at conceptualizing stress. American psychologist, 44(3), 513.

10) Hon, A. H. Y., & Chan, W. W. (2013). The Effects of Group Conflict and Work Stress on Employee Performance. Cornell Hospitality Quarterly, 54(2), 174-184.

11) Hunter, L. W., & Thatcher, S. M. B. (2007). FEELING THE HEAT: EFFECTS OF STRESS, COMMITMENT, AND JOB EXPERIENCE ON JOB PERFORMANCE. Academy of Management Journal, 50(4), 953-968.

12) Jex, S. M. (1998). Stress and job performance: Theory, research, and implications for managerial practice: Sage Publications Ltd.

13) Jia Lin, X., & Johns, G. (1995). Job scope and stress: can job scope be too high? Academy of Management Journal, 38(5), 1288-1309.

14) Khalid, A., Murtaza, G., Zafar, A., Zafar, M. A., Saqib, L., & Mushtaq, R. (2012). Role of Supportive Leadership as a Moderator between Job Stress and Job Performance. Information Management and Business Review, 4(9), 487-495.

15) Latack, J. C., & Havlovic, S. J. (1992). Coping with job stress: A conceptual evaluation framework for coping measures. Journal of Organizational Behavior, 13(5), 479-508.

16) Lazarus, R. S., Deese, J., & Osier, J. F. (1952). The effects of psychological stress upon performance. Psychological Bulletin, 49, 293-316.

17) Lily Mok, D. B. Survey Analysis: IT Organizations Need to Change Skills Mix and Staffing Models To Fulfill Business Needs [published abstract] from Gartner, Inc http://www.gartner.com/id=1724632

18) McGee, M. (1996). Burnout. Information Week, 569(4), 34-40.

19) Messersmith, J. (2007). Managing work-life conflict among information technology workers. Human Resource Management, 46(3), 429-451.

20) Mohsan, F., Nawaz, M. M., & Khan, M. S. (2011). Impact of Stress on Job Performance of Employees Working in Banking Sector of Pakistan. Interdisciplinary Journal of Contemporary Research In Business, 3(2), 1982-1991.

21) Montgomery, D. C., Blodgett, J. G., & Barnes, J. H. (1996). A model of financial securities salespersons' job stress. Journal of Services Marketing, 10(3), 21-38.

22) Morrison, E. W., & Phelps, C. C. (1999). Taking charge at work: Extrarole efforts to initiate workplace change. Academy of Management Journal, 42(4), 403-419.

23) Motowildo, S. J., Borman, W. C., & Schmit, M. J. (1997). A Theory of Individual Differences in Task and Contextual Performance. Human Performance, 10(2), 71-83.

24) Parker, S. K., & Collins, C. G. (2010). Taking stock: Integrating and differentiating multiple proactive behaviors. Journal of Management, 36(3), 633-662.

25) Pulakos, E. D., Arad, S., Donovan, M. A., & Plamondon, K. E. (2000). Adaptability in the workplace: development of a taxonomy of adaptive performance. Journal of applied psychology, 85(4), 612.

26) Rotundo, M., & Sackett, P. R. (2002). The relative importance of task, citizenship, and counterproductive performance to global ratings of job performance: a policy-capturing approach. Journal of applied psychology, 87(1), 66.

27) Salanova, Marisa, and W. B. Schaufeli. "A cross-national study of work engagement as a mediator between job resources and proactive behaviour."*The International Journal of Human Resource Management* 19.1 (2008): 116-131.

28) Schaubroeck, J., & Ganster, D. C. (1993). Chronic demands and responsivity to challenge. Journal of applied psychology, 78(1), 73.

29) Schwarzer, R. (2001). Stress, resources, and proactive coping. Applied Psychology: An International Review, 50(3), 400-407

30) Smith, C., Organ, D. W., & Near, J. P. (1983). Organizational citizenship behavior: Its nature and antecedents. Journal of applied psychology, 68(4), 653.

31) Trauth, E. M. (2006). Encyclopedia of gender and information technology. Hershey, PA [etc.]: Idea Group Reference. Pg 845

32) Weiss, M. (1983). Effects of Work Stress and Social Support on Information Systems Managers. MIS Quarterly, 7(1), 29-43.

33)   Wilkinson, R. (1969). Some factors influencing the effect of environmental stressors upon performance. *Psychological Bulletin, 72,* 260-272.

Technostressors and Job Stress: Examining the Role of Personality Traits

Shalini Chandra
S P Jain School
of Global Management
Singapore, Singapore
shalini.chandra@spjain.org

Anuragini Shirish
Telecom Ecole de Management
Institut Mines-Telecom
Evry, France
anu.paris11@gmail.com

Shirish C. Srivastava
HEC School
of Management, Paris
Jouy en Josas, France
srivastava@hec.fr

ABSTRACT

In the current scenario of globally distributed working, information and communications technologies (ICTs) are playing a key role in connecting the global workforce. Further, rapid technological advances have made it possible to get connected anytime anywhere, thereby delivering data and information in real time to support businesses, organizations and personal decisions. Though the ubiquity of ICTs is beneficial for organizations, it often promotes negative outcomes for the employees such as – increased work overload, increased stress, pressures due to excessive technology dependence and demands for enhanced productivity. Although prior research has examined the influence of technostressors on job stress, insights into the influence of personality traits on the perceptions of technostressors, and their consequent impacts on job stress, is rather limited. Such insights would enable a deeper understanding on the effects of individual differences on salient job related outcome.

In this research-in-progress, by leveraging the differences in personality traits offered by the Five-Factor Model (FFM) and grounding the research in Transactional Model of Stress and Coping (TMSC), we theorize the moderating influence of personality on the relationships between technostressors and job stress. Specifically, the study theorizes the mechanisms through which each of the specific personality traits of - openness-to-experience, neuroticism, agreeableness, conscientiousness and extraversion, interacts with technostressors to have a different influence on job stress. We plan to test the theorized model in a field study based on a survey of senior organizational managers, who regularly use information and communication technologies (ICTs) for professional tasks. Though technostressors are generally associated with negative job outcomes, we expect that for individuals with certain personality traits, the negative effect of technostressors may be mitigated. The study will thus contribute to the technostress literature – specifically by incorporating the salient role of individual differences into the nomological network linking technostressors to job stress. The study will also provide insights to managers for paying special attention to allocating specific job roles to employees with particular personality traits for maximizing job related outcomes.

Permission to make digital or hard copies of part or all of this work for personal or classroom use is granted without fee provided that copies are not made or distributed for profit or commercial advantage, and that copies bear this notice and the full citation on the first page. Copyrights for third-party components of this work must be honored. For all other uses, contact the owner/author(s). Copyright is held by the author/owner(s).
SIGMIS-CPR'14, May 29–31, 2014, Singapore, Singapore.
ACM 978-1-4503-2625-4/14/05.
http://dx.doi.org/10.1145/2599990.2599994

Factors Affecting Team Performance in Globally Distributed Setting

Ashay Saxena
Indian Institute of Management Bangalore
Bannerghatta Road
Bangalore, India
ashay.saxena@iimb.ernet.in

Johanna Burmann
University of Erlangen
Schloßplatz 4
Nuremberg, Germany
johanna.jb.burmann@studium.fau.de

ABSTRACT

Organizations are currently facing important and unprecedented challenges in an ever dynamic, constantly changing and complex environment. Groups of individuals working across time, space and organizational boundaries with links strengthened by webs of communication technology, commonly referred to as virtual team, have become a "norm" in order to cater to the needs of global market places. Thus, it becomes essential to understand those factors that impact some of the key team related measures like efficiency, effectiveness and productivity of this evolved team setting. This paper presents a conceptual model and develops testable propositions highlighting factors that affect team performance in globally distributed setting. The research focus of this paper is on the impact of diversity, distributedness and task characteristics on team performance in distributed settings. Analysis plan and directions for future research are also discussed in the paper.

Categories and Subject Descriptors

H.1.m [**Models and Principles**]: Miscellaneous – *team performance, virtual teams.*

Keywords

Virtual Teams; Team Performance; Software Development Work

1. INTRODUCTION

The increased globalization and advancement of information and communication technologies (ICTs) have meant that project teams distributed across the globe have become common place. In order to tackle the growing complexity of their operations, more and more firms now introduce virtual teams into their day-to-day operations. The advantage associated with distributed teamwork is that knowledge from diverse contexts can be aggregated and put to use, regardless of geographical separation between the team members. Organizations can draw the benefit of working round the clock by placing the members of virtual teams in time zones that span the globe (Griffith et al. 2003). As opposed to collocated teams where the team members draw upon similar social networks and sources of knowledge resulting in highly redundant task related information (Granovetter 1973), virtual teams have the advantage of having access to unique information and know-how

Permission to make digital or hard copies of all or part of this work for personal or classroom use is granted without fee provided that copies are not made or distributed for profit or commercial advantage and that copies bear this notice and the full citation on the first page. Copyrights for components of this work owned by others than the author(s) must be honored. Abstracting with credit is permitted. To copy otherwise, or republish, to post on servers or to redistribute to lists, requires prior specific permission and/or a fee. Request permissions from permissions@acm.org.
SIGMIS-CPR'14, May 29–31, 2014, Singapore, Singapore.
Copyright is held by the owner/author(s). Publication rights licensed to ACM.
ACM 978-1-4503-2625-4/14/05...$15.00.
http://dx.doi.org/10.1145/2599990.2599995

resulting in innovation and creativity (Ariel 2000). This has opened up opportunities for organizations to cater effectively to global market places by availing the best resources possible. However, these settings pose their own set of challenges. The major challenge associated with virtual teams is that there is lack of trust in team members (Jarvenpaa et al 1999). The geographic dispersion of team members poses constraining effects on spontaneous and frequent interaction. Other problems include heavy reliance on technology to address the problems of coordination and communication. Virtual teams tend to "adapt their interactions" depending on the availability of communication technologies. Despite these challenges, recent years have seen an upsurge in the occurrence of virtual teams in organizations, and consequently focus in research has also paid attention to this form of execution of teamwork.

However, in nearly all studies on virtual/distributed teams[1], the specific characteristics arising out of 'distributedness', such as dimension and degree of a team's dispersion have been overlooked (O'Leary et al. 2004). So far the construct of 'distributedness' has not been investigated properly. Though there are perceptual measures of dispersion in literature, however quantifiable measure of dispersion in terms of time, space, and distribution of team members across sites has been investigated in only two studies (O'Leary et al. 2004; Upadhyaya and Krishna 2007). It becomes imperative to develop clarity on the role of 'distributedness' in such a setting, which is radically different from usual co-located settings. This paper presents a conceptual model for team performance and develops testable propositions by identifying antecedents to communication extensiveness in distributed setting.

The contribution of this paper is primarily the conceptual model depicting role of various task related, cultural diversity related and distribution related factors that affect performance of virtual teams. This paper attempts to address communication as a holistic construct affecting team performance for the entire project, rather than just looking at some particular communication technology or some particular phase of project. Moreover, quantifiable measures of distribution index have been used in the model in order to aid empirical testing in future.

The next section presents a literature review on virtual teams and constructs related to performance of virtual teams. Following this, conceptual model has been presented and relevant propositions have been laid out. The final section presents the limitations of the work and future directions for empirically testing the proposed model.

---

[1] The terms virtual and distributed have been used interchangeably in the document. They stand for the same thing; structures which operate while being geographically separated

2. LITERATURE REVIEW

This section reviews the extant literature on virtual teams in general, dimensions of distributedness, communication and team performance in such settings.

2.1 Virtual Teams

Team based organizing has emerged to be one of the most dominant patterns in intra organizational initiatives (Devine et al. 1999; Guzzo et al. 1992; Townsend et al. 1998). Organizations increasingly use teams to accomplish tasks that are critical in nature (Campion et al. 1993; Cohen et al. 1997). Many companies today are struggling to adapt their organizations in a way which is flexible enough for them to effectively deal with ever-changing market requirements, employee expectations and customer needs. In order to tackle these challenges, the phenomenon of virtual teams is gaining importance in organizations amply supported by rise in outsourcing, globalization, alliances and joint ventures. A growing body of literature is on virtual teams. Several constructs have been studied at various levels to gain more clarity about the functioning of virtual teams such as *communication* (Hersleb et al. 2003; Im et al. 2005; Jarvenpaa et al. 1999; Maznevski et al. 2000; Sosa et al. 2002; Wiesenfeld et al. 1999), *trust* (Coppola et al. 2004; Iacono et al. 1997; Jarvenpaa et al. 1999; Wilson et al. 2006; Zolin et al. 2004), *task characteristics* (Bell et al. 2002; Rico et al. 2005), *role of leadership* (Bell at al. 2002; Davis 2004; Kayworth et al. 2001; Yoo et al. 2004) and *extent of virtuality* (Chudoba et al. 2005; Lu et al. 2003; Shin 2004). However, the conceptual understanding of these teams and its associated artifacts is still in its nascent stages (Badrinarayanan & Arnett, 2008, Prasad & Akhilesh, 2002).

The perceptions of exact definition of a virtual team are manifold. However, some common characteristics which all definitions have in common are highlighted by Townsend et al. (1998): "Virtual teams are groups of geographically and/or organizationally dispersed coworkers that are assembled using a combination of telecommunications and information technologies to accomplish an organizational task". While a few virtual teams are created to permanently work on certain ongoing issues within a company, in many cases, they only work on a temporary basis and are often assembled based on specific project or customer requirements (Powell et al., 2004).

Researchers and managers alike often point out how virtual teams "enable organizations to become more flexible by providing the impressive productivity of team-based designs in environments where teamwork would have once been impossible" (Townsend et al., 1998). However, the utilization of this new type of team comes with various challenges and its success greatly depends on numerous factors. While the use of ICT allows overcoming constraints like the geographic dispersion of the team members and enables the collaboration of individuals who might otherwise not have been able to work together, it also poses great barriers on the effectiveness of their communication. Many members of virtual teams might find it difficult to adapt to the technologies they are using and might struggle with the idea that other team members are not physically present (Townsend et al., 1998). Non-verbal communication, which forms an important component of effective communication, is missing in this context.

Aspects which are unique to virtual teams compared to traditional co-located teams, but especially crucial in the communication process of the former, include: "time delays in sending feedback, lack of a common frame of reference for all members, differences in salience and interpretation of written text, and assurance of participation from remote team members" (Crampton, 2001; Mark, 2001). Thus, it is extremely important in this context to ensure a fit between the task, the technology and the structure of the work which a virtual team is supposed to carry out. Only if virtual team members are "able to adapt the technology and match it to the communication requirements of the task at hand" (Maznevski & Chudoba, 2001), it is likely to be effective (Powell et al., 2004).

The collaboration of virtual teams is only made possible by recent developments in the communications and information technology, such as Desktop Videoconferencing Systems, Collaborative Software Systems, the Internet and Intranets. All these systems and technologies allow team members to communicate effectively, to share ideas, to jointly work on projects and to store and retrieve huge amounts of data. These new developments, however, also entail "new challenges in structure, technology and function" (Townsend et al., 1998). The fluid membership of team members and the high flexibility associated with virtual teams makes it necessary for individuals to quickly adapt to changing team compositions and altering responsibilities or task requirements. Increased flexibility also goes hand in hand with a more dynamic functional role of the virtual team within an organization. Since virtual teams also allow the inclusion of members from outside the company, team members will have various different skill sets and competencies which need to be combined effectively. Even more complexity is added to this task due to the various cultural backgrounds of virtual team members (Townsend et al., 1998).

2.2 Degree of Distributedness

The conceptualization of separation between virtual teams has been powerfully affected by Allen's (1977) work on geographical distance and dyadic communication, and has been carried forward by O'Leary (2004) and his colleagues. O'Leary's (2004) work on team based dispersion has looked at three dimensions of dispersion in virtual teams: (1) Spatial: the actual geographic separation between teams, (2) Temporal: the measure of actual overlap of normal work hours and (3) Configurational: the measure of distribution of team members across number of sites.

Based on the above three dimensions, five kinds of indexes have been developed: Mileage Index, Time Zone Index, Site Index, Isolation Index and Imbalance Index. Table 1 highlights these indexes with brief summaries of each index.

Table 1. Distribution Indices (adapted from O'Leary & Cummings, 2004)

Index	Summary	Dimension
Mileage Index	Average distance between the sites	Spatial
Time Zone Index	Average number of time zones between members	Temporal
Site Index	Number of sites across which the project is distributed	Configurational
Isolation Index	Percentage of team members with no other member at their site	Configurational
Imbalance Index	Relative balance of membership across sites	Configurational

Mileage Index: This index captures the geographical separation between the sites. It is based on Allen's (1977) measure of distances. People need to use media frequently to communicate when separated by large distances. In such a scenario, face-to-face meetings are often not possible.

Time Zone Index: This index is developed using the time zone difference between the two sites. Same time zones between sites would provide an option of making conference calls between members during work hours, as work hours would be same for two locations. Different time zones would mean extending the workday for some members located in different locations in order to make use of conferencing facilities.

Site Index: This index simply measures the number of different sites a team operates from (Upadhyaya and Krishna 2007). Greater number of sites would lead to communication being mostly asynchronous (and thus less effective), as synchrony between different dispersed sites would be difficult to establish.

Isolation Index: This index measures the number of sites with isolated individual in cases when rest of the team operates from a different location. Teams with high level of isolation will face the problem of co-ordination. Members who are isolated at sites may find it difficult to share and receive information.

Imbalance Index: This index measures the relative balance of proportion of team members across each site (Upadhyaya and Krishna 2007). Problems related to communication as well as coordination are common in cases when members are split unevenly across sites. This index is different from isolation index in the sense that isolation index can capture the effects only when one team member is isolated.

2.3 Communication in Virtual Teams

Communication technologies have evolved to an extent that it has enabled interaction between people separated across time and space (Espinosa et al. 2003). Communication is a prerequisite for cooperative activities such as software development (Hersleb et al. 2003).

Media richness theory, developed by Richard L. Daft and Robert H. Lengel, posits that communication-media vary in their capabilities to convey the communication cues, to resolve ambiguity, and facilitate understanding. The basic premise of this theory is that communication media differ from each other in their ability to: (1) Provide instant feedback, (2) Usage of natural language, (3) Transmission of multiple cues, such as, tone and pitch of the voice, body language, and (4) Personal focus of the medium. Hence, "richer" means of communication such as face-to-face interaction are more effective in task and conflict resolution, as compared to 'leaner' means of communication where merely exchange of written words or only vocal exchange of information is possible. The choice of media to communicate plays an important role in determining the effectiveness and efficiency of knowledge exchange between the team members. Communication is effective when there is balance between the richness of the communication medium and attributes of the message to be communicated (Daft et al. 1986).

For virtual teams, the choice of communication media is closely tied with the nature of task (Rico et al. 2005). Previous research has also suggested that apart from the nature of task, an important role is that of social context in which the communication is embedded (Markus 1994; Wiesenfeld et al. 1999). Hence, despite the convenience of face-to-face communication, some teams may use leaner media such as email to communicate (Wiesenfeld et al. 1999).

Previous research has looked at various aspect of communication such as choice of media, volume of communication, lateral communication, norms of technology use, etc. (DeSantis et al. 1999) but most of the work is done on student teams and hence corresponding validity in organizational work teams is difficult to establish.

In the context of offshore-onsite software development, a recent study (Vlaar et al, 2008) concluded that team members in distributed setting rated "quality of interaction" as the most important factor for successful collaboration and communication between onsite and offshore members. In such cases of virtual settings, where there is lot of ambiguity, communication and coordination mechanisms are technology dependent, and there are differences in perception and understanding among various stakeholders.

2.4 Team Performance

A uniform singular measure of group performance effectiveness is not available in literature (Guzzo et al. 1996). Cohen (1997) emphasizes that various types of team have different performance drivers. Factors affecting co-located team performance cannot be extended to virtual teams. Team performance in virtual teams is a function of team empowerment (Kirkman et al. 2004). Lu et al. (2006) reported that geographic dispersion of team members does not have any significant influence on team performance, whereas increased use of ICTs and greater variety of practice inhibited team performance. Some evidence in research exists towards identifying certain factors of effectiveness in virtual teams such as, social factors, task related factors, and the role of communication (Lin et al. 2008). The construct of team performance used in this paper is generalizable to a particular context in which efficiency or effectiveness is deemed more important.

The literature on virtual teams point out that team performance is affected by the *interaction style* of team members (Kankanhalli et al. 2006; Potter et al. 2002). The interaction style or the communication mode between the members of the virtual team is enabled through communication technologies. Usage of richer media enables better flow of information, and enables coordination easily than when leaner media is used. Hence when rich media is used team performance would be better than when reliance is more on leaner media.

Virtual teams are usually observed in global software development work. Due to the complex nature of software development work, rich communication exchanges becomes the need of the hour. This gets impacted by various factors like time zone difference, isolation of team members etc. For instance, if the teams are separated by large geographical distances, time of work does not overlap to a large extent. Hence, some forms of communication like tele-conferencing and instant messaging becomes a challenge. Similarly, if some of the team members are isolated at specific sites, it becomes difficult for such individuals to keep up with latest developments and simultaneously communicate frequently. These factors get covered in the distribution index constructs which have been used in this paper.

Another factor that seems to have significant impact on team performance in such a setting is team diversity. There seems to be slight inconsistency in the literature in trying to explain the impact of diversity on group performance. On one hand, arguments have been put forward that group diversity leads to misunderstanding & disagreement and hinders group performance (Jehn et al. 1999) whereas on the other hand, it has been argued that if the dysfunctional levels of misunderstanding & disagreement in a workgroup are not so high that they outweigh the benefits from informational diversity, the group's diversity can be associated instead with high group performance (Bunderson & Sutcliffe 2002, Jehn et al. 1999). In order to explain the inconsistency of the observed effects of diversity on group performance, Huber and Lewis (2010) articulated the construct of 'cross-understanding' to explain relevant inconsistencies in the literature on groups and how different levels and different distributions of cross-understanding affect group performance. Cross-understanding refers to the extent to which group members have an accurate understanding of one another's mental models (Huber 2004).

Based on the above arguments, there is clearly a need for closer investigation of the impact of team diversity on its performance. Since cultural diversity has been assumed to critically impact team effectiveness (Evaristo 2003), and aspects of diversity are likely to be amplified in the virtual setting (Hofstede et al. 1997), these findings call for explanation.

3. CONCEPTUAL MODEL

This section presents the conceptual model depicting factors that affect team performance in distributed setting. The research focus of this paper is on the impact of diversity, distributedness and task characteristics on team performance in distributed settings. The research is proposed in global software development context, which is typically executed through the use of virtual teams.

Globally distributed work such as software development requires heavy reliance on advance collaborative and communication technologies. Use of hi-tech media has implications on development of 'shared, common, or mutual understanding' (Vlaar et al. 2008) since episodes of face to face meetings are rare or impossible in distributed setting.

The research model proposed in this study is shown in Figure 1. The model incorporates the need for interaction between the communication technologies and task type (Bell et al 2002; Maznevski et al. 2000; Montoya-Weiss et al. 2001; Rico et al. 2005). The concept of communication extensiveness essentially means the degree, amount or volume of communication during the project/team work.

The extent of distributedness has been hypothesized to have an impact on the communication extensiveness of the team/work group, as the degree of distributedness would impact the choice of communication media for frequent use, which in turn could have an impact on communication extensiveness.

Since virtual teams often draw members from different cultures, cultural team diversity plays a significant role in the overall functioning of these teams. Individuals from different cultural backgrounds communicate and make decisions differently (Adler 1997) and their verbal and non-verbal communication styles differ (Gudykunst 1988). Hence, cultural team diversity has been hypothesized to have an overall impact on communication extensiveness.

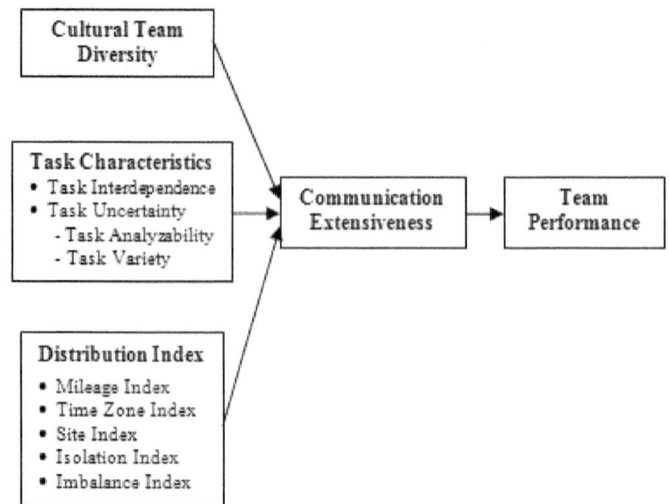

Figure 1. Conceptual Model

Table 2 below defines the scope of constructs and the source from literature, from where these definitions were adopted for the purpose of this study.

Table 2. Scope of Constructs

Constructs	Definition	Source
Cultural Team Diversity	Diversity due to differences in culture among team members	Kankanhalli et al. (2006)
Task Interdependence	Extent to which unit personnel are dependent upon one another to perform their individual jobs	Vegt et al. (2001)
Task Analyzability	Measure of how individuals respond to problems that arise	Daft & Macintosh (1981)
Task Variety	Frequency of unexpected and novel events that occur during information processing process	Daft & Macintosh (1981)
Distribution Index	Five indices of structural characteristics of distribution	O'Leary & Cummings (2004)
Communication Extensiveness	Cumulative score of media frequency weighted by media richness across all communication categories	Galvin (2000)
Team Performance	Effectiveness or Efficiency (based on specific context), are important dimensions used for defining this construct	Henderson & Lee (1992)

28

4. PROPOSITION DEVELOPMENT

This section discusses the links between various constructs presented in the conceptual model. Subsequently, it lays out relevant propositions between those links.

4.1 Distribution Index & Communication Extensiveness

We had earlier specified five key distribution indices (tabulated in Table 1). In this section, we take a closer look at all the indices and their implication on communication extensiveness.

4.1.1 Mileage Index

For higher values of mileage index, it is implied that the richer modes of communication, such as face to face interactions cannot take place at the same frequency as compared to teams which are low on mileage index. This has negative implication on the overall communication extensiveness of the team. People, in such scenarios, rely more on 'leaner media' to get their message across to other members. Subsequently, there is time delay in transmitting the entire communication cues and that invariably delays the entire process.

> **Proposition 1a:** Higher Mileage index of a virtual team will negatively affect the communication extensiveness between team members

4.1.2 Time Zone Index

Teams which are distributed more on the temporal index would use asynchronous media like e-mail, message boards, etc to communicate rather than tele/video conference. Use of synchronous media for communication such as tele/video conference would be contingent upon the number of overlapping work hours. Subsequently, the extent of communication would be severely impacted as almost all the communication is being done through the use of leaner media.

> **Proposition 1b:** Higher Time zone index of a virtual team will negatively affect the communication extensiveness between team members

4.1.3 Site Index

In distributed settings, teams usually operate from various cities across the globe. In these scenarios, face-to-face interaction is not usually possible. Hence, there is a significant dependence on digital means of communication, and a subsequent delay in communicating essential information.

> **Proposition 1c:** Higher Site index of a virtual team will negatively affect the communication extensiveness between team members

4.1.4 Isolation Index

In distributed settings, there could be instances of a single team member operating from a specific site whereas the entire team is operating from a different location. In such cases, isolation of that individual decreases other members' awareness of his activities. Moreover, isolated individual finds it difficult to share and receive information.

> **Proposition 1d:** Higher Isolation index of a virtual team will negatively affect the communication extensiveness between team members

4.1.5 Imbalance Index

If the proportion of team members across sites is not in balance, the minority team members feel out of loop and hesitate to share experiences. Hence, the extent of communication will go down. For teams which are distributed evenly, communication extensiveness should go up as members will be part of small sub-teams at their specific location.

> **Proposition 1e:** Higher Imbalance index of a virtual team will negatively affect the communication extensiveness between team members

4.2 Task Characteristics & Communication Extensiveness

Interaction between task type and communication technologies and its impact on team performance has been under investigated in literature (Bell et al. 2002; Maznevski et al. 2000; Montoya-Weiss et al. 2001; Rico et al. 2005). Since virtual teams rely heavily on communication technologies to coordinate their work, it is necessary to examine the relationship between nature of task and the effectiveness of communication which have an impact on team performance.

4.2.1 Task Interdependence

In collaborative software development environment, the nature of tasks performed by team members is highly interdependent. Task interdependence, the extent to which unit personnel are dependent upon one another to perform their individual jobs (Van de Ven 1976), is considered to be the most important structural variables that influence team performance (Langfred 2005). Higher levels of task interdependence means increased cooperation between the team members, as group members have to exchange information to complete the team's task. For lower levels of task interdependence, the need to exchange information is quite low (Vijfeiken et al. 2002).

The construct of task interdependence primarily focuses on the work flow (movement of ideas, resources, object and work) between the team members (Dailey 1978). In collaborative projects, the level of task interdependence is quite high (Vegt et al. 2001). In this context, high level of task interdependence would imply team members would interact frequently to share task related knowledge. Since the team members are distributed, they would rely on technology for communication exchanges.

> **Proposition 2:** Higher Task interdependence will positively affect communication extensiveness between team members in distributed work setting

4.2.2 Task Uncertainty

Software development projects are characterized by lot of uncertainty in terms of requirements and risk planning and followed by technological appropriateness till the project is completed. Uncertainty of tasks has been conceptualized using several dimensions of task complexity in literature. Some of the dimensions studied are task variety and task analyzability (Daft et al. 1981); variability (Ven et al. 1976); uniformity (Mohr 1971); predictability (Galbraith 1973) and complexity (Duncan 1972). The proposed model of information processing by Daft et al. (1981) is comprehensive and captures the nature of virtual team work effectively through the dimensions of task variety and task analyzability.

Task variety is the frequency of unexpected and novel events that occur during the information processing process. Low variety implies that team members know about the certainty with which future events will occur. High variety implies that team members will not be able to predict future activities. High variety would also imply lot of unplanned communication between team members. Communication frequency between team members will go up, resulting in overall high communication extensiveness.

> **Proposition 3:** Higher Task variety will positively affect communication extensiveness between team members in distributed work setting

Task analyzability is concerned with the way individuals respond to problems that arise. For analyzable process, task resolution is done objectively. Un-analyzable task require team members to think and find alternative methods for task resolution. For virtual teams, low levels of task analyzability would imply increase in knowledge exchanges between the team members for task resolution. Effective communication for difficult to analyze tasks would speed-up the process of task resolution.

> **Proposition 4:** Higher Task analyzability will negatively affect communication extensiveness between team members in distributed work setting

4.3 Team Diversity & Communication Extensiveness

Apart from highlighting the need for maintaining effective work environments, some of the researchers (Gruenfeld et al. 1996, Williams & O'Reilly 1998) have called for more team diversity to facilitate team performance. Looking at various conceptualizations of team diversity, two important types of team diversity proposed are functional (arising from differences in educational background, experience, and expertise among team members) and social category (arising from differences in race, culture, gender, and age among team members) (Pelled et al. 1999). The scope of this paper is focused on social category largely due to the fact that cultural differences play a significant and decisive role in distributed work settings (Fichman-Shachaf 2003).

An important aspect of social category diversity in virtual teams is *cultural diversity*. Cultural diversity includes national and linguistic differences among members as well as differences along broader cultural dimensions (Hofstede, 1991). Given that virtual team members bring their disparate cultural values to the team, it is important to know how cultural dimensions may affect communication extensiveness and subsequently performance in virtual teams.

Culture is a complex, multidimensional construct that can be studied on several levels: international, national, regional, business, and organizational (Shachaf 2008). Each individual is influenced by a wide range of cultural factors: ethnic, organizational, and national (Duarte & Snyder 2001, Schein 1992). Commonly used definitions of cultural diversity include racial, sexual, organizational, professional, and national heterogeneity (Shachaf 2008). Cultural diversity is here defined as heterogeneity of national cultures of team members; an individual's national culture is considered to be that of his or her country of residence.

Based on Hofstede's (1991) work, five bipolar dimensions of national culture have been identified—power distance, uncertainty avoidance, individualism, masculinity, and long-term orientation.

Power distance (PD) is a measure of the interpersonal power between a superior and a subordinate as perceived by the subordinate (Hofstede, 1991). PD dimension refers to the extent to which people accept inequality, as in hierarchy or a strict chain of command. The **Uncertainty avoidance** (UA) dimension determines the degree to which individuals feel threatened by, and try to avoid, ambiguous situations by establishing formal rules and rejecting deviant ideas and behaviours. **Individualism** implies belief in the primary importance of the individual as opposed to the group. **Masculinity** refers to cultures in which social gender roles are distinct. **Long-term orientation** is the degree to which people's efforts are focused toward the future rather than the present.

Of the five dimensions, individualism has been identified as particularly relevant in the context of studying teams (Paul et al. 2004, Sosik & Jung 2002). Prior research indicates that it influences cooperative behavior of individuals in a group and is likely to be the most important distinguishing feature of culture (Triandis, 1995). Alternatively, this dimension also impacts the extent of communication sought after by the specific team members. Team member, belonging to a culture which is high on individualism, is more likely to perform tasks independently and not share impediments of the process and discuss about the task with other members. On the other hand, individuals belonging to cultures high on collectivism/low on individualism would be more receptive to sharing ideas and hence would embrace more communication with other members for performing tasks.

> **Proposition 5:** Higher Cultural team diversity will negatively affect communication extensiveness among team members in distributed work setting

4.4 Communication Extensiveness & Team Performance

In congruence with the level of analysis of this paper, overall communication pattern between members at the team level is taken into account. Overall communication pattern over here refers to the extensiveness of communication through the use of several media for the project life cycle. Depending on the task characteristics, some communication medium may be more effective than the others. Several feedback loops between the members of virtual team across onsite and offsite occur with the intention of 'bridging information gaps', 'pre-empting and mitigating potential misunderstanding' and 'unearthing incorrect assumptions' (Vlaar et al. 2008).

The extent of communication would directly impact the team performance. Communication is seen as "most important factor that determined team success" (Suchan & Hayzak, 2001). Communication enhances team effectiveness if it is timely, helpful, and relevant to task at hand (Jarvenpaa & Leidner, 1999). Breakdown in communication can create duplication of effort and task overlaps.

> **Proposition 6:** Higher Communication extensiveness among team members will positively affect team performance in distributed work setting

Overall, Propositions (1-6) have attempted to capture the relationship established through various links in the conceptual model.

4.5 DATA COLLECTION & ANALYSIS PLAN

The proposed methodology for data collection is cross-sectional questionnaire based survey method. Survey research method is most prevalent in Information Systems (IS) area, as it allows for generalizability of the findings to the entire population apart from offering high level of reliability and validity which enables replication of the research (Balsley, 1970). The literature on virtual teams is mostly conceptual and majority of the empirical work is limited to student teams. There is a need to validate the conceptual understanding of virtual team dynamics. Hence, the sampling frame needs to be chosen as organizational work teams, which are distributed across sites.

The constructs used in the conceptual model are either quantifiable (distribution indices, communication extensiveness) or well established in the literature (task characteristics, cultural diversity) and hence empirically testable. Survey instrument needs to be designed by operationalizing the constructs from the respective sources mentioned in Table 2. Specifically, constructs related to task characteristics related scale can be adapted from Daft et al (1981) and Vegt et al (2001) work. Distribution Indices scale can be adapted from O'Leary & Cummings (2004) work. Cultural team Diversity related scale can be adapted from Hofstede (1991) work. Communication extensiveness can be measured by asking respondents to assign percentages to all available communication media on the basis of frequency of usage, weighed with a factor arrived from media richness theory, for a given communication category. Team performance related scale can be adapted from Henderson et al (1992) work.

Structural Equation Modeling (SEM) methodology is suited for the purpose of data analysis. SEM involves generalizations and extension from first generation techniques (PCA, factor analysis or multiple regressions) and when applied in the right manner they offer greater flexibility by simultaneously examining theory and measures (Hulland, 1999). Certain variables like *team size* and *project type* need to be controlled as these are not part of the proposed model. The measures of the constructs would be perceptual in nature (metric variables) and hence SEM would be useful in controlling the measurement errors. Validity and reliability of the developed scales need to be assessed using Partial Least Squares (PLS) analysis. In order to assess common method variance (CMV), as the study involves self-reported measures, Harman's one factor test and marker variable check needs to be deployed.

5. LIMITATIONS

Several limitations of this research should be noted. First, the focus of this paper is primarily on identifying team level factors, hence some of the individual level factors like task efficacy, motivation, satisfaction etc. have not been considered.

Second, the conceptual model described above does not consider elements of task conflict and subsequent role of conflict resolution impacting team performance. In instances of highly culturally diversified teams, researchers have looked at ways in which task conflict can arise and impact team performance (Kankanhalli et al. 2006, Hinds & Mortensen 2005). There is a need to further closely analyze this relationship between task conflict and team performance in distributed setting.

Third, the construct of cultural team diversity has been used in this paper based on Hofstede's dimensions of national culture. The complexity of culture is certainly not fully captured in a framework. One of the weaknesses of a dimensional approach is the underlying assumption that few dimensions can explain beliefs and values (Shachaf 2008). There is a need to use qualitative ethnographic methods in future to discover the significant components of culture.

Lastly, an empirical testing of the concepts is necessary to validate the proposed model. The findings from such an empirical testing will pave the way for further refinement and establishment of the model to analyze team performance in distributed setting.

6. ACKNOWLEDGMENTS

The authors would like to acknowledge the contribution of Prof. Mukta Kulkarni, IIMB for giving valuable feedback which helped in refining the conceptual model and propositions. The authors would also like to thank the two anonymous reviewers for their valued comments that helped in improving the quality of this paper.

7. REFERENCES

[1] Adler N.J. 1997. *International Dimensions of Organizational Behavior*, 3rd ed., PWS-Kent, Boston, MA

[2] Allen T.J. 1977. *Managing the Flow of Technology*, Cambridge, MA: MIT Press

[3] Ariel, S. 2000. Team Dispersion: The Effect of Geographical Dispersion on Team Process and Performance, In: Graduate School of Business, Stanford University

[4] Badrinarayanan, V. and D.B. Arnett, 2008. Effective virtual new product development teams: an integrated Framework *Journal of Business and Industrial Marketing*, 23, pp 242-248

[5] Balsley, H.L. 1970. *Quantitative Research Methods for Business and Economics*, Random House, New York

[6] Bell, B.S., and Kozlowski, S.W.J. 2002. A Typology of Virtual Teams: Implications for Effective Leadership, *Group and Organization Management* (27:1) , pp 14-50

[7] Bunderson, J. S., & Sutcliffe, K. M. 2002. Comparing alternative conceptualizations of functional diversity in management teams: Process and performance effects, *Academy of Management Journal*, 45, pp 875–893

[8] Campion, M.A., Medsker, G.J., and Higgs, A.C. 1993. Relations between work group characteristics and effectiveness: Implications for designing effective work groups, *Personnel Psychology* (46), pp 823-850

[9] Chudoba, K.M., Wynn, E., Lu, M., and Watson-Manheim, M.B., 2005. How Virtual Are We? Measuring Virtuality and Understanding Its Impact in a Global organization, *Information Systems Journal* (15), pp 279-306

[10] Cohen, S.G., and Bailey, D.E. 1997. What makes team work: Group effectiveness research from the shop floor to the executive suite, *Journal of Management* (23:3), pp 239-290

[11] Coppola, N.W., Hiltz, S.R. and Rotter, N.G. 2004. Building Trust in Virtual Teams, *IEEE Transactions on Professional Communication* (47:2), pp 95-104

[12] Crampton, C. 2001, The Mutual Knowledge Problem and its Consequences for Dispersed Collaboration, *Organization Science*, Vol. 12, No.3, pp. 346-371.

[13] Daft, R.L., and Lengel, R.H. 1986. Organizational Information Requirements, Media Richness and Structural Design, *Management Science* (32:5), pp 554-571

31

[14] Daft, R.L., and Macintosh, N.B. 1981. A Tentative Exploration into the Amount and Equivocality of Information Processing in Organizational Work Units, *Administrative Sciences Quarterly* (26), pp 207-224

[15] Dailey, R.C. 1978. The Role of Team and Task Characteristics in R&D Team Collaborative Problem Solving and Productivity, *Management Science* (24:15), pp 1579-1588

[16] Davis, D.D. 2004. The Tao of Leadership in Virtual Teams, *Organizational Dynamics* (33:1), pp 47-63

[17] DeSantis, G., and Monge, P. 1999. Introduction to the Special issue: Communication Processes for Virtual Organizations, *Organization Science* (10:6), pp 693-703

[18] Devine, D.J., Clayton, L.D., Philips, J.L., Dunford, B.B., and Melner, S.B. 1999. Teams in Organizations: Prevalence, Characteristics, and Effectiveness, *Small Group Research* 30, pp. 678-711

[19] Duarte, D., Snyder, N., 2001. *Mastering Virtual Teams: Strategies, Tools, and Techniques That Succeed*, Jossey-Bass, San Francisco, CA

[20] Duncan, R.B. 1972. Characteristics of Organizational Environment and Perceived Environmental Uncertainty, *Administrative Sciences Quarterly* 17, pp. 313-327

[21] Espinosa, J.A., Cummings, J.N., Wilson, J.M., and Pearce, B.M. 2003, Team Boundary Issues Across Multiple Global Firms, *Journal of Management Information Systems* (19:4), pp 157-190

[22] Evaristo, R., 2003. The management of distributed projects across cultures, *Journal of Global Information Management* 11 (4), pp. 58–70

[23] Fichman-Shachaf, P, 2003. Global Virtual Teams: The Impact of Cultural Diversity and Information and Communication Technology on Team Effectiveness. *School of Information and Library Science*, University of North Carolina, Chapel Hill, Doctor of Philosophy, 218

[24] Granovetter, M., 1973, The Strength of Weak Ties, *American Journal of Sociology* (78:6), pp 1360-1379

[25] Griffith, T.L., Sawyer, J.E., and Neale, M.A., 2003. Virtualness and Knowledge in Teams: Managing the Love Triangle of Organizations, Individuals and Information Technology, *MIS Quarterly* (27:2), pp 265-287

[26] Gruenfeld, D.H., Mannix, E.A., Williams, K.Y., and Neale, M.A., 1996. Group composition and decision making: How member familiarity and information distribution affect process and performance, *Organizational Behavior and Human Decision Processes*, 67, 1, pp. 1–15

[27] Gudykunst, W.B., and Ting-Toomey, S. 1988, *Culture and Interpersonal Communication*, Sage Publications, Newburry Park, CA

[28] Guzzo, R.A. and Dickson, M.W. 1996. Teams in Organizations: Recent Research on Performance and Effectiveness, *Annual Review of Psychology* (47), pp 307-338

[29] Guzzo, R.A. and Shea, G.P., 1992. Group Performance and Intergroup Relations in Organizations, *Handbook of Industrial and Organizational Psychology*, pp 269-313

[30] Hersleb, J.D., and Mockus, A., 2003. An Empirical Study of Speed and Communication in Globally Distributed Software Development, *IEEE Transactions on Engineering Management* (29:6), pp 481-494

[31] Hofstede, G.J., Vermunt, A., Smits M., and Noorderhaven N, 1997. Wired international teams: experiments in strategic decision making by multicultural virtual teams, in: *Proceedings of the 5th European Conference on Information Systems*, Vol. I, pp. 321–336

[32] Hofstede, G.H. 1991. *Cultures and Organizations: Software of the Mind.* London: McGraw- Hill

[33] Huber, G.P., 2004. *The necessary nature of future firms: Attributes of survivors in a changing world.* Thousand Oaks, CA: Sage

[34] Huber, G.P, and Lewis, K., 2010. Cross-understanding: Implications for group cognition and performance, *Academy of Management Review* (35:1), pp 6-26

[35] Hulland, J. 1999. Use of Partial Least Squares in Strategic Management Research: A review of four recent studies, *Strategic Management Journal*, Vol. 20, pp. 195-204

[36] Iacono, C.S., and Weisband, S. 1997. Developing trust in Virtual teams, *Proceedings of the Thirtieth Hawaii International Conference on System Sciences*, Wailea, HI, USA

[37] Im, H.G., Yates, J., and Orlikowski, W. 2005, Temporal Coordination through Communication: Using Genres in a Virtual Start-Up Organization, *Information Technology and People* (18:2), pp 89-119

[38] Jarvenpaa, S.L., and Leidner, D.E. 1999. Communication and Trust in Global Virtual Teams, *Organization Science* (10:6), pp. 791-815

[39] Jehn, K. A., Northcraft, G. B., and Neale, M. A., 1999. Why differences make a difference: A field study of diversity, conflict, and performance in workgroups, *Administrative Science Quarterly,* 44, pp 741–763

[40] Kankanhalli, A., Tan, B., and Wei, K., 2006. Conflict and Performance in Virtual Teams, *Journal of Management Information Systems*, (23:3), pp 237-274

[41] Kayworth, T.R., and Leidner, D.E., 2001. Leadership Effectiveness in Global Virtual Teams, *Journal of Management Information Systems* (18:3), pp 7-41

[42] Kirkman, B.L., Rosen, B., Tesluk, P.E., and Gibson, C.B. 2004. The Impact of Team Empowerment on Virtual Team Performance: The Moderating Role of Face-To-Face Interaction, *Academy of Management Journal* (47:2), pp 175-192

[43] Langfred, C.W. 2005. Autonomy and Performance in Teams: The Multilevel moderating Effect of Task Interdependence, *Journal of Management* (31:4), pp 513-529

[44] Lin, C., Standing, C., and Liu, Y. 2008. A Model to Develop Effective Virtual Teams, *Decision Support Systems*, 45, pp. 1031-1045

[45] Lu, M., Watson-Manheim, M.B., Chudoba, K.M., and Wynn, E. 2006. Virtuality and Team Performance: Understanding the Impact of Variety of Practice, *Journal of Global Information Technology Management* (9:1), pp 4-23

[46] Mark, G., 2001. Meeting Current Challenges for Virtually Collocated Teams: Participation, Culture, and Integration, in Chidambaram, L., and Zigures, I.(Eds.), *Our Virtual World: The Transformation of Work, Play and Life via Technology*, Hershey, PA: Idea Group Publishing, pp. 74-93.

[47] Markus, M.L., 1994. Electronic Mail as the Medium of Communication Choice, *Organization Science* (5), pp 502-527

[48] Maznevski, M.L., and Chudoba, K.M., 2000. Bridging Space Over Time: Global Virtual Team Dynamics and Effectiveness, *Organization Science* (11:5), pp 473-492

[49] Mohr, L.B., 1971. Organizational Technology and Organizational Structure, *Administrative Sciences Quarterly* (16), pp 444-459

[50] Montoya-Weiss, M.M., Massey, A.P., and Song, M., 2001. Getting It Together: Temporal Coordination and Conflict Management in Global Virtual Teams, *Academy of Management Journal* (44:6), pp 1251-1262

[51] Mortensen, M., and Hinds, P.J., 2001, Conflict and Shared Identity in Geographically Distributed Teams, *The International Journal of Conflict Management* (12:3), pp 212-238

[52] O'Leary, M.B. and Cummings, J.N., 2004. *Geographical Dispersion in Teams: The interplay of Theory and Methods*, MIT Sloan School of Management, 2004

[53] Paul, S., Samarah, I.M., Seetharaman, P., and Mykytyn, P.P., 2004. An empirical investigation of collaborative conflict management style in group support system-based global virtual teams, *Journal of Management Information Systems*, 21, 3, pp 185–222

[54] Pelled, L.H.; Eisenhardt, K.M.; and Xin, K.R., 1999. Exploring the black box: An analysis of work group diversity, conflict, and performance, *Administrative Science Quarterly*, 44, 1, pp 1–28

[55] Potter, R.E., and Balthazard, P.A., 2002. Virtual team Interaction Styles: Assessment and Effects, *International Journal of Human Computer Studies* (56:4), pp 423-443

[56] Powell, A., Piccoli, G., and Ives, B., 2004. Virtual Teams: Team Control Structure, Work Processes, and Team Effectiveness, *Information Technology & People* (17:4), pp 359-379

[57] Prasad, K. and K.B. Akhilesh, 2002. Global virtual teams: what impacts their design and performance? *Team Performance Management*, 8, pp 102 - 112

[58] Rico, R., and Cohen, S.G., 2005. Effects of Task Interdependence and Type of Communication on Performance in Virtual Teams, *Journal of Managerial Psychology* (20:3/4), pp 261-274

[59] Schein, E.H., 1992. *Organizational Culture and Leadership*, 2nd ed., Jossey-Bass, San Francisco, CA

[60] Shachaf, P., 2008. Cultural Diversity and information and communication technology impacts on global virtual teams: An exploratory study, *Information & Management* 45, pp 131-142

[61] Shin, Y., 2004. A Person-Environment Fit Model for Virtual Organizations, *Journal of Management* (30:5), pp 725-743

[62] Sosa, M.E., and Eppinger, S.D., 2002. Factors that Effect Technical Communication in Distributed Product Development: An Empirical Study in Telecommunications Industry, IEEE Transactions on Engineering Management (49:1), pp 45-58

[63] Sosik, J.J., and Jung, D.I., 2002. Work group characteristics and performance in collectivistic and individualistic cultures, *Journal of Social Psychology*, 142, 1, pp 5–24

[64] Suchan, J. & Hayzak, G., 2001. The Communication Characteristics of Virtual Teams: A Case Study, *IEEE transactions on Professional Communication*, 44(3), pp 174-186

[65] Townsend, A.M., DeMarie, S.M., and Hendrickson, A.R. 1998. Virtual Teams: Technology and the workplace of future, *Academy of Management Executive* (12:3), pp 17-29

[66] Triandis, H.C., 1995. *Individualism and Collectivism.* Boulder, CO: Westview

[67] Upadhyaya, A. and Krishna, S. 2007. Antecedents of knowledge sharing in globally distributed software development teams, *Proceedings of European Conference of Information Systems* (ECIS)

[68] Vegt, G.S.V.D., Emans, B.J.M., and Vliert, E.V.V.D., 2001. Patterns of Interdependence in Work Teams: A Two Level Investigation of the Relations with job and Team Satisfaction, *Personnel Psychology* (54:1), pp 51-69

[69] Ven, A.H.V.D., and Delbecq, A.L., 1976. Determinants of Coordination Modes Within Organizations, *American Sociological Review* 41, pp 322-338

[70] Vijfeiken, H.V., Kleingeld, A., Tuijl, H.V., Algera, J.A., and Thierry, H., 2002. Task Complexity and Task, Goal, and Reward Interdependence in Group Performance Management: A Prescriptive Model, *European Journal of Work and Organizational Psychology* (11:3), pp 363-383

[71] Vlaar, P.W.L., Van Fenema, P.C., and Tiwari V. 2008 Co-creating Understanding and Value in Distributed Work: How Members of Onsite and Offshore Vendor Teams Give, Make, Demand, or Break Sense *MIS Quarterly*, 32(2), pp 227-255

[72] Wiesenfeld, B.M., Raghuram, S., and Garud, R. 1999. Communication Patterns as Determinants of Organizational Identification in a Virtual Organization, *Organization Science* (10:6), pp 777-790

[73] Williams, K.Y., and O'Reilly, C.A., 1998. *Demography and diversity in organizations*, In B.M. Staw and R.M. Sutton (eds.), Research in Organizational Behavior. Stamford, CT: JAI Press, pp. 77–140

[74] Wilson, J.M., Straus, S.G., and McEvily, B., 2006. All in Due Time: Development of Trust in Computer Mediated and Face-To-Face Teams, *Organization Behaviour and Human Decision Process* (99:1), pp 16-33

[75] Yoo, Y., and Alavi, M., 2004. Ememrgent Leadership in Virtual Teams: What Do Emergent Leaders Do? *Information & Organization* (14:1), pp 27-59

[76] Zolin, R., Hinds, P.J., Fruchter, R., and Levitt, R.E., 2004. Interpersonal trust in cross-functional, geographically distributed work: A longitudinal study, *Information & Organization* (14:1)

Case Study: An Integrated First Year Experience and Tablet Program for Current Generations of Future IT Savvy Personnel

Malu Roldan, Ph.D.
Tanvi Kothari, Ph.D.
Lucas College and
Graduate School of Business
San Jose, CA 95192-0065
1-408-924-3411
malu.roldan@sjsu.edu
tanvi.kothari@sjsu.edu

EXTENDED ABSTRACT

College-goers have changed in a number of significant ways since the time when most current faculty were themselves undergraduates; various forms of demographic, personal, academic, and social analyses confirm that reality. Hence, it would be helpful to assess the value of program innovations for first year undergraduates to help faculty and administrators fully align them with the needs of current generations of students (e.g. Millennials). Coincidentally, the rise in penetration of tablets, smartphones and other mobile devices among students and instructors presents a unique opportunity to engage students by using such devices for both curricular and co-curricular activities. To maximize the impacts of these innovative platforms, it is ideal to integrate them into students' education at the earliest point, such as in a first year experience (FYE). At the Lucas College and Graduate School of Business, San Jose State University, we are leveraging these trends by building an integrated FYE facilitated with an iPad program with a focus on developing an IT savvy generation of graduates. To guide the implementation and evolution of the program we are employing a comprehensive set of measures, which include periodic surveys of students' technology skills and perspectives, an early warning system, learning goal assessments, student satisfaction surveys, and collection of curricular and co-curricular materials submitted by students.

Preliminary findings from a pre-test survey of students' technology skills and attitudes (n=329) show that the entering freshmen in this case study display high levels of self efficacy with their use of novel technologies for schoolwork, with scores averaging 7.2 to 9.15 (on a scale from 1 to 10) when asked to rate their confidence with using the novel technology with various types of support. The group's mean scores on self-efficacy with the use of productivity tools showed a progression from the highest confidence with word processing and web publishing, to less confidence with spreadsheets and the least confidence with databases. As expected, students display predominantly positive attitudes and low anxiety towards computers. Students tend to own and use mobile computing technologies, with more stating that they owned or used on a regular basis cellphones and laptops, and few stating the same for desktops, DVRs and fitness devices. Top ten ways students expect to use the iPads are: for research, taking notes, communication/networking, reading e-books/e-textbooks, using the learning management system, completing homework, time management, accessing productivity tools, replacing laptops, and web browsing.

The aforementioned findings point to a generation of students that already possess high levels of technology skills and great confidence and comfort with the use of technology. Our task is to enhance these skills to prepare them for even more sophisticated business technology applications. Aside from building their spreadsheet and database skills, there is an opportunity to steer students towards advanced tools for supporting their top ten expected uses for the iPad. As tablet technology and business adoption evolve, we expect to provide our students with training and guidance on new modes of authoring (e.g. greater use of multimedia), communication, and collaboration that they can expect to find (or perhaps introduce) in the organizations they join when they start their careers in a few years.

Categories and Subject Descriptors
K.3.1 [**Computers and Education**]: Computer Uses in Education – *collaborative learning, computer-assisted instruction*

General Terms
Management

Keywords
IT Education; Millennials; Computer Self Efficacy

Permission to make digital or hard copies of part or all of this work for personal or classroom use is granted without fee provided that copies are not made or distributed for profit or commercial advantage and that copies bear this notice and the full citation on the first page. Copyrights for third-party components of this work must be honored. For all other uses, contact the Owner/Author. Copyright is held by the owner/author(s).
SIGMIS-CPR '14, May 29–31 2014, Singapore, Singapore.
ACM 978-1-4503-2625-4/14/05.
http://dx.doi.org/10.1145/2599990.2599997

Developing a Well Employed IT Workforce in Pakistan

Dr. Malu Roldan
Dr. Ashraf Shirani
Lucas College and
Graduate School of Business
San Jose State University
San Jose, CA 95192-0244
1-408-924-7790
malu.roldan@sjsu.edu
ashraf.shirani@sjsu.edu

EXTENDED ABSTRACT

The Islamic Republic of Pakistan (Pakistan) represents a unique and important setting for IT workforce development and globalization. As an emerging economy with almost 40% of its population in the active workforce age range, Pakistan has the challenge of ensuring that both its sizable workforce develops the skills for gainful employment and that there are job opportunities that leverage the skills of this workforce. Gainful employment for a large majority of its population is key both to the economic development and stability of the country. The Pakistan government has implemented several programs to address labor force and education issues, most notably the 2010-2015 National Plan of Action for Decent Work, which aims to achieve "employment generation through human resource development, with a focus on employable skills [1]."

As part of the push to develop an IT workforce in Pakistan, The US State Department has funded a partnership between San Jose State University (SJSU) and Pakistan's Allama Iqbal Open University (AIOU). The partnership, called the Pakistan Distance Education Enhancement Program (PDEEP) is designed to build distance education capacity at AIOU, which serves more than 660,000 students throughout Pakistan through a correspondence program sending course materials via mail. In the current phase, SJSU is working with AIOU to build out its online delivery mode to build a foundation for an eCampus infrastructure. As part of this capacity building project, SJSU is also conducting a research study to develop recommendations on content to be delivered via this eCampus infrastructure.

To gain a better understanding of the Pakistan IT workforce needs and potential, SJSU researchers are conducting a survey of AIOU alumni, faculty, and Fulbright scholars. The survey aims to identify educational options, job search processes, career opportunities, and industry IT infrastructure from the point of view of workers who have been trained to enter the IT industry in Pakistan. Preliminary findings show that 84% of the survey respondents state that they have a full time job commensurate with their IT education. The majority of respondents have bachelors and/or master's degrees in Computer Science with a subset reporting additional certifications such as CCNA, MCP, OCP, MCSE, and MCDBA. Despite the successful employment of 84% of the respondents, only forty-nine percent rated Colleges and Universities in Pakistan as effective in preparing students for IT jobs and the job market and 42% of the respondents took 1 year or more to find a position that was commensurate with their IT training. Seventy one percent of respondents pointed to low salary and benefits as a major hurdle in finding suitable IT jobs.

An interesting finding that aligns well with the PDEEP project's focus on building an *eCampus* infrastructure at AIOU is the generally positive assessment of the Open University or online model by respondents. This points to the potential viability of this mode of instruction for reaching a greater number of the populace in Pakistan. Furthermore, graduates who are comfortable in an online environment will be ready for new, distributed modes of global talent sourcing such as *Odesk* and *eLance*. Respondent suggestions for improving the Open University offerings included: increased emphasis on problem solving and idea exploration, greater collaboration across universities and with industry, and greater alignment of offerings with current IT trends.

Categories and Subject Descriptors

K.3.2 [**Computer and Information Science Education**]: *Computer science education. Information systems education.*

General Terms

Management

Keywords

IT education; IT employment; IT workforce development; Pakistan

Permission to make digital or hard copies of part or all of this work for personal or classroom use is granted without fee provided that copies are not made or distributed for profit or commercial advantage and that copies bear this notice and the full citation on the first page. Copyrights for third-party components of this work must be honored. For all other uses, contact the Owner/Author. Copyright is held by the owner/author(s).

SIGMIS-CPR '14, May 29-31 2014, Singapore, Singapore.
ACM 978-1-4503-2625-4/14/05.
http://dx.doi.org/10.1145/2599990.2599997

REFERENCES

[1] International Labor Organization (2010). International Labor Organization, Decent Work Country Programme, ILO Country Office For Pakistan, 2010 – 2015. Retrieved July 25, 2013, from http://www.ilo.org/islamabad/country/lang--en/index.htm

Building Educational Capabilities through Information Technology in Developing Countries: It Takes a Village

Devinder Thapa
Luleå University of
Technology
Division of Computer and
Systems Science
Sweden
devinder.thapa@ltu.se

Maung K. Sein
University of Agder, Norway
Department of Information Systems
Luleå University of Technology
Sweden
maung.k.sein@uia.no

ABSTRACT

There is one aspect of globalization of IT work that appears only in fleeting glimpses in the mainstream IS literature and is sidelined in the discourse in general. If global IT work is painted mainly as outsourcing IT-infused work from developed countries to poorer countries (euphemistically referred to as "low income countries"), shouldn't the development of capabilities in these very same less-developed countries be a vital cog? Simply put, if these countries do not have a capable workforce, IT work, or any other work for that matter, cannot be outsourced to these countries. The question then is how can capabilities be developed in developing countries? In this research-in-progress paper, we address this question by examining a case of an activist-led initiative in Nepal called "Open Learning Exchange" (OLE in short) that used the capabilities of ICTs to deliver quality education to remote mountainous regions of Nepal. We collected data through interviews and group sessions as well as observations and document analyses. We are currently analyzing the data at both the micro and macro levels. At the micro level, we are using models from the IS training literature to gain an understanding of how training concepts developed in the West can explain the success of the initiative. Then we move to the macro level by shifting our interpretive gaze to the concept of "eco-system" in order to understand the role of the society and the surroundings in the implementation of capability building initiatives in developing countries and sustaining them.

Categories and Subject Descriptors

H.4 [**Information System applications**]: H.4.0 General
K.4 [**Computer and Society**]: Use of ICT for educational capabilities development – *teacher's training, collaboration, education.*

Keywords

Educational Capabilities; Information Ecology; OLE; Nepal; Rural Schools.

Permission to make digital or hard copies of all or part of this work for personal or classroom use is granted without fee provided that copies are not made or distributed for profit or commercial advantage and that copies bear this notice and the full citation on the first page. Copyrights for components of this work owned by others than ACM must be honored. Abstracting with credit is permitted. To copy otherwise, or republish, to post on servers or to redistribute to lists, requires prior specific permission and/or a fee. Request permissions from Permissions@acm.org.
SIGMIS-CPR '14, May 29–31 2014, Singapore, Singapore
Copyright 2014 ACM 978-1-4503-2625-4/14/05...$15.00.
http://dx.doi.org/10.1145/2599990.2599999

1. INTRODUCTION

If global IT work force has to become a viable proposition, the development of capabilities in developing countries is vital [1]. The groundwork for building this capability is arguably, education [2, 3]. Governments in developing countries are well aware of this. Providing quality education has become a high priority for governments who have set ambitious goals to raise the standard of mass education. However, they face massive challenges. Lack of resources, inadequate infrastructure, shortage of qualified teachers, outdated pedagogical approaches, lack of learning materials are just a few examples. These problems are multiplied many times over when the context is remote areas and particularly in mountainous regions. One answer to meet these challenges is using Information and Communication Technologies (ICT) [3, 4]. The question that arises is: *how can ICT be used to deliver quality education in remote mountain regions?*

In this paper, we seek to answer this question by examining how an non-government organization (NGO) called Open Learning Exchange (OLE) was successful raising the quality of education in a remote mountainous region of Nepal. OLE was launched by an activist in collaboration with a network infrastructure project called Nepal Wireless Network Project (NWNP), itself an activist led initiative [6]. Through the network, appropriate content based on the national curriculum was delivered to remote schools. In a setting where even basic learning materials, such as paper and pencil and text books, were scarce, such digitized content delivery was a huge leap. More importantly, it also changed the pedagogical approach from a teacher-centric paradigm to a student-centric (or self- learning) paradigm. The content was developed by OLE which was led by an enterprising ICT professional who had left a lucrative career in US to return to his homeland, Nepal. OLE collaborated with a number of key stakeholders, such as teachers who developed the learning material, the relevant government ministries and agencies and local district-level officials. At the delivery level, the project was a tight-knit collaboration between this NGO and the one that developed and maintained NWNP. At the local level, the project required tight collaboration with school officials, teachers and the community groups.

The success was based on a number of factors. Networking and community ownership and efficacious training approaches were key factors. We analyze these factors at the micro level through the interpretive lens of training models from IS literature and at the macro level through the interpretive lens of information ecology and eco-system. In the rest of this paper, we first briefly present the case, and then describe our data gathering process. We then provide our initial data analysis and findings.

2. The Case: OLE in Nepal

All Open Learning Exchange (OLE) was launched in September 2007 with the chief goal of using ICT to deliver quality education to remote mountainous regions of Nepal. The key initiators were two friends who had met while working in a technology firm in Silicon Valley in US. One was Rabi Karmacharya from Nepal who had graduated from MIT 3 years earlier. The other was Bryan Berry from US. As the first stage of the project, they targeted public schools in rural mountainous regions of the country. They quickly realized that at the core of the problem lay the lack of learning materials, such as text books. In schools where just a few years ago, basic materials such as pencils and papers were scarce, textbooks were a luxury. Even when textbooks were provided by the government, the delivery was often delayed by 2-3 months. To exacerbate the situation, there was also a dearth of qualified teachers. Most of the teachers were recruited from ex-Army personnel who had served in the famed Gurkha regiments of the British or Indian armies but had no formal teacher training and were not versed in pedagogical approaches.

The questions that OLE faced were: How could ICT be leveraged to meet its goals? More specifically, how could textbooks be delivered to students in rural schools? For OLE, the answer to these questions did not lie in textbooks per se: what was required was content. Once content was developed, there was a need for a medium to deliver the content. That meant a device (such as computer) and a network for transmission of the content. Fortunately, help was at hand for both. The well-known initiative, one laptop per child (OLPC) had been implemented in Nepal and many schools had benefited from it. That solved the medium problem. In Nepal, as in the rest of the world, OLPC was much hyped but was languishing with limited success. Partnering with OLE helped realize the promised benefits of the OLPC initiative.

The network problem was solved through partnering with the famous Nepal Wireless Network Project (NWNP). It was a mutually beneficial relationship. NWNP needed an application or service to deliver; OLE needed a network to transmit its material. It was a perfect match. NWNP was founded by another social activist, Mahabir Pun. Through the network, more than 160 villages had become connected to the Internet. To Pun though, mere connectivity was just the beginning: what was vital was what could be done with the connectivity. The affordance of connectivity was crucial. It had already provided healthcare and income generating activities to the villagers living in these remote mountainous regions [6]. Education was another affordance. It was here that partnering with OLE completed the picture.

All along the line, OLE enrolled various other actors such as Danish Government's local Grant authority, United Nations World Food Program (who provides free lunch to remote and rural public schools children), and Finnish Government's Funds for Local Cooperation.

Access was necessary, but far from sufficient. Content was crucial. To develop digital content appropriate to Nepal, OLE succeeded in enrolling the help and collaboration of the Nepal Government's Department of Education (DOE). The agreement was that OLE would develop interactive digital content which would be based on DOE's national curriculum. DOE would provide subject experts from its Curriculum Development Center who would help in the preparation and review of the educational material (named E-Paath). These interactive educational materials were thus designed to help teachers and students to meet the learning objectives outlined in the national curriculum.

These measures helped in meeting the challenge of accessibility and appropriate content. The next challenge for OLE was to develop skilled teachers who could realize the benefits of the digital content and the mode of delivery. As a prelude, OLE started to build confidence among public schools through discussions, and involving the teachers. Next, came the training to prepare teachers to integrate IT in daily teaching/learning activities. This was also collaboration between DOE and OLE. The training program was more focused on capacity building rather than teaching computer skills.

By 2008, OLE was ready to roll out the project as a pilot test in two rural public schools Bashuki and Bishwamitra. It was a success and also a learning experience. With teething problems solved, the initiative gradually expanded. By 2010, the project extended to 34 schools in ten districts and succeeded in providing quality education to more than 4000 children of public schools in rural and remote mountain areas of Nepal. OLE has installed local servers in all schools that contain digital library (E-Pustakalaya) and interactive learning resources (E-Paath). The schools are equipped with power backup and access points for students and teachers to easily access the materials in the servers. Currently, OLE's ICT based education programs are running in 50 schools in 16 districts across Nepal. The project provided benefits to more than 10,000 students, and trained over 300 school teachers.

In summary, the foundation of OLE Nepal was based on four principles:

- Development and distribution of free and open digital educational content
- Preparing teachers on effective integration of ICT in classroom teaching
- Research and development of appropriate technology and network infrastructure
- Building local capacity to monitor, support and sustain the program

3. DATA COLLECTION

The data collected is part of an ongoing larger case study on NWNP. Other aspects of the case have been reported elsewhere [6]. In this paper, we focus specifically on OLE. To do so, we collected additional data through a series of in-depth interviews with the founder of the OLE and NWNP projects, mainly in Kathmandu, the capital of Nepal. We visited several schools in three villages – Nangi, Tikot and Hetauda – and interviewed 40 stakeholders. The stakeholders included villagers, teachers, students, DOE officials, OLE content developers, district development officers, and chairperson of the village development committees. In addition, our direct observation of classroom activities, also added to our understanding. In Hetauda district, we conducted a focus group interviews with school board members, students and teachers. All the interviews and discussions were recorded with the permission of the participants. The recorded interviews were transcribed and analyzed using open coding and categorizing techniques taken partly from Strauss & Corbin [7].

4. ONGOING DATA ANALYSIS

We are currently analyzing the data at two levels. At the micro level, we are focusing on the training methods that have been used by OLE in training the teachers. To do so, we draw on the end-user training literature [8, 9, & 10]. Our initial analysis already reveals clear indications of normative and prescriptive concepts such as "training the trainers", "minimalist training", "motivational aspects". These concepts are parts of "training strategy" as postulated by Olfman et al. [11].

As our analysis progressed, it also became apparent to us that the micro – or training level – was only one part of the capacity building work achieved by OLE. The micro level was embedded in the larger context or the macro level. This embedded-ness of the micro in the macro is akin to Olfman et al. [11] notion of the "training strategy" being embedded in the organization's "learning strategy". When we therefore shifted our interpretive gaze to the contextual level, we found concept of "information ecology" to be an appropriate and useful lens for sense making [12]. *"An information ecology [is] a system of people, practices, values, and technologies in a particular local environment"* [12, p. 49]. The concept of information ecology particularly focuses on human activities that are served by technology. In applying the concept of information ecology, we cast OLE as an integral part, and perhaps the center, of an information eco-system. Our initial analysis reveals that OLE's achievements were made possible through its intricate and mutually beneficial network of relationships with other agencies, actors and stakeholders.

Our analysis has also revealed other intriguing aspects of the OLE initiative. There has been a fundamental change in pedagogical approach to primary education brought about by the use of ICTs. Chief amongst these changes is the move from teacher-centric to pupil-centric education. Two quotes from our respondents illustrate this change:

"Now students know more than teachers" (Pun)

"Things have changed. Now we have to prepare for classes" (A teacher)

Students have also become more creative by using the laptops in areas other than schoolwork. One student for example used his laptop to compose music.

These illustrations of preliminary findings bode well for a rich yield of both practical and theoretical insights from our study. At the conference, we plan to present the updated results of our ongoing analysis. Our findings are expected to provide some guidelines on how an ICT-based initiative can be successfully implemented to improve the quality of education in remote areas of a developing country. The consequences can make positive contributions towards developing a truly skilled global IT workforce.

5. REFERENCES

[1] Sen, A. 2000. Development as Freedom: Oxford University Press.

[2] Gulati, S. 2008. Technology-enhanced learning in developing nations: A review. The International Review of Research in Open and Distance Learning, 9(1), pp. 1-16.

[3] Haddad, W. D., Carnoy, M., Rinaldi, R., & Regel, O. 1990. Education and Development. Evidence for New Prioritie. Banque Mondiale Discussion Paper.

[4] Sife, A., Lwoga, E., & Sanga, C. 2007. New technologies for teaching and learning: Challenges for higher learning institutions in developing countries. International Journal of Education and Development using ICT, 3(2), pp. 57-67.

[5] Steinmueller, W. E. 2001. ICTs and the possibilities for leapfrogging by developing countries. International Labour Review, 140(2), pp. 193-210.

[6] Thapa, D., Sein, M. K., & Sæbø, Ø. 2012. Building collective capabilities through ICT in a mountain region of Nepal: where social capital leads to collective action. Information Technology for Development, 18(1), pp. 5-22.

[7] Strauss, A., & Corbin, J. 1994. Grounded theory methodology. Handbook of Qualitative Research, pp. 273-285.

[8] Sein, M. K., Bostrom, R. P., & Olfman, L. 1998. Rethinking end-user training strategy: applying a hierarchical knowledge-level model. Journal of End-User Computing, 9, pp. 32-39.

[9] Sein, M. K., & Simonsen, M. 2006. Effective training: applying frameworks to practice, Proceedings of the ACM SIGMIS CPR Conference, pp. 137-146.

[10] Simonsen, M., & Sein, M. K. 2004. Conceptual frameworks in practice: evaluating end-user training strategy in an organization. Proceedings of the ACM SIGMIS CPR Conference on computer personnel research: careers, culture, and ethics in a networked environment, pp. 14-24.

[11] Olfman, L., Bostrom, R. P., & Sein, M. K. 2006. Developing training strategies with an HCI perspective human-computer interaction and management information systems - applications. Advances in Management Information Systems, Vol. 5, pp. 258-283. NY: M. E. Sharpe: Armonk.

[12] Nardi, B. A., & O'Day, V. L. 1999. Information ecologies: Using Technology with Heart: The MIT press.

Learning in Knowledge Team: Can Passion in Teams' Activities Help?

Kyung Young Lee
Bishop's University
2600 College St.,
Lenoxville, Quebec, Canada
1-819-822-9600
klee@ubishops.ca

Geneviève Bassellier
McGill University
1001 Sherbrooke St. W.
Montreal Quebec, Canada
1-514-398-4221
genevieve.bassellier@mcgill.ca

ABSTRACT

This study investigates the antecedents of individual learning under knowledge team environments, where team members work together for a limited time period, share knowledge informally and eventually create a knowledge outcome that is beneficial for an organization. Participating in a knowledge team provides individual members with a good opportunity to learn during a short period of time, since they work on novel and creative tasks. However, because knowledge team activities are often non-routine for each member, their attitudes toward and psychological involvement with their knowledge team activities vary among different individuals. In this study, we suggest that *individual passion about knowledge team activities* is an important psychological input for *individual members' external knowledge sourcing, internal knowledge sharing, and helping behaviors*, which eventually lead to improving an individual's *learning outcomes* through knowledge team activities. We hypothesize that *individual passion about the activities in a knowledge team* positively influences both *1) knowledge management (sourcing and sharing) behavior; and 2) the organizational citizenship behavior – helping (OCB-helping)* of individuals, and these behaviors, in turn, result in their learning outcomes. Also, members' *perceived psychological safety within knowledge teams* positively moderates *the impact of members' passion on internal knowledge sharing and helping behavior on learning outcomes*. The research model will be tested with survey data from the knowledge team participants. We conclude with potential contributions of this study for the academy and practice.

Keywords

Individual learning, passion, knowledge teams, knowledge sourcing, knowledge sharing, organizational citizenship behavior, helping, and psychological safety

Permission to make digital or hard copies of all or part of this work for personal or classroom use is granted without fee provided that copies are not made or distributed for profit or commercial advantage and that copies bear this notice and the full citation on the first page. Copyrights for components of this work owned by others than ACM must be honored. Abstracting with credit is permitted. To copy otherwise, or republish, to post on servers or to redistribute to lists, requires prior specific permission and/or a fee. Request permissions from permissions@acm.org.
SIGMIS-CPR'14, May 29–31, 2014, Singapore, Singapore.
Copyright © 2014 ACM 978-1-4503-2625-4/14/05...$15.00.
http://dx.doi.org/10.1145/2599990.2600000

1. INTRODUCTION

Nowadays, in order to confront the fast-changing business environment, organizations often need to combine knowledge from different parts of organization in order to create something novel. With the help of advanced Information Communication Technologies (ICT) such as Wikis, virtual workplaces, (cloud) file sharing systems, and other various communication tools, it is now easier for organizations to form knowledge teams [16]. This form of team is prevalent in the current business environment, since it helps companies create something new without hiring additional human resources, and it combines and creates new knowledge from different geographical or functional areas within or across organizations [4; 17].

Participating in knowledge teams is also an important opportunity to learn from engaging in non-routine tasks with members of various areas of expertise. That is, in a team environment, individuals can learn from interaction with others [1]. To further investigate how professionals learn from participating in knowledge team activities, we take the perspective that one's psychological input influences individual learning outcomes through participating in learning behavior [37], while this link (individual input – behavior – learning outcome) is moderated by environmental factors in teams [21], such as the psychological environment in a team. Thus, this study aims to investigate the role of an individual's psychological input, behaviors, and team's psychological environment on *individual learning outcomes* in the context of knowledge teams. More specifically, we introduce the concept of *passion* in the knowledge team context and suggest that *passion about the activities of a knowledge team,* which refers to "the degree with which an individual has love, enthusiasm, and attachment to the activities (tasks) of the knowledge team [6], is an important individual input factor that influences three individual-level behaviors in knowledge teams; 1) knowledge sharing with other team members; 2) knowledge sourcing from external knowledge sources; and 3) organizational citizenship behavior of helping other team members (OCB-helping) [7; 36; 38], all of which should influence individual learning outcome. We also argue that the relationship between passion and members' internal behaviors (internal knowledge sharing and OCB-helping) is moderated by *psychological safety* [15].

This research aims to answer the following two questions: *"Is an individual's passion about knowledge team activities associated with her/his learning outcomes through learning and helping behaviors?"* and, *"Does psychological safety in a knowledge team improve the relationships between passion and knowledge sharing (and helping) behaviors?"*

To answer these research questions, we first review studies on passion and learning behaviors and outcome. Then, we develop a research model and briefly describe this study methodology.

2. THEORETICAL BACKGROUND

2.1 Passion as an important antecedent for learning behavior in knowledge teams

In extant literature, the term "passion" has been defined in several ways. For example, it is defined as the "persistent desire to succeed" [33], "intense positive feelings by engaging in an activity" [8], an "intense affective state" [11], and "attachment to a certain object", which is also referred to as a "reference target" [9]. In the organizational context, passion has been defined as *strong likeness, enthusiasm, and attachment to the activities individuals are doing* [6; 19].

Since passion entails *psychological attachment and strong likeness* to a reference target, and this feeling of attachment is supposed to come from a certain degree of experience with the reference target [3], passion originates from experience rather than inherently disposed feelings [8]. For example, an individual could have good feelings about playing tennis before s/he can actually play it, but it may not be possible to identify her/himself as a passionate tennis player without actually having the experience of playing this sport. With this in mind, we define an *individual's passion about her/his activities* as the degree with which an individual has experienced love, enthusiasm, and attachment to the activities (tasks) of the team [6].

In knowledge teams, by engaging in goal-setting, brainstorming, fulfilling team tasks, and interacting with other members, passion about some aspects of knowledge teams (e.g., on team activities) can be formed by the knowledge teams members during the tenure of their team. When active involvement in knowledge teams is not strictly mandated, knowledge team members will have different degrees of experience from team activities and thus varying degrees of passion about team activities. We argue that this variation in individuals' passion about team activities will eventually lead to how much they engage in team interaction behaviors.

2.2 Individuals' learning behaviors and OCB-helping behavior for team tasks

In the context of knowledge teams, we argue that there are three important individual behaviors that make a difference in individual learning outcomes: 1) internal knowledge sharing; 2) external knowledge sourcing; and 3) OCB-helping.

First, in a knowledge team, in order to create a novel outcome by combining the knowledge and experience of each member, team members' knowledge should be shared within the team. *Internal knowledge sharing* is defined as the activity of exchanging knowledge with the other members of a knowledge team [38]. Previous studies also argue that *knowledge sharing* within a work group is beneficial to group performance, and it can also help an individual obtain broader insights and skills [2; 34; 38].

Second, *external knowledge sourcing*, which refers to the activity of obtaining knowledge from external knowledge sources of a team [7; 18; 38], is important because knowledge teams are formed to create something new, whether the team goal is to produce a completely new business idea or to improve current

work processes. For this, members should look for appropriate knowledge and skills outside of their teams, using various knowledge sources [29; 39].

Third, *organizational citizenship behavior – helping* occurs when an individual uses discretion and decides to assist co-workers in their work or when they volunteer to do things that benefit the teams. It is defined as voluntarily assisting other group members in work-related areas [26; 36]. Within organizational teams, such behavior builds and preserves relationships among team members and improves the collective harmony of the members [36]. This helping behavior can be another important factor for accomplishing goals in knowledge teams, where members have never worked together before. In this study, we define *OCB-helping* as an individual team member's behavior that not only helps the other members fulfill their tasks in her/his team, but also helps the knowledge team accomplish its goal. This form of behavior is distinct from knowledge sharing with other members because helping behavior can go beyond merely sharing knowledge and skills. It helps members work together by improving collective harmony.

2.3 Individual learning outcomes as an accumulation of knowledge

Studies on learning clearly differentiate between *learning processes and learning outcomes*. Individuals' learning can be conceptualized as the *outcome* of the acquisition of knowledge or skills, while it can also be conceptualized as the *process* of acquiring knowledge [23]. Another distinction is that a learning outcome can be interpreted as *accumulation of new knowledge and skills* [1] and as *enhanced productivity* which focuses on the enhancement of productivity (reducing completion time) on group members' tasks, implying that a "learning curve" is involved due to the antecedents (e.g., exercise or previous experience on similar tasks) of this type of learning [24; 31]. From these two distinctions in the definitions of learning, this study looks at individuals' learning outcomes as the accumulation of new knowledge and skills, which results from individuals' participation in knowledge teams. Therefore, based on the definition of a learning outcome by Alavi et al. [1], we define an *individual learning outcome in a knowledge team* as an individual's change in knowledge representation as a result of the activities of her/his knowledge teams.

3. RESEARCH MODEL AND HYPOTHESIS

Based on the theoretical perspectives we introduced in previous section, we developed our research model in order to investigate the role of passion, knowledge management and helping behaviors and perceived psychological safety on individual's learning outcome. Our research model is depicted in Figure 1.

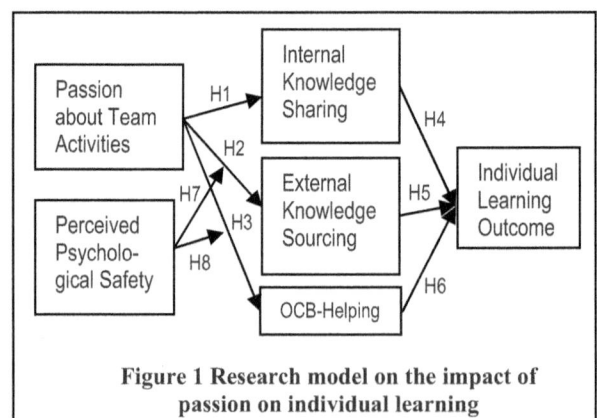

Figure 1 Research model on the impact of passion on individual learning

3.1 The impact of passion on individuals' knowledge management and helping behavior

Individual passion toward a certain object entails a high-level of liking [8], a desire to succeed [33], and deep psychological involvement [35]. Thus, when individual team members become excited about the goals and tasks of a knowledge team, they will not only try to engage in the activities to accomplish their sub-tasks as much as possible, but they will also put forth their extra time and effort to improve team outcomes by 1) sharing knowledge with other team members, 2) sourcing new knowledge externally, and 3) helping other members fulfill their tasks.

First, research suggests that passionate people like to share their seeds of ideas in order for others to add and reincorporate them [20]. In addition, they are willing to transfer and share their expertise [32]. Since members of a knowledge team have different background knowledge and interest in their topic, sharing knowledge within the knowledge team requires significant effort by its members. Thus, sharing knowledge in this environment may require one's deliberate effort to transfer, translate, and transform ideas that are from different knowledge sources [10]. An individual with passion about team activities will go through long and frustrating activities to engage in knowledge sharing, in order to make their team outcomes successful [35]. Therefore, we hypothesize that:

H1: Individual passion about knowledge team activities is positively associated with internal knowledge sharing behavior in one's knowledge team.

Second, to produce successful team outcome, passionate team members will broaden their social networks to reach out various knowledge sources. That is, they will try to use or expand their social networks to those who may help their team tasks [5]. For example, a passionate team member will reach out to people who have successfully done knowledge team activities previously to obtain their know-how from their experiences. Also, because s/he wants team outcomes to come out perfectly, s/he may reach out to industry experts for their group tasks, or may consult an online community that contains useful information for team outcomes. S/he will also spend time looking for the best examples related to their self-selected goals. As such, individual passion encourages an individual to engage in various external knowledge sourcing activities. With these perspectives, we hypothesize that:

H2: Individual passion about knowledge team activities is positively associated with external knowledge sourcing behavior.

Third, when an individual within a knowledge team becomes excited about the activities and goals of the team, s/he will not only try to engage in the activities to accomplish her/his own tasks in the team, but s/he will also put forth extra time and effort to improve the outcomes generated by the team as a whole. That is, a passionate individual will put in a great deal of effort to perform her/his sub-tasks, as well as to do her/his teamwork, nurture team members' relationships, and maintain collective harmony, whichever aspects of the team that help it move forward. Thus, s/he will voluntarily help others' work, which will be combined into one team outcome. The helping behavior within a team is manifested by "Organizational Citizenship Behavior-Helping," which includes volunteering to do things in the team, orienting others within the team, and assisting others' work that could benefit the outcomes of the team [26], which can be facilitated by passionate individuals. Therefore, we hypothesize that:

H3: Individual passion about knowledge team activities is positively associated with OCB-helping in one's knowledge team.

3.2 The impact of learning and helping behaviors on individual learning outcomes

Accumulation of knowledge occurs with the various activities of individuals. Professionals can learn from formal educational sessions or from learning materials, such as manuals, books, and trade journals. Further, they can learn by working on their tasks. In team environment, learning by doing one's tasks happens not only from an individual's interaction with the tasks themselves, but also through formal and informal communication among the team members [27; 30]. It is suggested that in order for an individual to achieve learning, two processes should occur: reception – perception of information in the learner's short-term memory – and structuring – mental activity of processing the information and connecting it to appropriate prerequisite concepts retrieved from the long-term memory to form new (or modified) knowledge [1] (P.406). As such, in team environment, an individual's learning starts with *reception* by communicating with other members and is achieved through *structuring* by challenging her/his initial understanding with others' points-of-view, clarifying her/his understanding of new perspectives and enhancing the comprehension of new information [1]. According to the perspective of communities of practice [22], learning is situated in practice and results from participating in communities of practitioners.

When an individual team member shares knowledge with the other team members as a group by exchanging her/his expertise, experiences and feedback, s/he can become engaged in an inflow of knowledge from other members to her/him, as well as an outflow of her/his knowledge to other members. The inflow of knowledge corresponds to the reception of new information from other team members while structuring occurs as he/she also processes the shared knowledge and connects it to his/her prerequisite concepts to modify his/her long-term memory [1]. In addition, while sharing one's knowledge with others – outflow – an individual participant in a knowledge team may often spend time with those who receive knowledge from her/him. By engaging in conversation to share one's knowledge with the others in their team, individuals get to know what the other members are working on, what kind of information and knowledge they need, and what concerns they have to improve their work performance. Thus, in both ways (inflow and outflow of knowledge), the activities of internal knowledge sharing make her/him become involved with many different aspects of the activities related to the team, which will eventually improve learning. Therefore, we hypothesize that:

H4: Internal knowledge sharing behavior positively influences individual learning outcomes.

As in the context of a community of practice where learning is situated in practice, individual learning in knowledge team is improved as a person actually engage in knowledge sourcing in teams. By participating in external knowledge sourcing for team tasks, a professional improves the reception of new information from external sources. This reception of new perspectives can be restructured when an individual actually applies the knowledge to team activities, which leads to learning outcomes [1; 18]. Research has also found that external knowledge sourcing behaviors help individuals learn new perspectives from various views and from external sources [7; 14]. Therefore, we hypothesize that:

H5: External knowledge sourcing behavior positively influences individual learning outcomes.

Helping is important to teams in organizations, especially when roles are interdependent and employee cooperation facilitates overall performance [36]. A knowledge team is a team that is composed with individuals from different backgrounds and is formed to produce a new aggregated outcome. Thus, the team's tasks are interdependent, and helping one another will create great synergy for final outcome. In this study we suggest that individual OCB-helping not only improves team outcomes but also enhances help-givers' individual learning outcomes. Indeed, as OCB-helping consists – among other things – in helping to orient other members [36] and with the interdependence nature of the tasks, a member will get to learn many aspects of her/his team tasks by helping to orient other members which requires reviewing the overall goals of one's team. Also, when individuals help others to learn and fulfill their responsibilities, they get to work on tasks that have the potential to help their own tasks, and they get to reflect on their own experiences. Moreover, an individual showing helping behavior for her/his team as a whole tends to become more involved in the task of finalizing team output. These activities eventually make an individual learn more about the tasks in the knowledge team. Therefore, we hypothesize that:

H6: OCB-helping behavior positively influences individual learning outcomes.

3.3 The moderation impact of psychological safety

Based on Webb's [37] framework of individuals' informal learning in team environments, we argue that environmental factors within a team should moderate the link between an individual's psychological input and his/her interaction behaviors or the link between the interaction behaviors and the learning outcomes. As this study contributes to the literature on learning by introducing "passion" as an important antecedent of learning, it focuses on a moderating factor that enhances *the impact of passion on individuals' interaction behaviors.*

In knowledge teams, where members are gathered from different parts of an organization, an *individual's perceived psychological safety* (the extent that an individual participant feels comfortable (safe) for interpersonal interaction and risk-taking within the team) should vary among different individuals [15]. It is found that psychological safety within a team encourages team members' learning behavior [15]. Also, it is found that psychological safety helps individuals in teams engage in quality improvement work [25]. We also believe that psychological safety have a direct effect on an individual's interaction behaviors in knowledge teams. However, instead of its direct impact on learning behaviors, we focus on its moderating effect on the relationship between individuals' passion about their team activities and their internal interaction behaviors (internal knowledge sharing and OCB helping) in knowledge teams, since we are interested in how an individual's perceived team environment affects the role of passion on his/her interaction behavior.

First, if an individual feels safe about interpersonal risk-taking, her/his passion about team activity will more strongly encourage her/him to share knowledge with team members. That is, if an individual team member with a high level of passion about his/her team work feels that s/he is comfortable with making a mistake in interpersonal interaction and asking other members questions, knowing that s/he will not be rejected by the other members for

being different in opinion, then s/he will contribute more time to looking for solutions to others' work and sharing their experiences, opinions, and knowledge about others' jobs. On the other hand, if s/he has passion about team activities, but perceives that the team environment is not safe enough to freely express her/his opinion or to share her/his knowledge about the team work, s/he may work hard to achieve good team outcomes by her/himself (because s/he has passion about team activities), but will not actively share her/his knowledge due to psychological fear about expressing her/his knowledge. With these perspectives, we hypothesize the following:

H7: Perceived psychological safety within a knowledge team positively moderates the relationship between passion about team activities and internal knowledge sharing behavior.

Second, in the same vein, we argue that psychological safety should enhance the relationship between passion and OCB-helping behavior within the team. In knowledge team environments, helping others entails not only an individual assisting others in doing their work, but also in taking the role of moving team work forward, persuading others' participation, and even finalizing team outcomes. If s/he feels that the psychological safety of her/his team is low, s/he may be passionate enough to do things in the team, but s/he will be reluctant to take on the role of making an extra effort to help others, persuade others' participation, and finalize team outcomes, because of her/his fear of being rejected by other members. However, if an individual participant of a knowledge team perceives that his/her team is a safe place to express opinions and make mistakes in trying different things, s/he will make more of an effort in helping others and taking the role of facilitating team work, as well as finalizing team outcomes, as long as s/he is willing to make an extra effort for the knowledge team. Therefore, we hypothesize that:

H8: Perceived psychological safety within a knowledge team positively moderates the relationship between passion about team activities and OCB-helping behavior.

4. METHODOLOGY

4.1 An overview of the research site

Survey data by the individuals who participate in knowledge teams were collected at a large South Korean firm operating in the educational service industry. This firm offers "home visiting private-tutoring services" and "book publishing". This research site is chosen because the participation in this knowledge team is not strictly mandated; thus, the individual's psychological attachment to the team activities varies among different individuals. The members in most knowledge teams in this research site have never worked together before; as a result, we can see the variation in their psychological safety

4.2 Item development procedure and pilot test

When not available, scales for the different constructs were developed. A pilot survey was performed with 94 respondents and results were used to refine the measures.

4.3 Measures

Measures will be presented at the conference.

4.4 Full scale test

The survey was administered to 1,300 individuals and a total of 402 completed the survey and 393 were usable response, for a response rate of 30.2%. Approximately 81% of the respondents were female, 85% were between 25 and 44 years old and had on average 64 months of tenure in their function. 86% had a university degree.

4.5 Data Analysis

Data will be analyzed for presentation at the conference. The analysis will test the measurement and structural model using Partial Least Squares (PLS) analysis with SmartPLS [28]. PLS analysis is chosen because we have a multi-path research model. In addition, the data for this study contain non-normal data, and PLS analysis also supports testing moderation effects [12; 13].

5. POTENTIAL CONTRIBUTION

The prospective results of our empirical study will contribute to the literature in several ways. First, broadly, we investigate the role of passion in the area of the knowledge management field. Passion has been studied frequently in the field of entrepreneurship and has explained the variance of the success of entrepreneurs [8] has not been studied much in the field of knowledge management. Second, the impact of knowledge management and helping behavior on individual's learning outcome will re-confirm the notion of learning from the perspective of Community of Practice (CoP), which posits that individual learning results from participating in communities of practitioners [22]. Finally, although individual's learning achieved from organizational activities is considered as an important outcome from team activities [15; 23], individual learning in teams have not been much focused on as compared to team-level outcomes such as effectiveness and creativity. Therefore, the result of this study will provide a practical implication that learning in knowledge teams is achieved from knowledge sharing activities and OCB activities, under psychologically safe environment. That is, the result will help general managers who facilitate knowledge team activities understand how to facilitate this type of team in order to improve employees' learning in a number of ways.

6. LIMITATION AND FUTURE RESEARCH SUGGESTION

There are some limitations of this study. First, we considered only positive side of passion in this study, although passion can cause negative outcomes if they are obsessive [35]. Also, if overall team activities are evolved into areas where an individual team member is not very passionate about, then the individual who might have been passionate about a certain aspect of team activities at the early stages of the team may not get engaged in team activities eventually, so that s/he may not be able to learn from team activities. Thus, future research should look at the negative impact of obsessive passion on individual's learning outcome as well as the impact of the fit between overall activities of a team and a specific activity that an individual is passionate about. Second, although we included psychological safety as an important team environmental (moderating) factor, when investigating a phenomenon in team environment, the characteristics of team tasks should also be considered. Thus, future research should look at the impact of task characteristics on the relationship among passion, knowledge management and OCB behaviors, and learning or other team level outcomes.

7. REFERENCES

[1] Alavi, M., Marakas, G.M., and Yoo, Y., 2002. A Comparative Study of Distributed Learning Environments on Learning Outcomes. *Information Systems Journal* 13, 4, 404-415.

[2] Allen, T.J., 1977. *Managing the Flow of Technology: Technology Transfer and the Dissemination of Technological Information Within the R&D Organization*. MIT Press, Cambridge, MA.

[3] Ashforth, B.E. and Mael, F., 1989. Social Identity Theory and the Organization. *Academy of Management Review* 14, 1, 20-39.

[4] Bakker, M., Leenders, R.T.A.J., Gabbay, S.M., Kratzer, J., and Engelen, J.M.L.V., 2006. Is trust really social capital? Knowledge sharing in product development projects. *Learning Organizations* 13, 6, 594 - 605.

[5] Baron, R.A., 2008. The role of affect in the entrepreneurial process. *Academy of Management Review* 33, 328-340.

[6] Baum, J.R. and Locke, E.A., 2004. The Relationship of Entrepreneurial Traits, Skill, and Motivation to Subsequent Venture Growth. *Journal of Applied Psychology* 89, 4, 587-598.

[7] Bresman, H., 2010. External Learning Activities and Team Performance: A Multimethod Field Study. *Organization Science 21*, 1, 81-96.

[8] Cardon, M.S., Wincent, J., Singh, J., and Drnovsek, M., 2009. The nature and experience of entrepreneurial passion. *Academy of Management Review* 34, 3, 511-532.

[9] Cardon, M.S., Zietsma, C., Saparito, P., Matherne, B., and Davis, C., 2005. A tale of passion: New insights into entrepreneurship from a parenthood metaphor. *Journal of Business Venturing* 20, 23-45.

[10] Carlile, P.R., 2004. Transferring, translating, and transforming: An integrative framework for managing knowledge across boundaries. *Organization Science* 15, 5, 555-568.

[11] Chen, X., Yao, X., and Kotha, S., 2009. Entrepreneur Passion and Preparedness in Business Plan Presentations: A Persuation Analysis of Venture Capitalists' Funding Decisions. *Academy of Management Journal* 199-214, 52, 1.

[12] Cummings, J.N., 2004. Work Groups, Structural Diversity, and Knowledge Sharing in a Global Organization. *Management Science* 50, 3, 352–364.

[13] Chin, W.W., 1998. Issues and Opinion on Structural Equation Modeling. *Mis Quarterly* 22, 1, vii-xvi.

[14] Chin, W.W., Marcolin, B.L., and Newsted, P.R., 2003. A Partial Least Squares Latent Variable Modeling Approach for Measuring Interaction Effects: Results from a Monte Carlo Simulation Study and an Electronic-Mail Emotion/Adoption Study *Information Systems Research* 14, 2, 189-217.

[15] Edmondson, A.C., 1999. Psychological safety and learning behavior in work teams. *Administrative Science Quarterly* 44, 350-383.

[16] Faraj, S. and Yan, A., 2009. Boundary Work in Knowledge Teams. *Journal of Applied Psychology* 94, 3, 604-617.

[17] Grawitch, M.J., Munz, D.C., Elliott, E.K., and Mathis, A., 2003. Promoting Creativity in Temporary Problem-Solving Groups: The Effects of Positive Mood and Autonomy in Problem Definition on Idea-Generating Performance. *Group Dynamics: Theory, Research, and Practice* 7, 3, 200-213.

[18] Gray, P.H. and Meister, D.B., 2004. Knowledge sourcing effectiveness. *Management Science* 50, 6, 821-834.

[19] Hagel, J., 2012. Exploring passion – what kind of passion do you have? *Edge Perspectives with John Hagel*, Permalink.

[20] Kane, G.C., Majchrzak, A., Johson, J., and Chen, G., 2009. Theorizing perspective development in fluid online collectives. In *Proceedings of the Web 2.0 Research Workshop* (Boston, MA, USA).

[21] Katz-Navon, T., Naveh, E., and Stern, Z., 2009. Active Learning: When Is More Better? The Case of Resident Physicians' Medical Errors. *Journal of Applied Psychology* 94, 5, 1200-1209.

[22] Lave, J. and Wenger, E., 1991. *Situated Learning: Legitimate Peripheral Participation*. Cambridge University Press, Cambridge, UK.

[23] Levitt, B. and March, J.G., 1988. Organizational learning. *Annual review of sociology*, 14, 319-340.

[24] Narayanan,S., Balasubramanian, S., and Swaminathan, J.M., 2009. A Matter of Balance: Specialization, Task Variety, and Individual Learning in a Software Maintenance Environment *Management Science* 55, 11, 1861-1876.

[25] Nembhard, I.M. and Edmondson, A.C., 2006. Making it safe: the effects of leader inclusiveness and professional status on psychological safety and improvement efforts in health care teams. *Journal of Organizational Behavior* 27, 7, 941-966.

[26] Ng, K.Y. and Van Dyne, L., 2005. Antecedents and Performance Consequences of Helping Behavior in Work Groups : A Multilevel Analysis. *Group Organization Management* 30, 5, 514-540.

[27] Reagans, R., Argote, L., and Brooks, D., 2005. Individual experience and experience working together: Predicting learning rates from knowing who knows what and knowing how to work together. *Management Science* 51, 6, 869-881.

[28] Ringle, C.M., Wende, S., and Will, A., 2005. *SmartPLS*, Hamburg, Germany.

[29] Rulke, D.L., Zaheer, S., and Anderson, M.H., 2000. Sources of managers' knowledge of organizational capabilities. *Organizational Behavior and Human Decision Processes* 82, 134-149.

[30] Ryu, C., Kim, Y.J., Chaudhury, A., and Rao, H.R., 2005. Knowledge acquisition via three learning processes in enterprise information portals: Learning-by-investment, learning-by-doing, and learning-from-others. *Mis Quarterly* 29, 2, 245-278.

[31] Schilling, M.A., Vidal, P., Ployhart, R.E., and Marangoni, A., 2003. Learning by doing something else: Variation, relatedness, and the learning curve. *Management Science* 49, 1, 39-56.

[32] Sie, L. and Yakhlef, A., 2009. Passion and expertise knowledge transfer. *Journal of Knowledge Management* 13, 4, 175-186.

[33] Smilor, R.W., 1997. Entrepreneurship: Reflections on a subversive activity. *Journal of Business Venturing* 12, 341-346.

[34] Tushman, M., 1977. Special boundary roles in the innovation process. *Administrative Science Quarterly* 22, 4, 587-605.

[35] Vallerand, R.J., Blanchard, C., Mageau, G.A., Koestner, R., Ratelle, C., Leonard, M., Gagne, M., and Marsolais, J., 2003. Les passions de l'ame: On obsessive and harmonious passion. *Journal of Personality and Social Psychology* 85, 756-767.

[36] Van Dyne, L. and Lepine, J.A., 1998. Helping and Voice Extra-Role Behaviors: Evidence of Construct and Predictive Validity. *Academy of Management Journal* 41, 1, 108-119.

[37] Webb, N.M., 1982. Student Interaction and Learning in Small Groups. *Review of Educational Research* 52, 3, 421-445.

[38] Wong, S. S., 2004. Distal and Local Group Learning: Performance Trade-Offs and Tensions. *Organization Science* 15, 6, 645-656.

[39] Zimmer, J.C., Henry, R.M., and Butler, B.S., 2007. Determinants of the use of relational and nonrelational information sources. *Journal of Management Information Systems* 24, 3, 297-331.

Knowledge Management and Consumerization of Information Technology: Opportunities and Challenges

Benyawarath Nithithanatchinnapat
College of Business
Washington State University
Pullman, Washington, USA 99164
1-509-715-7684 (phone)
b.nithithanatchinna@wsu.edu

K. D. Joshi
College of Business
Washington State University
Pullman, Washington, USA 99164
1-509-335-5722 (phone)
joshi@wsu.edu

ABSTRACT

The conduct of knowledge management (KM) is changing fundamentally due to consumerization of Information Technology. The consumerization of Information Technology (CoIT) is transforming the way knowledge workers conduct work and share knowledge and information. Therefore, knowledge management activities in an organization are no longer only supported by traditional Information and Communications Technologies (ICTs) (such as DB, DSS, data warehouses, email), but are also enabled through new forms of ICTs commonly referred to as social software or Web 2.0 technologies. Although, the ubiquitous and pervasive nature of these new forms of ICTs are creating a flexible KM environment, these digitized workspaces are also creating challenges. This study examines the following research question, *what opportunities and challenges do knowledge-intensive organizations face during the conduct of KM in a multiple platform technology environment?* In this research in progress, the preliminary findings (emerging research themes and potential research questions) from our pilot test are presented. When the study is completed, the multiple and diverse perspectives from the practitioner and scholarly journals plus interviews with knowledge workers and providers will be compared and contrasted to posit a more complete research agenda and management implications.

Categories and Subject Descriptors

K.4.3 Organizational Impacts; K.6.4 System Management

General Terms

Management, Design, Human Factors

Keywords

Mobile technology; social media; consumerization of IT; multiple technology platforms; knowledge management; social software

1. INTRODUCTION

The conduct of knowledge management (KM) is changing fundamentally due to consumerization of Information Technology [11]. The consumerization of Information Technology (CoIT), which refers to a phenomenon where new technologies emerge first in the consumer market and then get diffused into organizations, is transforming the way knowledge workers conduct work and share knowledge and information [10]. Therefore, knowledge management activities in an organization are no longer only supported by traditional Information and Communications Technologies (ICTs) (such as DB, DSS, data warehouses, email), but are also enabled through new forms of ICTs commonly referred to as social software or Web 2.0 technologies. As a result, the workspace of today's knowledge worker is not constrained by a desktop or even a particular technological platform, but instead, involves multitudes of devices and applications. Although, the ubiquitous and pervasive nature of these new forms of ICTs are making knowledge workers' workspaces more flexible, these digitized workspaces are also creating challenges for the workers because they are expected to work, learn, and share knowledge effectively, no matter where they are or what device they are using. We use the term multiple platform technology environment (MPTE) to characterize the work environments where workers use multiple applications (such as social software) that can be accessed via multiple devices (such as PCs, server, smartphone, tablets) which are running on multiple operating systems. MPTE is not new, but the pervasiveness of smartphone and online services (such as social software and online storage) have made these environments very ubiquitous[1].

Toyota Australia rolled out a tablet mobility strategy to its travelling sales workforce who while visiting 200 Australian dealerships used to carry a laptop and 3G dongle which constrained both IT asset utilization and knowledge workers' productivity [3]. The new tablet mobile strategy allows each sales staff to use a mobile device enabled with social software. This has resulted in increase in workers' productivity, professionalism, presentation and morale [3]. According to the 2012 consumerization of IT survey by InformationWeek, the obvious trend is the increased use of mobile devices and applications (such as Instant Messaging, videoconferencing, and enterprise social networking) in work environment [7]. From the perspective of an information technology research company, Mark McDonald, a group vice president and head of research in Gartner Executive Programs, said that CoIT is changing the nature of work by creating highly networked and digitized working environments that allow for knowledge flows among people without constraints based on position in the organization[2].

Permission to make digital or hard copies of all or part of this work for personal or classroom use is granted without fee provided that copies are not made or distributed for profit or commercial advantage and that copies bear this notice and the full citation on the first page. Copyrights for components of this work owned by others than ACM must be honored. Abstracting with credit is permitted. To copy otherwise, or republish, to post on servers or to redistribute to lists, requires prior specific permission and/or a fee. Request permissions from Permissions@acm.org.

SIGMIS-CPR '14, May 29 - 31 2014, Singapore, Singapore
Copyright 2014 ACM 978-1-4503-2625-4/14/05...$15.00.
http://dx.doi.org/10.1145/2599990.2600001

---

[1]www.webopedia.com/TERM/C/consumerization_of_it.html retrieved February 20, 2014

[2]From Gartner Blog Network, a page of a Mark McDonald, a group vice president and head of research in Gartner Executive

Similarly, the public and non-profit sectors are also realizing the benefits of CoIT in the context of knowledge management. According to a recent report by the European Union Agency for Network and Information Security, CoIT enables increased access, mobility, and work flexibility allowing for communication and collaboration among knowledge workers. This in turn could increase peer influence and knowledge sharing through modern channels, such as social networking, blogging, and chatting [4]. In addition, inside the United Nations Development Programme (UNDP), social software, such as social media tools and social networking sites, is bringing people together so that they can learn from each other through informal knowledge exchanges [9].

The aforementioned examples provide anecdotal evidence of the potential KM benefits social software provisioned through CoIT could bestow within both private and public sectors. However, it is not clear whether these new social software are substituting and thus cannibalizing the traditional ICTs implemented in organizations to enable the conduct of KM. Or do they have complementary effects and thus can co-exist? Therefore, the emerging relationship between the traditional technologies (such as knowledge repositories, knowledge portals) and contemporary social software (such as Web 2.0 technologies) is not clear and needs to be systematically examined by KM researchers [11]. This relationship between traditional and contemporary technologies used for conducting KM within the organizational boundaries is complex, not only because it introduces disparate technological platforms, but also because it changes the power dynamics among the users of KM technologies (i.e., organizational knowledge workers) and providers of KM technologies (such as organizational IT units). In this work, we attempt to throw some light on this complex relationship by uncovering the challenges and opportunities organizations face while conducting KM in multiple platform technology environments resulting from the use of both the traditional technologies and emerging social software enabled by Web 2.0 technologies.

Next we summarize the limited academic research conducted to examine the effects of CoIT on the conduct of KM within the organizational boundaries. Andriole [2] conducted an empirical study to examine the business impacts of Web 2.0 technologies and found that formal KM tools are replacing more informal Web 2.0 tools, a substitution trend he expects will continue. Harris et al. [6] uncovered how businesses deal with the KM challenges due to CoIT by minimizing its risk and maximizing its benefits. Using the knowledge based view of the firm, Von Krogh [11] posit a KM research agenda developed around five fundamental issues arising from the complexities of using social software for KM activities within profit-making organizations. This research agenda is built on the premise that organizations can garner rent from its knowledge resources and thus they need to develop institutional capabilities that focus on protecting and maintaining the value of its knowledge resources, an assumption not valid for not-for-profit organizations. Ford and Mason [5] look at how organizations maximize the benefits of social media applications and traditional KM systems, and conclude that social media could be very useful in knowledge sharing at multiple levels, such as in organizations, between groups, and among individual if the

Programs and co-author of The Social Organization with Anthony Bradley. Retrieved October 29, 2013, from http://blogs.gartner.com/mark_mcdonald/2012/06/21/the-consumerization-of-management-part-1/

tension induced by multiple platform technology environment (MPTE) regarding the roles, ownership, control, and value of knowledge are appropriately addressed.

The limited extant literature on the conduct of KM in MPTE primarily focus on profit-making organizations. We premise that because of differential knowledge management objectives, organizations in different industries (financial, education, retail) and sectors (public, private) are likely to encounter different opportunities and challenges in managing knowledge in MPTE. A very thorough review of KM research issues was done by Alavi and Leidner [1], since the technological landscape has changed significantly, we argue there is a need to re-examine the conduct of KM in the age of CoIT Therefore, in this study, we attempts to answer the following research question: *What opportunities and challenges do knowledge-intensive organizations face during the conduct of KM in a multiple platform technology environment?*

In this research in progress, the preliminary findings in form of emerging research themes and potential research questions) from our pilot test are presented. When the study is completed, the multiple and diverse perspectives from practitioner and scholarly journals plus interviews with knowledge workers and providers will be compared and contrasted to posit a more complete research agenda and management implications. The remainder of the paper is organized as follows. Section two explains our methodological approach. Section three summarizes the study's preliminary findings. And section four describes our next steps.

2. METHODOLOGY

2.1 Sampling

A pilot study was conducted to explore the phenomenon. For our pilot test, four research sites from both private and public sectors were included in our sample. The sample is comprised of knowledge-intensive organizations that offer products and services in form of knowledge representations (such as financial advice, innovation, and training) that heavily depend on organizational knowledge resources Holsapple and Joshi [8]. A total of nine participants who either performed the role of KM providers and/or KM users were interviewed. Table 1 summarizes our research sites and participants. Three sites are located in Thailand, those include (1) an internet-banking innovation unit within an IT department in a commercial bank (site A), (2) a research institute within a public university (site B), and (3) a nationwide project involving the government and a non-profit organization (site C). The fourth one is a research and development (R&D) unit in one of the US polymer company (site D).

Table 1: research sites and participants

Research site	Industry	Number of Participants	Participants' Roles
A – Private Sector	Banking	2	KM Users - 1 unit manager and 1 team lead
B – Public Sector	Public research institute	3	KM Users and Providers - 2 senior and 1 junior Scientists
C – Public Sector	Government and non-profits	3	KM Users and Providers - 2 project leaders

Research site	Industry	Number of Participants	Participants' Roles
			and 1 administrator
D – Private Sector	R&D intensive, startup company	1	KM User - Head of R&D

Moving forward, we plan on using a similar convenient sampling strategy to fully address the posited research question. Our research sample will include knowledge-intensive organizations included in the pilot. Organizational perspectives from two categories of knowledge workers, namely KM providers and KM users, will be captured. KM providers are knowledge workers responsible for provisioning IT enabled KM solutions in an organization, and could be people working in an IT department. For KM users, we will sample the participants who can provide an organizational level view of the opportunities and challenges in managing knowledge in MPTE. In addition, care will be taken to ensure that participants included in the study are aware of both the traditional and contemporary technologies used to support organizational KM activities.

2.2 Data Collection
The data was collected using unstructured interviews. We asked all nine participants opened-ended questions regarding (1) the benefits, positive impact, and/or opportunities of using social software supported by Web 2.0 technologies to conduct KM within a team/group, (2) the challenges or negative impact, or constraints imposed by these new technologies in the conduct of KM. Before the next round of interviews, the interview script will be revised and validated by two KM experts. For the pilot test, we decided to use note taking to make our participants feel comfortable. A combination of face-face and phone interviews were conducted to collect data. Each interview was typed up and sent back to the participants for verification, then it was translated from Thai to English. Each interview ranged from one to two hours.

2.3 Data Coding and Analysis
For the pilot test, one author coded all the interview transcripts to extract key challenges and opportunities. The second author reviewed all the coding and all the disagreements were resolved through discourse. After all the interviews was coded, the individually coded challenges and opportunities were iteratively analyzed to construct meaning. The first level of meaning was constructed by extracting all the coded instantiations and labeling them with brief descriptions that summarized the nature of challenge (or opportunity). These descriptions were then used to frame potential research questions which are listed in Table 2. In the second level of meaning making process, these descriptions were clustered into broader themes which are labelled as research themes.

3. PRELIMINARY FINDINGS
In this research in progress, we uncovered challenges and opportunities (framed as potential research questions) which fell into five research themes found in the extant literature. Even though the themes are not novel to the KM domain, the potential research questions that emerge from our analysis of the interview data are unique to the conduct of KM in MPTE. More specifically, the research questions focus on the issues that knowledge workers face while using technologies to conduct their work in a multiple-platform technology environment

3.1 Knowledge Flows within MPTE
Multiple knowledge flows related issues emerged in our data. The interview data suggests that the flow of knowledge between employees' personal devices and organizational systems is not smooth. This may result in loss of knowledge that is valuable to an organization. As one knowledge worker from site A indicates, *"If we could have something like LINE and [also] be able to link with the company knowledge base, that would be even better;"* implying a disconnect between the social software (i.e., LINE) and organizational knowledge base. The use of social software could also mitigate barriers to information flow created by bureaucratic hierarchies. This is reflected in the sentiments shared by a knowledge worker in site C who suggests that *"Reduced barriers to reach management staff which creates team unity is also the obvious benefit of LINE."* The interview data also revealed that some knowledge workers resist the use of new forms of ICTs and thus are in danger of being "socially isolated" from their peers. This is reflected in the following quote from a knowledge worker in site B, *"We feel closer to our LINE friends, than our friends that are not on LINE, there are a few scientists here who don't use [LINE]. Some have been very quiet and they don't use the technology, and thus now they seem to [work] in silos."* The sociality is being enacted in or through social software, therefore employees who are not participating in the digital interactions lose the ability to garner social capital thorough informal interactions. Future research needs to examine the presence and effects of this social isolation on employee turnover, morale, and productivity.

3.2 Knowledge Security
Securing organizational knowledge assets emerged as a challenge only in the interviews conducted at for-profit organizations. These organizations felt the need for institutionalizing security policies and legal contractual agreements with their employees to protect knowledge. One company mitigated the security risks by providing appropriate employee training regarding organizational policies. Whereas the second company protected its knowledge secrets legally by contractually not allowing their employees to work for their competitions for 3-5 years if they left the company. In the R&D intensive company, the risks of using social media outweighed the benefits, therefore only the use of Twitter was allowed.

3.3 Changing Nature of IT Work
As users are becoming more dependent on social software, they are becoming less dependent on their organizational IT units. This is evident in the following two quotes provided by knowledge workers at two separate sites, *"With Google Apps/Docs, we no longer have to beg for help from our busy web developers. Non-technical person can create an ad hoc web database like in a matter of few minutes;"* and *"It is tedious to request one from the university. So, we just figure out on our own, it's quicker."* How does this shift in the dependencies on IT unit's resources and capabilities affect the roles and responsibilities of IT workforce within organizations? What strategic value do IT units provide to an organization in the era of CoIT? Does the phenomenon of CoIT which empowers knowledge workers, marginalize IT units?

3.4 Social Software Designs

Our data also reveals knowledge workers' social software preferences during the conduct of KM. The workers' preferences suggest that different social software are suitable for different kinds of KM activities. In addition, participants' responses also suggest that the selection of social software is contingent on the nature of the device being used during the conduct of KM. For instance, one knowledge worker shared the rationale for their team's preferences as follows, *"There are so many functions available on Facebook, it's good on PC, but it's not good for team privacy. LINE is much better for teamwork because it gives us much more privacy. Plus, we can share emotions and pictures which creates a relaxed environment that helps with discussion, allows us to show our respect to our seniors, and our care for other team members"*

3.5 IT and Innovation

Our participants perceived that the use of social software and personal devices can help accelerate an organization's innovative processes. The participants mentioned that the use of social software positively affect innovation because these technologies expedite knowledge sharing and search. For instance, a knowledge worker at a research intensive company indicated, *"Mobile technology is very beneficial because it speeds up knowledge search and sharing, and of course speeds up the innovation. Features of mobile devices (specifically iPad and iPhone) help a lot. [They are] Not just useful in the meetings."*

Table 2 summarizes research questions related to the themes discussed above. These are the areas in which we believe further research is warranted

Table 2: Research themes and potential research questions

Research Themes	Potential Research Questions Derived from Our Data
Knowledge Flows within MPTE	• How can organizations transfer the knowledge assets and resources that are generated through the use of social software on knowledge workers' personal devices into organizational memory systems? Are the knowledge resources embedded in the newly created knowledge flows worth capturing? Are the new knowledge flows replacing (and possibly destroying) existing more formal knowledge flows institutionalized within the organizations or are they complementing them? • Can the use of social software help mitigate the impediments to work flows due to constraining information flows created by bureaucratic hierarchies? Can informal knowledge flows supported by social software help attenuate information asymmetry often created within the organizations to maintain control and power?
	• What are the effects of digital social isolation on knowledge workers' job satisfaction, performance, and development?
Changing Nature of IT Work	• How does this shift in the dependencies on IT unit's resources and capabilities affect the roles and responsibilities of IT workforce within organizations? • What strategic value do IT units provide to an organization in the era of CoIT? • Does the phenomenon of CoIT which empowers knowledge workers, marginalize IT units?
Knowledge Security	• Are the traditional legal and procedural agreements institutionalized to protect knowledge assets sufficient in the era of CoIT? • How can knowledge intensive organizations harness the benefits of online services (such as social media and storage) and mitigate the spill over risks of proprietary knowledge?
Social Software Design	• What factors shape a knowledge worker's design preferences?
IT and Innovation	• Can the adoption and use of social software accelerate firm innovation? • What knowledge processes can social software enable that could facilitate firm innovation?

4. CONCLUSION

Our preliminary findings reveal that the conduct of KM within MPTE creates novel and unique opportunities and challenges that the knowledge management and IT communities need to investigate. The sample size used to uncover the findings in this research in progress study is small. In order for this work to offer a systematic and unified research agenda for the conduct of KM in the era of CoIT, we need to not only conduct more interviews (i.e., increase the sample size), but also triangulate our findings by reviewing practitioner literature. In addition, emerging scholarly literature will also be reviewed to find out which of the issues revealed in our work are being addressed by the academic community. We are in the process of revising the script based on our preliminary findings which we will use to collect additional data. We hope to present a more complete research agenda at the conference.

5. REFERENCES

[1] ALAVI, M. and LEIDNER, D.E., 2001. Review: Knowledge management and knowledge management systems:

Conceptual foundations and research issues. *MIS quarterly*, 107-136.

[2] ANDRIOLE, S.J., 2010. Business impact of Web 2.0 technologies. *Communications of the ACM 53*, 12, 67-79.

[3] CLARKE, T., 2013. Car maker gets on the mobility bandwagon Sydney Morning Herald.

[4] ENISA, 2012. *Consumerization of IT: Top Risks and Opportunities.*

[5] FORD, D.P. and MASON, R.M., 2013. A Multilevel Perspective of Tensions Between Knowledge Management and Social Media. *Journal of Organizational Computing and Electronic Commerce 23*, 1-2, 7-33.

[6] HARRIS, J., IVES, B., and JUNGLAS, I., 2012. IT consumerization: when gadgets turn into enterprise IT tools. *MIS Quarterly Executive 11*, 3, 99-111.

[7] HEALEY, M., 2012. *Research: 2012 Consumerization of IT Survey.*

[8] HOLSAPPLE, C.W. and JOSHI, K.D., 2004. A formal knowledge management ontology: Conduct, activities, resources, and influences. *Journal of the American Society for Information Science and Technology 55*, 7, 593-612.

[9] UNDP, 2011. Inside UNDP Managing Knowledge, UNPD.

[10] VAR, C., 2013. Consumerization of IT Paves Way for Disruptive Technologies Wired.

[11] VON KROGH, G., 2012. How does social software change knowledge management? Toward a strategic research agenda. *The Journal of Strategic Information Systems 21*, 2, 154-164.

Cultural Richness versus Cultural Large Scale Insights: Culture, Globalization, and IT Workers

Extended Abstract

Michelle L. Kaarst-Brown
School of Information Studies
Syracuse University
Syracuse, NY 13244 USA
+1.315.443.1892
Mlbrow03@syr.edu

Indira R. Guzman
College of Information Systems
Trident University International
Cypress, CA 90630, USA
+1.714.816.0366
indira.guzman@trident.edu

ABSTRACT
The increasing globalization of business and of the Information Technology (IT) workforce has increased interest in cross-cultural issues associated with distributed software development, virtual teams, and cultural conflict or collaboration using information and communication technologies (ICT's) [6]. We continue to see a reliance on studies using quantitative methods that compare a limited number of cultural variables (such as Hofstede's 1984), often because of the challenges associated with richer interpretive or ethnographic studies. Ethnography is a traditional design approach when studying rich cultural issues, deeply rooted in anthropology and goals of rich, emic description, and understanding [1]. Unfortunately, in information systems (IS) research, there is a predominant emphasis on quantitative survey designs, sacrificing cultural richness for broader sampling of more limited variables. Our extended abstract proposes mixed method designs that incorporate both quantitative and qualitative methods as a viable, richer alternative to survey research of cultural studies. For purposes of our presentation at ACM SIGMIS-CPR, we are providing some preliminary arguments from our larger study where additional research is analyzed and compared. To illustrate our points, however, we briefly compare two IS cultural studies, one using comparative ethnography and one using a sequential, phased mixed method design. Our goal is not to discourage rich cultural ethnographies, but to provide a viable alternative approach that may enable more culture research in IS.

Categories and Subject Descriptors
H.0 Information Systems – General; K.4.0 Computers in Society – General; K.4.2 Computers in Society – Social Issues;

General Terms
Measurement, Human Factors, Design, Reliability, Verification.

Keywords
Research Design Choices, Culture, Ethnography, Mixed Method

Permission to make digital or hard copies of part or all of this work for personal or classroom use is granted without fee provided that copies are not made or distributed for profit or commercial advantage, and that copies bear this notice and the full citation on the first page. Copyrights for third-party components of this work must be honored. For all other uses, contact the owner/author(s). Copyright is held by the author/owner(s).
SIGMIS-CPR'14, May 29–31, 2014, Singapore, Singapore.
ACM 978-1-4503-2625-4/14/05
http://dx.doi.org/10.1145/2599990.2600002

1. INTRODUCTION
The increasing globalization of business and of the Information Technology (IT) workforce has increased interest in cross-cultural issues associated with distributed software development, virtual teams, and cultural conflict or collaboration using ICT's [6]. We continue to see a reliance on studies that consider quantitative methods that compare a limited number of cultural variables (such as Hofstede's 1984) to study cross cultural teams and other IS issues, often because of the many challenges associated with richer interpretive or ethnographic studies. For example, all researchers continue to face the methodological and design debate of whether to focus on a deep, rich ethnographic or interpretive study of a limited phenomenon, or try to gain broader, more generalizable insights by using survey or other large-scale research approaches. They further deal with challenges associated with access, time, and resources required for different designs, with ethnographic and other field based qualitative designs acknowledged as very time intensive, costly, and difficult to identify and gain access to suitable research sites [8].

1.1 New Considerations in Cultural Research in IS
There are many important cultural questions in information systems, and especially when considering the IT workforce. Domains and scope are evolving. We are studying more than organizations; we are moving from villages and small local firms to huge global firms and online communities. We are shifting from micro and local studies to macro and global and societal settings. Our data sources are expanding to include audio, video, online-real time, blogs, and twitter feeds. Yet the same basic challenges exist:

- Richness and depth versus parsimony and breadth
- What question do we want to answer?
- What story do we want to tell?
- Who will publish it?

There are hosts of compromises that we make, even as we seek to match the research question to the design [2].

1.2 Surveys versus Ethnography
One point we wish to make clear is that we are not arguing against survey design or discouraging ethnographic or other rich, field studies. Rather, when trying to integrate culture, globalization,

and the IT workforce, our consideration of cultural richness versus would benefit from moving away from paradigmatic debates to consider other issues and options than survey based designs.

With the increasing use of online data collection, the costs of survey studies have decreased in some ways, although incentive payments have become increasingly common and can certainly add up. Access issues also exist in obtaining a large enough sample size for statistically significant survey results, however, options for sampling are often varied and considerable. In comparison, field based qualitative methods such as ethnography often require the researcher to travel significant distances and incur high costs while they emerge in the cultural experiences of their chosen site. This is especially the case with cross-cultural studies where travel is not measured just in miles, but in number of countries involved.

While differences in total amount of time required surveying IT workers around the world is likely considerably shorter and less expensive the conducting a field-based ethnography of these same IT workers, there are other time related differences to these designs. This reflects in both the length of time from beginning to end of a project, but also in the phasing of the various stages of a study. Survey designs require much thinking in advance to identify theory, variables and measures, question wording, and sampling criteria. This is balanced by the relatively straightforward data entry, automated analysis, and write-up of findings. In comparison, ethnographic and other rich field based qualitative designs often have shorter periods prior to the start of data gathering, but the data collection period, analysis, and writing stages are laborious and intensive.

Unfortunately, not all cultural settings are ideal for survey research. From an organizational perspective, Schein [5] argued strongly that cultural studies must use qualitative methods in order to tap and understand deep structure issues. Unfortunately, within the IS discipline, Leidner and Kayworth [9] found that there is a predominance of survey designs and positivist case studies in IS culture research, with very few ethnographies or other interpretive designs. This predominance of quantitative survey design sacrifices cultural richness for broader sampling of more limited variables. To complicate the issue, researchers in different countries face their own discipline's preferences and legitimacy for quantitative versus qualitative research in cultural studies.

We hope that we can move this debate beyond the extremes of quantitative versus qualitative designs to study culture and IT workforce issues, and consider "mixed method design" a viable alternative that may bridge legitimacy gaps across countries and journals, while providing richer studies.

2. WHY MIXED METHOD DESIGNS IN CULTURAL STUDIES?

So, if there are weaknesses to survey designs when studying cultural issues in IS, and challenges in conducting richer, field based studies, then how can the case be made for using mixed methods for conducting research dealing with culture and information systems? To address this question, it helps to review briefly some specific characteristics and challenges of Ethnography and Mixed Method designs.

2.1 Ethnography versus Mixed Method Designs

Although there are many types of rich, field-based designs, we will focus here on the more traditional ethnographic cultural

studies as a point of comparison. Similar to surveys at one end of the paradigmatic debate, ethnography is often viewed as being on the other extreme. We have mentioned the value of a deep, rich study, but this takes time. The result of many interviews and long periods of fieldwork can be data overload. It can also be very difficult to narrow down a rich study into short articles [10, 13, 14, 16]. Figure 1 summarizes some key advantages and disadvantages of ethnographic design.

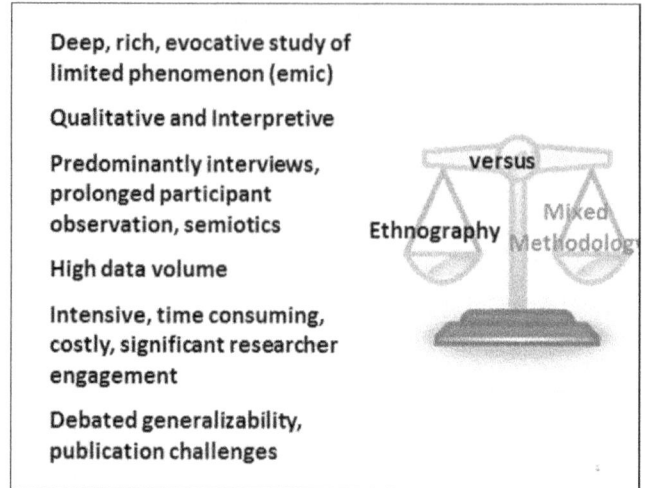

Figure 1: Ethnography: Summary of Pros and Cons

Mixed method approaches often can compensate for the leanness of traditional quantitative methods, but there are potential challenges in integrating data across methods, units of analysis, types of data, let alone different paradigms [2, 3, 4, 11, 12, 15, 17]. Still, the research and analysis can be accomplished in a much shorter time, on a smaller budget, and may be easier to access data sources. In many case, publication opportunities exist at each of the stages of the study, or for each of the methods used. Figure 2 summarizes some of the main advantages and disadvantages of mixed method designs.

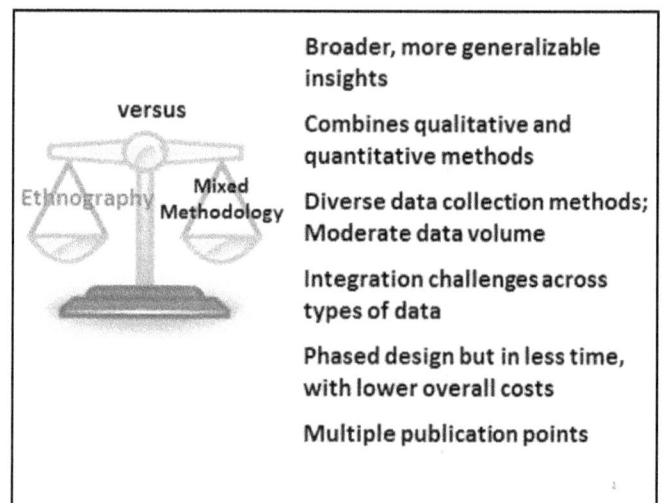

Figure 2: Mixed Method Design: Summary of Pros and Cons

3. A COMPARISON OF TWO STUDIES

We propose here that mixed method designs that incorporate both quantitative and qualitative methods offer a viable, richer alternative to pure survey research. While not replacing or equaling the depth provided by ethnographies, they balance researcher choices of breadth versus depth, and increase the viability of cultural studies in the IS field. While adding data collection and analysis steps to the design, they are less resource demanding than traditional ethnographies while delivering rich and compelling results. To illustrate this, we briefly compare two IS cultural studies, Kaarst-Brown's "IT Culture" study [7] using comparative ethnography of two large firms, and Guzman's [5] IT Occupation Culture and Commitment study using a sequential, phased mixed method design.

These dissertation studies were conducted by the authors some years ago, but are publicly available. As such, they provide the authors and the readers with some distance from original events as well as insights that go beyond what is in print. We hope that this evaluation will enrich discussion for researchers around the globe about culture, technology, and associated methodological decisions. Ultimately, we hope to show that beyond simple encouragement of more research into culture and information systems, richer cultural studies using mixed method designs are a viable area of inquiry that may overcome legitimacy or practical constraints.

As summarized above, ethnographic studies typically focus on a narrow aspect of the cultural phenomenon being studied (but delve much deeper into it), and survey-based quantitative studies are broader in scope (but limited in the amount of richness and insight they provide into the cultural phenomenon). Given this, how can the results of two studies that use these two very disparate approaches with different goals be compared?

We share with you two approaches to comparison; based on:

1. Goals, Assumptions, Paradigm, Research Stream Contributions

2. Challenges drawn from both mixed method and ethnographic designs: Complexity of Presentation, Legitimacy, Transferability or Generalizability, Integration of Data Across Methods, and the Politics of Acceptance/Usage [1, 10, 12]

In terms of their research methods, Kaarst-Brown [7] chose a comparative ethnography of two large companies, using multiple data collection and analysis methods. One site was on the east coast and one site on the west coast, requiring considerable travel for almost two years. Guzman [5] conducted a sequential, phased, mixed method design using both qualitative (focus groups, interviews) and quantitative methods [survey]. We want to point out that although Guzman drew largely upon a student sample, she was able to use an online service that accessed students from many universities throughout the US, and studied IT professionals relatively new to the IT field. (She later went on to replicate the study using the same survey with participants in four other countries.) Both researchers sought to investigate new concepts that had little a priori research to build upon: IT Culture (underlying assumptions about IT) and IT Occupational Culture and Commitment.

Table 1 summarizes across the goals, assumptions, paradigms and research streams to which these studies contribute. It is interesting to note that one studied embraced the subjective and irrational aspects of IT workers assumptions about IT, while the other focused on a rational view. As noted earlier, the challenges of writing ethnography are great. Writing *two* rich comparative ethnographies (almost 300 typed pages of the 700 page dissertation), and comparing them added to Kaarst-Brown's challenge.

Table 1: Comparison of Two Dissertations

	Kaarst-Brown (1995/1999) "IT Culture	Guzman (2006) "IT Occupational Culture"
Goals	Explore underlying assumptions about IT and their impact	Explore enculturation to IT work as it impacts commitment to IT career
Assumptions	Irrationality; sense making	Rationality
Tradition/ Paradigm	Anthropological & Interpretive	Applied Psychology & Social Sciences; Positivist
Research Streams/ Contributions	IT Governance & Strategic Mgmt.; IT Workforce; IT in Society	IT Governance & Strategic Mgmt.; IT Workforce & HR; IT in Society

Both studies seem to have been accepted by their peers as both have spawned follow-up studies and dissertations by other researchers. The Kaarst-Brown research has been referred to as groundbreaking and a foundation for future research [9], and has been reprinted several times in popular textbooks and collections of readings. Different parts of the Guzman study continue to be published in quality journals, and citations are mounting.

While Guzman's study did not provide long ethnographic case studies, her combined approach of focus groups and interviews yielded deep understanding of student and new IT worker's cultural conflict as they were enculturated to the IT occupation. Her survey results added breadth and confirmatory data, in a different way from Kaarst-Brown's literal replication with a second ethnography.

Both studies have high transferability to practical settings, both authors faced challenges associated with integrating data from multiple methods, and both faced the usual challenges associated with acceptance of new concepts and new approaches to IS research. As such, they seem quite comparable. The author's argue that the research designs could potentially have been reversed.

Table 2 summarizes our second approach to comparing these two studies, drawing upon and integrating key challenges presented in both the ethnography and mixed method literature [1, 10, 12].

4. CLOSING COMMENTS

Culture researchers studying IT workforce issues in the global context should not limit themselves to the most common survey/case study approaches (60%) using scales that are well known, but are not necessarily adapted to today's reality. With information and communications technology, our reality changes very rapidly and purely quantitative approaches may not always address the depth of "cultural" studies. Research design must be carefully matched to the research question. Ethnography provides rich, compelling insight to culture, however, mixed method designs that combine both qualitative and quantitative methods may be a viable alternative for many culture researchers. If you believe that ethnographic and other purely qualitative approaches are the only way to answer the cultural questions you pursue, but struggle with resources, we again encourage you to consider if a mixed-method design might help you achieve your goals.

Table 2. Comparison Criteria (Adapted from Bernard 1988; Leininger 1994, Onwuegbuzie and Leech 2004)

	Kaarst-Brown (1995)	Guzman (2006)
Complexity of Representation	High	Moderate
Legitimacy	High, but paradigm challenges still exit	Paradigm challenges reduced due to quantitative methods; Legitimacy for mixed methods increasing
Transferability or Validity and Generalizability	High	High
Integration Across Data Methods	High – Iterative & complimentary	High – Sequential and integrated
Politics of Acceptance and Use of Findings	High acceptance of findings from triangulated methods; Good citation count; Articles reprinted multiple times in IS text books	Moderate to High Acceptance of sequential mixed methods; (Some criticism of student sample but complementary use of IT workers; Good citation count

We hope you will consider pragmatic issues when choosing research designs for cultural studies in IS, and move beyond the dichotomy of depth versus breadth, to explore alternatives. As we see increased globalization of the IT workforce, we will all benefit by increasing our body of knowledge about cultural issues in IS research [Heinz and Leidner].

5. ACKNOWLEDGMENTS

Our thanks to the anonymous reviewers who provided valuable feedback and encouragement. We would also like to thank the program committee of ACM SIGMIS-CPR for allowing us to share our ideas virtually with the SIGMIS-CPR community.

6. REFERENCES

[1] Bernard, H. R. (1988) Cultural Anthropology. Sage, Beverly Hills, CA.

[2] Creswell, J. W. (1994) Research Design: Qualitative and Quantitative Approaches. Sage.

[3] Green, Jennifer D. (2008) Is Mixed Methods Social Inquiry a Distinctive Methodology? Journal of Mixed Methods Research, Vol. 2(1), 7-22. Sage.

[4] Greene, J. C., Caracelli, V. J. and Graham, W. F. (1989) Toward a Conceptual Framework for Mixed-Method Evaluation Designs. Educational Evaluation and Policy Analysis, Vol. 11, 255-274.

[5] Guzman, I. (2006) As you like I.T.: Occupational Culture and Commitment of New Information Technologists. Syracuse University, Syracuse, NY

[6] Heinzl, A. and Leidner, D (2012) "Information Systems and Culture - The World Might be Flat, but It is Culturally Rich (Editorial)". Business and Information Systems Engineering, Vol. 3, 109-110.

[7] Kaarst-Brown, M. (1995) A Theory of Information Technology Cultures: Magic Dragons, Wizards, and Archetypal Patterns, York University (Released 1999), Toronto, ON Canada.

[8] Kaarst-Brown, M.L. & Guzman, I.R. (2008) "Decisions, Decisions: Ethnography or mixed-method approaches to study cultural issues in IS Research". Cultural Attitudes Toward Technology and Communication (CATaC) 2008, Editors, F. Sudweeks, H. Hrochovec, and C. Ess. Nimes, France. June 24-27.

[9] Leidner, D. E. and Kayworth, T. (2006) Review: A Review of Culture in Information Systems Research: Toward a Theory of Information Technology Culture Conflict. MIS Quarterly, 30, 357.

[10] Leininger, M. (1994) Evaluation Criteria and Critique of Qualitative Research Studies. In Critical Issues in Qualitative Research Methods (Ed, Morse, J. M.). Sage, 95-115.

[11] Mingers, J. (2001) Combining IS research methods: Towards a pluralist methodology. Information Systems Research, 12, 240-259.

[12] Onwuegbuzie, A. J. and Leech, N. L. (2004) Enhancing the Interpretation of "Significant" Findings: The Role of Mixed Methods Research. The Qualitative Report, 9, 770-792.

[13] Schein, E. H. (1985) Organizational Culture and Leadership: A Dynamic View. Jossey Bass, San Francisco, CA.

[14] Schwartzman, H. B. (1993) Ethnography in Organizations. Sage.

[15] Tashakkori, A. and Teddlie, C. (1998) Combining Qualitative and Quantitative Approaches. Sage.

[16] Tedlock, B. (2003) Ethnography and Ethnographic Representation. In Strategies of Qualitative Inquiry (Ed, Lincoln, Y. S.), Sage, 165-213.

[17] Venkatesh, V., Brown, S.A. and Bala, H. (2013) Bridging the Qualitative-Quantitative Divide: Guidelines for Conducting Mixed Methods Research in Information Systems. MIS Quarterly, Vol. 37(1), 21-54.

Differences in Approach to and Output of Innovation: Study of "Established" and "New Entrant" Small Software Businesses in India

K.G. Satheesh Kumar
Asian School of Business
Technocity
Trivandrum, India
91-9847-060-016
k.g.kumar@ieee.org

Amalendu Jyotishi
Amrita School of Business
Kasavanahali
Bangalore, India
91-9900-213-825
amalendu_jyotishi@blr.amrita.edu

ABSTRACT
This paper examines whether and how established or incumbent firms and new entrants differ in their approach to innovation and innovation output. Analyzing three streams of theory we argue that established firms base their approach to innovation strategy on their resources, capabilities, technologies, and existing markets, while new entrants approach innovation from emerging customer needs and new markets. We also view that established companies are more likely to produce innovation related to new technology, products, and processes, while new entrants are more likely to perform marketing or business model innovations. Indepth qualitative interviews with CEOs and CEO- level officials in a sample of small software businesses in India produce results that support the conclusions from theory. These results have implications for industry and policy makers and open up avenues for further research.

Categories and Subject Descriptors
K.1: The Computing Industry
K.4.1: Public Policy Issues

General Terms
Management, Performance

Keywords
Incumbents; small business; established firms; new entrants; innovation strategy; Indian software industry

1. INTRODUCTION
This paper examines whether and how incumbent firms and new entrants differ in their approach to innovation strategy. Based on three strands of theory we argue that incumbent firms tend to

Permission to make digital or hard copies of all or part of this work for personal or classroom use is granted without fee provided that copies are not made or distributed for profit or commercial advantage and that copies bear this notice and the full citation on the first page. Copyrights for components of this work owned by others than ACM must be honored. Abstracting with credit is permitted. To copy otherwise, or republish, to post on servers or to redistribute to lists, requires prior specific permission and/or a fee. Request permissions from permissions@acm.org.

SIGMIS-CPR '14, May 29 - 31 2014, Singapore, Singapore
Copyright © 2014 ACM 978-1-4503-2625-4/14/05...$15.00.
http://dx.doi.org/10.1145/2599990.2600003

work forward from their resources, capabilities, technologies, and existing markets, while new entrants tend to work backwards from emerging customer needs and new markets; and that incumbent companies are more likely to do technology / product / process innovation, while new entrants are more likely to do marketing / business model innovation. We then analyze these on a sample of small software businesses employing the qualitative method of unstructured interviews. The findings agree with the premises based on theory, and may be further verified using more rigorous quantitative methods. They are important and relevant due to their implications on firm-level innovativeness, especially for incumbent firms who should avoid the problem of innovator's dilemma [12, 13]. Innovator's dilemma has been mostly researched as a large-company phenomenon, leaving out small businesses, and has been attributed more to the organizational structural and cultural inertia than to strategic capacity. By examining the approaches to innovation strategy in the small business sector, this paper attempts to understand these two knowledge gaps.

The relevance of this work lies in the increasing role of small businesses, world-over, in creating jobs and supporting supply chains. The micro, small, and medium enterprises (MSME) sector is the engine of economic growth in most economies, constituting a large fraction of the total number of enterprises. According to India's National Association of Software and Service Companies (NASSCOM), small businesses in Indian software industry introduce new products, services, and processes and develop breadth as well as depth in the industry's offerings (http://nasscom.org/will-small-be-big). This is important because large software companies in India already face an innovation challenge even as their software services outsourcing model, in operation for nearly three decades, nears its end-of-life. As computing moves onto mobile platforms with operating systems like Android and iOS, substantial innovation is being performed by small firms. It is in this context that this work, which attempts to understand the differences in innovation approaches of incumbent and new small businesses, becomes relevant and useful for the industry as well as for policy makers.

It is well-acknowledged that incumbent companies have a preference for incremental or sustaining innovations and become vulnerable to disruptive innovations by new entrants [12, 24, 40]. A range of reasons have been cited for this preference, including structural rigidities, dependence on investors and customers, system of performance appraisal and reward, financial evaluation process, short-term priorities, and culture. Studies in this regard have mostly focused on the innovation process in large firms with organizational inertia [25]. In line with this, the solutions prescribed include creating external small environments [8, 22], fringe or networked innovation [21], open innovation [11], external innovation [6], transaction cost leveling [27], and acquisition of innovative companies. Peripheral, fringe, external, or open innovation models are good for isolated product or service innovations, but not for strategic or business model innovations that create new businesses. Further they may be unsuitable for small firms.

Extant prescriptions avoid the fundamental issue of a firm's approach to innovation strategy. If incumbent organizations are skewed in their approach, their ability to develop new businesses will be limited. Firms basing innovation purely on one competence may soon find themselves at a competitive disadvantage with respect to others. A balanced approach is needed.

Many studies consider small firm environment to be agile in exploiting innovation opportunities [38], but does this imply a balanced approach to innovation? Do small firms, over time, acquire strategic rigidity and develop preferences to some innovation approaches, leaving gaps for new entrants to disrupt? Do their innovation strategies consciously or otherwise become based on technology prowess and existing markets, letting new unmet markets slip beyond their radar? Do they tend to become too confident of their technological competence, that they ignore the complementary role of marketing competence (ability to enter new markets)?

In the Indian software industry, where quality systems like ISO and CMM have created standardized, efficient and process-driven production environments, strategic capacity makes the difference between innovative and non-innovative firms [28]. While strategic capacity creates several innovation options, firm's structural context selects the options actually available to it [8]. Strategic capacity can generate a range of options only if it is well-rounded, else it will leave out opportunities. Extant studies have focused on structural context as the determinant of innovation [24, 37] paying less attention to the role of the approach to innovation, which arises from strategic capacity. This gap is addressed in this paper, in small businesses where structural context is likely to be less rigid, allowing strategy to play a more decisive role in the firm's innovation performance.

In the subsequent sections we bring out the theoretical aspects of the innovation approaches of incumbent firms and new entrants. Following this, a brief overview of Indian software industry is presented. We then present the findings of an in-depth qualitative study of twelve small software businesses: six incumbent and six new entrants. In this paper we use the terms "established" and "incumbent" interchangeably, to mean firms in business for over five years.

2. THEORETICAL BUILD-UP

We present below three streams of theory that suggest a preference by incumbent companies to pursue innovation strategies within their comfort zones of existing markets and technological competencies, even as new entrants venture out into uncharted territories of unmet customer needs, with potential disruptive effects on incumbents. These streams are: (1) dilemma of dichotomous choices, (2) the innovation process, innovative capability and innovation value chain, and (3) fundamental approaches to innovation strategies

Dichotomous choices create dilemma for incumbent firms, but not so much for new entrants. These include choosing between exploration and exploitation, induced and autonomous strategic processes, sustaining and disruptive innovations, and competency-enhancing and competence-destroying innovations [10, 13, 20, 35, 40]. The underlying difficulty that firms face in dichotomous situations is choosing between short term and long term objectives, which are often inconsistent, yet compete for the same scarce resources [30]. While short-term rewards are based on tactical choices and exploitation of assets, resources, and capabilities, long-term benefits are based on exploration and strategic decisions to build new assets, new resources and new capabilities to exploit future opportunities. Investors of incumbent firms expect them to generate short-term returns and hence managers have incentives to emphasize exploitation. Further, customers prefer continuous improvements in existing products and services, rather than pursuit of new areas of no immediate interest to them. Forced thus by investors and customers to chase immediate goals, incumbent firms often lose sight of long-term options. New entrants, on the other hand, are expected to invest in exploration, rather than immediate exploitation. Investors allow them time to build assets, resources, and capabilities that lead to future revenue flows. New entrants are encouraged to explore new business models, while incumbent firms need to maximize the exploitation of present business model and investments therein.

Innovation strategies based on exploitation of technological competencies and existing markets help increase the level of product integration, while innovation strategies based on exploration of new user segments tend to reduce it. Incumbent firms in the industry have a motivation to increase the level of integration, while new entrants have the opposite goal of disintegrating the vertical chain [29].

Organizational leadership has an important role in managing the challenge of dichotomous choices [33]. However, unlike new entrants, leadership interventions are not easy in incumbent firms because of hierarchy and process standardization. In the absence of intervention, middle level managers follow exploitative paths due to their predictable results and returns, rather than the risky, unsure path of exploration.

Notwithstanding a wide range of innovation theories and prescriptions, incumbent's dilemma remains real and unresolved, argues Steve [38], to the disadvantage of incumbent firms. Campbell and Park [9] found that the failure rate of incumbent companies attempting to grow new businesses has been 90% or sometimes even 99%. Disruptive innovations require offering products and services or doing activities fundamentally different and most existing companies find this painful. Unless absolutely unavoidable, incumbents tend to avoid doing that. New entrants do not have problem pursuing disruptive opportunities or new business models.

The second theoretical stream is related to managing innovative capabilities and the innovation process. Smith et al. [37] attempt a structured literature review and present a conceptual model of the factors influencing the ability of an organization to manage innovation. They conceptualize culture as the primary determinant of innovation. Other authors have looked at innovative capability as a function of the strategic, structural, technological and competitive context of a firm, and the ability of the business unit to understand these environments and their evolutions, as well as to respond to them effectively. Burgelman et al. [8] offer a framework for innovative capabilities audit, which groups variables influencing innovation strategies into five broad categories: resource availability, knowledge of the industry context and its evolution, knowledge of technological environment and its evolution, structural context, and managerial capacity to execute. The first three factors are related to the formulation of innovation strategies and the last two to strategy implementation.

Akman and Yilmaz [2] examine how innovation strategy, market orientation, and technological orientation influence innovative capability and innovation success of small and medium enterprises (SME) in a developing country. They found that market orientation, particularly customer orientation, is more relevant than technological orientation, for innovative capability of software SMEs.

Processes in the innovation value chain also determine the innovativeness and innovation success of an organization. FORA, the research and analysis division of the Danish Authority for Enterprise and Construction, identifies eight stages of innovation, classified broadly into "what to innovate" and "how to innovate" [34]. Software industry emphasizes the elements of "what to innovate", more than the elements of "how to innovate" [2]. A study of software firms in India by Kumar et al. [28] proposes a framework to assess innovative capability of a business unit in relation to its strategic innovation priorities. They found that innovative organizations significantly differed from less innovative ones in strategic and ideation capabilities, but not in implementation and commercialization capabilities, a finding similar to that of Akman and Yilmaz [2]. For incumbent companies and new entrants alike, conversion of ideas into products or services hardly differs, being fairly standardized and accessible at competitive rates. The difference between innovative and less-innovative companies lies in their strategic capacity and the related competence to generate and screen ideas. The first three factors of the framework for innovative capability audit [8] discussed earlier, related to the formulation of innovation strategy, work differently for new entrants and incumbent companies because they differ in their resources, knowledge of industry and technology contexts, and their evolutions. Incumbent companies would be at an advantage in existing markets where their knowledge lies. They may also control technologies, complementary assets, intellectual property, and technology development / R&D assets. Hence they will be in a better position to initiate innovation based on technology and existing markets. New entrants on the other hand will be at a disadvantage on these aspects and will need to search for opportunities elsewhere in new markets.

The third stream of innovation theory relates to the fundamental innovation approaches or strategies available to firms and how incumbent players and new entrants differ in conducting the processes of idea selection and screening. Christensen [13] envisioned two broad approaches to innovation: one starting with technology as given and seeking markets, and the other starting with markets as given and seeking new technologies. Their subsequent work, "Innovator's Solution" [15] expands the idea to include new market disruptions. Narasimhalu [31] also identifies innovation perspectives as market-driven or resource-driven. Rosted [36] observes an increasing emphasis on user-centric and user-driven innovation, over technology-driven innovation. NESTA [34], based on five case studies, identifies customers' ideas, demand, and experiences as sources of innovation. Akman and Yilmaz [2] found customer orientation (behavior directed at understanding customer needs and creating value for the customer) to be an important factor. Keskin [26] found that firm innovativeness was influenced by learning-orientation, which was, in turn, influenced by market-orientation.

The external environment of innovation, which partly shapes a firm's innovation strategy, includes forces that may be macro or micro in nature. Public policy is an important environmental input that plays a role in fostering innovation [39]. Government can promote innovation through policies that support revenue streams; through collaborative projects involving universities, R&D institutions and industries; and by improving the overall environment through creation of clusters [3]. In India, the National Innovation Council envisages creating an ecosystem of institutions, policies, incentives and tools to spur innovation. Interventions and macro-environmental changes lead to new user needs and new markets. EIU [19] identifies several direct and indirect macro-level factors driving innovation in an economy including R&D spend, quality of infrastructure, education and skill of workforce, political and microeconomic stability, regulatory environment, etc. CII & INSEAD [16] identifies five macro-level enablers namely, institutions, human capacity, infrastructure, market sophistication and business. At the micro-level the environmental factors driving innovation relate to competitors, collaborators, and customers [1]. At the firm-level, the key drivers of innovation success are resources and capabilities, structured processes of idea generation, screening and execution, and organizational leadership and skilled human resources [3, 14, 23].

Summarizing the above discussion, three fundamental approaches are available, to innovation strategy: (1) based on resources, capabilities, and technologies (RCT), (2) based on existing markets and industry (EM), and (3) based on new unmet user needs and emerging markets/industries (NM). In the first approach, technological competencies, resources, patents, and experience can lead firms to introduce new products, services, or businesses into the market. Using their technology prowess firms may introduce products even before customers have articulated or even identified a need [7]. The second approach to innovation strategy is by following the changes in the existing market trends, which may create new innovation opportunities. This requires close and careful attention of existing customers and their requirements, as well as competitors' responses. The third approach to innovation is based on new or unmet customer needs. This approach is prone to be risky and challenging as customer needs as well as innovations to satisfy them will remain fluid in a pre-paradigmatic phase [39] for a period of time.

Existing firms might consider the third innovation strategy an unnecessary risk, difficult to assess or inadequately rewarding on the basis of their financial metrics, and not compatible with their resources, capabilities and complementary assets [39]. Campbell and Park [9] argue that promising growth opportunities are rare for mature companies and hence they may reject new projects till a really good one emerges. Many established companies have considerations like BET (break-even-time) and opportunity costs which prevent them from waiting too long for a venture to turn profitable. They may also be constrained by a minimum acceptable level of return [14]. New entrants are usually free from such considerations and will be more risk-taking and willing to allow themselves the time it takes for the rewards to come. They will be more willing to embrace a new business opportunity, pursuing the third innovation approach (NM), while existing companies limit themselves to the more familiar turfs of technology and existing markets by following the first two approaches (RCT and EM).

All the three threads of innovation theory discussed above point in the same direction: incumbent companies and new entrants have reasons and incentives to adopt different approaches to innovation strategy, the former basing their approach on familiar territories of existing markets and resources / capabilities, and the latter willing to try uncharted waters.

3. THE INDIAN SOFTWARE INDUSTRY

The rationale for choosing the Indian software industry for this study is mainly two-fold: first, the software industry has, in recent decades, emerged an important sector of the Indian economy contributing significantly to its growth, and second, it currently seems to be facing severe innovation challenges, addressing which is crucial to its continued success and growth. The sector has triggered growth in several other areas too, notably real estate, transportation, communication and infrastructure. The software industry emerged to be the most promising and glamorous mainstream industrial sector in India in the 1990s and 2000s, employing millions of graduates directly and many times more indirectly.

The performance of the Indian software industry during the 1990s and the first decade of 2000s have been phenomenal [5, 17]. Between 1998 and 2012, the software sector grew its share of Indian GDP from 1.2% to 7.5% and share of Indian exports from below 4% to about 25% [32]. Arora and Athreye [4] attributes the success of the software industry to two mutually reinforcing wage advantages: low wage costs of Indian programmers compared to their counterparts in North America or Europe or Japan, and the high wages received by software programmers in India in comparison with other industry professionals of comparable qualification and experience. Other success factors included the ability of Indian professionals to read, write and speak in English, the availability of a wide range of skills across multiple hardware and software platforms, an entrepreneurial ability to customize to the needs of each client, project management skills, quality systems, scalability in volume and scope, ability to quickly assemble teams with diverse talents, and a successful software services model. These have been further aided by the presence and track record of Indian software professionals in North America.

Notwithstanding its phenomenal success, the industry did not acquire any significant competitive advantage or core competency to ensure long-term sustainability. Software is a fast evolving industry with short technology life cycles and hence firms need to reinvent competitive advantage regularly through innovation. There is little opportunity for software service firms to compete on capabilities, which are usually generic and widely available. Entry barriers are low, location advantage is nearly absent, and projects can be switched from one location to another with ease and speed. The maturing Indian software industry faces increasing competitive pressures due to rising costs in India and the emergence of new locations. The industry grew through an innovative "onsite plus offshore outsourcing" model, developed in the 1990s and perfected over the years through incremental improvements. Over the last two decades, the model has been exploited with great success, but with no radical innovation. Today there is hardly any novelty or inimitable value in this model. The nature of work undertaken by Indian companies, namely customized services, maintenance and production support, and business process outsourcing, provide little room for innovation, except for improvements in process, quality and reliability. In fact many large clients are highly concerned about business continuity, conformity and reliability that they tend to be wary of change. Software service firms dependent on such clients tend to be unwilling to try out new things or to experiment, impeding the flow of creative ideas. Quite often, winning a customer will require getting things right at the first time, which makes companies risk-averse. This influences the organization's innovation priorities.

Several barriers stand in the way of the Indian software industry's efforts to ramp up innovation, especially product and business model innovation. These include the large distances to the global product markets, the high cost structure of inputs that impedes the growth of domestic markets, shortage of product conceptualization and architecting competences, and the high opportunity cost arising from attractive services exports revenues. Grown through exports and high margins, Indian software industry has out-priced itself in the domestic market.

Nevertheless, over the last 5-8 years, partly due to the various e-Governance initiatives of central and state governments, there has been a growth in the domestic software market in India. Government of India actively promotes new ventures and entrepreneurship in software through a range of technology and business incubation programs. A new breed of entrepreneurial software ventures have sprung up and these firms are exploring far more new opportunities in the domestic and global markets for innovative software products and services. Unlike established software companies, these new entrants have been very innovative, customer-oriented and conscious of cutting costs, a necessary prerequisite to succeed in India's domestic markets. They have been further helped by the abundance of human resources graduating from the large number of engineering courses that have started in India during the past decade. Not used to the luxury of assured export markets, these new ventures have struggled during their emergence and developed far superior marketing competencies than those who grew in the hay days of the industry. These entrepreneurial firms appear to have taken on the challenge of innovation much more effectively than established companies. Recently these new entrants have also been able to access international markets.

4. THE QUALITATIVE STUDY

The qualitative study presented below attempts to bring out how the innovation approaches of new entrants differ from that of incumbent companies. The study is limited to small businesses in the Indian software industry.

4.1 Methodology

Twelve small software businesses were studied in depth as part of the qualitative study, 6 new entrants (5 years or less in software business) and 6 incumbent firms (more than 5 years in software business). Companies were selected purposefully ensuring good diversity of domains and markets of operation, both Indian and overseas.

Interviews were held with chief executives or other top level officers in these firms. Each interview was held in an unstructured manner using an interview guide. A typical interview lasted two hours.

Table 1 lists the companies (names replaced with codes for confidentiality), years in business and areas of activity. Companies 1a, 1b, 1c, 1d, 1e, 1f were new entrants and 2a, 2b, 2c, 2d, 2e, 2f incumbent firms.

Table 1. Companies Studied

Company Code	Years in Business	Activity
1a	5 years	Digital marketing platform for a range of brick and mortar businesses
1b	3 years	Smart school ERP and learning management system
1c	3 years	SaaS (software as a service) tour platform
1d	4 years	VOIP (voice over internet protocol) platform
1e	3 years	Web-based ERP (Enterprise Resources Planning)
1f	1.5 years	Bidding eCommerce
2a	12 years	Software solutions (development and support)
2b	15 years	Travel, transportation and logistics software
2c	20 years	Billing software for telecom and finance
2d	14 years	Software solutions
2e	10 years	Revenue product suite
2f	15 years	Software solutions

4.2 Interview Guide

Qualitative interviews that are unstructured and exploratory in nature are helpful in theory building. Following the suggestions in the literature [18], some a-priori interview questions were developed for conducting the interviews. The respondents (CEOs or senior functionaries at similar level) were allowed to reply at length to each question. They were encouraged to give examples and to go beyond specific answers. Apart from briefly asking each question, the interviewer was mostly a patient listener.

The questions broadly covered the following:

- Firm's major area(s) of activity, years in software business, nature of the firm (captive use of a parent / dedicated development facility, and ownership)

- Major area(s) of strength leveraged for innovations

- Where innovations impacted and how, whether they led to new industry, new business model in an existing industry, market entry into an existing industry, or new product(s) for company's existing markets

- Major source of innovation ideas; departments and/or functions that generated such ideas

- Sources of resources and capabilities for executing innovations (internal, external)

4.3 Categorization of Information

Interview transcripts, being responses to open-ended questions, were long and narrative. These transcripts were analyzed, and information was categorized and coded into tables 2.1 and 2.2, using keywords listed in tables 3.1, 3.2, and 3.3.

Table 2.1. Keywords Classified by Interview Questions

Question	Responses from new entrants	Responses from incumbents
What has been the firm's major area of strength that was leveraged to perform innovations?	Entre (1a), MarkDev (1a), Network (1b), MarkDev (1b), DomKnow (1c) Observ (1d), MarkDev (1d), CusBase(1d), MarqueeCus (1e), Entre (1f)	Tech (2a), CusBase (2a), Entre (2b), CusBase (2b), ProdMgt (2c), Tech (2c), CusBase (2c), MarqueeCus (2d), Entre (2e), Parent (2f)
Where have firm's high-impact innovations been?	NewBiz (1a), BizMod (1b), BizMod (1c), Feature (1c), NewBiz (1d), BizMod (1d), Product (1e), BizMod (1f)	Process (2a), Process (2b), MarkEntry (2b), Product (2b), Quality (2b), Feature (2c), Process (2d), Product (2e), Feature (2e), Product (2f), Process (2f)
Where have firm's low-impact innovations been?	Feature (1a), Process (1b), Feature (1b), Product (1c), Process (1d), Feature (1d), Process (1e), Process (1f)	Quality (2a), Process (2b), Process (2c), Quality (2d), Process (2e), Product (2f)

Continued in Table 2.2

Table 2.2. Keywords Classified by Interview Questions

Question	Responses from new entrants	Responses from incumbent companies
What have been the major sources of innovation ideas that succeeded? Where did ideas originate?	Non-cust (1a), Network (1b), DomKnow (1c), Entre (1c), Entre (1d), Int_Res (1e), Network (1e), Int_Res (1f)	CusBase (2a), CusBase (2b), Adjacencies (2b), CusBase (2c), Adjacencies (2c), CusBase (2d), Sales (2e), Int_Res (2f)
Did innovations create new industry, new business model in an existing industry, market-entry for into an existing industry, or new product for company's existing markets?	NewBiz (1a), BizMod (1b), BizMod (1c), BizMod (1d), MarkEntry (1e), MarkEntry (1f)	MarkEntry (2a), MarkEntry (2b), NewCus (2b), BizMod (2c), MarkEntry (2c), NewCus (2d), MarEntry (2e), NewProd (2f)
Where did the resources and capabilities to execute innovations come from (internal, external, networks etc.)?	Ext-Res (1a), Network (1a), Int_Res (1b), Int_Res (1c), Ext_Res (1d), Int_Res (1e), Ext_Res (1f)	Int_Res (2a), Int_Res (2b), Network (2b), Int_Res (2c), Int_Res (2d), Network (2d), Int_Res (2e), Int_Res (2f), Ext_Res (2f)
Which department or function contributed most to innovation ideas?	Mark (1a), Mark (1b), Mark (1c), Tech (1c), Entre (1d), .Mark (1d), Tech (1e), Entre (1f), Mark (1f)	Tech (2a), Sales (2a), Sales (2b), Tech (2b), Pre-Sales (2c), Sales (2d), Sales (2e), Tech (2e)

In tables 3.1, 3.2, and 3.3, explanations are offered for each keyword listed in tables 2.1 and 2.2 along with its implication on the approach to innovation or on the type of innovation.

Three approaches are considered: Resources, capabilities, technologies (RCT), Existing markets or industries (EM), and Emerging customer needs/new markets (NM).

Innovation types are classified broadly into two: Technology / product / process innovation (TPP), and Marketing / business model innovation (Biz).

Table 3.1. Keywords and Explanations

Keyword	Explanation (based on words used by the respondent)	Implication on approach to innovation	Implication on type of innovation
Adjacencies	New markets adjacent to the company's existing markets, where the firm's existing resources, capabilities, and technologies can be leveraged	RCT	
BizMod	Business model innovation, new way of delivering value / service / product, new way of capturing value		Biz
CusBase	Exiting customer base which can be leveraged for innovation	EM	
DomKnow	Knowledge of new domains which can aid access to new markets	NM	
Entre	Entrepreneurial, enterprising, risk-taking behavior by owner / CEO which help access new markets	NM	
Ext_Res	External resources, technology collaborators etc., which usually help the firm to access new markets.	NM	
Feature	Features or attributes added to an existing product / service		TPP

Continued in Table 3.2

Table 3.2. Keywords and Explanations

Keyword	Explanation (based on words used by the respondent)	Implication on approach to innovation	Implication on type of innovation
Int_Res	Internal resources, know-how, capability	RCT	
Mark	Marketing function, which usually develops new markets, existing markets being left to sales	NM	
MarkDev	New market development	NM	
MarkEntry	Market entry by the company (not new market creation)	EM	
MarqueeCus	An initial avid customer or the first large and helpful customer who helps get similar customers	EM	
Network	Networks, groups, associations etc. cooperating to pool resources to access new markets to grow	NM	
NewBiz	New business or new market created, that did not exist before		Biz
NewCus	New customers in a market in which the firm already operates	EM	
NewProd	New Products for existing customers		TPP

Continued in Table 3.3

Table 3.3. Keywords and Explanations

Keyword	Explanation (based on words used by the respondent)	Implication on approach to innovation	Implication on type of innovation
Non-cust	Non-customers or potential customers with unmet needs or pain-points, unaware of a need or a product they could use	NM	
Observ	Observation or scanning of environment for opportunities to develop new markets	NM	
Parent	A strong parent which helps with resources and markets	RCT	
Pre-Sales	Consulting function that educates prospects on company's products	EM	
Process	Process improvements to improve efficiency, performance etc.		TPP
Product	Product innovations or improvements		TPP
ProdMgt	Product management team in the company	RCT	
Quality	Quality systems, process maturity		TPP
Sales	Sales function which pushes products into existing markets	EM	
Tech	Technology or R&D department/function	RCT	

5. RESULTS AND DISCUSSIONS

The qualitative study attempts to understand how the innovation approaches of new entrants differ from that of incumbents. The study is limited to small businesses in the Indian software industry.

In tables 4 and 5, we group the responses: on the input side based on approach to innovation (RCT, EM, or NM), and on the output side based on type of innovation performed (TPP or Biz). This data is plotted in figure 1 onto a matrix of three columns and two rows, showing how new entrants and incumbent companies differ in their approach to innovation strategy and type of innovation.

Table 4. Classification of Responses by Innovation Approach

Innovation approach	Keywords and companies whose responses contained these keywords
Based on resources, capabilities, and technologies (RCT)	Adjacencies: 2b, 2c
	Int_Res: 1b, 1c, 1e, 1f, 2a, 2b, 2c, 2d, 2e, 2f
	Parent: 2f
	Tech: 1c, 1e, 2a, 2b, 2c, 2e
Based on existing markets (EM)	CusBase: 1d, 2a, 2b, 2c, 2d
	MarkEntry: 1e, 1f, 2a, 2b, 2c
	MarqueeCus: 1e, 2d
	NewCus: 2b, 2d:
	Pre-Sales: 2c
	Sales: 2a, 2b, 2c, 2d, 2e
Based on emerging customer needs / new markets (NM)	DomKnow: 1c
	Entre: 1a, 1c, 1d, 1f, 2b. 2e
	Ext_Res: 1d, 1f, 2f
	Mark: 1a, 1b, 1c, 1d, 1f
	MarkDev: 1a, 1b, 1d
	Network: 1a, 1b, 1e, 2b, 2d
	Non-Cust: 1a
	Observ: 1d

The results of the qualitative interviews, summarized in Figure 1 indicate a marked difference between new entrants (1a, 1b, 1c, 1d, 1e, 1f) and incumbents (2a, 2b, 2c, 2d, 2e, 2f).

While all incumbent firms in the sample approached innovation based on their resources, capabilities, and technologies, and many based on existing markets, only two-thirds based their innovations on new markets. On the other hand, all the new entrants in the sample approached innovation based on new markets, and only two-thirds leveraged their resources and capabilities.

Table 5. Classification of Responses by Innovation Type

Innovation type	Keywords and companies whose responses contained these keywords
Technology / product / process innovation (TPP).	Feature: 1c, 2c, 2e
	NewProd: 2f
	Process: 2a, 2b, 2d, 2f
	Product: 1e, 2b, 2e, 2f
	Quality: 2b
Marketing / business model innovation (Biz)	BizMod: 1b, 1c, 1d, 1f, 2c
	NewBiz: 1a, 1d

Note: Responses regarding low-impact innovations excluded

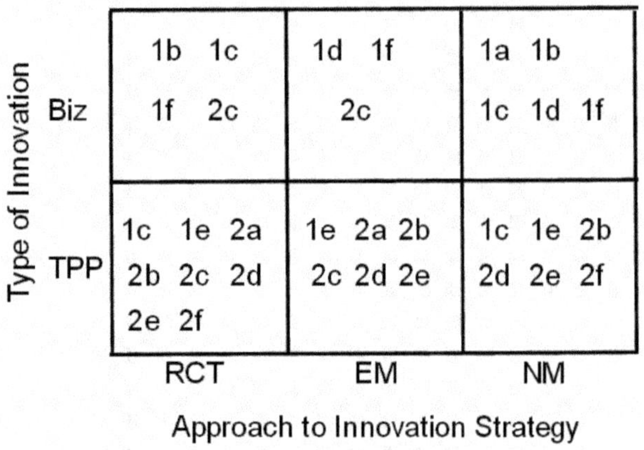

Figure 1. Grouping of new entrants and incumbents on the basis of approach to innovation and type of innovation

In terms of type of innovation, 83% of the new entrants performed innovations related to marketing and business models, as against only 17% of incumbent firms. Technology, product and process innovations were pursued by all incumbent firms as against only one-third of new entrants.

It is to be expected that incumbents leverage their technologies, experiences from past projects, skills available with their human resources and pursue opportunities that match these resources and capabilities. The results reflect this. New entrants are not worried about their lack of resources or capabilities, but are confident that required resources and capabilities can be accessed as needed through back-to-back tie-ups with incumbent companies. In fact a new trend in the industry has been the emergence of open labs and open office spaces where infrastructure and resources are accessible at short notice for a cost. Several software companies in India have developed infrastructure provisioning as a new business activity.

Many of the established companies in India are ISO-certified or CMM-assessed, and hence their processes are well standardized. This is because they have found certification a pre-requisite for exporting outsourced services. The availability of such well developed, certified/assessed, and standardized software development facilities with established companies is a resource which new entrant may access. The new entrants who participated in the interviews indicated that they had the comfort that they need not invest in creating facilities, and may outsource work to a firm with facilities. Such standardized software development facilities are not only reliable, but can also be trusted with confidentiality and non-disclosure agreements, because of the way their business practices have evolved over years of doing business with international clients.

Many new entrants work on web-based and mobile applications and products, taking pains to find unique user needs and markets. The ability to identify and develop unmet and unstated user needs appear to be a key competence of successful new entrants.

While new entrants widely networked with each other and with established firms, the extent of networking among established firms was much less. Networking is used as a resource for accessing markets as well as complementary capabilities. Incubators provide an environment for such collaborative relationships and for growing together. The respondents reported that new entrants in incubators had a high survival rate.

New entrants had what one of them described as "experimentation mentality". They were willing to experiment and prod markets. Uncertainty was welcome and provided the thrust and energy to move forwarded. One new entrant said, "we know where we want to reach, but we do not know how". Incumbent companies held nearly opposite view. They were less willing to experiment. They preferred certainty. New entrants were not concerned about today, as they held hopes of tomorrow. Incumbent companies were overly concerned about today, that they had little time to think about tomorrow. Their appetite for risk-taking was lower than that of new entrants despite resourcefulness.

In conclusion, this paper has attempted to explore the key differences in the innovation approaches and innovation outputs of incumbent firms and new entrants among small software businesses. As is the case of most qualitative studies, the above findings are useful to generate hypotheses that need to be tested through more robust quantitative analyses. Our objective in this paper has been to develop some pointers towards theory building, by converging existing theoretical streams and following it up with further evidence through in-depth exploratory qualitative interviews. The empirical study has reinforced the premises generated through review of theory, opening up new areas for research.

6. REFERENCES

[1] Afuah, A. 2009. *Strategic Innovation: New Game Strategies for Competitive Advantage*. Routledge, New York.

[2] Akman, G. and Yilmaz, C. 2008. Innovative capability, innovation strategy and market orientation: an empirical analysis in Turkish software industry. *International Journal of Innovation Management* 12, 1, 69–111.

[3] Andrew, J.P., DeRocco, E.S., and Taylor, A. 2009. *The Innovation Imperative in Manufacturing: How the United States can Restore its Edge*. The Boston Consulting Group, Boston.

[4] Arora, A. and Athreye, S. 2002. The software industry and India's economic development. *Information Economics and Policy* 14, 253-273.

[5] Athreye, S. 2005. The Indian software industry and its evolving service capability. *Industrial and Corporate Change* 14, 3, 393–418.

[6] Boudreau, K.J. and Lakhani, K.R. 2009. How to manage outside innovation. *Sloan Management Review* 50, 4, 69-76.

[7] Broring, S., Leker, J., and Ruhmer, S. 2006. Radical or not? Assesing innovativeness and its organizational implications, *International Journal of Product Development* 3,2, 152-166.

[8] Burgelman, R. A., Christensen, C. M., and Wheelwright, S.C. 2004. *Strategic Management of Technology and Innovation, 4th ed*, McGraw-Hill/Irwin, New York

[9] Campbell, A. and Park, R. 2004. Stop kissing frogs. *Harvard Business Review* 82 (July-Aug 2004), 27-28.

[10] Chandy, R.K. and Tellis, G.J. 2000. The incumbent's curse? Incumbency, size and radical Innovation. *Journal of Marketing* 64, 1-17.

[11] Chesbrough, H. 2003. *Open Innovation: The New Imperative for Creating and Profiting from Technology*. HBS Press, MA

[12] Christensen, C. M. and Bower, J.L. 1996. Customer power, strategic investment, and the failure of leading firms. *Strategic Management Journal* 17, 197–218.

[13] Christensen, C. M. 1997. *The Innovator's Dilemma: When New Technologies Cause Great Firms to Fail*. HBS Press, MA.

[14] Christensen, C.M. and Overdorf, M. 2000. Meeting the challenge of disruptive innovation. *Harvard Business Review* 78, 2, 67-76.

[15] Christensen, C..M., and Raynor, M.E. 2003. *The Innovator's Solution: Creating and Sustaining Successful Growth*, HBS Press, Cambridge, MA.

[16] CII and INSEAD. 2010. *Global Innovation Index and Report, 2009-10*. INSEAD.

[17] Dossani, R. 2003. *The Evolution of the IT Industry in India*, Asia-Pacific Research Center, Stanford University.

[18] Eisenhardt, K.M. 1989. Building theories from case study research. *Academy of Management Review* 14, 4, 532-550.

[19] EIU. 2007. *Innovation: Transforming the Way Business Creates*. The Economist Intelligence Unit.

[20] Foster, R.N. 1986. Innovation: *The Attacker's Advantage*, Summit Books, NY.

[21] Freeman, C. 1991. Networks of innovators: A synthesis. *Research Policy* 20, 499-514.

[22] Govindarajan, V. and Trimble, C. 2010. *The Other Side of Innovation: Solving the Execution Challenge*, HBR Press.

[23] Gumusluolu, L. and Ilsev, A. 2009. Transformational leadership and organizational innovation: the roles of internal and external support for innovation, *Journal of Product Innovation Management* 26, 3, 264–277.

[24] Henderson, R. and Clark, K. 1990. Architectural innovation: the reconfiguration of existing product technologies and the failure of established firms. *Administrative Science Quarterly* 35, 9-30.

[25] Isary, D. and Pontiggia, A. 2010. What's new in innovation? A contribution to the novelty of innovation management approaches, SSRN: http://ssrn.com/abstract=1585843

[26] Keskin, H. 2006. Market orientation, learning orientation, and innovation capabilities in SMEs: An extended model. *European Journal of Innovation Management* 9,4, 396–417.

[27] Kumar, K.G.S. and Jyotishi, A. 2013. Transaction cost leveling to reduce incumbent's difficulty in innovation: a heuristic approach through critical review, *International Journal of Knowledge, Innovation, and Entrepreneurship* 1, 1-2), 25-39.

[28] Kumar, K.G.S., Thampi, P.P., Jyotishi, A., and Bishu, R. 2013. Toward strategically aligned innovative capability: a QFD-based approach, *Quality Management Journal* 20,4, 37-50.

[29] Kumar, K.G.S. and Rajeev, S. 2013. Managing exploration and exploitation using industry-level integration as a guide. Paper presented the Fifth International Conference on Role of Innovation in Business, Bangalore 16-17, May 2013.

[30] March, J.G. 1991. Exploration and exploitation in organizational learning. *Organization Science*, 2, 71-87.

[31] Narasimhalu, A.D. 2005. Innovation cube: Triggers, drivers and enablers for successful innovations. ISIPM, 2005.

[32] NASSCOM. 2012. *The IT-BPO Sector in India: Strategic Review 2012*. NASSCOM, New Delhi.

[33] Nemanich, L.A., Keller, R.T., and Vera, D. 2007. Managing the exploration/exploitation paradox in new product development: how top executives define their firm's innovation trajectory. *International Journal of Innovation and Technology Management* 4, 3, 351-374.

[34] NESTA. 2010. Demand and innovation: how customer preferences shape the innovation process," [Working Paper]. NESTA, London.

[35] Pfeffer, J. and Salancik, G.R. 1978. *The External Control of Organizations: A Resource Dependence Perspective*. Harper & Row, New York.

[36] Rosted, J. 2005. *User-driven innovation: Results and recommendations*. FORA.

[37] Smith, M., Busi, M., Ball, P., and van der Meer, R. 2008. Factors influencing an organization's ability to manage innovation: a structured literature review and conceptual model. *International Journal of Innovation Management* 12, 4, 655-678.

[38] Steve, D. 2005. Why the best and brightest approaches don't solve the innovation dilemma. *Strategy & Leadership* 33, 1, 4-11.

[39] Teece, D. J. 1986. Profiting from technological innovation, *Research Policy* 15, 6, 285-330.

[40] Tushman, M. L. and Anderson, P. 1986. Technological discontinuities and organizational environments. *Administrative Science Quarterly* 31, 439–65

Impacts of Globalization on Indian Industry:
Case of Financialization in IT and Non IT Sectors

Upasana Mishra
Amrita School of Business
Kasavanahali
Bangalore, India
91-9449020272
dr.upasana.m@gmail.com

Sashi Sivramkrishna
Narsee Monjee Institute
for Management Studies
Bangalore, India
9198450 22272
sashi.sivramkrishna@gmail.com

Karthik R
Amrtia School of Business
Bangalore
India
91-9686-041-700
rk.b728@gmail.com

Amalendu Jyotishi
Amrita School of Business
Kasavanahali
Bangalore, India
91-9900-213-825
amalendu_jyotishi@blr.amrita.edu

ABSTRACT

This paper endeavors to understand the aspect of financialization that exists in companies, and study the possibility of an increase in an organization's profitability due to accessibility of financial instruments and other investment decisions that can sustain the net margins to meet market expectations and falling operational revenues by the real sector. Our objective is to observe the financial and investment activities of different real sector companies and relate the impact of their existence over the organization's net profits. The study also attempts to seek a further understanding upon the question of its exposure towards IT Service Organizations. With Information Technology reigning as a paramount factor in the Indian Economic context, the question of how financialization applies to the comparison of IT sector *vis-à-vis* other sectors is the highlight of this paper.

This study after an extensive review of literature considers the reported items of the financial statements of 56 companies and analyze the various Non-Operational Items as independent variables that impact the Profit after Tax component of the Income Statement. These variables include income from financial services, other income, interest income, R&D expenditure and workforce and IT service as a dummy variable. The analysis was performed using multiple regression technique. The study overwhelmingly supports significant impact of non-operating income on profit of the organization though there is no statistical difference across IT and non-IT sectors. However, one has to bear in mind the limitation and cross-sectional nature of data before generalizing these results.

Permission to make digital or hard copies of all or part of this work for personal or classroom use is granted without fee provided that copies are not made or distributed for profit or commercial advantage and that copies bear this notice and the full citation on the first page. Copyrights for components of this work owned by others than ACM must be honored. Abstracting with credit is permitted. To copy otherwise, or republish, to post on servers or to redistribute to lists, requires prior specific permission and/or a fee. Request permissions from permissions@acm.org.
SIGMIS-CPR'14, May 29–31, 2014, Singapore, Singapore.
Copyright © 2014 ACM 978-1-4503-2625-4/14/05...$15.00.

Categories and Subject Descriptors
K.1:The Computing Industry
K.4.1: Public Policy Issues

General Terms
Management, Performance

Keywords: Financialization, Non-Operating Income, Net Profit, Information Technology, Econometric Analysis, India

"When the capital development of a country becomes the byproduct of the activities of a casino, the job is not likely to be well done."- John Maynard Keynes

1. INTRODUCTION: Financialization
"His continued presence is the biggest overhang on Microsoft's stock." This was one of the most influential hedge fund manager's, David Einhorn's comment on Steve Ballmer, CEO of Microsoft. Einhorn's comment caused a stir on Wall Street and helped Microsoft shares climb 2 percent to $24.67 the same day (Reuters, 26.05.2011). While many believe that Einhorn's concerns are well founded and appropriate action by Microsoft would result in a positive outcome, there are others gravely apprehensive of the expanding and overwhelming influence of finance capital over corporations or what has come to be called, financialization.

To the latter faction, this event is but one amongst a growing trend, an intensifying reality in many advanced nations of the world and cause for concern. This paper is an attempt to bring this debate over financialization into the Indian context; to identify indicators that can tell us whether the process has already taken root and to delineate some of its possible consequences. While many of the concerns raised in the West cannot be simply transplanted on to developing countries like India, it would, at the same time, be imprudent to dismiss them off as irrelevant. In fact, in an age of fluid global capital it is imperative to begin understanding financialization and its possible consequences for developing economies, not merely as a cause for concern but to identify both, positive and negative impact on responses of various stakeholders to this emerging and perhaps inevitable, reality.

Financialization was once considered to be a concept that had been mainly a subject of academic interest. Financialization has evolved over the decades with the evolution of financial markets and financial institutions across the industries. It has generated a new dimension of behavioral finance in corporate sector; that uses the pattern of profit enhancement through financial channels rather than operationalization of prime areas in business [1]

The study of financialization is a broader scope and is inclusive of various investing and financial activities of the business that generate cash flows that maybe imperative to increase profitability on short run which can determine the shareholder value [2].

Before delving on financialization in India, we begin with a survey of meaning/s, indicators and impacts of financialization in the U.S. and other advanced nations of the world. Financialization has no unique definition; the difficulty in pinning it down to a single meaning has led some researchers to conclude that the term "remains imbued with an almost atmospheric quality, omnipresent but absent of context or cause" [3](p. 664). Nonetheless, the various definitions attempted by researchers *taken together* do give us a better understanding of what financialization is. Implicitly, the term articulates the emergence of a "new" reality which can be better understood with reference to a pre-financialized condition. A rather trendy expression which succinctly captures the essence of financialization and the situation which prevailed prior to this transformation is "Wall Street vs. Main Street". There are of course the more academically oriented definitions that describe different facets of the phenomenon; a few of these are mentioned below.

To Lazonick [4](p. 701), financialization is "the evaluation of the performance of a company by a financial measure, such as earnings per share" that manifests itself with an obsession to "distribute value to shareholders." Although quantifiable, Lazonick's definition does not adequately bring out the essential features of financialization *as an enduring process*. Epstein [5], going beyond shareholder value to a more qualitative definition, captures this aspect of financialization; "the increasing role of financial motives, financial markets, financial actors and financial institutions in the operation of domestic and international economies." (p. 3). Montgomerie [6] highlights the systemic and relational aspects of present day capitalist dynamics in a financialized world "...where individuals, firms, and the macroeconomy are increasingly mediated by new relationships within financial markets" (p.234). What these definitions are driving at is "the ever greater importance of *strictly financial considerations*[1] in economic affairs" [7] of and between all stakeholders in society. At the corporate level, this directional shift in a firm's objectives towards financial gains may come at the cost of other economic priorities including technological innovation, R&D outlays, product quality, long-term investment in fixed assets, employment and/or the environment. Consider, for instance, the following news from a business daily;

> "Pfizer Inc. is looking for $1 billion in extra yearly cost cuts on top of the billions of dollars in cuts to research and development that it was already making, according to people familiar with the matter" (Mint, June 9, 2011, p. 20)

---

[1] Emphases in italics are our own.

Jensen [8], however, asserts that multi-stakeholder (de)centered theories "fail to provide a *complete* specification of the corporate purpose or objective function" (p.8) and could therefore, "without the clarity of mission provided by a single-valued objective function", lead companies to "... experience managerial confusion, conflict, inefficiency, and perhaps even competitive failure" [8]. Narayanan and Nanda [9] reiterate this view that stakeholder value maximization makes little sense; for instance, a firm cannot give away its products for free to consumers. However, shareholder value maximization is possible only by "optimizing the value to other stakeholders" [9]. Irrespective of whether a single objective function for the firm (as maximization of shareholder value) is superior to a multiple objectives, there is no doubt that the financial sector has grown phenomenally in the US and is influencing corporate decision-making. Krippner [10] and Kedrosky and Dangler [11] provide stylized facts and empirical evidence pertaining to the ascending position of the financial sector in the US economy; just as a case in point, the relative share of the FIRE sector (finance, insurance and real estate) in the US economy increased from ~12% in 1950 to more than 22% in 2000, whereas that of manufacturing declined from ~32% to ~16% over the same period[10,11] (p. 178).

Lazonick [4] locates the commencement of the process in the employee stock options given to young professional in the ICT sector to attract them from jobs in the "old economy" that ensured lifetime employment. High share prices became the objective of managers and employees, thereby aligning decisions to this ultimate goal. The declining profits of Main Street since the 1970s and the Internet boom of the 1990s brought large volumes of speculative capital into this sector seeking maximum gains from rapid stock price increases. Institutional and individual investors were more interested in actual value creation (that directly reflected in share prices) than diversification and expansion for their own sake. Another critical factor that facilitated the process of financialization was adoption of neoliberal policies across the Western world embedded in Reaganism and Thatcherism, the Washington Consensus of the early 1980s, the repealing of the Glass-Steagall Act of 1933 (which had separated commercial and investment banking operations post-Great Depression) in 1999, and deregulation of all sectors of the economy including the financial sector. Post the dot.com burst and 9-11, easy monetary policy adopted by the Fed in the early 2000s pushed bank rates of interest to almost zero; this not only increased circulation of money through financial sector directly but also indirectly by weaning individuals from holding savings in bank deposits and into the market.

Whatever may be proposed as a definition and/or whatever may be the true basis for its rise and intensification, financialization, like globalization, manifests itself perceptibly in the "subsumption" of non-financial companies to interests of financial capital. The passage below, extracted from a popular book on "Financial Intelligence", illustrates the almost commonsensical level to which the notion of financialization has now percolated.

> "...suppose your company did well and grew fast. Potential acquirers came shopping, and you sold the business to a large corporation, one that makes earning predictions to Wall Street. The folks in the corporate office, *like the folks in just about every publicly traded company, want to keep Wall Street happy*. This quarter, alas, it looks as if the parent corporation is going to miss

its earnings-per-share estimate by *one penny*[2]. If it does, Wall Street will not be happy. And when Wall Street isn't happy, the company's stock gets hammered." [12] (p. 40).

To return to our phrase, Wall Street is gaining significant control over decisions of Main Street. While a fuller study of this process will continue to throw up important questions in the West, we can nonetheless begin an inquiry into its relevance to developing economies like India. In this paper, we do so by focusing on impact of Non-Operational Income factors on profitability of the corporate organizations, especially the organization not in Banking and financial domain and compare the results of information technology vis-a-vis other organisations.

2. Financialization in the Indian Context

The following reports culled out from an Indian business are a sign that the financialization narrative may well have taken root in India. While there is no doubt that we must go beyond newspaper reports to actually ascertain the advancement of financialization in India at the economy, firm and individual level, it is nonetheless important to consider part of media as an integral character in the financialization narrative.

"With this transaction (sale of Intelenet Global Services Pvt. Ltd.), Blackstone Advisors India Pvt. Ltd. will sell its entire 67% holding in Intelenet, at estimated returns of almost three times. The private equity firm had invested $150-160 million in the outsourcing firm in 2007 (and sold it at £375 million)." (Mint, June 1, 2011, p. 09)

"How do you bring back investor confidence?

We are doing an analysts meet within a week to explain threadbare all the detail …"

(Interview with State Bank of India Chairman, Mr. Pratik Chaudhuri, Mint, June 3, 2011, p. 09)

"MukeshAmbani, chairman of India's most valuable company, Reliance Industries Ltd (RIL), spoke of doubling its enterprise value to $160 billion in less than a decade … With Ambani having elaborated on RIL's long-term objective last year, analysts now expect him to offer details on the short-term steps the company intends to take to get there, beginning with plans for this fiscal year." (Mint, June 3, 2011, p. 06)

"Television content provider and film producer Balaji Telefilms Ltd is planning to launch a film-focused private equity (PE) firm … the plan is to invest in Hindi films, television content and educational media … (it) wants to tap foreign investors and rich individuals to raise money." (Mint, June 6, 2011, p. 07)

"Union KBC Asset Management will sell its MF (mutual fund) schemes mainly through its parent bank UBI (Union Bank of India) in the initial years … Unlike private sector banks that have well-established departments for selling third party products, government-owned banks have only recently started to catch up." (Mint, June 7, 2011, p. 16)

"The fall in market value and investor base of some of the (Reliance) group's companies is also reflected in the number of employees on its rolls. According to the May 2011 presentation, this number is 120,000. The May 2010 presentation mentions the number as 130,000." (Mint, June 8, 2011, p. 05)

"American hedge fund Tiger Global Management LLC … returned (to India) after about a year's absence and, while the investments between then and now have been carefully selected, they reflect a significant shift in the India strategy – a preference for striking deals through co-investments and in e-commerce start-ups." (Mint, June 8, 2011, p. 06)

"Analysts who track Tata Motors are baffled as the company posted good earnings for fiscal 2011 (FY11), even though March quarter results did not meet Street expectations …The Tata Motors stock has lost 11.51% since earnings were announced on 27 May, while Sensex has gained 1.94%." (Mint, June 9, 2011, p. 02)

"In another month that saw more than $1 billion in private equity/venture capital (PE/VC) investments, May accounted for $1.14 billion in Indian companies across 39 deals; around 180% increase over $408 million across 17 deals in the same period last year." (Mint, June 11, 2011, p. 07)

This selection of reports gives us an idea of how the language of financialization is now entrenched in Indian economic and business discourse. But does this mean that it has actually reached proportions spoken about in the West? Or is this just hype and content for business dailies and television programs? We use the some of the indicators culled out above to go below the surface to identify relevant facts that could give us more concrete evidence on the extent of financialization in India. Obviously, we do not expect to arrive at definitive yes/no conclusions; however, the strength of these indicators has a direct bearing on the relevance of anticipated consequences of financialization in India.

At the core of financialization is the transformation of the banking system in channelizing flow of funds from savings to investment. In India, however, priority sector lending as well as underdeveloped corporate debt markets would necessitate that the traditional role of banks must continue. In spite of this it would be interesting to track broad changes in inter-sectoral money flows in the Indian economy. The Reserve Bank of India does compile flow of funds accounts, which is available from 1950-51 onwards; however, and unfortunately, these accounts are at a highly aggregated level and with a significantly high level of discrepancy that makes it difficult to utilize them even to make superficial inferences on the changing trends in roles of banks.

Instead of using the flow of funds accounts it would be appropriate to study the changing pattern of bank credit from data pertaining to "Gross Bank Credit by Major Sectors"; the sectors being agriculture, industry, personal loans and services. One major concern over financialization of the banking sector in developing countries is the increasing priority to "personal loans" at the cost of credit to small industries[13]. Although priority sector lending (small enterprises are included in priority sector lending), this data would throw light over this aspect in the Indian context. Times series data of "Flow of Financial Resources to the Commercial Sector" could be indispensable in monitoring trends in fund flows to non-financial commercial sector.

---

[2] Emphases in italics are our own.

Since a substantial portion of the banking sector is controlled by the government (public sector banks), a more realistic picture of the underlying trends in banking would be to compare differences in the nature of core banking operations between private and public sector banks. Here the proportion of retail/wholesale banking and proportion of non-interest/interest income would be critical parameters in assessing the changing pattern of bank credit in the Indian economy. More comprehensive or aggregate figures across the Indian banking system would be necessary to make valid generalizations.

At the corporate-level, as we have seen above, although the narrative clearly conforms to the financialization narrative, we must go below the surface to unravel the degree of control exerted by finance capital over top management decision-making. Macro level data pertaining to several indicators need to be compiled from company balance sheet and other financial reports; quantitative data would include growth in number of financial subsidiaries of non-financial companies, share of profits of such subsidiaries to total profits, share buy backs and trends in distribution of dividends, performance-based remuneration and stock market reactions to mergers and acquisitions. Qualitative indicators of financialization are equally important and the changing language of managers and media, the rise of CFOs in the corporate hierarchy and general finance-focus of top management merits serious deliberation.

Although broad trends in financialization at the corporate level may be inferred from macro-level data, a deeper understanding of the impact of financialization would require individual case studies like those carried out for Boeing, and Nestle and Kraft. The recent (June 2011) pressure exerted on Reliance Industries Limited on account of a lack of confidence could push the company to shift focus from oil and natural gas to more consumer-centric businesses that are seen as having greater possibilities to create shareholder value.

3. Non Operational Income: A case for IT and Non IT Companies

The information brings in the various instances that researchers and economists have put forth to supplement the broader theory of financialization, it is also understood that no instance can singularly define what financialization does to the corporate sector. In order to delve our own study into identifying the presence of financialization in the corporate sector we search for its presence in the disclosure of a company's earnings.

The Financial imperatives that focus on value maximization to the shareholders can be determined through various parameters such as dividend payments, seen as the decision to appease shareholders in the event of recessionary phase. The real sector of the economy is mostly concerned with managing earnings and stakeholder demands. In the short run, the management of cash flows and development financial strategies can be obtained through access towards Financial Market Channels[14].

Non-operational incomes (NOI) are earnings that are obtained by the investment or strategy made for the purpose of business expansion or development. However, financialization attempts to dominate the financial activities of the firm over their production activities. The financial investment is more powerful in accumulation of wealth in the short run due to the large presence of financial institutions and instruments that can act as a multipliers over the margins earned by a company[15].Some of the non-operating transactions can include sustained dividend and interest income from investment and advances, capital gains on sale of assets, gains on share buybacks, mergers and acquisitions of businesses and patented income through research and development.

Most of the non-operational items are statutorily reported in the firm's financial statements and they form an integral part of a company's balance sheet income, statement and cash flows. Non-operating items are imperative to the real sector as they represent the other sources of earnings apart from revenues from operations. The real sectors of an economy are organizations that apply land, labor and raw materials determined through production factors through which products or services can be generated to the economy as opposed to the financial sector.

In the study, we intended to find the variables indicating financialization that impact the profitability of the organization. We consider non-financial organizations for this study. The dependent variable in our study is adjusted net profit. The independent variables are the non-operational items in the financial statements that are aligned with our analysis of financialization apart from a few firm specific characters. Of these, IT and non-IT is an important category. Since, India has shown high level of growth as well as higher degree of globalization in IT services as compared to other groups of organizations (namely the manufacturing organizations), we expect that there would be statistically significant difference in both these categories of organizations.

It is important to note that the profitability of a company is increased or decreased reasonably due to the presence of these variables in a company's books. The reported profit of a company would be significantly affected in the absence of such variables leading to a lower measure of a firm's EPS. A firm with a positive EPS component is a better signal to an increased shareholder value, albeit not all the times.

The major source of literature reference has been used to analyse the compatibility of the variables to the study of financialization in the economy. Our prime objective is to assimilate the knowledge for the study and investigate whether the company earnings are significantly related to the presence of interest and dividend incomes, capital gains, investment gains.

3.1 Methodology Data and Variables

The study is conducted based on the information extracted from the Prowess database provided by Center for Monitoring Indian Economy (CMIE). Our sample selection was based on the following criteria. We selected the listed companies[3] in National Stock Exchange (NSE) for our study. Our sample consists of the firms in the Nifty 50 (NFT) index and IT (IT) index. We have excluded the banking and financial companies (NBFC) from this list. Therefore, our final sample is [NFT]+[IT]-[NFT∩IT]-[NBFC]. Our final sample size is 56 whose financial statements were observed and analyzed. The sample size is inclusive of 20 sample companies which are primarily into Information Technology, Telecommunication or IT enabled services. The adjusted net profit for a company is the final value that a company reports as its earnings for the current financial year. This net profit is considered as the dependent variable in our econometric model.

---

[3] Listed companies are important for the study of financialization as the financialization indicators are based on the market perception of profitability of the organization that in turn influence the strategy of it.

Data on the independent variables are collected from the notes in the financial statements given in the company's Profit and Loss Account. The selected variables are the resultant sources of income from the company's Non-Operational activities during the financial year in 2012-2013. Some of the companies differ with respect to the actual period of a year-end being December 31st of 2012.

The interest income is the fixed fee on any financial lending or advances that the company has made to other organizations. This forms an important aspect of NOI. Other important aspect of NOI is reflected in the variable 'other incomes' found in profit and loss account of the company's financial statement. Income from subsidiaries or institutions and financial activities referred to as the incomes like dividend income or miscellaneous income. These incomes are bundled as income from financial services. We have also considered R&D expenditure as an important variable. We assume that with the pressure of financialization, company's would minimize in-house R & D activities and would prefer to fund start-up or other organizations to do the necessary development with an agenda of merger or acquisition of the successful venture. Apart from these three important variables we have also considered workforce and a dummy variable denoting the orientation of the firm as IT or others. We attempted to considered a few other variables related to NOI aspect of business influencing profit or, factors explaining financialization. These include merger and acquisitions, patents, dividend paid, global or domestic orientation of the organization, being listed in a off shore stock exchange etc. However, lack of data across samples and statistically insignificant results led us to the final model that we describe in the next section.

3.2 Method and Analysis

This paper analyzes whether a relationship of Non-Operating component variables viz. Interest Income in the income statement of a sample company to its reported net profits.

The analysis takes into consideration the case of companies in IT sector and Real sector companies in order to identify the various aspect of financialization is found more in the IT sector.

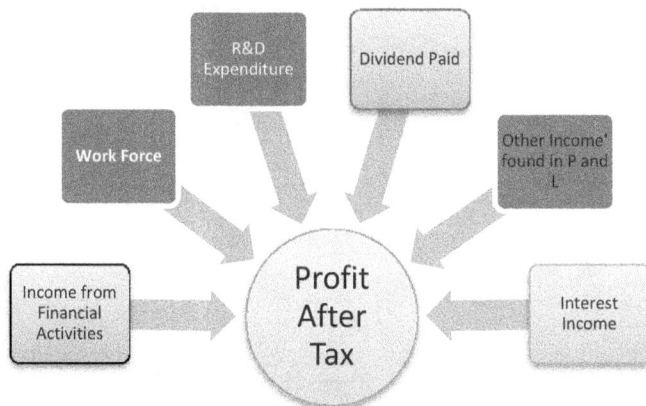

Figure 1. Financialization Factors influencing Profit

For our final analysis we used a log-linear model that was identified as the most appropriate model. We attempted various models for our analysis, before arriving at this final model. Based on review we had also considered non-operating incomes as ratio to total profit as dependent variable. This, however, did not yield statistically significant results. However, after subjecting the models into various tests, including normality of error term, multicolinearity, autocorrelation and hetroscadasticity, the log linear (also known as double log or Cobb-Douglas function) model was identified to be appropriate.

$$Y_i = \beta_0 \prod_{j=1}^{n} x_{ij}^{\beta_j} e_i^{\varepsilon}$$

This model can be expressed in log linear form as follows,

$$\ln Y_i = \beta_0 + \beta_j \sum_{j=1}^{n} \ln x_{ij} + \varepsilon_i$$

Where,
Y_i=Total sales of ith observation.
x_{ii}= jth input for ith observation
β_j = Coefficients of different inputs
ε_i= Error term

This model can be expressed in following way

$$y = \beta_0 + \sum \beta_j x_{ij} + \varepsilon_i$$

At a first step, above equation is estimated using ordinary least square (OLS) technique to yield best linear unbiased estimates of ß coefficients.

$$\hat{y} = \hat{\beta}_0 + \hat{\beta}_j x_{ij}$$

Results obtained using this model are analyzed in the next section.

4. RESULTS AND DISCUSSIONS

The results pertaining to the regression analysis are discussed in this section. In table 1 we provide the descriptive statistics of the variables considered in the model. Table 2 provides the regression results. Robustness of the model can be identified from the results shown in table 2 as well as in figure 2 and 3.

Table 1. Descriptive Statistics of the variables studied

	Mean	Std. Deviation	N
Profit after Tax(Y)	34378.5	48809.794	56
Income from financial services (X1)	10104	18595.543	56
Other Income' found in P and L (X2)	837.11	1730.586	56
Interest Income(X3)	5060.89	10355.671	56
Work Force(X5)	24249.2	43419.035	56
R and D Expenditure (X6)	1661.75	3266.242	56
Dummy1	0.3571	0.48349	56

Table 2. Regression Results

Model	Unstandardized Coefficients		Standardized Coefficients	t-stat	Collinearity Statistics	
	B	Std. Error	Beta		Tolerance	VIF
(Constant)	4889	3957		1.24		
Income from financial services (X1)	0.221	0.21	0.084	1.07	0.37	2.71
Other Incomes (X2)	11.65	1.47	0.413	7.94*	0.84	1.19
Interest Income (X3)	2.807	0.36	0.596	7.84*	0.395	2.53
Workforce (X5)	0.346	0.06	0.307	5.7*	0.783	1.28
R & D Expenditure (X6)	-1.574	0.77	-0.105	-2.06**	0.868	1.15
Dummy 1	-6913	5678	-0.068	-1.22	0.72	1.39

Note: Dependent Variable: Profit After Tax; Independent Variable: Interest Income(X3), R and D Expenditure (X6), Work Force(X5), Other Income found in Profit and Loss account (X2), Income from financial services (X1), Dummy Variable: Dummy 1 is industry type (1= IT industry; 0 otherwise)

F-Statistics is significant at 1 percent level; R-Square=0.88 ; Durbin-Watson= 1.999

* Significant at 1 percent level; ** significant at 5 percent level

The regression equation of the observations yield:

Profit after Tax (Y) = 4889+0.221*Income from Financial Services (X1) + 11.65*Other Income found in P&L (X2) + Interest Income (X3) + 0.346*Work Force (X5) - 1.574*R&D Expenditure (X6) – 6913 * Dummy1

Our results show a robust R square value of 0.888. F-Statistics being significant suggest the appropriateness of the model and choice of variables..

Durbin Watson Value being 1.999 shows that there is no auto-correlation among the error terms. Variance Inflating Factor is well within the limit for all the variables [VIF,8]implies Multi-Collinearity problem is not a matter of concern. The Scatter Plot of error terms not having any pattern evades the heteroschedasticity problem. The Normal probability plot shows the normal distribution of error terms. Therefore, overall the model seems to be robust and hence the inferences drawn from the results make statistical sense.

Figure 2. Scatter Plot of Error Terms

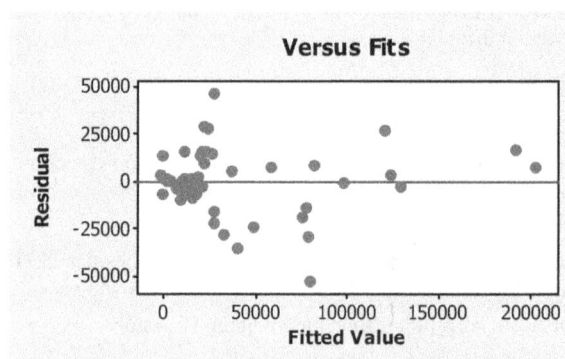

Figure 3. Testing of Normality of Error Terms

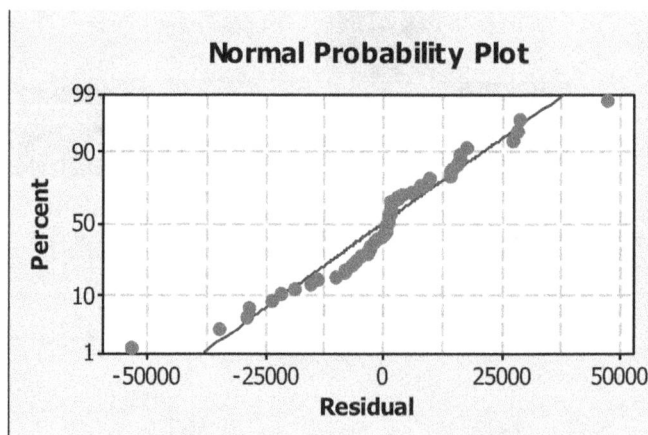

Our analysis provides some interesting results though we do not find any statistically significant difference across IT and non-IT industry. Other income and interest income factors positively and significantly impact the profitability of the organizations. The negative and significant beta coefficient of R&D expenditure possibly is one of the important indicator of financialization in Indian corporate. The standardized beta coefficient suggest that interest income, other income and work force are respectively the three most important factors influencing profitability of the corporate.

CONCLUSION

Our results from the limited sample study are suggestive towards the financialization in corporate India. However, we did not find any statistically significant difference across IT and non-IT industry. It is possibly to carry out more empirical investigation on financialization across various sectors, micro as well as at macro level. It is also possible to conduct such empirical study by bringing in diverse range of variables explaining financialization. On a further study we would be interested to introduced panel data analysis using data over a relatively longer period to indicate of the presence of financialization factors reflected in financial statements of the corporate sector. Longitudinal data would provide better understanding on financialization as compared to cross-sectional data.

5. REFERENCES

[1] Epstein, G. 2002. Financialization, Rentier Interests and Central Bank Policy. *Political economy Research Institute*

[2] Newberry, S and Robb, A. 2008. Financialization: Constructing Shareholder value for some. *Critical Perspectives of Accounting*

[3] Muellerleile, C. 2009. Financialization takes off at Boeing. *Journal of Economic Geography 664*

[4] Lazonick, W. 2002. Marketization, Globalization, Financialization: The Fragility of U.S. Economy in an era of Global Change.

[5] Epstein, G. 2005. Introduction: Financialization and the World Economy. *Political Economy Research Institute*

[6] Montgomerie, J. 2008. Bridging the Capital Divide: Global Finance, Financialization and Contemporary Capitalism

[7] Marangoni, G and Stefano, S. nd. The 'Good' Company and Financialization: Corporate Choices, Institutional Environment and Catholic Social Thought

[8] Jensen, M.C. 2001. Value Maximization, Stakeholder Theory and the Corporate Objective Function. *European Financial Management, 7,3,8*

[9] Narayanan, M.P and Nanda, V.K. 2004. Finance for Strategic Decision Making. What Non-Financial Managers need to know? *University of Michigan Business School Management Series.* 5-10

[10] Krippner, G. 2005. The Financialization of the American Economy. *Socio-Econ Rev. 3,173-208*

[11] Kedrosky,P and Dangler, S. 2011. Financialization and its Entrepreneurial Consequences. *Erwin Marion Kauffman Foundation Research Paper, 1-20*

[12] Berman et al. 2008. Financial Intelligence for Entrepreneurs: what you really need to know about the number*s. Harvard Business School Press, USA, p.40*

[13] Elkholy, S.H. 2010. Modern Finance and Transformation of Financial Systems: Key considerations of Egypt in light of Global Crisis. *Inauguration Conference for launching information and decision support Centre. Working Paper Series, 4, 1-29.*

[14] IUF. 2006. Feeding Financial Markets: Financialization and Restructuring. *International Union of Food* retrieved from *www.iuf.org*

[15] Vargas, G. Luna, A. nd. Theory of the Firm, Financialization and the Crisis of CEMEX

Sourcing Strategy and Cross-Organizational Career Development

Mohan Tanniru
Oakland University
200 I Elliott Hall, Rochester MI 48309
520-405-6845
tanniru@oakland.edu

ABSTRACT

IT departments have gone through many ups and downs in recruiting IT talent due to changes in the focus of IT departments over the last three decades, from back-office application development to strategic exploration of applications/technologies today.

Complicating the recruitment and retention of IT talent may include several factors such as:

- Rapid changes in technologies and the lag between the talent needs and educational institutions' ability to provide this talent

- The evolving sourcing (outsourcing as well as insourcing trends) and how it disrupts a reasonable career development path for professional growth for new IT recruits

- Significant amount of IT investment is tied to the maintenance of current infrastructure and staying current with the changing technology related threats (e.g. security) and opportunities (e.g. social media) calls for different types of talent that is becoming hard to recruit and retain

- Lack of effective knowledge retention or management strategies to capture the expertise of those that leave an IT department

- Loss of knowledge associated with application/technology that has been outsourced to external partners

- Inadequate resource and time needed to support the development of talent as they seek to professionally grow, and others

Peter Cappelli of Wharton bemoans the fact that US has moved today to "just-in-time" approach to recruit talent, as opposed to an "organization man" approach, where firms have made long term investments on human capital development. Is there a hybrid model more appropriate for IT (a cross-organizational approach), where some of the human capital development occurs at the organizational intersection? Such models are used in special cases such as: cross-disciplinary teams to solve specific business problems, joint appointments in academia, talent acquired from different organizations to create movies in film industry, etc.

Can IT departments leverage cross-organizational partnerships to retain talent that is crucial for innovation, support joint development, access unique talent for specific purposes (e.g. legacy system maintenance, social media, open source, cloud computing, etc.)?

This presentation will discuss a multi-university research effort that is currently being undertaken to understand the issues and challenges in developing such a cross organizational approach to retaining and growing IT talent. Preliminary data from interviews conducted with several senior level IT executives will be analyzed and presented at the conference.

ACM Classification

H.1.0 General, H.5.3 Organizational Design, Theory and Models, J.0 General, K.3.0 General, and K.6.1 Staffing

Keywords

Talent management; sourcing strategy; Inter-organizational partnerships; knowledge retention

Speaker's Bio

Mohan Tanniru, Ph.D. is a Professor of MIS at the School of Business Administration at Oakland University, Rochester, Michigan. Prior to Aug 2013, he was the Dean of School of Business at OU, Dept. Head of the MIS program at the University of Arizona, and Director of Applied Technology Program at Oakland University. He also taught at Syracuse University and U of WI-Madison. He received Ph.D. in MIS from Northwestern University and published over 90 articles in various journals, books and conference proceedings. He also worked with major corporations in Syracuse (Carrier-UTC, Bristol Myers Squibb, etc.), SE Michigan (GM, EDS/HP, Comerica, Chrysler, Compuware, St Joe Mercy-Oakland, Crittenton, Beaumont, etc.), and Arizona/California (Honeywell, Intel, Kaiser Permanente, Sanofi-Aventis, etc.) through corporate sponsored graduate and under-graduate student projects.

Permission to make digital or hard copies of part or all of this work for personal or classroom use is granted without fee provided that copies are not made or distributed for profit or commercial advantage, and that copies bear this notice and the full citation on the first page. Copyrights for third-party components of this work must be honored. For all other uses, contact the owner/author(s). Copyright is held by the author/owner(s).

SIGMIS-CPR'14, May 29–31, 2014, Singapore, Singapore.
ACM 978-1-4503-2625-4/14/05.
http://dx.doi.org/10.1145/2599990.2602230

Getting IT Together: Linking Computing Intervention Camps with Computing Careers

Christina N. Outlay
University of Wisconsin - Whitewater
Dept of Information Technology
Whitewater, WI 53190
00 1 242-472-7034
outlayc@uww.edu

Alana J. Platt
University of Wisconsin - Whitewater
Dept of Information Technology
Whitewater, WI 53190
00 1 242-472-1258
platta@uww.edu

Kacie Conroy
Girls Educating Themselves
about Information Technology
Madison, Wisconsin

kconroy@gmail.com

ABSTRACT

The dearth of women choosing computing careers has been identified as a national problem in the United States. Efforts have been made to combat this by educating girls at a young age about technology. Recent research demonstrates that exposure to technology is insufficient to change young girls' attitudes towards computing careers and that interventions must explicitly tie technology activities to careers. Faculty and staff of a Midwestern University modified a computing summer camp for middle school girls to include career specific programming. . The camp partnered with the *Girls Educating Themselves about Information Technology* (GET IT) program to garner interest among middle school girls in computing careers. This exploratory paper describes the impact of this summer camp on girls' interest in pursuing careers in computing.

Categories and Subject Descriptors

K.3.2 [**Computers and Education**]: Computer and Information Science Education—*Curriculum; Computer science education; Information systems education* K.4.0 [**Computers and Society**]: General

General Terms

Human Factors.

Keywords

Middle school, computing programs, summer technology camps, STEM education, K-12 CS Education, girls in computing, IT careers, broadening participation in computing.

Permission to make digital or hard copies of all or part of this work for personal or classroom use is granted without fee provided that copies are not made or distributed for profit or commercial advantage and that copies bear this notice and the full citation on the first page. Copyrights for components of this work owned by others than the author(s) must be honored. Abstracting with credit is permitted. To copy otherwise, or republish, to post on servers or to redistribute to lists, requires prior specific permission and/or a fee. Request permissions from permissions@acm.org.
SIGMIS-CPR'14, May 29–31, 2014, Singapore, Singapore.
Copyright is held by the owner/author(s). Publication rights licensed to ACM.
ACM 978-1-4503-2625-4/14/05...$15.00.
http://dx.doi.org/10.1145/2599990.2600005

1. INTRODUCTION

According to the National Center for Women in Technology (NCWIT), women earn fewer than 21 percent of computing degrees (DuBow 2011). Recognizing this lack of representation, multiple universities, corporations and not-for-profit institutions have begun offering intervention programs targeting girls in middle school, high school or both, with varying degrees of success. Faculty and staff of a Midwestern University had organized a computing summer camp for middle school girls for 5 years but changed the activities in response to research suggesting stronger ties between camp activities and the nature of computing careers (i.e., Taub et al. 2012).The summer camp partnered with the *Girls Educating Themselves about Information Technology* (GET IT) program. GET IT was founded in 2007 to educate middle school girls about Information Technology (IT) careers. GET IT works with various organizations, including Girls Scouts, middle school summer tech camps, and college preparatory programs to educate young girls about IT career opportunities.

2. BACKGROUND

Girls are up to five times less likely than boys to consider computing careers or to major in computing related fields in college (Melymuka 2001). This is due in part to negative influences conveyed by society, specifically representing computing as "men's work". This attitude is often adopted by young girls in the early stages of their educational career (Ramsey et al. 2005).

Educational programs geared toward attracting girls to computing seek to provide positive experiences with technology and education to address the perception that computing is a male-only field. Existing programs target girls as young as middle school using a variety of approaches, such as classes introduced as part of the school curriculum, after school programs and/or summer camps, support groups and Girl Scout programs (Bruckman et al. 2009; Craig et al. 2009; Doerschuk et al. 2007; Hu 2008; Ramsey et al. 2005; Webb et al. 2011).

A common element of educational programs is the recognition that interventions must start early in order to spark young girls' interest in computing and to maintain that interest throughout their middle and high school years. Existing camps and similar programs have largely focused their programing on exposing girls to different technologies. The results achieved by the camps have been mostly positive, with examples such as improved campers' attitudes toward computer science (Craig et al. 2009), and campers developing a positive image of programming and computers after working with programming software (Hu 2008). In another camp (Doerschuk et al. 2007), results were mostly positive, with improved campers' interest levels for topics like robotics programming and web page development, but not computer operations.

While girls reported enjoying the camp activities in some camps, there was no significant impact on computer science career attitudes (Webb et al. 2011). In other camps, the girls appeared more interested in non-computing topics rather than computing topics (Franklin et al. 2011). The varied results from different types of camps suggest that simply introducing campers to technologies is insufficient to capture the interest of girls towards computing careers. Effectively capturing and retaining girls' interest in computing careers remains a challenge.

A proposed solution to this challenge is to explicitly link the technology-based activities in camps to the related computing constructs and IT careers (Taub et al. 2012). This paper describes initial efforts to ascertain the effectiveness of a summer camp for girls consisting of programming dedicated to linking fun technology with computing careers. The GET IT program was a central piece of the camp's career oriented programming along with sessions designed to introduce girls to computing topics.

3. CAREER ORIENTED INTERVENTIONS
3.1 The GET IT Program
The GET IT program was started in 2007 by a female IT college graduate and IT professional in an effort to provide positive images to girls about computing careers. Since 2007, the GET IT program has expanded beyond middle school girls to include high school girls, educational professionals, as well as boys. The focus of the GET IT program is to break down the complex topic of IT careers into easy to understand concepts.

The GET IT program is a multi-phase interactive presentation. The program begins with the presenter asking questions about the girls' knowledge of technology careers (e.g., Project Manager, Business Analyst, Quality Assurance Analyst, Database Analyst, Software Engineer, Graphics Designer, and Tech Writer) and the impact of gendered attitudes on their perceptions. The aim of this phase is to get the girls questioning their preconceived notions about computing careers. The presenter then introduces various IT careers utilizing an accessible metaphor – specifically, a sandwich shop. The presenter describes the sandwich-making process from customer order, to sandwich preparation and quality control, and sandwich delivery back to the customer. Along the way, the presenter relates employee roles within the sandwich shop to similar roles in IT (i.e., sandwich shop manager to a IT project manager; sandwich maker to an IT developer).

A second activity allows girls to role-play as a Business Analyst. The presenter holds a picture hidden in a folder, and the campers are tasked with figuring out the picture by asking a series of questions. Campers then draw an image based on the new information they gathered, and at the end the presenter reveals the actual picture for comparison. The presenter then facilitates a discussion correlating the activity with gathering IT project requirements. The activity ends with campers receiving additional information about IT careers (Figure 1). The session concludes with the presenter asking campers if they are interested in the careers discussed at the beginning of the session.

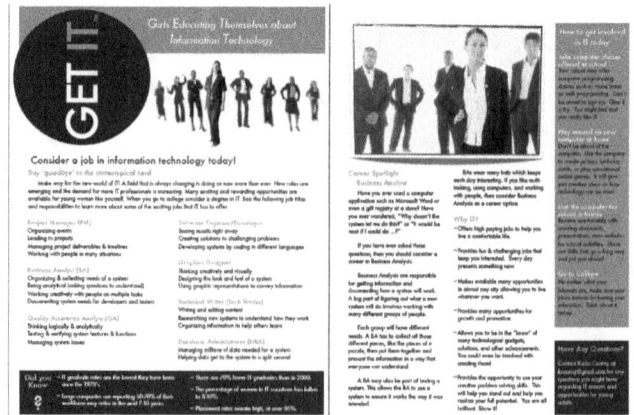

Figure 1. GET IT handout describing IT careers ©Kacie Conroy, GET IT.

3.2 Other Interventions
In addition to programs such as GET IT, there are various ways to introduce computing careers to girls at the middle school level, particularly 7th and 8th grades. Talking with female professionals working in different careers can cause girls to consider those fields for themselves (Campbell 1991). Allowing girls to visit computing environments, either in person or through virtual tours, can also prompt girls to consider future careers. Showing people working across fields using technology, especially young women below the age of 35, also proves effective to generate interest in computing among middle school girls (dotdiva.org).

4. RESEARCH METHOD
This study tested the impact on girls' attitudes towards computing careers by including career-oriented programming in a summer technology camp. The camp is an annual camp offered at a Midwestern University targeting middle school girls entering 6th, 7th and 8th grades. Most camp attendees traveled to the camp from neighboring cities within a 60-mile radius of the University. Campers enrolled into the camp on a voluntary basis by accessing an online registration page when open enrollment began a few months prior to the start of camp. There were a total of 80 girls in the camp across all three grade levels during the summer of 2013.

The camp occurs across two days and is divided into separate tracks for 6th, 7th and 8th grades. On each day of the camp, campers complete two major activities, such as learning a new skill (i.e., web programming) in the morning session, then completing a project using the new skill in the afternoon. In addition to breaks for snacks and lunch, campers tour different areas of campus to show workers using technology. To tie camp activities to computing careers, 6th grade campers participate in the GET IT program. 7th graders tour a multimedia recording studio and hear from a female guest speaker who works in IT. 8th graders also hear from a female IT worker guest speaker.

To test the effectiveness of explicitly tying camp activities to jobs in order to impact girls' attitudes towards computing careers, a survey was administered with relevant questions twice: at the start of camp and at its conclusion. All girls who participated in the camp were invited to complete the surveys describing their attitudes towards computing and computer careers. For the purposes of this paper, the results of comparing two sixth grade groups of campers are only reported. All survey participants were first-time camp participants. One group of campers attended camp during a prior year and did not participate in GET IT. The other group of campers participated in the same camp sessions the following year and also attended GET IT. In both camps, campers participated in sessions on computer programming, digital video and digital animation and toured an on-campus radio station.

5. RESULTS

Twenty-three 6th graders attended the camp in 2012. Thirty 6th graders attended in 2013. Research consent was obtained from the parents of all campers as well as child assent from the campers themselves. Across both groups, a total of 53 girls were invited to participate in the research. Campers completed the same surveys prior to the start of camp activities. Each camper received a camper number prior to the start of camp so that pre- and post-camper responses could be matched.. All thirty campers completed the pre-camp survey and twenty-six campers completed the post-camp survey in 2013. All twenty-three campers completed both the pre-camp and post-camp surveys in 2012. Two campers did not include their camper number on the post-camp survey..

5.1 Camper characteristics – Attitudes toward computers and computing careers (based on Pre- Camp survey)

A series of Likert-type questions were compiled from several sources. Two introductory questions were included to assess each camper's feelings toward and perceived skills with computers (Adams, 2007). Items to measure computer playfulness (Webster et al. 1992), positive stereotypes (Webb and Rosson, 2011), and college and career plans (Hu, 2008) were also adapted to this study. Campers also rated separately their level of interest and their level of knowledge for a variety of computing related areas (Doerschuck et al 2007). Tables 1 and 2 list the means and standard deviations for each characteristic variable. Cronbach's alpha is also shown for the scale variables. Tables 3 and 4 list the means and standard deviations for the interest and knowledge variables.

Since each group of campers attended the camp during a different time period, independent samples t-tests were conducted against all campers' characteristics (including interest and knowledge levels) to determine whether there were significant differences between the two groups. There was a significant difference $(t(51)=-2.878, p=.006)$ in the scores for interest in Web Page Development between the 2012 group (M=4.04, sd=1.186) and 2013 group (M=3.13, sd=1.106). There were no significant differences in the scores for any of the other pre-camp variables. The groups were similar enough to use for comparison despite the time difference in camp attendance.

Table 1. 2012 Camper Characteristics (n=23)

Playfulness (a=.768, n=23)	Positive Stereotypes (a=.861, n=23)	Skill Level (n=23)	Feelings toward Computers (n=23)	Interest in Computing Career (n=23)	Fun (n=23)
3.96 (sd=.75)	3.86 (sd=.98)	4.17 (sd=.834)	4.09 (sd=.515)	3.00 (sd=1.348)	4.13 (sd=.815)

Table 2. 2013 Camper Characteristics (n=30)

Playfulness (a=.723, n=27)	Positive Stereotypes (a=.878, n=30)	Skill Level (n=28)	Feelings toward Computers (n=30)	Interest in Computing Career (n=28)	Fun (n=30)
3.67 (sd=.60)	3.64 (sd=.87)	4.04 (sd=.922)	4.07 (sd=.45)	2.59 (sd=.907)	4.47 (sd=.730)

Table 3. 2012 and 2013 campers' interest in computing related topics

Topic	2012 Pre-camp Interest Level	2013 Pre-camp Interest Level
Computer Science	2.52 (n=23, sd=1.238)	2.41 (n=29, sd=.946)
Computer Programming	3.04 (n=23, sd=1.261)	3.0 (n=29, sd=1.035)
Web Page Development	4.04 (n=23, sd=1.186)	3.13 (n=30, sd=1.106)
Computer Graphics and Media	3.74 (n=23, sd=1.356)	3.21 (n=28, sd=1.397)
Developing Software Programs	3.30 (n=23, sd=1.396)	2.63 (n=30, sd=1.245)
Creating Mobile Apps	4.35 (n=23, sd=.885)	3.80 (n=30, sd=1.126)
Creating and Editing Digital Music	4.09 (n=23, sd=1.083)	3.60 (n=30, sd=1.545)
Creating and Editing Digital Video	4.35 (n=23, sd=.885)	4.03 (n=29, sd=1.149)
Producing Animated Movies	4.09 (n=23, sd=1.125)	4.00 (n=30, sd=1.145)
Designing and Building Video Games	3.65 (n=23, sd=1.369)	3.24 (n=29, sd=1.405)
Working with Business and Technical Staff	2.48 (n=23, sd=1.473)	2.38 (n=29, sd=.942)
Leading Teams to Develop New Technology	2.83 (n=23, sd=1.557)	2.86 (n=29, sd=1.060)

Table 4. 2012 and 2013 campers' knowledge in computing related topics

Topic	2012 Pre-camp Knowledge Level	2013 Pre-camp Knowledge Level
Computer Science	2.04 (n=23, sd=.928)	1.90 (n=30, sd=.960)
Computer Programming	2.39 (n=23, sd=1.118)	2.10 (n=30, sd=.995)
Web Page Development	2.65 (n=23, sd=1.369)	2.33 (n=30, sd=1.124)
Computer Graphics and Media	2.74 (n=23, sd=1.137)	2.30 (n=30, sd=1.179)
Developing Software Programs	2.00 (n=23, sd=1.044)	2.10 (n=30, sd=1.125)
Creating Mobile Apps	2.00 (n=23, sd=1.414)	2.33 (n=30, sd=1.241)
Creating and Editing Digital Music	2.83 (n=23, sd=1.527)	2.67 (n=30, sd=1.322)
Creating and Editing Digital Video	3.17 (n=23, sd=1.527)	3.07 (n=30, sd=1.311)
Producing Animated Movies	2.52 (n=23, sd=1.410)	2.76 (n=29, sd=1.123)
Designing and Building Video Games	2.13 (n=23, sd=1.290)	1.93 (n=29, sd=1.100)
Working with Business and Technical Staff	1.74 (n=23, sd=1.096)	2.00 (n=30, sd=1.174)
Leading Teams to Develop New Technology	2.00 (n=23, sd=1.168)	1.93 (n=30, sd=1.230)

5.2 Post Camp Results – Interest in Computing Topics

Campers in both groups were asked to indicate their interest on a number of different computer-related topics before the start of camp and again after the camp completion. Within each group, matched pair t-tests were used to determine whether there was a measurable change in campers' interest and/or knowledge levels for each computing topic.

5.2.1 2012 Campers – no GET IT

No significant changes in camper attitudes existed toward viewing computers as fun, interest in computing careers or positive stereotypes. No significant changes existed in campers' interest scores on any of the computing topics. A significant and positive change existed in campers' knowledge scores for Creating and Editing Digital Video (mean difference=1.000, sd=1.342, t(20)=3.416, p=.003), Producing Animated Movies (mean difference=1.000, sd=1.342, t(20)=4.126, p=.003) and Working with Business and Technical staff (mean difference=.476, sd=1.209, t(20)=1.805, p=.086).

5.2.1.1 2013 Campers – GET IT

No significant changes in camper attitudes existed toward viewing computers as fun or positive stereotypes. A significant change did exist in campers' interest in computing careers (mean

difference=.654, sd=.629, p=.000). A significant and positive change existed in the campers' interest scores for Computer Science (mean difference=.625, sd=1.173, t(25)=2.611, p=.016), Web Page Development (mean difference=.5, sd=1.068, t(25)=2.388, p=0.25), Software Development (mean difference=.538, sd=1.104, t(25)=2.487, p=.020), Creating and Editing Digital Video (mean difference=.462, sd=1.240, t(25)=1.897, p=.069), and working with Business and Technical Staff (mean difference=.833, sd=1.204, t(23)=3.391, p=.003). 2013 campers also reported significant and positive changes in the knowledge levels for all of the computing topics on the survey, as shown in Table 5.

Table 5. 2013 Campers' difference in pre- and post-camp computing knowledge scores

Item	Mean difference	SD	T(df)	p-value
Computer Science	.769	1.032	3.801 (25)	.001
Computer Programming	1.000	1.443	2.464 (24)	.002
Web Page Development	.462	1.334	1.765 (25)	.090
Computer Graphics and Media	1.038	1.311	4.039 (25)	.000
Developing Software Programs	.692	1.350	2.616 (25)	.015
Creating Mobile Apps	.760	1.363	2.789 (24)	.010
Creating and Editing Digital Music	.600	1.041	2.882 (24)	.008
Creating and Editing Digital Video	1.346	1.231	5.576 (25)	.000
Producing Animated Movies	1.167	1.685	3.391 (23)	.003
Designing and Building Video Games	.720	1.339	2.688 (24)	.013
Working with Business and Technical Staff	1.080	1.470	3.674 (24)	.001
Leading Teams to Develop New Technology	1.080	1.077	5.014 (24)	.000

5.2.2 Comparing the Two Groups

Independent sample t-tests were used to check for differences between the group that participated in GET IT (experimental group) and the group that did not participate in GET IT (control group). We excluded the campers' interest and knowledge of Web Page Development from the post-camp comparison between the groups. No significant differences existed between the two groups' post-camp scores for interest in computing careers or positive stereotypes of computer workers. Significant differences did exist in the two groups' post-camp scores for interest in Computer Graphics/Media and Working with Business and Technical Staff. Significant differences also existed in the two groups' post-camp scores for Knowledge of Computer Science, Computer Programming, Developing Software Programs, Developing Mobile Apps, Working with Business and Technical Staff and Leading Teams to Develop New Technology. Table 5 below shows the differences in means, standard deviations and t-test results for each item.

Table 6. Differences in post-camp interest and knowledge levels for GET IT vs non GET IT groups

Item	2012 Mean (Non GET IT)	2013 Mean (GET IT)	T (df)	P-value
Interest in Computer Graphics and Media	4.22 (n=23, sd=1.085)	3.61 (n=27, sd=1.100)	1.986 (47)	.053
Interest in Working with Business and Technical Staff	2.52 (n=23, sd=1.344)	3.23 (n=26, sd=1.142)	1.996 (47)	.052
Knowledge of Computer Science	2.09 (n=23, sd=1.345)	2.74 (n=27, sd=1.196)	1.819 (48)	.075
Knowledge of Computer Programming	2.48 (n=23, sd=1.377)	3.23 (n=26, sd=1.275)	1.986(47)	.053
Knowledge of Developing Software Programs	2.13(n=23, sd=1.180)	2.96 (n=27, sd=1.400)	2.251(48)	.029
Knowledge of Developing Mobile Apps	2.04 (n=23, sd=1.331)	3.12 (n=26, sd=1.275)	2.877 (47)	.006
Knowledge of Working with Business and Technical Staff	2.17 (n=23, sd=1.267)	3.19 (n=27, sd=1.241)	2.844(48)	.007
Knowledge of Leading Teams to Develop New Technology	2.04 (n=23, sd=1.364)	3.12 (n=26, sd=1.275)	2.842(47)	.007

6. DISCUSSION

This study offers evidence that incorporating GET IT helped to increase campers' knowledge of career-related items such as working with business and technical staff and leading teams to create new technologies. Participating in GET IT increased campers' reported knowledge of computing areas that were taught in the camp; moreover, the campers gained exposure to computing areas that were not taught in sessions during the camp. The campers' increased knowledge in any particular topic did not necessarily result in increased interest in the same topic. Additional observations include:

- *Girls who attend IT and Computing camps already like computers*

  Girls who attended camp already had some computer skills and positive attitudes toward computers and computer workers. This was true for both groups of campers and it is anticipated that this trend will continue in future years' camp participants.

- *Girls who like computers don't necessarily want a career in computers*

  Camp attendees who expressed interest in computers do not necessarily view computing careers as desirable career options. It is unclear if this is due to a genuine lack of interest in computing careers. Perhaps the campers' young age (entering sixth grade) may be responsible for the girls not yet having a clear vision of any specific career path. This possibility will be explored in a future camp.

- *Goal of computing camps should be to get girls who already like computers interested in computing careers*

  Given that the girls who attend our camp already demonstrate a predisposition to computing, the focus of the camp may shift again. The camp currently attempts to attract middle school girls to develop positive attitudes toward and experience with computing topics. A more effective focus would be to increase campers' interests in working in computing careers. Since most girls in the camp are already interested in computing, it will be fruitful to examine ways to incorporate more information on computing careers into the camp activities while maintaining a positive and fun atmosphere.

There are several limitations to this research that currently affect its generalizability. First, despite our initial tests to rule out any significant differences between the two groups, the campers in each group attended camp during different time periods and there might be other differences in the camp atmosphere that could have affected our results. Second, our sample size is relatively small. Third, the camp draws from a local, rather than national, population and therefore the camper characteristics may only be representative of the nearby area.

While our sample size and characteristics are determined by camp attendance, we have several next steps in mind. In conjunction with the summer camp and the GET IT program, we intend to further explore the impacts of exposing girls to fun technology activities while emphasizing the focus on computing careers. We intend to do this in several ways: we are currently working with the Midwestern University to plan the 2014 camp, during which additional data will be collected across a larger group of campers attending during the same year and across multiple grade levels. We will continue to partner with GET IT to gather data from participants in other intervention programs to identify common factors from a larger, more varied sample of participants. We will also incorporate other methods of explicitly linking fun computer topics with related computing careers.

7. REFERENCES

[1] Bruckman, A., Biggers, M., Ericson, B., McKlin, T., Dimond, J., DiSalvo, B., Hewner, M., Ni, L., and Yardi, S. 2009. "Georgia Computes!": Improving the Computing Education Pipeline. *ACM SIGCSE Bulletin 41, 1,* 86-90.

[2] Campbell, P. 1991. Girls and math: Enough is known for action. *WEEA Digest.*

[3] Craig, M., and Horton, D. 2009. Gr8 Designs for Gr8 Girls: A Middle-School Program and its Evaluation. *ACM SIGCSE Bulletin 41, 1,* 221-225.

[4] Doerschuk, P., Liu, J., and Mann, J. 2007. Pilot Summer Camps in Computing for Middle School Girls: From Organization Through Assessment. *ACM SIGCSE Bulletin 39, 3,* 4-8.

[5] DuBow, W. 2011. NCWIT Scorecard: A report on the status of women in Information Technology. *NCWIT Conference, Boulder, CO.*

[6] Franklin, D., Conrad, P., Aldana, G., and Hough, S. 2011. Animal Tlatoque: Attracting Middle School Students to Computing through Culturally-Relevant Themes. *Proceedings of the 42nd ACM technical symposium on Computer science education,* 453-458.

[7] Hu, H. H. 2008. A Summer Programming Workshop for Middle School Girls. *Journal of Computing Sciences in Colleges,* 23, 6, 194-202.

[8] Melymuka, K. 2001. If girls don't get IT, IT won't get girls. *Computerworld,* 35, 2, p 44.

[9] Ramsey, N., and McCorduck, P. 2005. Where are the Women in Information Technology? *Report of Literature Search and Interviews. Prepared for the National Center for Women & Information Technology.*

[10] Taub, R., Armoni, M., and Ben-Ari, M. 2012. CS Unplugged and Middle-School Students' Views, Attitudes, and Intentions Regarding CS. *ACM Transactions on Computing Education,* 12, 2, 1-29.

[11] Webb, H. C., and Rosson, M. B. 2011. Exploring Careers While Learning Alice 3D: A Summer Camp for Middle School Girls. *Proceedings of the 42nd ACM technical symposium on Computer science education,* 377-382.

[12] Webster, J., and Martocchio, J. J. 1992. Microcomputer playfulness: development of a measure with workplace implications. *MIS quarterly,* 201-226.

The Barriers Facing Women in the Information Technology Profession: An Exploratory Investigation of Ahuja's Model

Deborah J. Armstrong
Florida State University
College of Business
Department of Entrepreneurship, Strategy
and Information Systems
01-850-644-8228
djarmstrong@cob.fsu.edu

Cindy K. Riemenschneider
Baylor University
Hankamer School of Business
Department of Information Systems
01- 254-710-4061
c_riemenschneider@baylor.edu

ABSTRACT

In 2002, Ahuja conducted an extensive literature review and proposed a model of the challenges and barriers facing women in the information technology (IT) profession [3]. Her goal was to develop a model that might be used to stop the exodus of women from IT. While Ahuja's model has been consistently cited in the IT workforce literature (citation count as of 1/30/2014 ~ 65 utilizing ISI Web of Science and ~ 230 utilizing Google Scholar), women are still leaving the IT profession at an alarming rate. Using Ahuja's model as the impetus, the current investigation asked women working in the IT department at a Fortune 500 company what unique workplace challenges and barriers they faced that had influenced their voluntary turnover decisions at two time periods. The insights from this exploratory study are applied to Ahuja's model to propose an updated model that may be used to further explore the challenges and barriers facing women, and ultimately perhaps increase the retention of women in the IT field. The proposed model may be used to re-energize the dialogue regarding creating a more diversified IT work environment.

Categories and Subject Descriptors

K.7.1 [Computing Milieu]: The Computing Profession – *occupations*.

General Terms

Management.

Keywords

IT workforce, gender, barriers, qualitative, interpretivist approach.

1. INTRODUCTION

In 2002, Manju Ahuja proposed a model of the barriers faced by women in the information technology (IT) field at three distinct career stages (*choice*, *persistence* and *advancement*). At each stage, she outlined social (the social and cultural views/biases held by society in general) and structural (the structure/hierarchy of the institution) factors that may act as barriers to success (i.e., advancement and persistence). Her goal was to develop a model

Permission to make digital or hard copies of all or part of this work for personal or classroom use is granted without fee provided that copies are not made or distributed for profit or commercial advantage and that copies bear this notice and the full citation on the first page. Copyrights for components of this work owned by others than ACM must be honored. Abstracting with credit is permitted. To copy otherwise, or republish, to post on servers or to redistribute to lists, requires prior specific permission and/or a fee. Request permissions from permissions@acm.org.
SIGMIS-CPR'14, May 29–31, 2014, Singapore, Singapore.
Copyright is held by the owner/author(s). Publication rights licensed to ACM.
ACM 978-1-4503-2625-4/14/05...$15.00.

to help researchers and practitioners "reduce the leakage in the IT career paths of women" [3, p. 20].

For over a decade, various researchers have sought to identify the barriers to the retention of female IT employees (e.g., [6, 48]). To date Ahuja's article has been cited over 65 times according to the ISI Web of Science database, and over 230 times according to Google Scholar. While strides have been made in the area, to date Ahuja's model remains under-studied. In addition, women are significantly underrepresented in the IT field (e.g., [36, 47]), and the number of women in IT positions continues to decline. "In 1985, 37% of Computer and Information Science undergraduate degree recipients were women. By 2011 this proportion had dropped to 18%" [50]. Clearly, more research is needed in this area to aid our understanding of the underlying factors influencing the retention of women in IT (and stop the exodus).

We consider Ahuja's model at two time periods and gather data from women working in a Fortune 500 company. We use our insights to propose a possible update to Ahuja's model [3]. As we are looking at women working in the IT field, we focus on the *persistence* and *advancement* career stages, and limit our discussion to factors affecting those stages.

Social Factors include social expectations (cultural values that shape expectations about women) and work-family conflict (when the demands of participation in one domain are incompatible with demands of another domain). Ahuja [3] contends that social factors can influence whether or not women decide to remain (i.e., persist) in the IT field. Structural Factors include occupational culture (a masculine occupation which includes aspects such as a rigorous engineering approach, long hours, late nights, individual focused behavior), lack of role models (absence of evidence that a successful career in IT is a typical occurrence), presence of informal networks ('good old boy' network; traditional means of building camaraderie), lack of mentors (developmental relationship of long duration in which protégé receives career and psychosocial help from a senior person), and institutional structures (globalization; flattening of organizational structures). Within the structural factor, occupational culture and lack of role models are proposed to influence persistence in an IT career, while informal networks, lack of mentors, and institutional structures are proposed to influence advancement in an IT career. See Figure 1 for a graphical representation of Ahuja's model [3]. Note the grayed out portions of the model are not under study, and the propositions listed are from Ahuja's original model.

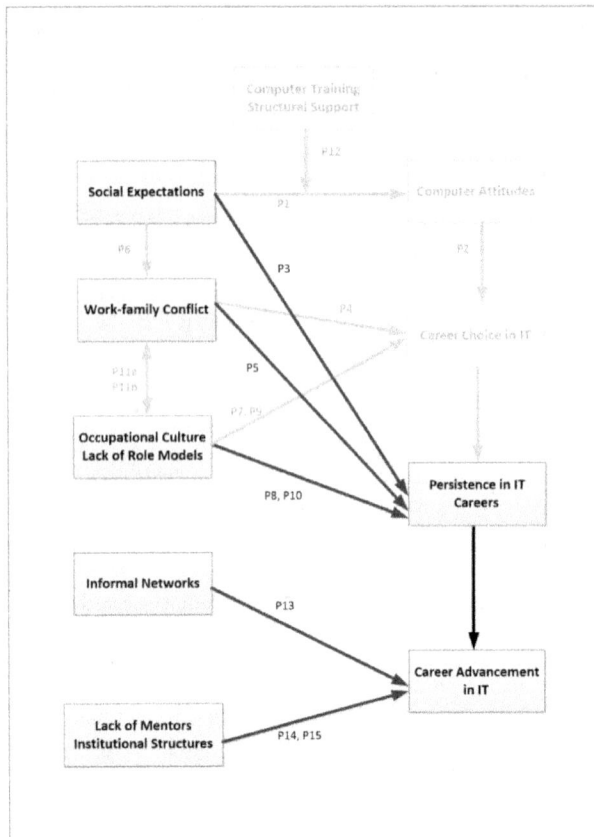

Figure 1. Ahuja's original model

This research contributes to the ongoing investigation of women's participation (and/or lack of participation) in the IT field. Answers to these questions may aid our understanding of the environment faced by women in IT and encourage future research to validate or refute the findings so as to aid organizations (and others such as universities) in developing appropriate interventions to retain a diversified IT work environment.

2. LITERATURE REVIEW

Using Ahuja's model as a starting point, we focus on working professionals in the IT field, and thus review the appropriate literature regarding persistence and advancement for this population.

2.1 Persistence / Turnover

Numerous studies have examined the antecedents to turnover among IT employees [13, 20, 25, 41], ranging from organizational context [2, 4, 27, 28], career advancement opportunities [12], and work exhaustion [27], to personal characteristics such as education and intrinsic values [14]. Niederman, Sumner, and Maertz [35] found that IT employees take numerous routes to deciding to leave their current employment and Jing and Hoon [24] found that IT professionals have a greater desire to move than non-IS professionals, citing a "turnover culture" as a possible cause of the difference.

When we look at gender within the context of IT turnover and persistence findings indicate that men and women view the IT environment and turnover differently. For example, Wickramasinghe [52] found that although organizational tenure

negatively affects job satisfaction among women, many female IT workers wish to remain in their current positions and workplaces. This intention to remain may be a result of improved job embeddedness [46], a strong organizational subculture [30], or perhaps high organizational commitment [43]. In contrast, using data from the Scientists and Engineers Statistical Data System (SESTAT) Stephan and Levin [45] found that retention varied by gender and that a large percentage of IT-trained women leave the labor force rather than take positions in other occupations. Positive and negative workplace culture characteristics such as the 24/7 nature of the job or autonomy seem to affect women's career development and turnover intention within IT [5, 7, 51]. One possible explanation for this may be found in the work of Trauth, Quesenberry and Huang, "In theory, a woman's personal profile - her demographic characteristics such as parenthood status, her personality, and her support system - has been shown to interact with the particular characteristics of her IT job and the culture of her IT workplace to influence her satisfaction and, ultimately, her retention." [49, p. 494].

2.2 Advancement

Research on advancement within the IT field has primarily focused on the challenges and barriers facing women in the workplace and only eludes to its influence on advancement. Research directly assessing barriers facing women in the IT workforce ranges from the topics of gender and race barriers to communication issues within the workplace. These barriers appear to exist at different stages throughout a career in IT [34] as women (and minorities) continue to be underrepresented in positions of power [23, 37, 38]. Studies reveal a persistent view that women 'fit' better with the softer side of IT (e.g., support functions, user relationships) [13, 29].

A consistent barrier to advancement found in the literature is gender-related discrimination [7]. Perceived barriers to advancement have been linked to a lack of respect, ageism, stress, and work schedule flexibility [5]. Adya's [2] interviews revealed that while most women from South Asia did not identify career genderization in the workplace, American IT professionals perceived greater stereotyping and discrimination based on gender. Although men in the IT workplace generally realize that women face challenges and barriers [39], discriminatory practices continue to inhibit career progression for many targeted groups [38, 42].

The literature informs us that men and women may perceive the IT work environment differently, and that the IT work environment has an influence on women's retention and career advancement. As women remain under-represented in the IT field, and in leadership positions within IT, this topic is worthy of continued research efforts. This research attempts to further explore the challenges and barriers facing women in IT and the influence these challenges and barriers have on advancement and persistence with the following research questions. Using Ahuja's model [3] as our guide we explore the following:

1. *What are women's perceptions of workplace challenges and barriers they face that are impediments to their career advancement in the IT field?*

2. *What are women's perceptions of workplace challenges and barriers they face that are impediments to their persistence in the IT field?*

The next section details the method that was employed to explore the research questions.

3. METHOD

Believing that much of our social reality is constructed and perpetuated through discourse [11], using an interpretive perspective, qualitative data collection and analysis we sought to elucidate the emergent cognitions evoked from group interaction.

3.1 Data Source and Procedure

The organization, FoodCo (a pseudonym), founded in the 1930s, is one of the world's largest processors of protein. Information about FoodCo was gathered directly from multiple corporate representatives at two time periods, and supplemented via corporate website, annual reports and news articles. During the T1 (time 1) data collection, FoodCo had over 125,000 employees and 300 facilities in the United States and around the world, with sales of over $20 billion. At the time the IT department was in the midst of a major systems integration initiative.

There were three years between the data collections. At the time of the second data collection (T2) FoodCo had just over 100,000 employees at more than 300 facilities in the United States and around the world, with sales of over $25 billion. In response to a financially tough year, FoodCo cut overhead costs and increased efficiencies to become more agile. FoodCo was engaged in a multi-pronged change process with initiatives ranging from expansion in production capacity to turnover within the Board of Directors and executive personnel.

Focus group interviews were utilized because they have high face validity, capture real-life data, are flexible [9], and provide a more relaxed context, thereby increasing the chance of spontaneous responses [31]. We conducted focus group interviews with women working in the IT department at the headquarters of FoodCo. As this exploratory research was focused on generating insights, we believe this sampling approach is acceptable.

The initial contact with the organization was the CIO who identified the participants as IT personnel. Participants were recruited via email invitation and the contact person within the organization handled the room scheduling and invitation process. The focus groups were held during working hours in on-site conference rooms. Job titles of the participants in T1 included Programmer, Business Analyst, and Project Lead. Job titles of the participants in T2 were Business Analyst, Database Administrator, and Director of Business Process Change, to name a few. While the focus groups in T1 and T2 differed in terms of the proportion of managerial, technical and business-related participants, as the recruitment process was identical, and participation was voluntary, rather than a limitation, we feel this is a contextual factor that added richness to our study. Due to the nature of some topics discussed in the larger study, concerns regarding the identifiability of certain participants, and to increase interviewee trust in the researchers, a decision was made not to gather additional demographic information.

The focus group interviews ranged from 45 to 65 minutes, were tape recorded and transcribed verbatim. The interview transcripts averaged 12 pages in length (range 7-17). The total number of participants from T1 was 39 and 15 from T2. The participants discussed several open-ended questions of relevance to the research questions. Follow up questions were asked as prompted by the participant responses. To ensure confidentiality each participant was assigned a number, and asked not to use each other's names in the conversation. In the quotes provided later in the manuscript, the reader will note that the focus group and participant number are provided to identify the speaker.

The researchers were trained in group interview techniques to promote consistency and reduce interviewer variance. The interview guide (see Appendix) was strictly adhered to by the researchers as confirmed in the transcriptions. While steps were taken to mitigate researcher bias in the data collection and analysis processes (e.g., tape recording interviews as opposed to only researcher notes), the authors acknowledge that they are representing the participant's concepts as experienced through their own subjectivity.

3.2 Coding Process

Content analysis was used to make inferences from the verbatim transcriptions. Content analysis is, "any technique for making inferences by objectively and systematically identifying specified characteristics of messages" [15, p. 14]. In recent years, content analysis has emerged as a common methodology for aggregating and drawing inferences from textual material in organizational research [10]. Content analysis is appropriate for examining whether patterns in the content support research questions, and can be used to code responses to open-ended questions [33] from a variety of sources (e.g., surveys, interviews, texts).

The researchers systematically examined the interview transcriptions to identify the concepts. During the data analysis process the researchers developed a coding scheme. Similar to other researchers (e.g., [17, 32]) a phrase was used as the base unit of analysis to develop the coding scheme. The researchers chose not to develop a coding scheme a priori for the T1 data analysis, but inductively as the concepts emerged from the interview transcripts. To guide the coding process, the authors started with a broad definition of the problem which became more focused as relevant literature was analyzed, data collection was undertaken, and the transcripts were repeatedly read, analyzed and extensively discussed (e.g., [18, 19]). Thus, the emergent coding scheme is not a-theoretical, but grounded in theory and organic in nature [26]. With emergent coding each of the researchers independently coded the texts using her research perspective and grounding in the literature base. In the coding process, words that are frequently mentioned in the statements are grouped together, and a word or word group is created to summarize the meaning of the phrase. The researchers developed the 'labels'; however the concepts emerged from the participants. The individually coded phrases were discussed and all discrepancies were resolved through discussion to reach 100% agreement. At the T2 data analysis the coding scheme developed at T1 was used as the foundation. Any new concepts that emerged from the T2 transcripts were vetted using the same process as at T1. The emergent concepts with descriptive phrases from the participants are provided in Table 1.

Table 1. Concepts with sample phrases

Concept Label	Description and Sample Phrases from Participants
Actions the Company Can Take	Actions the company takes to solve problems, increase performance, etc… Example: "Stagnant management are moved out"
Barriers: Discrimination	People not being treated equally; how things are not fair; discrimination. Example: "They don't see that we need to be paid for what we do for our position"
Barriers: General	Barriers experienced in the workplace that do not fit into any of the more specific barriers. Example: "I don't live really close"
Barriers: Management	Upper management's attitudes, beliefs and actions which seem problematic for women. Example: "Then there's also management, higher up that I deal with"
Barriers: Politics	Need to schmooze, be political. Example: "I wouldn't be able to go out to lunch with my team"
Barriers: Promotion	Problems being promoted; lack of criteria for promotion; references to glass ceiling. Example: "How they decide who gets promoted isn't really clear to everyone"
Barriers: Respect	Feeling not listened to or not treated with consideration. Example: "Some of the men overpower and step in and compensate," "I had enough of not being recognized."
Barriers: Women's Characteristics	Failure to communicate effectively; personality traits; self-doubt. Example: "If they are teary-eyed, then its frowned upon by the male peers"
Change	References to the rate, pace, or amount of change faced. Examples: "I think the change is ever increasing"
Cultural Norms	Informal knowledge that shapes employee behavior; how things are done. Examples: "you're just gonna put in 45 hours"
Gender Differences	Statements about how genders are treated, interest areas they like, and the way they deal with stress. Direct comparisons of men and women. Example: "Women kind of have a different mindset than men do"
Information Technology (IT)	Getting the job done; characteristic of IT. Example: "If you are developing systems"
Job Qualities	Positive job-related qualities; needed skill sets. Example: "go those extra hours to meet that customer demand"
Lack of Control	This is how things are; can't change it, take what you can get; situation out of control, just coincidence. Example: "You can't change it"
Managing Family Responsibility	Women do the most of the child rearing; The choice to have a family being a decision they made. Examples: "It's kind of expected that the Mom will take care of things,"
Men	Male activities and interests. Example: "They tend to play golf and baseball together"
My Situation is Different	Cannot relate to what is being discussed; includes mentioning a situation facing a specific individual or individuals. Example: "She had different circumstances,"
Negative Descriptions	Negative situations: beat down, irritated. Example: "turmoil creates demoralization"
Opportunities	New, growth or promotion opportunities; challenging job. Example: "We don't do the same thing two days in a row"
Organization	References to company size, changes, number of buildings. Example: "the whole matrix organization"
Positive Descriptions	Positive emotions; like what I do; feel better. Example: "we were successful"
Result of Own Decision	Responsible for own decisions; taking control of own career. Example: "I made that decision [choose family]"
Time	Time either as problems or hours worked. Example: "Now you have to work just 6:30am until 3:30pm or 7:00am to 4:00pm"
Turnover	Leaving an organization. Example: "they just come in, get the training, and go"
Turnover: Family	Left organization or IT due to family considerations or family pressure. Example: "A few women have left when they've had their second child"
Turnover: Job Characteristics	Left a job because she was bored, stressed out, overloaded, not acquiring new skills, worked long hours. Example: "If you are stuck in old technology,"
Turnover: Management	Left organization or IT because management was unfair, ineffective or inappropriate. Example: "The good ol' boy thing kind of shoved her out of IT"
Work Schedule Flexibility	Ability to have flexible work schedules; asking for flexibility; autonomy. Example: "If they have personal things that they need to leave and do, then they go do it"
Work Stress	Stress or descriptions of elements in the work environment that are stressful; long work hours. Example: "I'm definitely over committed"

Table 2. Mapping Concepts to Ahuja's Model

Factor	Barrier	T1 Concepts	T2 Concepts
Social	Social Expectations	My Situation is Different	My Situation is Different
		Gender Differences	Gender Differences
	Work-family Conflict	Managing Family Responsibilities	Managing Family Responsibilities
		Work Schedule Flexibility	Work Schedule Flexibility
Structural	Occupational Culture	Work Stress	Work Stress
		Time	Time
		Lack of Control	Negative Descriptions
			Positive Descriptions
			Change
			Cultural Norms
	Lack of Role Models		
	Lack of Informal Networks		Men
	Lack of Mentors		
	Institutional Structures	IT	IT
		Organization	Organization
		Opportunities	Opportunities
		Actions Company Can Take	
		Job Qualities	
Career Stage	Persistence In IT Career	Result of Own Decision	Turnover
		Turnover	Turnover: Management
		Turnover: Job Characteristics	Turnover: Family
	Career Advancement in IS	Barriers: General	Barriers: General
		Barriers: Promotion	Barriers: Promotion
		Barriers: Discrimination	Barriers: Respect
			Barriers: Politics
			Barriers: Women's Characteristics
			Barriers: Management

4. RESULTS AND DISCUSSION

Based on the descriptions provided by Ahuja [3] and our participant statements, we mapped the concepts evoked at T1 and T2 to a corresponding factor (social or structural), or career stage (e.g., persistence in IT). For example, the T1 and T2 concepts identified as *Barriers* were mapped to the advancement career stage (bottom of Table 2).

Relationships between the concepts were identified when two concepts (phrases) were linked by a verbal connector such as if/then, because or so (e.g., if [phrase 1] then [phrase 2]). By overlaying our data onto the Ahuja model [3] we see patterns in the relationships and changes in those patterns over time. For example, in the T1 data we found support for the relationship between the social expectations barrier (social factor) and the persistence career stage (see the dashed line from *My Situation is Different* to *Turnover* in Figure 2a). In the T2 data, we found support for the relationship between the work-family conflict barrier and the persistence career stage (see the dashed line from *Managing Family Responsibilities* to *Turnover* in Figure 2b). We use the term support, not in the analytical (traditional) sense, but as in 'lending credence to.' If we found that a barrier-career stage relationship existed in our data, we classify the relationship as supported. The relationships found at T1 and T2 are summarized in Table 3. In addition to outlining these relationships, Ahuja [3] presented propositions regarding the relationships which are also

illustrated with our data in Table 3. The values in the last column represent a rough measure of the strength of the 'support'.

So what have we learned from these results? Looking at Figures 2 and 3 we can see two potential insights from this study: 1) social expectations and work-family conflict seem to have become less of a barrier to women's persistence in IT while occupational culture remains an influence; and 2) institutional structures seem to carry less influence, while informal networks may be becoming more important to the advancement of women within IT. These findings are discussed below and then placed within Ahuja's model [3].

4.1 Social factor

Our findings indicate that in this organization, over time, perhaps social expectations and work-family conflict are becoming less of a barrier to women's persistence in IS (i.e., retention). Even though gender differences persist as T2, focus group 2, participant 1 stated, "Women are usually more emotional and more timid and so we have to get through those barriers with whoever you're working with in the workplace," it does not seem as central a barrier to the women as found in T1. From the perspective of our participants it seems that the social expectations with regard to work are becoming more balanced. As T2, focus group 5, participant 1 stated, "…one of them [male] works for me who does their equal share in staying home with the sick child. I think that's becoming very common because their wives work and they totally share those responsibilities."

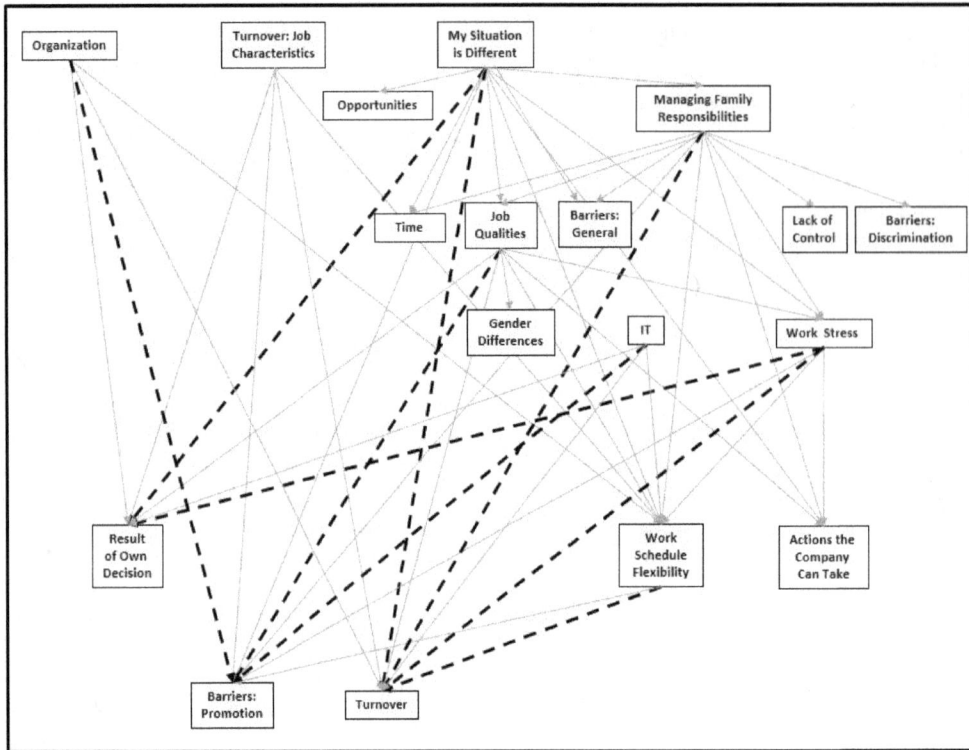

Figure 2a. Time 1 concept map

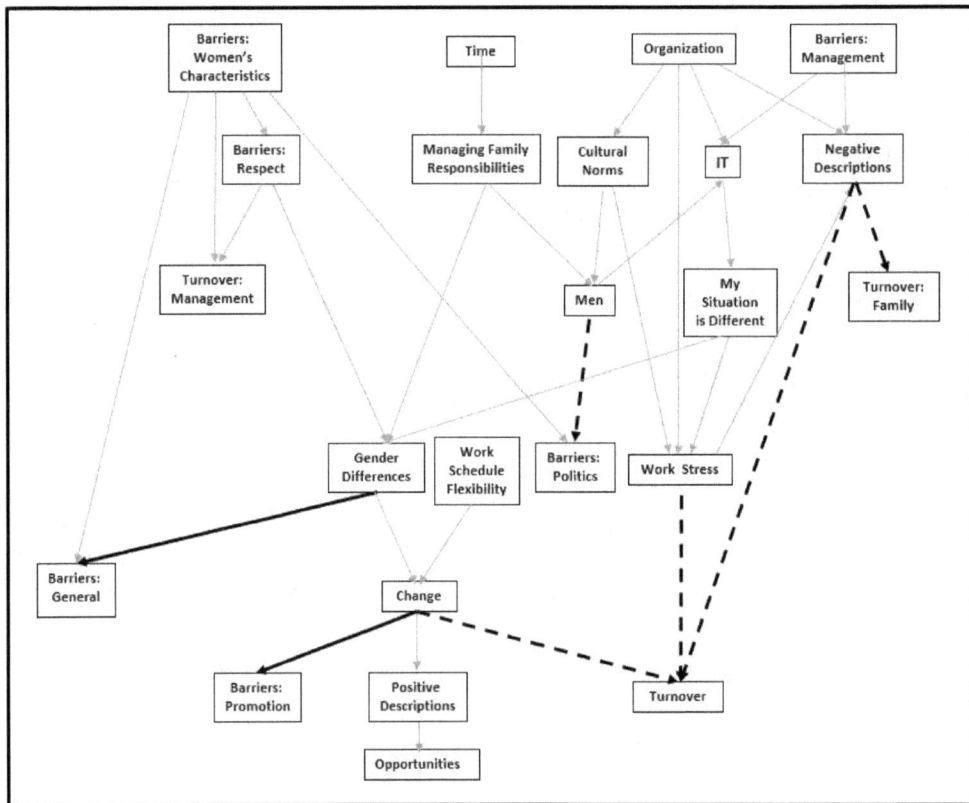

Figure 2b. Time 2 concept map

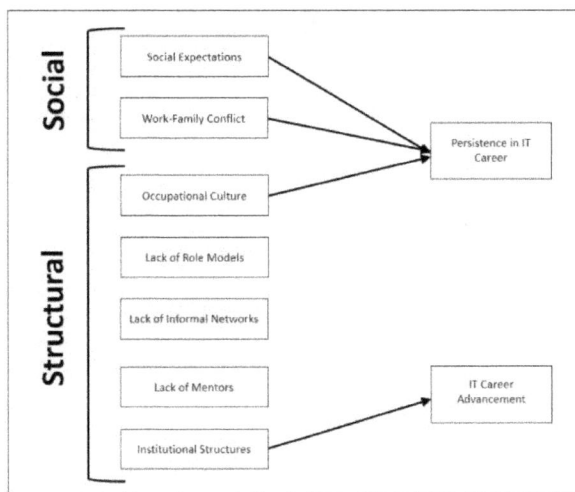

Figure 3a. Time 1 mapping to Ahuja model

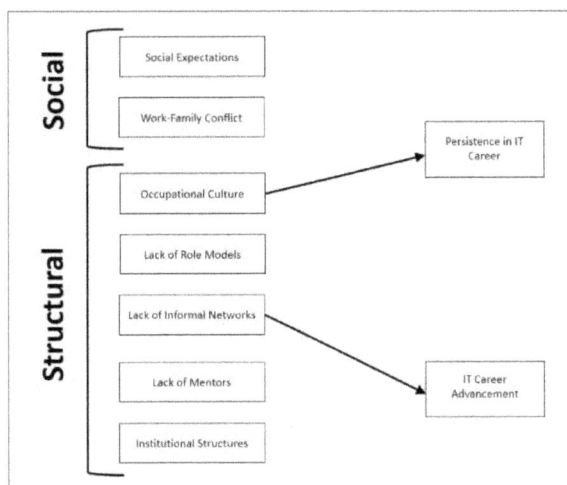

Figure 3b. Time 2 mapping to Ahuja model

It seems that work-family conflict is trending toward being less of a barrier to the persistence of women in IS as well. For example, T2 focus group 1, participant 9 stated,

Well, I think one of the things that in today men have more of a role at home than they did 30 years ago… so for the men to have to rush out of here to take a child to a baseball game or something, that happens much more frequently today than it did 30 years ago.

In addition to the changes in social norms, the diminished influence of work-family conflict may be explained by T2 focus group 3, participant 9 who stated, "The amount of guilt that I feel if I have to stay home with a sick child is unbelievable. But at least I have my laptop. If it wasn't for the laptop… I can take care of both while I'm at home." Thus the availability of telecommuting, even on an ad hoc basis may provide the flexibility to be able to attenuate the conflicting demands of work and family. Another participant in T2 focus group 5 stated, "… just in the past couple of years, it's become so much easier for women to take care of their family responsibilities." This finding may also be influenced by the composition of our T2 participants

having different jobs from those in T1 that were more conducive to telecommuting, but we propose that technological advances (e.g., telecommuting, VPN) may be providing opportunities for women to manage work and family responsibilities more seamlessly.

4.2 Structural factor

While the influence of the social factor may be decreasing, it appears that the structural factor is still an issue, and within that structural factor occupational culture (the assumptions, values and norms that are broad and systemic in the occupation) [40] is a contextual layer that sits atop the organization and society. These layers may be interdependent and to some extent self-reinforcing, and thus change at one layer is difficult because the other layers often counter the attempted change [44, p. 184].

Our results indicate that institutional structures (e.g., *Organization, Opportunities*) seem to be a less important and informal networks (which are focused on *Men*) are trending to be important for advancement in the IT profession. Research has found that even seemingly neutral features of organizations (e.g., structure) may not gender neutral [1]. Some of the participants still see the outcomes of structural inequities, as T2 focus group 5, participant 9 stated, "No one in key positions has worked up through the ranks because all of the senior women have been brought in from the outside. Women are not promoted from within, but men were." In contrast, others noted a shift in attitudes based on structural changes as T2 focus group 5, participant 1 shared, "I think it used to be extremely male dominated and it was very difficult for a woman to have any opportunities and I've seen that change a lot in the past 2 or 3 years."

With regard to the informal networks, the participants mentioned issues related to men "hanging out together" after hours, or the positive exposure to management by working late. Several women addressed trying to connect with men on an interpersonal level in an attempt to find common ground and build a rapport. As T2 focus group 3, participant 1 commented:

Well, just in my group, if I didn't like sports, I wouldn't be able to go out to lunch with my team because they talk about sports at lunch… and it really helps that I like science fiction and things like that you can relate to a lot of other people that work in IT.

One interpretation may be that women are discovering that they can rely less on the policies, procedures and structures of the organization to assist with their advancement and retention needs and may need to rely more on building their personal networks. The next section addresses the implications of this research.

5. IMPLICATIONS

What does this mean for women in the IT field and for research about women in IS? When we map our data to Ahuja's model, we speculate that changes in society and the IT work environment over the 10+ years since Ahuja published her model may have an impact. We begin by applying our findings to Ahuja's model with occupational culture directly (and negatively) influencing persistence in IT careers. We assert that because the influence of social expectations and work-family conflict as barriers to an individual's intention to remain in the profession decreased from T1 to T2 (as indicated by their lack of relationship in T2), that perhaps the expectations that society places on women (both work and family related) indirectly influences their persistence in IT via

Table 3. Propositions from Ahuja's Model

Proposition	Time	Factor Concept	Career Stage Concept	Support*
P3: Social expectations will negatively influence women's persistence in IT careers.	T1	My Situation is Different	Result of Own Decision	.50
			Turnover	
		Gender Differences (NS)		
	T2	Gender Differences (NS)		NS
		My Situation is Different (NS)		
P5: Work-family conflict will negatively influence women's persistence in IT careers.	T1	Managing Family Responsibility	Turnover	1.00
		Work Schedule Flexibility	Turnover	
	T2	Managing Family Responsibility (NS)		NS
		Work Schedule Flexibility (NS)		
P8: Perceived occupational culture will negatively influence women's persistence in IT careers.	T1	Work Stress	Turnover	.33
			Result of Own Decision	
		Time (NS)		
		Lack of Control (NS)		
	T2	Negative Descriptions	Turnover	.50
			Turnover: Family	
		Work Stress	Turnover	
		Change	Turnover	
		Positive Descriptions (NS)		
		Time (NS)		
		Cultural Norms (NS)		
P10: A lack of role models will negatively influence women's persistence in IT careers	T1			NS
	T2			NS

Table 3. Propositions from Ahuja's Model

Proposition	Time	Factor Concept	Career Stage Concept	Support*
P13: A lack of informal networks will negatively influence women's career advancement in the IT field.	T1			NS
	T2	Men	Barriers: Politics	1.00
P14: A lack of mentors will negatively influence women's career advancement in the IT field.	T1			NS
	T2			NS
P15: Institutional structures will negatively influence women's career advancement in the IT field.	T1	IT	Barriers: Promotion	.60
		Job Qualities	Barriers: Promotion	
		Organization	Barriers: Promotion	
		Actions Company Can Take (NS)		
		Opportunities (NS)		
	T2	IT (NS)		NS
		Opportunities (NS)		
		Organization (NS)		

their perceptions of the occupational culture in IT. Technological advances have changed the need to be physically located at the office, and it has become more acceptable to have your laptop at Jane's soccer game. Perhaps the combination of these factors can help IT professionals better manage work and family demands. Thus social expectations and work-family conflict may serve as distal antecedents of persistence in IT careers and as proximal antecedents of perceived occupational culture.

To affirm or refute our assertion, we looked for a relationship between social expectations and occupational culture and between work-family conflict and occupational culture in the T2 data. This is accomplished by looking at the relationships identified (via arrows connecting appropriate concepts) in the concept mapping in Figure 2b. The social expectations – occupational culture relationship is found in the linkage between *My Situation is Different* and *Work Stress* and *Gender Differences* and *Change*.

The work family conflict - occupational culture relationship is found in the linkage between *Gender Expectations* and *Change*.

The same logic can be applied to the advancement career stage. As institutional structure was becoming less of an influence on advancement, perhaps the organizational structure is indirectly influencing advancement via informal networks. As the lack of informal networks to advancement career stage was indicated by the linkage between *Men* and *Barriers: Politics*, we began with this relationship. We assert that because the influence of institutional structures as a barrier to an individual's advancement within the profession may be decreasing, that perhaps the institutional structures within the organization and IT department influence the women's perceptions of informal networks which in turn influences advancement opportunities. Thus we assert that institutional structures serve as a distal antecedent of advancement in IT and a proximal antecedent of informal networks. To affirm or refute this assertion, we looked for a relationship between institutional structures and informal networks (e.g., IT to *Men*). Once again, a relationship was indicated by our qualitative data (see Figure 2b).

In addition, we believe that while the lack of role models and mentoring were not directly addressed by our participants, the aspects of mentoring identified by Ahuja (e.g., developmental relationship of long duration; help from a senior person) may be encompassed within the concept of informal networks, especially in organizations that have not adopted a formal mentoring program. Finally, while not proposed by Ahuja [3], we looked for any evidence of a link between social expectations, work-family conflict, occupational culture, lack of role models and advancement in IT careers; and if informal networks, lack of mentors and institutional structures were linked with persistence in IT careers. We found a connection between social expectations and advancement in IT careers (*Gender Differences* to *Barriers: General*); and between occupational culture and advancement in IT careers (*Change* to *Barriers: Promotion*). Figure 4 graphically represents our proposed changes to the Ahuja model [3].

Our primary contribution is the exploration of a portion of Ahuja's model [3] regarding the challenges and barriers potentially affecting women's advancement and persistence in the IT field. While Ahuja's model has been cited in the IT workforce literature, an in-depth exploration of the conceptual model has been lacking. We begin to address this gap by assessing the applicability of the model and highlight the barriers that over time may be decreasing (e.g., social expectations) and the barriers that remain (e.g., occupational culture).

Our findings provide insights into the applicability of the model for the current IT work environment. We believe the barriers experienced by women in IT may be shifting from more distant sources (e.g., society) to more intimate sources (e.g., interpersonal). We capture this shift by illustrating potential proximal and distal antecedents to advancement and persistence for women in IT careers. We encourage future research to further explore Ahuja's model moving from a more exploratory perspective to a more explanatory one.

From a practitioner perspective, the model illustrated here may be utilized to assist organizations in their advancement and retention initiatives. The findings of this study allude to changing gender roles in the work-family relationship. Where gender roles have traditionally placed the majority of child-rearing responsibilities on women, men appear to be embracing more family-oriented responsibilities. In addition, societal and technological advances are changing views of the permeability of work and family boundaries. Practitioners may benefit from these findings by adapting work-family initiatives to fit the changing needs of IT professionals (e.g., creating programs benefiting both men and women, or providing more flexible work schedule/telecommuting options). Ultimately, effective interventions should be systemic in nature, focusing on reshaping assumptions, values and culture addressing the underlying issue(s) not merely the symptom(s).

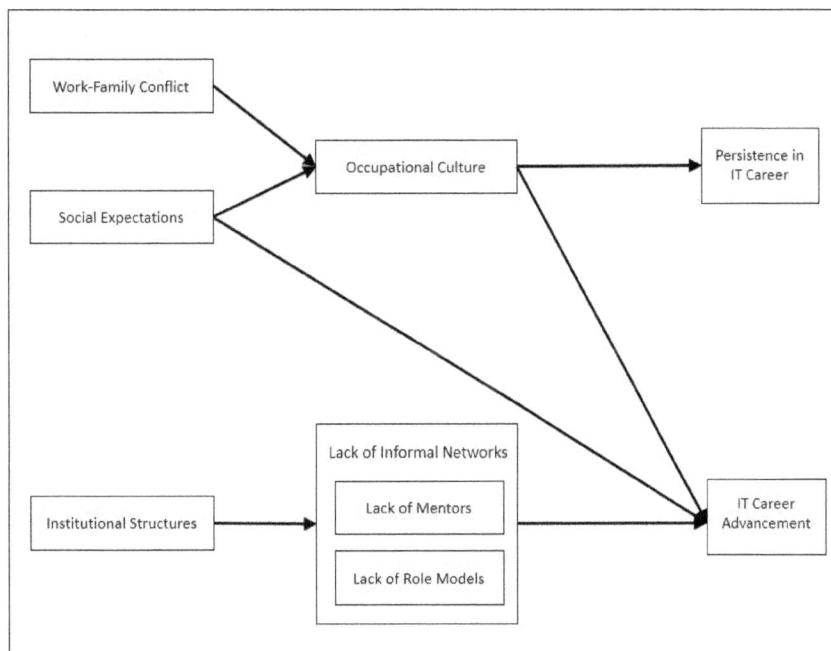

Figure 4. Proposed Adaptation of Ahuja's Model

5.1 Limitations

The research design choices and methodology of this study create certain limitations which should be addressed. Qualitative research often relies on small convenience samples which limits traditional generalizability (e.g., [21]), a criticism which may applies to this context because participants were obtained from IT personnel in one organization and the number of participants is low; as such, the results are not generalizable in the same sense as quantitative studies. However, Altheide and Johnson [8] tell us that providing a map that helps readers understand similar situations constitutes a dimension of generalizability within qualitative studies. This research is designed to provide this map. There may be different issues in other industries, locations and types of organizations such as startups and public institutions, and thus future research should explore a variety of contexts.

The data collection method could also pose a limitation. Using focus groups implies data aggregation, a process that treats the participants as a group rather than examining individual differences [47]. Further, the organizational constraints imposed meant that the researchers could not fully investigate all individual contextual factors (e.g., marital status) that might shape the participants experiences. While extensive information was collected on the organization, data were collected from active IT professionals and there are gaps in the demographic data. Future research could further detail the characteristics of women and interview individuals that have left the IT field to compare the findings of those who have left the field with the results of this study.

6. CONCLUSION

We used qualitative data to explore propositions that Ahuja initially presented in her model of the challenges and barriers facing women in different IT career stages. Our findings indicate that changes in perceptions of structural and social factors have occurred over time for women in the organization under study. By overlaying our data onto Ahuja's model [3] we provide a potential version of an updated model that may be used to explore the challenges and barriers facing women in IT. The proposed model may be useful as a tool to re-energize the dialogue regarding creating a more diversified IT work environment.

7. REFERENCES

[1] Acker J. 2006. Inequality regimes. *Gender & Society* 20, 4 (Aug. 2006), 441-464.

[2] Adya, M. P. 2008. Women at work: Difference in IT career experiences and perceptions between South Asian and American women. *Human Resource Management* 47, 3 (Fall 2008), 601-635.

[3] Ahuja M. K. 2002. Women in the information technology profession: A literature review, synthesis, and research agenda. *European Journal of Information Systems* 11, 1 (Mar. 2002), 20-34.

[4] Ahuja M. K., Chudoba K. M., Kacmar C. J., Mcknight D. H., and George J. F. 2007. IT road warriors: Balancing work-family conflict, job autonomy, and work overload to mitigate turnover intentions. *MIS Quarterly* 31, 1 (Mar. 2007), 1-17.

[5] Allen, M. W., Armstrong, D. J., Riemenschneider, C. K., and Reid, M. F. 2006. Making sense of the barriers women face in the information technology work force: Standpoint theory, self-disclosure, and causal maps. *Sex Roles: A Journal of Research* 54, 11-12 (Jun. 2006), 831-844.

[6] Armstrong, D. J., Riemenschneider, C. K., Nelms, J., and Reid, M. F. 2012. Revisiting the barriers facing women in information systems. *Journal of Computer Information Systems* 53, 2 (Winter 2012), 65-74.

[7] Armstrong, D. J., Riemenschneider, C. K., Reid, M. F. and Allen, M. 2007. Advancement, voluntary turnover and women in IT: A cognitive study of work-family conflict. *Information and Management* 44, 2 (Mar. 2007), 142-153.

[8] Altheide, D. L., and Johnson, J. M. 1994. Criteria for assessing interpretive validity in qualitative research. In *Handbook of Qualitative Research,* N. K. Denzin and Y. S. Lincoln Eds. Sage, Thousand Oaks, CA, 485-499,.

[9] Babbie E. 1995. *The Practice of Social Research*, 7th ed. Wadsworth, New York, NY.

[10] Backhouse, J., Hsu, C. W., and Silva L. 2006. Circuits of power in creating de jure standards: Shaping an international information systems security standard. *MIS Quarterly* 30: Supplement (Aug. 2006), 413-418.

[11] Berger, P. L., and Luckmann, T. 1966. *The Social Construction of Reality*, Doubleday & Co, New York, NY.

[12] Bidwell, M. and Briscoe, F. 2010. The dynamics of interorganizational careers. *Organization Science* 21, 5 (Sep-Oct. 2010), 1034-1053.

[13] Carayon, P., Schoepke, J., Hoonakker, P. L. T., and Haims, M. C. 2006. Evaluating causes and consequences of turnover intention among IT workers: The development of a questionnaire study. *Behaviour & Information Technology* 25, 5 (Sep. 2006), 381-397.

[14] Chang, J. Y., Choi, J. N., and Kim, M. U. 2008. Turnover of highly educated R&D professionals: The role of pre-entry cognitive style, work values and career orientation. *Journal of Occupational and Organizational Psychology* 81, 2 (Jun. 2008), 299-317.

[15] Conant, J. S., Mokwa, M. P., and Rajan, V. P. 1990. Strategic types, distinctive marketing competencies and organizational performance: a multiple measures-based study. *Strategic Management Journal* 11, 5 (Sep. 1990), 365–383.

[16] Crump, B. J., Logan, K., and McIllroy, A. 2007. Does gender still matter? A study of the views of women in the ICT industry in New Zealand. *Gender, Work, and Organization* 14, 4 (Jul. 2007), 349-370.

[17] Denzin, N., and Lincoln, Y. 2000. *Handbook of Qualitative Research*. Sage, Thousand Oaks, CA.

[18] Eden, C., Ackerman, F. and Cropper, S. 1992. The analysis of cause maps. *Journal of Management Studies* 29, 3 (May. 1992), 309-324.

[19] Ely, R., and Padavic, I. 2007. A feminist analysis of organizational research on sex differences. *Academy of Management Review* 32, 4 (Oct. 2007), 1121-1143.

[20] Ghapanchi, A. H. and Aurum, A. 2011 Antecedents to IT personnel's intentions to leave: A systematic literature review. *The Journal of Systems and Software* 84, 2 (2011), 238-259.

[21] Hamel, J., Dufour, S. and Fortin, D. 1993. *Case Study Methods*. Sage, Newbury Park, CA.

[22] Ho, L. 2011. Meditation, learning, organizational innovation and performance. *Industrial Management + Data Systems* 111, 1 (2011), 113-131.

[23] Igbaria, M., and Shayo, C. 1997. The impact of race and gender difference on job performance evaluations and career success. *Equality, Diversity and Inclusion: An International Journal* 16, 8 (1997), 12-23.

[24] Jing, Q., and Cha, H. 2010. IT certifications, outsourcing and information systems personnel turnover. *Information Technology & People* 23, 4 (2010), 330-351.

[25] Joseph, D., Kok-Yee, N., Koh, C. and Ang, S. 2007. Turnover of information technology professionals: a narrative review, meta-analytic structural equation modeling, and model development. *MIS Quarterly* 31, 3 (Sep. 2007), 547-577.

[26] Kearns, G. S. 2005. An electronic commerce strategic typology: Insights from case studies. *Information & Management* 42, 7 (Oct. 2005), 1023–1036.

[27] Kim, S., and Wright, B. E. 2007. IT employee work exhaustion: Toward an integrated model of antecedents and consequences. *Review of Public Personnel Administration* 27, 2 (Jun. 2007), 147-170.

[28] Korunka, C., Hoonakker, P. and Carayon, P. 2008. Quality of work life and turnover intention in information technology work. *Human Factors and Ergonomics in Manufacturing* 18, 4 (Jul-Aug. 2008), 409-423.

[29] Kuhn, S. and Rayman, P. 2007. Women on the edge of change. In *Reconfiguring the Firewall: Recruiting Women in Information Technology Across Cultures and Continents,* C. J. Burger, E. G. Creamer, and P. S. Meszaros, Eds. AK Peters, Ltd, Wellesley, MA, pp. 191-210.

[30] Lemons, M. A. and Parzinger, M. J. 2008. Psychological congruence: The impact of organizational context on job satisfaction and retention of women in technology. *Advancing Women in Leadership* 28, 1 (mon. 2008), Retrieved on 05/20/May 2011 from: http://advancingwomen.com.proxy.lib.fsu.edu/awl/awl_wordpress/psychological-congruence-the-impact-of-organizational-context-on-job-satisfaction-and-retention-of-women-in-technology/.

[31] Madriz, E. 2000. Focus groups in feminist research. In, *Handbook of Qualitative Research*, N. K. Denzin, and Y. S. Lincoln, Eds., Sage, Thousand Oaks, CA, pp. 835-850.

[32] Magenau, J., and Hunt, R. 1989. Sociopolitical networks for police role-making. *Human Relations* 42, 6 (1989), 547-561.

[33] McLaughlin, J. 1999. Gendering occupational identities and IT in the retail sector. *New Technology, Work and Employment* 14, 2 (1999), 143-156.

[34] Michie, S. and Nelson, D. 2006. Barriers women face in information technology careers: Self efficacy, passion and gender biases. *Women in Management Review* 21, 1 (2006), 10-27.

[35] Niederman, F., Sumner, M., and Maertz, C. P. 2007. Testing and extending the unfolding model of voluntary turnover to IT professionals. *Human Resources Management* 46, 3 (Fall 2007), 331-347.

[36] Panko, R. R. 2008. IT employment prospects: Beyond the dotcom bubble. *European Journal of Information Systems* 17, 3 (Jun. 2008), 182-197.

[37] Ragins, B. R., Townsend, B. and Mattison, M. 1998. Gender gap in the executive suite: CEOs and female executives report on breaking the glass ceiling. *The Academy of Management Executive* 12, 1 (Feb. 1998), 28-42.

[38] Regmi, K., Naidoo, J., and Regmi, S. 2009. Understanding the effect of discrimination in the workplace: A case study amongst Nepalese immigrants in the UK. *Equal Opportunities International* 28, 5-6 (2009), 398-414.

[39] Reid, M. F., Allen, M. W., Armstrong, D. J. and Riemenschneider, C. K. 2010. Perspectives on challenges facing women in IS: The cognitive gender gap. *European Journal of Information Systems* 19, 5 (Oct. 2010), 526-539.

[40] Ridgeway, C. L., and Correll, S. J. 2004. Unpacking the gender system: a theoretical perspective on gender beliefs and social relations. *Gender and Society* 18, 4 (Aug. 2004), 510-531.

[41] Rigas, P. P. 2009. A model of turnover intention among technically-oriented information systems professionals. *Information Resources Management Journal* 22, 1 (Jan. 2009), 1-23.

[42] Ryan, M. K., Haslam, S. A. and Postmes, T. 2007. Reactions to the glass cliff: gender differences in the explanations for the precariousness of women's leaderships positions. *Journal of Organizational Change Management* 20, 2 (2007), 182-197.

[43] SamGnanakkan, S. 2010. Mediating role of organizational commitment on HR practices and turnover intention among ICT professionals. *Journal of Management Research* 10, 1 (Apr. 2010), 39-61.

[44] Soe, L. and Yakura, E. 2008. What's wrong with the pipeline? Assumptions about gender and culture in IT work. *Women's Studies* 37, 3 (Apr. 2008), 176-201.

[45] Stephan, P. E. and Levin, S. G. 2005. Leaving careers in IT: Gender differences in retention. *Journal of Technology Transfer* 30, 4 (Oct. 2005), 383-396.

[46] Tanova, C., and Holtom, B. C. 2008. Using job embeddedness factors to explain voluntary turnover in four European countries. *The International Journal of Human Resource Management* 19, 9 (Sep. 2008), 1553-1568.

[47] Trauth, E. M. 2002. Odd girl out: An individual differences perspective on women in the IT profession. *Information Technology & People* 15, 1 (2002), 98-118.

[48] Trauth, E. M., and Howcroft, D. 2006. Critical empirical research in IS: An example of gender and the IT workforce. *Information Technology & People* 19, 3 (2006), 272-292.

[49] Trauth, E. M., Quesenberry, J. L., and Huang, H. 2009. Retaining women in the U.S. IT workforce: Theorizing the influence of organizational factors. *European Journal of Information Systems* 18, 5 (Oct. 2009), 476-497.

[50] Wadhwa, V. 2014. Steps to increasing the number of women in IT. *The Wall Street Journal* (Jan. 22, 2014) retrieved on 01/27/2014 from http://blogs.wsj.com/accelerators/2014/01/22/vivek-wadhwa-steps-to-increasing-the-number-of-women-in-tech/.

[51] Wentling, R. M., and Thomas, S. 2009. Workplace culture that hinders and assists the career development of women in information technology. *Information Technology, Learning, and Performance Journal* 25, 1 (Spring 2009), 25-42.

[52] Wickramasinghe, V. 2009. dPredictors job satisfaction among IT graduates in offshore outsource IT firms. *Personnel Review* 38, 4 (2009), 413-431.

Appendix: Partial Interview Guide

Introduction protocol: Thank you for your willingness to participate in this focus group. We are researchers from the University of ___ who are conducting a research project investigating the working conditions facing Information Technology professionals. For about 45 minutes we'll be asking you to share your experiences working in IS. Your participation is voluntary. Anything you tell us will be kept confidential. Thank you in advance for your assistance.

1. Think back to why you left other IT positions in the past and what your colleagues told you when they decided to leave an organization. What caused you, your colleagues, or friends to decide to leave the organization?

2. Did they move to an IT job in another organization, or leave IT completely?

3. Did management provide a public explanation for why that person left?

   - If yes, ask participant to elaborate (e.g., who provided the explanation, did they announce it verbally or in writing, what reason did they give).

4. Do you think women in the IT workplace face different challenges than men? Please explain.

5. Do you think men in the IT workplace face different challenges than women? Please explain.

6. How do you manage your family responsibilities so you can meet the unique aspects of your IT job?

7. What makes your job in IT unique from people who work in other professions?

8. What keeps you working in the IT field?

Perceptions of Malaysian Female School Children Towards Higher Education in Information Technology

Ven Yu Sien
HELP University
Pusat Bandar Damansara
Kuala Lumpur, Malaysia
+6-0320942000
sienvy@help.edu.my

Grace Yanchi Mui
Thye & Associates
Bandar Bukit Raja
Klang, Malaysia
+6-0196716093
gymui@yahoo.com

Eugene Yu Jin Tee
HELP University
Wisma HELP
Kuala Lumpur, Malaysia
+6-0327112000
teey@help.edu.my

Diljit Singh
University of Malaya
Lembah Pantai
Kuala Lumpur, Malaysia
+6-0379676357
diljit@um.edu.my

ABSTRACT

Malaysia, like many countries, faces a shortage of students enrolling in computing undergraduate programs. This paper investigates the impact of technology on female secondary school children's choice of studying information technology (IT) in higher education. Malaysian female secondary school students from various ethnicities participated in a proprietary survey conducted in various cities in both East and West Malaysia. Despite the lack of technological support provided by government funded schools in terms of functioning computers and access to computers, there is a strong and encouraging trend in the respondents' interests in wishing to learn more about IT and their intentions to study an IT-related undergraduate degree. The respondents' perceptions on careers in IT are largely positive – unlike the generally held belief that there are not many available jobs in the industry, and IT is a male-dominated field, difficult and boring. This is the first known Malaysian study that focuses on the perceptions of female indigenous school students towards higher education and careers in IT.

Categories and Subject Descriptors

K.3.2 [**Computer and Education**]: Computer and Information Science Education – *Computer Science Education*.

General Terms

Measurement, Design, Human Factors.

Keywords

IT education, IT careers, female school children, female indigenous school children.

Permission to make digital or hard copies of all or part of this work for personal or classroom use is granted without fee provided that copies are not made or distributed for profit or commercial advantage and that copies bear this notice and the full citation on the first page. Copyrights for components of this work owned by others than ACM must be honored. Abstracting with credit is permitted. To copy otherwise, or republish, to post on servers or to redistribute to lists, requires prior specific permission and/or a fee. Request permissions from Permissions@acm.org.
SIGMIS-CPR '14, May 29 - 31 2014, Singapore, Singapore
Copyright 2014 ACM 978-1-4503-2625-4/14/05...$15.00.
http://dx.doi.org/10.1145/2599990.2600007

1. INTRODUCTION

Low enrolment in computing undergraduate programs is a pervasive and persistent problem in many countries (South Africa: [1]; Canada: [2]; United States: [3],[4]; Germany: [5]; Australia: [6] – and Malaysia is not spared from this problem [7]. There is a pressing demand for knowledge workers in the Malaysian information and communications technology (ICT) services sector [7], [8].

The supply of information technology (IT) workers is generally reflected in university enrolments. In Malaysia, private university computing enrolments are reflective of demand for careers in technology because students are able to enroll in computing undergraduate degree programs as long as they meet the necessary entry requirements. In contrast, public university computing enrolments remain relatively stable due to the limited capacity of public universities to absorb students [9]. Malaysian university computing enrolments are illustrated in Fig. 1. The downward supply trend of computing graduates is most evident in the reduction of almost 50% in private university computing enrolments from 2002 to 2011.

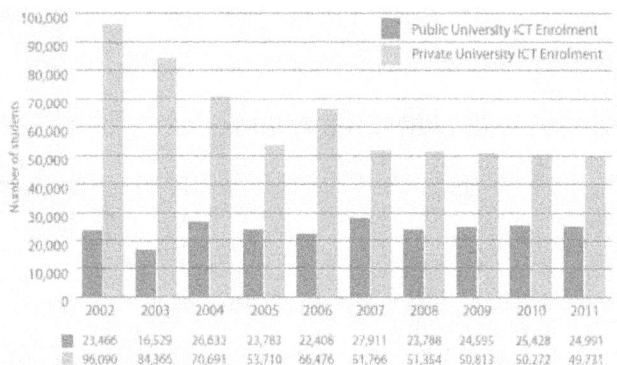

Figure 1. ICT enrolment in Higher Education Institutions (HEIs) [7]

Addressing the supply for IT workers begins at the secondary school level. Adya and Kaiser [10] and Downes and Looker [6] reported that increased secondary school student access to and usage of computers is a contributing factor to students' choice of computing education at tertiary level. In Malaysia, there are other unique contributing factors to the declining supply of IT workers. In a study on IT undergraduate students' perceptions of computing education Mui, Tee and Sien [11] identified that secondary school teachers, school career counsellors, and the secondary school environment – such as the availability of functional computer laboratories and the use of technology in classroom teaching – play an important role in encouraging or discouraging the student from learning about technology and deciding whether or not to enroll in IT at tertiary level. Conceptions and attitudes about IT are developed through a learning process based on various factors, e.g. personal interests, peers, school environment, access to computers, media. Therefore, students' interest in IT is invariably influenced by their exposure and interaction with technology in both formal and informal settings (school and leisure).

In this paper, we focus on the role of IT and its impact on female secondary school children's choice of pursuing information technology in higher education. We will focus on government-funded schools only since they are directly affected by government intiatives and policies to increase ICT use in government-funded schools. We will also be paying particular attention to the responses from the indigenous students.

2. MISCONCEPTIONS OF IT TERTIARY EDUCATION

Today's secondary school students have grown up with technology. They have spent their entire lives surrounded by and using computers, videogames, digital music players, mobile phones, and toys and tools of the digital age [12]. Computer games, email, the Internet, social media and mobile phones form an integral part of their lives. Through their experiences and exposure to technology, the students have come to view IT as fast-paced, interesting and exciting. Yet, they do not seem to show a significant interest in pursuing higher education and careers in IT.

As employment demand for IT graduates increases, the number of students enrolling in computing undergraduate degrees seems to be declining. Many studies have been conducted to investigate a better understanding towards the perceptions of students concerning this decline and some of the results are presented in this section.

2.1 Prevailing Misconceptions

Students' interests and motivation to pursue a career in technology related areas are highly influenced by the experience and knowledge of their teachers [4], [11], [13]. School teachers however may not be aware of the prospects and diversity of IT careers that are available in the industry, and are hence handicapped in their advice to students on their choice of appropriate careers.

Computing subjects may not be offered as part of the overall curriculum in schools [4]. Therefore, students are not exposed to computing subjects during their time in school and this may have a direct effect on their choice of undergraduate program at universities. Carter [14] found that school curricula contain very little computing content. Consequently, students have very little appreciation of what computing is. In Malaysia, schools that offer computing subjects usually teach students basic computing skills like word processing and spreadsheet. Students invariably find this boring and unchallenging. This negative perception of computing subjects may contribute to the prevailing misconception that an undergraduate degree in computing is an extension of these basic skills.

Previous research found (see [5], [13]) that students chose not to study computing undergraduate degrees because they either have an incorrect or no perception of what computing is all about. Schulte & Knobelsdorf [5] report that 50% of the students they surveyed are opposed to a career in computing because they perceive a computing professional to be sitting in front of computers and programming all day. In an earlier study [11], we identified some common misconceptions that Malaysian secondary school students have in not choosing to study an IT undergraduate degree:

- There are no jobs in the IT industry. The effects of the dot com crash continue to have a negative effect on parents who are primarily responsible for financing students' tertiary education. The belief about the lack of jobs available in the IT industry is the overriding reason for parents not encouraging their children to study IT. However, Malaysian government initiatives have increased the demand for IT workers [7], [8]. In terms of entry-level monthly average salary scales, the ICT industry is consistently ranked as one of the top five amongst twenty-five industries [7].

- IT undergraduate degrees are only for secondary school students in the science stream. This misconception precludes secondary school students in the arts stream who may have an interest in IT from enrolling in an IT undergraduate degree. Further, the secondary school examination system does not allow arts stream students to enroll in the ICT subject in Form 5, the most common exit point from secondary school.

- Societal pressure not to pursue IT careers. Among some Malaysian parents, teachers and career counselors, IT careers are considered to be less prestigious and clerical in nature.

Other reasons identified for low IT enrolments at Malaysian universities are the relative difficulty of computing programs, low passing rates, narrow scope and lack of computing facilities at universities [7].

2.2 Gender Differences

There is essentially an imbalance between the genders in computing with a great under representation of girls enrolled in computing programs [1], [3], [15], [16]. Black et al. [15] reports that women have mostly been a minority in computing; with female enrolment in computing undergraduate programs declining in many countries, with no promised change in sight.

Furthermore, there is a general lack of information or inaccurate perceptions about IT and careers in IT. First, misconceptions [17] about the lack of social interactions, few job opportunities, and computing being a difficult academic discipline are common. Second, women suffer from a lack of confidence – consequently, they believe that they lack the ability to succeed in IT [3], [5], [14], [15], [17]. Third, there is unequal treatment and discrimination both at home and at school [5], [15], [17], [18]. Such treatment and discrimination includes women being treated as not suited to using computers: discrimination within the classroom as teachers rarely interact with female students; discriminations within the family e.g. placing the family computer in the boy's room. Fourth, there also seems to be a lack of influencers and female role models [3], [5], [14], [17], [19]. Fifth, the negative stereotyping of computing as "nerdy", "geeky" and boring has put women off from considering a career in IT [3], [5], [14], [17]. The media has also contributed to the formation of this stereotype: more men than women are portrayed using computers; the users generally appear to be myopically focused on their computers and lack other social interests. Consequently, the pervasive stereotype is that the computing domain is essentially male and this has projected negative effects on young women's choice of computing in education and as a career.

There are now even fewer women in computing than in the late 1980s and early 1990s [16]. However, Mellstrom [16] and Adya [10] found that this trend is not applicable to developing countries like Malaysia. Adya [20] reported that under representation of women in the IT industry seem to apply to the United States, Australia, New Zealand and Ireland; whereas Asian countries like India, China and Malaysia have a greater number of female IT employees. She attributes this to the growth and demand for talent in the IT sector. Mellstrom [16] attributes this phenomenon to the fact *that gender and technology relations are deeply embedded in cultural contexts shaping the use, design and production of technologies and their co-production of gender and technology'*. In terms of technology and relations, he argues that Malaysian women's education and positions in the IT industry is equivalent to those of men – and this contributes to the relative optimism about gender and technology relations in developing countries. Furthermore, technology, specifically IT holds highly positive connotations and is seen as major sources of individual and national empowerment especially within the Malaysian society of social and ethnic identities. There is also a high proportion of leading female professionals occupying executive positions within the Malaysian IT industry. Although the Malaysia Education Statistics [21] does not provide a breakdown of statistics for specific academic disciplines, the 2011 enrolment in the Science, Mathematics and Computer category consists of a high proportion of women (63% in private universities and 62% in public universities); and an equally high proportion of women graduates within this category (64% from private universities and 65% from public universities).

3. MALAYSIAN EDUCATION SYSTEM

The education structure in Malaysia was established during colonial rule under the United Kingdom (from the 18th Century to 1957). Students attend six years of primary school (aged 7 to 12 years) followed by five years of secondary school (aged 13 to 17 years). Students who intend to pursue a university degree can continue at secondary school for two more years or enroll in a matriculation program offered by universities. Thereafter, they are eligible to enroll for an undergraduate program. Most universities offer three-year programs for a Bachelor's degree.

At government-funded schools, a non-examinable IT subject is usually offered at the lower secondary level (Forms 1 to 3) where students are usually taught fundamental computer skills (e.g. Microsoft Office) for at least 40 minutes a week. IT is offered as an elective examinable subject for the Form 5 and 6 examinations. The majority of students taking this subject are from the Science stream. Teachers conducting these classes may have had no formal training on the use of the software.

Almost all secondary schools have at least one computer laboratory. Depending on the school and its locality (urban or rural), the computer laboratory may still be equipped with outdated computers and CRT monitors. Since 2011, the Ministry of Education has embarked on an initiative to upgrade

technology access and facilities in all government schools. However, this initiative is in its initial stages.

4. THE SURVEY

The survey instrument consisted of 17 questions. Four of these questions captured demographic data. The remaining questions were either yes/no questions or the level of agreement (5-point Likert scale). The Likert scale had strongly disagree (1) and strongly agree (5) as endpoints and neutral (3) as the centre point. Previously established scales were used whenever possible. New items were developed based on our earlier study [11]. These new items are the inclusion of first computer learning experience (Part A Question 6); family members (other than family members) as a social influencer who encouraged the participant to learn about IT (Part B Question 1); and intention to enroll for an IT subject for school leaving examinations (Form 5 or Form 6) (Part B Question 3). See Appendix.

This study investigates the role technology plays in the lives of female secondary students and their perceptions towards higher education in IT. A proprietary survey was designed from preliminary interviews with IT undergraduate students (see [11]). This survey was pilot tested in a Malaysian secondary school for girls before it was administered to other Malaysian secondary schools in cities and towns in both East and West Malaysia. The inclusion of secondary school students from East Malaysia ensured that the sample included indigenous students.

The survey addressed the students' usage of computers at home and at school; their IT learning experience; their intention to pursue IT at university; and their perceptions of IT careers.

We conducted a nation-wide survey amongst 616 female secondary school students on their perceptions of IT education. Data were collected over a course of six months, from seven government secondary schools in both East and West Malaysia. The schools represent two Chinese medium national schools, two Malay medium national schools, and three mission schools. The first two types of schools are fully funded by the Malaysian government and the mission schools are partially funded by the government. The details of the respondents are shown in Table 1.

Table 1. Participating schools

School	School Type	District and State	Number of respondents
A	Chinese	Teluk Intan, Perak	46
B	Malay	Kota Kinabalu, Sabah	136
C	Mission	Kuala Lumpur, W Persekutuan	222
D	Chinese	Klang, Selangor	7
E	Mission	Kuala Lumpur, W Persekutuan	128
F	Mission	Mukah, Sarawak	45
G	Malay	Petaling Jaya, Selangor	32
		Total	**616**

Fig. 2 shows the breakdown of participants by race. Multiple ethnic groups represent the demographics of Malaysia. The participants comprise Malays (31.3%), Chinese (29.1%), Indians (17%) and indigenous communities (22.6%). The indigenous communities make up the third largest group of survey participants. The indigenous groups that participated in this survey are from East Malaysia: Kadazan Dusun, Melanau, and Bajau.

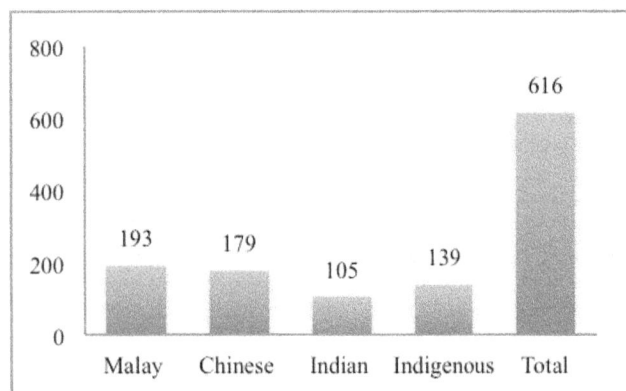

Figure 2. Participants by race

The majority of respondents identified themselves to be in Forms 4 (247 girls) and 5 (284 girls), which accounts for 86% of total respondents. The remaining participants are in Form 6.

5 Discussion and Results

The results suggest that female students in Malaysian schools are exposed to computers at an early age; and encouragement from their friends, schoolteachers and the influence of the media are major factors in instilling a personal interest for further studies in IT. In general, students held favorable perceptions towards IT careers, together with positive intentions to pursue IT-related studies at the university level. This survey also reveals that the majority of the respondents spend a minimum of 8 hours a week on the computer when they are home whilst access to computers at school are limited to less than 2 hours a week. This limited access to computers and computer facilities at the school level may be the contributory factor to low intentions to enroll in the IT examinable subjects at Forms 5 and 6; and the low IT club memberships. A more detailed discussion follows.

5.1 Computer Related Experience

Personal computers are the most commonly used technology gadget across all races. The majority of students (55%) have one computer with Internet access at home. Table 2 shows that computer usage in the home is widespread with only 0.5% of respondents reporting that they do not use a computer at home. This may be because they do not own a computer. The most commonly reported uses of computers in the home by rank for Malay, Chinese and Indigenous communities are to access social media sites; watch movies; and to do homework and assignments. The Indian students reported that they use computers at home (by rank) for study and research; access social media sites; and watch movies.

Table 2. Usage of computers at home (by race)

	Malay	Chinese	Indig-enous	Indian	Total
Social media sites	171	162	82	117	532
Blogs	67	55	24	38	184
Email	104	86	73	68	331
Games	95	84	48	71	298
Movies, You-Tube, etc	168	153	81	111	513
Study and research	156	111	89	103	459
Home-work, assign-ments	160	124	71	108	463
Do not use comput-ers	4	6	2	3	15

In terms of computer usage at home, 67% of the students surveyed use computers for a minimum of four hours per week. The Malay, Indigenous, and Indian females tend to use computers for two to four hours per week. The highest proportion of Chinese females tends to use computers at home for at least eight hours per week.

These students have grown up in a technology-pervasive world and it is therefore expected that they have computers and mobile devices for work and play. It is however surprising that they have not recorded more time spent on these devices. Predictably, the predominant use of devices reported in this survey is for social media access.

5.2 IT Experience at School

A reported 60% of the respondents do not use computers at school. This could be due to the lack of access to computers in the school. Those who do have access to computers in schools use them for no longer than 2 hours per week. The majority of respondents (83.6%) indicated that their first exposure to computers was at the primary school while only 16.1% were first exposed to computers in secondary school.

The Malay, Indigenous and Indian students reported that the primary party that encouraged them to learn about IT is secondary school teachers. Chinese students reported that their parents encouraged them to learn about IT.

Most respondents reported that their school teachers use computers to teach in classes. It is not within the scope of this study to investigate how technology has been integrated into the curriculum – but from interviews with secondary school teachers, the most common practices seem to be PowerPoint slides and YouTube videos in classrooms. Some more 'tech-savvy' Science teachers have incorporated appropriate educational software and online tutorial in their teaching materials. Table 3 shows the mean values of the responses by ethnic groups.

Table 3. IT learning experience in school

	Malay	Chinese	Indian	Indig-enous	Total
My school has good functional computer labs	3.66	3.11	3.72	3.29	3.43
My school teachers use computers to teach lessons	3.68	3.15	3.56	3.71	3.51
There is an IT club (or equivalent) at my school	3.72	3.22	3.13	3.65	3.46

Only 7% of respondents were members of their school's IT club. The highest percentage of membership amongst the various groups is the indigenous students (10%).This is followed by Indian students (7.6%), Chinese students (6.7%), and Malay students (5.7%).

There is a very high percentage of indigenous (62.6%) and Malay (53.9%) students who indicated that they had enrolled or planned to enroll in IT for their Forms 5 and 6 examinations. Only 22.9% of Chinese students and 44.8% of Indian students stated that they would enroll, or were planning to enroll in IT subject(s) for their Form 5 and 6 examinations.

Based on the results from the questions in this sub-section, it would seem that schools (taking part in this survey) are not providing their students a conducive environment in which to study IT – 57% of the students do not have access to computers. Even though 83.6% of the respondents are exposed to computers during their time at primary schools, only 45% or respondents are enrolled (or interested in enrolling) in IT subjects at secondary school level; and registration in IT clubs is particularly low (7.3%).

5.3 Intentions to Study IT at HEIs

About 64.2% of Malay, 56.2% of Indians and 74.8% indigenous students are interested in studying an IT related undergraduate degree. Only 36.9% of Chinese students indicated an interest in studying an IT related degree in university whilst 55% preferred to study a non-IT related degree. See Fig.3 for details.

Figure 3. Perceptions of students towards an IT undergraduate degree

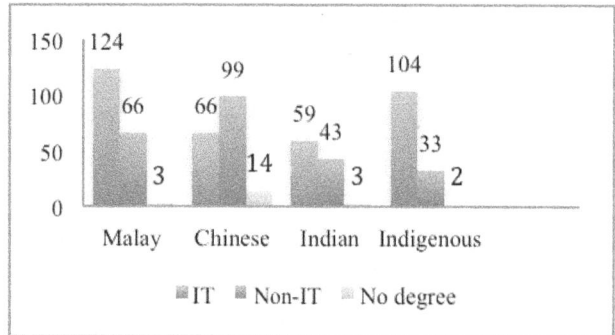

The strongest source of encouragement for students to learn IT came from their teachers, followed by their family and school career counselors. See Table 4.

Table 4: Sources of encouragement towards IT studies

	Malay	Chinese	Indian	Indig-enous	Total
Friends	3	4	2	2	11
Parents	5	7	12	6	30
Family	48	68	24	24	164
Teachers	77	65	37	68	247
Counsel-ors	60	35	30	39	164
Total	193	179	105	139	616

Despite the lack of technological support provided by the schools in terms of functioning computers and access to computers, there is a strong and encouraging trend in the respondents' interests in wishing to learn more about IT and their intentions to study an IT-related degree at HEIs. The respondents' perceptions on careers in IT are generally positive and upbeat – unlike the generally held belief that IT is difficult, boring and there are not many available jobs in the industry.

The majority of students believe that IT jobs and careers are *creative*, *fun* and *interesting*. The Malay students are most enthusiastic about IT jobs and careers – followed closely by the Indians and Indigenous students. Most of the indigenous females perceive IT jobs or careers to have high salaries with a big impact on the world. Other races did not have such a strong perception for these two factors. The Chinese students tend to be less positive in their responses compared to the other races. Of all the factors in this category, the perception that IT careers are stable had the lowest rankings for all students. See Table 5.

Table 5. Perceptions of IT jobs/careers

	Malay	Chinese	Indian	Indig-enous	Total
Easy to find	3.8	3.4	3.7	3.7	3.7
Pay high salaries	4.0	3.8	4.0	4.0	4.0
Secure/ Stable	3.6	3.4	3.7	3.5	3.5
Very creative	4.2	3.7	4.2	4.0	4.0
Very cool	4.1	3.4	3.9	4.0	3.8
Very interesting	4.2	3.6	4.1	4.1	4.0
Very fun	4.2	3.8	4.1	4.1	4.0
Very easy/straight forward	3.6	3.2	3.8	3.7	3.5
Very challenging	3.8	3.5	3.9	3.6	3.7
Jobs that allow me to travel	3.6	3.3	3.8	3.5	3.5
Jobs that allow me to meet many people	3.9	3.7	3.9	3.8	3.8
Jobs with a *big* impact on the world	4.1	3.8	4.0	4.0	4.0
Jobs with *lots* of promotion opportunit-ies	3.8	3.5	3.78	3.4	3.6

6. THREATS TO VALIDITY

This section discusses some threats to validity that may affect this study.

This study does not capture whether these students' intention to enroll in ICT programs at tertiary level will translate into actual enrolments. This is a potential topic for future research.

The participants may be influenced by social desirability response bias, and hence try to portray themselves in the best possible light. Therefore the students could have felt that they should respond in a particular way – they could have responded in ways, which they think are socially desirable or acceptable. At the beginning of the survey, the students were assured that their responses will be held in strict confidence and used only for the purposes of the research.

The main threat to external validity is generalizing our results as our sample may not be representative of all female Malaysian secondary school students at government funded schools. It has to be noted that the studies conducted at this stage are exploratory in nature.

7. CONCLUSION

The survey results provide evidence that there is a high level of interest in IT education and careers amongst the female Malaysian secondary students who participated in this study. Despite the less than conducive technological learning environment in the schools, and low student recruitment in school IT clubs, there is an encouraging tendency amongst the students to want to learn more about IT, and their intentions to study an IT related degree at HEIs. There is a general belief that possessing some technological skills will enhance their chances in getting jobs and helping them when they are at universities. Therefore students' intentions to study IT may be spurred by their innate interest in technology supported by encouragement from their friends, teachers and the media.

It is also particularly interesting and encouraging to note that female indigenous students do not seem to be marginalized by their heritage and gender – based on their positive responses, they seem to be more interested in pursuing an IT related undergraduate degree than the Chinese students. One of the reasons that may attribute to the low interest amongst the Chinese students in studying IT at a HEI could possibly be the strong Chinese culture amongst parents in wanting their children to pursue more 'prestigious' careers e.g. medicine, law or engineering [11].

However, despite the positive interest that we have found amongst the female students in this study towards studying IT in higher education, a current and future shortage of IT resources still exists. In order to encourage youths to take up education and careers in IT, IT advocates must interact directly with the youths and their parents – teachers and guidance counselors cannot fulfill this role alone; schools and the government must play their part in providing skilled IT teachers to incorporate technology into their teaching to make their lessons interesting and fun; the government and educational authorities have to relook at curriculum and start engaging students in IT classes from the primary school levels [2].

8. ACKNOWLEDGEMENTS

The authors would like to extend their thanks to all the school children who took part in the survey. Also special thanks to Ms Hai Bee Goh, Principal of SMK St Mary for making the necessary introductions to the Principals of the participating schools.

9. REFERENCES

[1] Alexander P.M., Holmner M., Lotriet H.H., Matthee M.C., Pieterse H.V., Nidoo, S., Twinomurinzi H. and Jordaan D. 2011. Factors affecting career choice: Comparison between students from computer and other disciplines. In *Journal of Science Education and Technology,* 20, 3 (June 2011), 300-315.

[2] Babin, R.,Grant, K.A. and Sawal, L. Identifying influencers in high school student ICT career choice. In *Information Systems Education Journal*, 8, 26, 1-18

[3] Heersink, D. and Moskal, B.M. 2010. Measuring high school students' attitudes toward computing. In *Proceedings of the 41st ACM Technical Symposium on Computer Science Education.*

[4] Morreale, P. Joiner and Chang 2010. Connecting undergraduate programs to high school students: teacher workshops on computational thinking and computer science. In *Journal of Computing Sciences in Colleges*, 25, 6, (June 2010), 191-197.

[5] Schulte, C. and Knobelsdorf, M. 2007. Attitudes towards computer science-computing experiences as a starting point and barrier to computer science. In *Proceedings of the 3rd International Workshop on Computing Education Research.*

[6] Downes, T. and Looker, D. 2011. Factors that influence students' plans to take computing and information technology subjects in senior secondary school. In *Computer Science Education*, 21, 2, 175–199.

[7] PIKOM, Jobstreet.com and KPMG 2012. In *ICT Job Market Outlook in Malaysia.*

[8] MDeC 2011. MSC Malaysia talent supply-demand study 2010-2013, Putrajaya: Multimedia Development Corporation.

[9] Wilkinson, R. and Yussof, I. 2005. Public and private provision of higher education in Malaysia: A comparative analysis. In *Higher Education*, *50*, 361–386.

[10] Adya, M.P. and Kaiser, K. 2005. Early determinants of women in the IT workforce: A model of girls' career choices. In *Information Technology and People*, 18, 3, 230–259.

[11] Mui, G.Y.,Tee, Y.J. and Sien, V.Y. 2013. Perceptions of information communication technologies: A supply-side case of Malaysian private education. In *Proceedings of the 2013 Pacific Asia Conference on Information Systems (PACIS).*

[12] Prensky, M. 2001. Digital natives, digital immigrants. In *On the Horizon*, 9, 5

[13] Brinda, T., Puhlmann, H., and Schulte, C. 2009. Bridging ICT and CS – Educational standards for computer science in lower secondary education. In *Proceedings of the 14th annual ACM SIGCSE Conference on Innovation and Technology in Computer Science Education*, 288-292.

[14] Carter, L. 2006. Why Students with an apparent aptitude for computer science don't choose to major in computer science. In *Proceedings of the 37th SIGCSE Technical Symposium on Computer Science Education*, 27-31.

[15] Black, J., Curzon, P., Myketiak, C. and McOwan, P.W. 2011. A study in engaging female students in computer science using role models. In *Proceedings of the 16th Annual Joint Conference on Innovation and Technology in Computer Science Education*, 63-67.

[16] Mellström, U. 2009. The intersection of gender, race and cultural boundaries, or why is computer science in Malaysia dominated by women? In *Social Studies of Science,* 39, 6, 885–907.

[17] MacIntyre, K. 2009. Increasing the enrolment of women in IT at Fanshawe College. DOI= http://www.fanshawec.ca/sites/default/files/file_attachments/macintyre09.pdf.

[18] Galpin, V. 2002. Women in computing around the world. In *Women and Computing*, 34, 2, 94-100.

[19] Buzzetto-More, N., Ukoha and O. Rustagi, N. 2010. Unlocking the barriers to women and minorities in computer science and information systems studies: Results from a multi-methodolical study conducted at two minority serving institutions. In Journal of *Information Technology Education*, (2010), 115-131.

[20] Adya, M.P. 2008. Women at work: Differences in IT career experiences and perceptions between South Asian and American Women. In *Human Resource Management,* 47, 3, 601-635.

[21] Malaysia Educational Statistics, QUICK FACTS 2012, Educational Planning and Research Division, Ministry of Education Malaysia population distribution and basic demographic characteristic report 2010. DOI= http://www.statistics.gov.my/portal/index.php?option=com_content&id=1215&Itemid=89&lang=en

APPENDIX: SURVEY INSTRUMENT

A) Use of Technology

1) At home I use computers to: (Choose all relevant items)
   a) Access social media sites
   b) Update and read blogs
   c) Access email
   d) Play games
   e) Watch movies, YouTube, etc.
   f) Study and research
   g) Do my homework, assignments
   h) I do not use computers at home

2) I use the following technology gadgets regularly: (Choose all relevant items)
   a) Personal Computer/Notebook
   b) iPAD/Tablet or equivalent
   c) Smartphone

3) At home I have access to: (Choose one option only)
   a) Computers but not the Internet
   b) One computer with Internet access
   c) More than one coputer with Internet access
   d) I don not have access to computers at home

4) On average, in a week, I use computers at home for: (Choose one option only)
   a) 0.1 – 2 hours
   b) 2 – 4 hours
   c) 4 – 6 hours
   d) 6 – 8 hours
   e) More than 8 hours
   f) I do not use computers at home

5) On average, in a week, I use computers at school for: (Choose one option only)
   a) 0.1 – 2 hours
   b) 2 – 4 hours
   c) 4 – 6 hours
   d) 6 – 8 hours
   e) More than 8 hours
   f) I do not use computers at home

6) I first learnt how to use computers at: (Choose one option only)
   a) Primary school
   b) Secondary school
   c) I do not know how to use computers

B) IT Learning Experience

1) I received encouragement to learn about IT from: (1 = strongly disagree; 5 = strongly agree)
   a) My friends
   b) My parents
   c) My family members (other than parents)
   d) My secondary school teachers
   e) My school counsellors
   f) A television program/movie

2) The following statements indicate my IT learning experience at school: (1 = strongly disagree; 5 = strongly agree)
   a) My school has good (functional) coputer laboratories
   b) My school teachers use computers to teach lessons
   c) There is an IT club (or equivalent) at my school

3) I am enrolled or planning to enrol for an information technology subject(s) for SPM / STPM (school leaving examinations at Form 5 and Form 6) (Yes/No)

4) I am a member of my school IT club (Yes/No)

5) The following statements indicate my opinion of learning about IT: (1 = strongly disagree; 5 = strongly agree)
   a) I want to learn more about IT
   b) I find IT interesting
   c) I find that knowledge of IT will help me to get a job
   d) I find that knowledge of IT will help me to get into university

6) I intend to study the following course at university: (Choose one option only)
   a) IT-related degree program
   b) Non-IT related degree program
   c) I do not intend to study at university

C) Opinion of IT Jobs or Careers

1) I think IT jobs or careers are: (1 = strongly disagree; 5 = strongly agree)
   a) Easy to find
   b) Pay high salaries
   c) Secure/stable
   d) Very creative
   e) Very cool
   f) Very interesting
   g) Very fun
   h) Very easy/straightforwards
   i) Very challenging
   j) Jobs that allow me to travel
   k) Jobs that allow me to meet many people
   l) Jobs with a big impact on the world
   m) Jobs with lots of promotion opportunities

Great Expectations:
What Do Children Expect From Their Technology?

Jessica Korte
Griffith University
170 Kessels Road
Nathan, Queensland, Australia
+61 7 3735 5191
jessica.korte@griffithuni.edu.au

Leigh Ellen Potter
Griffith University
170 Kessels Road
Nathan, Queensland, Australia
+61 7 3735 5191
l.potter@griffith.edu.au

Sue Nielsen
Griffith University
170 Kessels Road
Nathan, Queensland, Australia
+61 7 3735 5025
s.nielsen@griffith.edu.au

ABSTRACT

Children of the digital generation have expectations of technology that may or may not reflect the expectations of the adults around them. This paper explores the expectations of and attitudes towards technology of a group of young Deaf children while interacting with a computer game application. We found that the children expect seamless, intuitive behaviour from technology in part based on their existing experience with game platforms, mobile technology, and other computer games. In addition to high expectations of the technology, the children were highly adaptive to unfamiliar interfaces, tolerant of prototype deficiencies once they were familiar with the prototyping approach and could readily interact with new game elements. The challenge for developers is to create applications that harness the creativity of the digital generation and meet their high expectations. We suggest that involvement of children within the development approach will assist in meeting these goals.

Categories and Subject Descriptors

H.5.2 User Interfaces: [**Information Interfaces and Presentation**]: User Interfaces – *graphical user interfaces (GUI), prototyping, screen design, user centered design.*

General Terms

Design, Human Factors

Keywords

Child Computer Interaction; Attitude towards technology; Deaf Children; Deaf; Children

Permission to make digital or hard copies of all or part of this work for personal or classroom use is granted without fee provided that copies are not made or distributed for profit or commercial advantage and that copies bear this notice and the full citation on the first page. Copyrights for components of this work owned by others than the author(s) must be honored. Abstracting with credit is permitted. To copy otherwise, or republish, to post on servers or to redistribute to lists, requires prior specific permission and/or a fee. Request permissions from Permissions@acm.org.

SIGMIS-CPR '14, May 29 - 31 2014, Singapore, Singapore
Copyright is held by the owner/author(s). Publication rights licensed to ACM.
ACM 978-1-4503-2625-4/14/05...$15.00.
http://dx.doi.org/10.1145/2599990.2600008

1. INTRODUCTION

Children expect an "interconnectedness of experience" - to be able to intuitively and immediately interact with the media that they use [2], whether that is by touching the pictures in a reading book, or by interacting with media elements using technology such as computers, tablets and smart phones. This technology is increasingly available to children as part of their everyday lives, and software applications are specifically developed for children from pre-school age through to adulthood.

While research has been conducted into how technology can be used to support children in a range of activities, much of this research comes from adult choices and approaches on behalf of children. The view of adults is frequently different from that of the child [22] as the child has differing expectations and desires [15]. This paper presents the experience of the child in their interactions with technology and software applications designed for children.

In an increasingly digitalized world, designing with and for children takes on new significance, as not only are these children current technology users but they are also potential future technology developers. Early exposure to technology has been shown to influence the level of intrinsic motivation that an individual has towards interacting with technology and the consideration of the Information Technology area as a career choice [21]. Game design and game play is suggested as a motivating factor for interest in computing and the production of technology [5]. A better understanding of children's expectations of technology may allow the development of approaches to encourage an interest in technology, and advance Information Technology as an attractive career choice.

This paper seeks to describe the way several young children interacted with a game-based technology application and their experience with that interaction and with the technology they used. In doing so we will explore the children's expectations of how the game would work based on their experience with the internet and mobile technologies.

We present a narrative discussing the experience and expectations of these children, and the observations that we noted during the experience. A narrative as it is used here is defined in its simplest terms as a "tale, story, recital of facts" [18], with our experience presented as such a story. Our observations represent 'lessons learned', which in this context is taken to mean "knowledge gained through experience, which if shared, would benefit the work of others" [1].

2. THE CHILD

The word 'child' can be applied to a range of ages, with many sub-categories possible. For the purpose of this paper, the focus will be on younger children under the age of twelve. This choice is a convenience choice made to match the focus of the author's larger research project, which seeks to assist young and very young children in learning signs in Australian Sign Language (Auslan).

The children who participated in this project are Deaf, and it is important to clarify the appropriate terminology for the Deaf community. Individuals who have some form of hearing loss may be described as 'deaf'. The capitalised 'Deaf' describes individuals who identify as belonging to the signing Deaf community and who communicate using Auslan. Deaf individuals may describe themselves as "Culturally Deaf." The term 'hard of hearing' is a broader term describing individuals with a hearing loss who usually communicate with speech [25]. This paper will follow the conventions of Deaf Australia and use the term ""deaf" when referring to all Deaf and hard of hearing groups at once."

3. THE TECHNOLOGY EXPERIENCE FOR THE CHILD

Children from developed nations are commonly described as the digital generation, or "digital natives" – the generation born into a digital world with access to networked, digital technologies [20]. With this label comes assumptions around children's competence with and attitudes towards technology [13]. A comparison of children's attitudes in 1999 and again in 2009 found that children are able to conceptualise both technology and the concept of computers from as young as six years old, and that they can create these ideas at a younger age now compared to 1999. In 2009 children were more likely to describe entertainment, communication and game based activities when describing technology, whereas in 1999 descriptions were related to the physical nature of the computer itself [19]. Children's conceptualisation of technology has moved to include a broad range of devices such as mobile phones in addition to a computer.

These conceptualisations may stem in part from the ubiquity of technology within the home. According to the Australian Bureau of Statistics, 79% of Australian households had access to the internet at home in the 2010-2011 period, with high income households reaching as high as 95%. Households with children under the age of fifteen were reported as more likely to have home internet access, with this group at 93%, and 90% of children aged five to fourteen had accessed the internet in the twelve months to April 2012. This percentage was lower for the five to eight year old group (79%) and higher for the twelve to fourteen year old group (98%). 29% of children owned a mobile phone, with percentages again increasing with age. 95% of households with children under fifteen have a personal computer [12].

Coupled with technology in the home is the global rise of technology in study environments. In Australia, government policy has focused on providing children with individual access to computers, with initiatives such as the Digital Education Revolution (DER). This initiative ran from 2008 until mid-2013, and aimed to give all students from grade 9 to grade 12 access to technology such as a laptop or PC. This would then support the development of an online national curriculum and the development of online and digital learning resources. It was reviewed in 2013 and "broadly regarded as a major success." [4].

Current technology initiatives involve the deployment of tablet computers to both primary and secondary school students. This is consistent with the Tablets for Schools initiative in the United Kingdom. In the United States, 43% of students and teachers are reported to use tablet technology in education, supported by the ConnectED program bringing broadband to schools.

Attitudes held by children towards technology do of course vary between populations. A study of children aged eleven to fourteen found that children from a lower socio economic background were more cautious towards computers than children from wealthier families [9]. However, they were also positive about the importance of technology, especially at younger ages [9, 16].

Studies of very young children's interaction with multimedia found that the children were enthusiastic and needed little encouragement to interact with the technology. Even at two years of age, these children were able to interact independently with a customised laptop and software [9]. This finding is supported in part by Mcknight and Fitton [17], who found that young children were able to comfortably use touch screen devices from the age of six, and were familiar with a range of on-screen gestures. They did find that younger children were more prone to unintentional screen touches, resulting in minor errors.

McKenny and Voogt [16] found similar positive attitudes in a group of four to seven year old children. These children stated that they were able to independently or with help complete a range of computer tasks, such as game play, drawing, and internet search, with proficiency increasing with age. The amount of computer use also increased with age. Children described their primary computer activity as playing games, with school related activities become more common as children progressed through school. This is consistent with the activities listed by the ABS Australian surveys [12].

A study of children's interactions with tablet computers found that the children were motivated and enthusiastic about the technology. They were comfortable in exploring the application on the tablet and in making mistakes, persisting with their interaction regardless [3]. One child involved in the study observed: "Sometimes the computer doesn't hear you.... I just keep trying and trying until it [the computer] gets it right." (p. 91). This is in contrast to the reactions shown by many adults, who tend to blame themselves for errors.

4. DEVELOPING TECHNOLOGIES FOR DEAF CHILDREN AROUND THE WORLD

There has been very little development of technologies for Deaf children learning sign language in Australia. Some multimedia tools have been created in recent years for hearing and deaf children [8], and a number of tools exist for adult and/or hearing audiences; but nothing until the Seek and Sign project has focused on creating technologies specifically for Deaf children.

International efforts also seem rather sparse. American Sign Language (ASL) has fared the best, with a number of research projects being completed over the last decade. Key examples are CopyCat [10, 14], the iSign Bear [11] and PlayWare [26]. All three of these programs present non-standard technology interfaces. The iSign Bear and PlayWare are not intended to be treated as technological artefacts, but rather to integrate into the already existing physical world of the child. CopyCat has an interface which is controlled by sign-like gestures. Each of these approaches has benefits, and potential to help young Deaf children acquiring a sign language. However, it is less helpful for this investigation of children's use of "standard" technologies – technologies and programs which are designed for children, but still rely on their skills and knowledge with existing hardware interfaces.

5. OBSERVING CHILDREN'S EXPECTATIONS OF INTERACTION

In the next two sections, we will describe the Sign My World case study. Sign My World is an application intended to aid young Deaf children in learning signs from Auslan. We included members of our target audience, preliterate deaf children and children in their early years of schooling, in the development of the Sign My World application. This was in order to realistically address their expectations. To do this, we took a child-as-informant approach to requirements elicitation, as described within the Cooperative Inquiry approach [6, 24]. As a preliminary study we conducted a series of prototyping sessions with a small number of Deaf children from the target audience, recording their comments and observations about their behaviour. These were used to identify new requirements and changes to existing requirements, which were used in turn to modify the prototype for the next testing session. Discussion of the results of the prototyping sessions, with particular focus on the children's interface expectations, is in the next section.

Eight prototyping sessions were conducted with three participants, who we will call "Pat", "Roger" and "Richard", where the children interacted with an evolving prototype of the application. All three of the participants were familiar with computers, both desktop and laptop, and iPads, to which they had access at home and school. Roger's parents also reported that he played console games.

Pat was a profoundly deaf seven year old boy who had had a working cochlear implant for the preceding two years. Pat attended a Special Education Program; however sessions with Pat took place at his home. Roger and Richard were two hearing-impaired boys who were also aged seven. Both boys wore hearing aids and were learning vocalised English through a Special Education Program attached to an Education Queensland school. All three of the boys were learning Auslan.

Pat's mother and grandmother were present for his prototyping session. His grandmother acted as Auslan interpreter for the application developer for his session. The sessions with Roger and Richard took place within the dedicated Special Education Program building at their school. Roger and Richard sat on adjacent edges of a small, square table, with an Auslan interpreter from the school sitting at one of the opposite sides of the table. This afforded the interpreter a place where she could see and be seen by Roger and Richard. The application developer sat beside the participants, so that their interaction with the prototype was visible. All eight of the sessions were conducted with the prototype presented to the children on a laptop computer.

The prototype was built in Adobe Flash, as this program allowed our requirements elicitor to create dynamic, interactive prototypes quickly.

The initial prototype used in testing consisted of a single virtual area which users could explore, as shown in figure 1. Clicking on animated item buttons would trigger a video flash card, displaying

the item which had been clicked, the English word for the item, and an Auslan sign video for the item, as shown in figure 2. When the flash card first opened, the image of the item clicked was displayed in the centre of the screen for two seconds. Then it would resize and relocate to the top of the screen, and an Auslan sign video would be displayed at the centre of the screen. The video could be replayed after it had finished, by clicking the play button. Clicking on the image icon would display the image in the centre of the screen at full size once more.

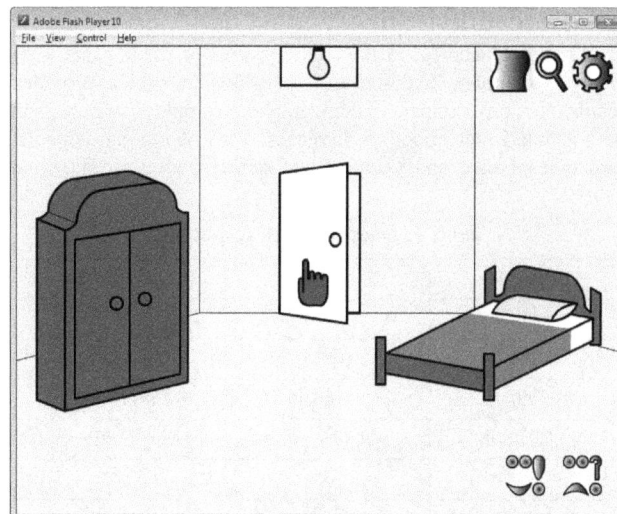

Figure 1. Prototype initial screen. © Seek and Sign

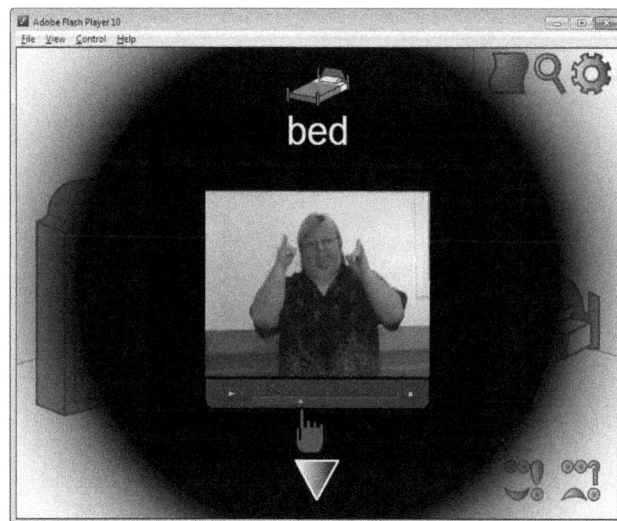

Figure 2. Video flash card. © Seek and Sign

During every prototype testing session, the children would interact with a new version of the prototype. In most sessions, this was the sole tool used for information gathering. However, in Session 2 with Richard and Roger, a small paper prototyping activity was also conducted. This will be described in more detail below.

6. LIMITATIONS

It is acknowledged that these sessions were conducted with only three children. The purpose of the sessions was to prototype an initial application for the Sign My World game, and further development is currently ongoing. Subsequent sessions with more children will be required, and the story told here is specific to the participants in this prototyping round. We will describe the children's interaction with the technology used in the prototyping sessions and with the application in narrative form, and our aim is to generate insight that will influence future prototyping rounds.

7. SIGN MY WORLD PROTOTYPING SESSION OBSERVATIONS

7.1 Descriptive Survey

At the commencement of the study, parents of participants were asked to complete a descriptive questionnaire which provided details about participants' demographic, computer access, and demonstrated recreational preferences. Two of our participants' parents responded, and a summary of their responses are shown in Table 1.

Table 1. Questionnaire responses.

Question	Roger	Richard
Age	7	7
Gender	M	M
Languages	English	English
Home computer?	Yes	Yes
Home internet?	Yes	Yes
Supervised home computer / internet time (hours/week)	1-2	2-3
Unsupervised home computer / internet time (hours/week)	0	0
Smartphone/tablet device?	No	Yes, iPad
Conditions of smartphone / tablet use?	-	No conditions – most apps are learning games or drawing/photography
Supervised smartphone / tablet time (hours/week)	-	3-4
Unsupervised smartphone / tablet time (hours/week)	-	2
Technology use at school?	Unknown	Unknown
Computer activities?	Artwork, learning games, photography, music	Artwork, learning games, videos, recreational games
Use of non-computer gaming platforms?	Yes	Yes
Choice of games	Puzzles, sport, Lego, Wii, PlayStation	Puzzles, adventure

7.2 Sessions with Pat

The pilot session was conducted with Pat. He was presented with the initial prototype on a laptop computer. It had been assumed that, due to his reported familiarity with technology, presenting the prototype on a laptop would not present a problem. However, he had some difficulties, because he had not encountered a laptop touch pad before. He had difficulty controlling the pointer, and using the left- and right-click, as the button did not have a clear separator between the two. After a short demonstration, he adapted quickly to using it, however general assumptions often attributed to 'digital natives' were incorrect in Pat's case.

Pat quickly worked out that the animated item buttons in the prototype could be clicked on. He ignored the smaller, static 'tutorial' button that had been included (visible in Figure 1).

The first time he viewed a video flash card -- which greys out the area of the interface not covered by the video -- and tried to exit, he was surprised to see that it did not work as he expected. There was a 'back' button, shown in figure 2; he was trying to return to the 'room' by clicking on the greyed-out area. He became rather frustrated that the interface did not work as he expected it to. This navigation was simplified in future versions of the prototype in response to his frustration.

When Pat had explored the entire prototype, roughly 10 minutes into the session, he began exploring the laptop desktop and looking for other programs. It was at this point that the session was ended.

At the beginning of the session, Pat was told to play with the prototype and share his thoughts about it, as per the procedure of gestural think-aloud protocol [23]. He was not prompted again throughout the session, and did not provide many utterances. Therefore, the majority of data gathered from this session came from researcher observations of his reactions.

From this first session, we observed that assumptions regarding technology familiarity needed to be confirmed with the children prior to introducing them to the prototype. Pat expected to be able to click on a button, just as he could in other applications. He was frustrated when the application did not behave as he expected, based on his experience with other games. It appears that he expected a degree of consistency in his interaction with the technology.

7.3 Sessions with Richard and Roger

Using the lessons learned from the pilot session, the laptop used for testing sessions with Richard and Roger had the desktop icons and taskbar hidden so that the boys were not distracted. Richard and Roger were also supplied with a plug-in mouse, which was familiar from their existing experience with laptops at school. In later sessions, it would be revealed that Roger was also familiar with the touch pad.

Richard and Roger attended all but one session together – the exception being when Roger missed a day of school due to illness – and would take turns controlling the prototype. They would often offer input or suggestions to one another on what to do while using the other was controlling the prototype.

At the start of the sessions, Richard and Roger were instructed in English and Auslan to play with the prototype and to vocalise or sign what they thought of it. This is in line with usability testing think-aloud and gestural think-aloud protocols [23], and matched the introduction Pat was given in the pilot session. Unlike the pilot session, however, Richard and Roger were prompted throughout the sessions to share their thoughts when their reactions were particularly emotional.

7.3.1 Session One

Initially, neither child clicked on any of the animated buttons until prompted by the designer, although they were delighted by the animations themselves. This might have been due to nervousness about the unfamiliar situation they found themselves in.

Richard had more experience using computers than Roger did, and began to use the interface more quickly. He showed Roger how to replay videos and attempted to demonstrate button hit zones when Roger had trouble clicking directly on the area he wanted, again challenging the 'digital native' assumptions.

When prompted for thoughts and suggestions at the end of the session, Roger suggested that the prototype should be expanded to include a kitchen, and listed some signs he would like to see there. When asked for ideas on how navigation between different rooms could be introduced, Roger drew on his real-world experiences rather than his knowledge of technology, because he said he would "walk downstairs".

Based on these early observations, it appeared that pre-existing familiarity with technology was an influence on the children's interaction with the laptops and with this application. The boys appeared happy to interact with the prototype, and to blend their understanding of games and technology with real-world experience, as shown in the case of Roger's suggestion of the kitchen.

7.3.2 Session Two

In session two, Roger and Richard quickly identified the only change made to the beginning interface between sessions -- a new button which allowed them to navigate between rooms, as shown in Figure 3. This easy identification of visual change may be specific to these boys, as Deaf children rely largely on visual-spatial cognitive perception and processing [7]. The boys readily identified any visual changes to the application, no matter how minor. Further comparison with hearing children would need to be undertaken to compare this skill.

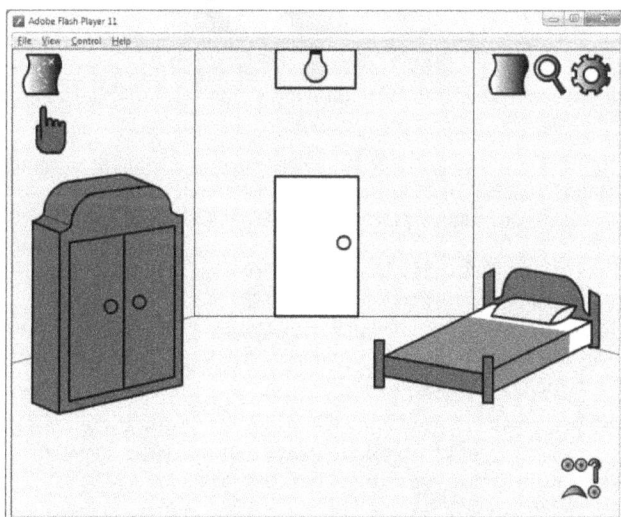

Figure 3. Updated prototype initial screen. © Seek and Sign

The new button led to a map screen, shown in Figure 4. The participants' behaviour on viewing this screen demonstrated their pre-existing familiarity with technology and the effect this had on their expectations once more. Each room was represented by a white parallelogram with a symbol representing the room on it. The boys were surprised when the parallelogram was not part of the clickable area. They were also surprised that the roof, which had a similar appearance to the item buttons in the bedroom, was not clickable. Both of these issues were addressed in future prototypes.

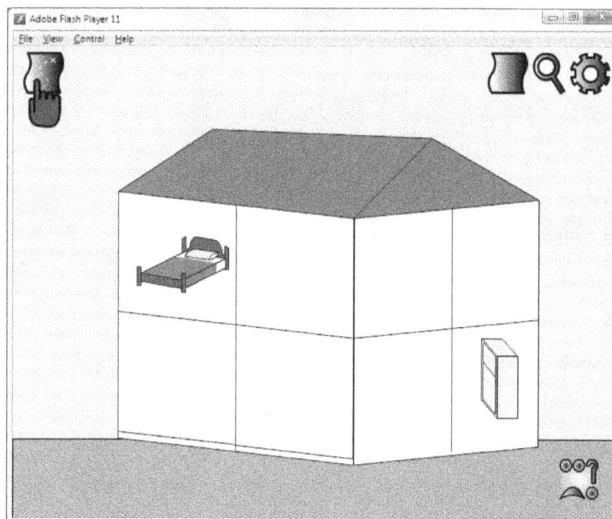

Figure 4. New 'map' screen. © Seek and Sign

This prototype also introduced a new room, the Kitchen, as per Roger's suggestion in the previous session. His suggestion, which included a number of food items, had not been completely implemented in code. Instead, the participants were presented with a paper prototype of how food items might be found "inside" objects such as the fridge. Once the boys approved of the paper prototype, it was implemented, as shown in Figure 5, and was present in the prototype tested in Session Three.

Figure 5. Items "in" the fridge are accessed by scrolling through a list. © Seek and Sign

7.3.3 Session Three

During session three, Richard revealed that he was familiar with how laptop touchpads worked by trying to control the mouse while it was Roger's turn. Roger was interacting with the game using the mouse, and Richard stepped in and started using the touchpad to try to control the interaction.

7.3.4 Session Four

During session four, the participants were mostly understanding about an interface bug, especially as it was one that was easily fixed. They also demonstrated that they understood the concept of scrolling, by being able to find all the items "in" the fridge, as shown in figure 5.

7.3.5 Session Five

In session five, Richard decided he would rather use the laptop touch pad than the mouse. He had no problems in using it. Roger, on the other hand, experienced some frustration. His cursor movements were unsteady, and he had some difficulty focusing on the items he wanted to click on. Despite this, he did not want to use the plug-in mouse when it was offered.

7.3.6 Session Six

In session six, both participants demonstrated once again that they expect consistency from the interface. They were dismayed to see that some new item buttons were not animated, as the previous ones had been.

Both participants seemed to have realised how the requirement elicitation sessions worked by session seven, and were excited to realise their input really was being used to change the prototype. They were keen to give suggestions during the final two sessions, and both listed a large number of things they would like to see included in the game. They became active participants in the process and were enthusiastic in their participation.

They had also realised that interface bugs were fixable, and when they occurred calmly asked for them to be fixed.

At one point, Roger tried to replay a video by clicking on the video itself. Due to the way Adobe Flash treats videos, this was registered as a click on the background, and the video flash card was closed. He was surprised and annoyed by that, and clicked on the triggering item again to access the same video flash card.

7.3.7 Session Seven

During the final session, the participants revealed that they were aware of customisable avatars in other games and programs, and when asked, said they would enjoy something similar in Sign My World. The prototype for this session had a partial implementation of this, as shown in figure 6. The way the avatar creation was set up to work was that the user should be able to select a part of the face to see the sign for it, in a predetermined part of the screen, and then they would be able to make changes to it. This did not match the way Richard expected it to work. Because there was a loading bar where the video would appear, and the changing arrows did not work (because he had not selected a body part), he declared it to be "not working" and returned to the main part of the house. After the way it worked was explained to him, he tried it again, and quickly got it working. Roger had a little more trouble during his turn, as he kept attempting to double-click on the arrows, and got frustrated when it changed twice.

Figure 6. Avatar personalisation screen. © Seek and Sign

7.3.8 General Observations

Throughout the sessions, none of the participants clicked on the symbol icon for the sign they were viewing; nor did they seem to realise when an extra set of 'verb' buttons were unlocked and appeared on the 'door' video flash card (see figure 7), as these remained unclicked.

Figure 7. Video flash card showing verb buttons. © Seek and Sign

Further work would need to be undertaken to ascertain the reasons behind this lack of interaction with the icons, and whether this stemmed from a lack of familiarity or from another reason.

8. CONCLUSION

In this paper we aimed to present the experience of several children with a game based technology application, and to explore their expectations of and attitude towards their interaction with the technology that they used.

Our participants' interactions with Sign My World demonstrated in-depth knowledge of technological norms. Their interactions with the interface seem to suggest an expectation of seamless, intuitive behaviour from technology. Some of these expectations seem to have been shaped by previous exposure to computer games, smart phone apps and online content. This presents a challenge for developers for children - how can you ensure that an implementation which seems logical to you will be truly intuitive to your users? The answer would seem to be to involve members of your target audience in the design throughout the design of the application. In the development of the Sign My World prototype, participant feedback and reactions were key in streamlining the interface, and ensuring user expectations were met. It is possible that this involvement may also encourage a further interest in Information Technology, and the enthusiasm and level of participation by our participants is a positive indicator.

Some observations of the children using technology challenge the assumptions associated with 'digital natives'. Balancing this, it was also noticeable that, in addition to their high expectations, our participants were highly adaptable when it came to encountering software or hardware interfaces they were unfamiliar with, once the underlying logic had been explained or demonstrated. The inclusion of short, visual, interface tutorials could help to ensure that users are not distracted from content by frustration with the interface; although of course, the best interface is one that needs no explanation.

The children in the prototyping sessions encountered some challenges with mouse control and this is consistent with experiences described by Ellis and Blashki [9]. Sign My World is currently being redeveloped for deployment to tablet devices. This will enable a comparison between the child's game experience using a mouse and their experience using touch.

9. REFERENCES

[1] Abecker, A. and van Elst, L. 2009. Ontologies for Knowledge Management. *Handbook on Ontologies*. S. Staab and R. Studer, eds. Springer. 713–734.

[2] Bearne, E. 2003. Rethinking Literacy: Communication, Representation and Text. *Literacy*. 37, 3 (2003), 98–103.

[3] Couse, L.J. and Chen, D.W. 2010. A Tablet Computer for Young Children? Exploring Its Viability for Early Childhood Education. *Journal of Research on Technology in Education*. 43, 1 (2010), 75–98.

[4] danolopartners 2013. *DER Mid-Program Review: Assessing Progress of the DER and Potential Future Directions – Final Report*.

[5] Denner, J. 2007. The Girls Creating Games Program: An Innovative Approach to Integrating Technology into Middle School Jill Denner. *Meridian: A Middle School Computer Technologies Journal*. 10, 1 (2007).

[6] Druin, A. 2002. The role of children in the design of new technology. *Behaviour and Information Technology*. 21, 1 (2002), 1–25.

[7] Ebrahim, F. 2006. Comparing Creative Thinking Abilities and Reasoning Ability of Deaf and Hearing Children. *Roeper Review*. 28, 3 (2006), 140.

[8] Ellis, K. and Blashki, K. 2007. The Digital Playground: Kindergarten Children Learning Sign Language Through Multimedia. *Education*. 15, (2007).

[9] Ellis, K. and Blashki, K. 2004. Toddler Techies: A Study of Young Children's Interaction with Computers. *Information technology in childhood education annual*. 1, (2004), 77–96.

[10] Henderson, V., Lee, S., Brashear, H., Hamilton, H., Starner, T. and Hamilton, S. 2005. Development of an American sign language game for deaf children. *Proceedings of IDC 2005* (Jun. 2005), 70–79.

[11] Huang, K., Smith, J., Spreen, K. and Jones, M.F. 2008. Breaking the sound barrier: designing an interactive tool for language acquisition in preschool deaf children. *Proceedings of IDC 2008* (Sep. 2008), 210–216.

[12] Internet and Mobile Phones: 2012. *http://www.abs.gov.au/AUSSTATS/abs@.nsf/Latestproducts/4901.0Main Features7Apr 2012?opendocument&tabname=Summary&prodno=4901.0&issue=Apr 2012&num=&view=*. Accessed: 2013-10-29.

[13] Lebens, M., Graff, M. and Mayer, P. 2009. Access, Attitudes and the Digital Divide: Children's Attitudes Towards Computers in a Technology-Rich Environment. *Educational Media International*. 46, 3 (2009), 255–266.

[14] Lee, S., Henderson, V., Brashear, H., Starner, T., Hamilton, S. and Hamilton, H. 2005. User-centered development of a gesture-based American Sign Language game. *Instructional Technology and Education of the Deaf Symposium, Rochester, NY* (2005), 1–8.

[15] Markopoulos, P., Read, J.., MacFarlane, S. and Hoysniemi, J. 2008. *Evaluating Children's Interactive Products: Principles and Practices for Interaction Designers*. Morgan Kaufmann.

[16] McKenney, S. and Voogt, J. 2010. Technology and young children: How 4–7 year olds perceive their own use of computers. *Computers in Human Behavior*. 26, 4 (Jul. 2010), 656–664.

[17] Mcknight, L. and Fitton, D. 2010. Touch-screen Technology for Children: Giving the Right Instructions and Getting the Right Responses. *Proceedings of Interaction Design and Children* (Barcelona, Spain, Jun. 2010), 238–241.

[18] Myers, M.D. and Avison, D. 2002. *Qualitative Research in Information Systems*. Sage Publications.

[19] Oleson, K.E., Sims, V.K., Chin, M.G., Lum, H.. and Sinatra, A. 2010. Developmental Human Factors: Children's Mental Models of Computers. *Proceedings of the Human Factors and Ergonomics Society Annual Meeting*. 54, 19 (2010), 1450–1453.

[20] Palfrey, J. and Gasser, U. 2010. *Born Digital*. Basic Books.

[21] Potter, L.E., von Hellens, L. and Nielsen, S. 2009. Childhood Interest in IT and the Choice of IT as a Career: The Experiences of a Group of IT Professionals. *Proceedings of the special interest group on management information system's 47th annual conference on Computer personnel research* (Limerick, Ireland, 2009), 33–40.

[22] Rabiee, P., Sloper, P. and Beresford, B. 2005. Doing research with children and young people who do not use speech for communication. *Children & Society*. 19, 5 (Nov. 2005), 385–396.

[23] Roberts, V.L. and Fels, D.I. 2006. Methods for inclusion: Employing think aloud protocols in software usability studies with individuals who are deaf. *International Journal of Human-Computer Studies*. 64, 6 (2006), 489–501.

[24] Scaife, M. and Rogers, Y. 1999. Kids as Informants: Telling us what we didn't know or confirming what we knew already? *The Design of Children's Technology*. A. Druin, ed. Morgan Kaufmann. 28–50.

[25] Terminology: 2010. *http://www.deafau.org.au/info/terminology.php*. Accessed: 2013-10-29.

[26] Yarosh, S., Huang, K., Mosher, I. and Topping, M. 2008. Playware: augmenting natural play to teach sign language. *Proceedings of CHI 2008* (Apr. 2008), 3249–3254.

Active Learning Approaches in Information Technology (IT) Pedagogy

Benjamin Gan Kok Siew
Singapore Management University
80 Stamford Road
Singapore 178902
+65 6828-0267
benjamingan@smu.edu.sg

K.D. Joshi
Washington State University
PO Box 644750
Pullman, WA 99164
1-509-335-5722
joshi@wsu.edu

Diane Lending
James Madison University
MSC 0203, 342 Zane Showker Hall
Harrisonburg, VA 22807
1-540-568-3273
lendindc@jmu.edu

Christina Outlay
University of Wisconsin-Whitewater
809 W. Starin Road
Whitewater, WI 53190
1-262-472-7034
outlay@uww.edu

Jeria Quesenberry
Carnegie Mellon University
5000 Forbes Avenue
Pittsburgh, PA 15213
1-412-268-4573
jquesenberry@cmu.edu

Randy Weinberg
Carnegie Mellon University
5000 Forbes Avenue
Pittsburgh, PA 15213
1-412-268-9593
rweinberg@cmu.edu

ABSTRACT

The purpose of this panel is to take stock of the various active learning approaches in IT pedagogy at the post-secondary level being employed in the SIGMIS CPR community. The ultimate goal is to better understand the various active learning tools and techniques and when it makes sense to employ such approaches in the classroom. The panelists will give an overview of specific approaches they have employed in the classroom and share their insights from the experience. The panelists will also provide suggestions and examples for those who are interested in incorporating these pedagogical approaches in their teaching.

Categories and Subject Descriptors

K.3.2 Computer and Information Science Education

General Terms

Management, Human Factors, Theory

Keywords

Active learning; curriculum; post-secondary education; pedagogy

1. INTRODUCTION

Professors at colleges and universities around the world are abandoning traditional 'chalk and talk' teaching methods in favor of alternative approaches to education. Likewise, recreating the context of the information technology (IT) workforce – one where the problem space is often complex and ill defined– is difficult in the undergraduate classroom environment. Research on IT pedagogy has demonstrated support of innovative active learning approaches that include elements of: problem-based, team-based, experiential and service-learning, just-in-time teaching, case-

based teaching, hands-on / simulation activities, flipped classroom scenarios, and distributed / global projects. The SIGMIS CPR community is at the center of research that examines post-secondary education pedagogy and approaches used to prepare tomorrow's leaders in the IT workforce. So it is fitting that the conference continues its leadership role by investigating and assessing new and innovative paradigms in IT pedagogy approaches and research.

Hence, the purpose of this panel is to take stock of the various techniques and approaches to new paradigms in IT pedagogy at the post-secondary level being employed in the SIGMIS CPR community. The ultimate goal is to better understand the various tools and techniques in the paradigm of IT pedagogy and when it makes sense to employ such approaches in the classroom.

During the panel, Jeria will serve as the moderator, and will provide an introduction to the session. Afterwards, each panelist will give a summary of his/her experiences with active learning (detailed abstract by each panelist are included in this article). The panelist presentations will address the following discussion questions:

1. What active learning teaching approaches have you used and why do you consider these to be appropriate for your topics, courses, and/or students?

2. What key insights have resulted from your active-learning teaching / research?

3. What suggestions or examples can you share with audience members who might want to explore these teaching approaches in their classrooms?

4. What are some important areas of IT pedagogy research that should be pursued in the future – how can the research body move forward given these innovations in education?

The panelist presentations will be followed by a general discussion of the questions with the audience.

Permission to make digital or hard copies of part or all of this work for personal or classroom use is granted without fee provided that copies are not made or distributed for profit or commercial advantage, and that copies bear this notice and the full citation on the first page. Copyrights for third-party components of this work must be honored. For all other uses, contact the owner/author(s). Copyright is held by the author/owner(s).
SIGMIS-CPR'14, May 29–31, 2014, Singapore, Singapore.
ACM 978-1-4503-2625-4/14/05.
http://dx.doi.org/10.1145/2599990.2600016

2. PANELIST ABSTRACTS

2.1 Benjamin Gan Kok Siew

I have been learning IT with undergraduates, graduates and professional participants for about 20 years. My topic of interest ranges from technical areas such as programming languages to more soft skills area such as global software project management. While lecturing allow for a large-scale dissemination of information efficiently, active learning, where student do more than just listen, are able to better retain student interest in the subject. My experience in active learning includes but not limited to team-based, global project-oriented learning.

At Singapore Management University, I teach an IS elective course, Global Software Project Management with panelist, Prof Jeria Quesenberry and CMU Qatar Prof Selma Mansar. In this course, students learn by actively working on a team project, either writing a report for a case study or implementing a system code with students from other countries. Instead of just reading a case on chasing the sun, they experience how effective working around the global clock can be. Or how ineffective they are if the team is not prepared with a well defined set of roles and process. Besides gathering knowledge about what works in a global project, students are involved in higher order thinking, such as having the right attitude to meet challenges of work-life imbalance or burnout IT professions in the globalized IT industry.

Another active learning course that I teach is the Application project course or more commonly know as the final year project course. Like most fyp course, there is very little lecturing. In fact, only 1 hour briefing is done early to present the structure and assessment of the course. Students meet in a team, with sponsors, with supervisors and conduct testing with end users. Students are able to apply what they learn in other courses in a real project. In most cases, they are actively learning while engaging in these meeting. The reflection comes during supervisor meeting sessions or milestone presentations. This reinforces the claim that active learning results in deeper learning if the activities are done before the reflection.

Programming concept courses are especially difficult due to student motivation issues. Disseminating the required information needed before student can practice to acquire skills in programming can be done by lecture or virtually. Various active learning methods such as team assignments for discussions, pair programming, learning by teaching when student present their solutions, etc. have produce degrees of success but they sometimes introduce other problems. These problems include free loaders in team assignments, permanent leader in pair programming and shyness in teaching by weaker students. In addition, it takes a longer time to cover the fundamental concepts.

Finally, I bring a group of students to Seoul on a study mission to learn about technopreneurship in Seoul. It helps student understand another higher learning analysis of entrepreneur culture and motivation. Reflections are discussed after the trip.

I believe that active learning is important to motivate and help improve retention of knowledge, skills and attitudes, especially coupled with outside classroom projects.

2.2 K.D. Joshi

My teaching philosophy is based on the famous saying by Confucius, "*I hear and I forget. I see and I remember. I do and I understand.*" I incorporate the concept of "doing" in my classes by designing numerous learn by doing (LBD) activities that build on each other. These activities are done in class where we all do the LBD together. I will use my undergraduate Business Intelligence (BI) course as an example to illustrate how the LBD oriented course design help in achieving my course objectives. My BI course is designed around four capabilities that are necessary in order for organizations to successfully implement a data driven performance management solution. These capabilities include, Datawarehousing Capability that provides companies with the ability to structure a data repository in a standardized and integrated manner; Data Cleaning and Integration Capability that allows companies to profile, clean, map, and load the transactional data into data repositories; Analytical Capability that allows companies to grow into an analytical company which is data and fact-driven in its approach to decision making; and Visualization and Intelligence Delivery Capability allows companies to monitor and assess progress towards its strategic goals. The overall course objective is to learn to design and build a BI system that has all of the aforementioned capabilities. The system developed in class has both - rigor and realism.

The course contains five modules. In the first module, the students acts as end-users of a BI system that they will be building in class. They do LBD exercises in class where they engage in data driven decision-making. By allowing them to access and use the BI system that they will be building, they are not only able to understand the role of BI systems (i.e., how they are structurally different than online transaction systems), but also get some sense of what they will be accomplishing at the end of the class. The in class LBDs are followed up with HWs and group projects where they are again receiving lots of hands on experience by replicating what is learned in the class but using a different data scenario (See Figure 1). In the second module, the students act as designers where they learn to design datamarts using the dimensional modeling technique. In class they learn design concepts by first developing design documents for four different BI system scenarios, but the majority of the time is devoted to the system they used in the first module. After developing the logical designs, the physical designs are created using the DB engine feature in Microsoft's BI stack. In module three, the students act as data integration specialist. They learn to conduct an ETL process by profiling, cleaning, and loading data from relevant OLTP datasets into their datamarts that they designed and created in module 2. First, the source-to-target mapping documents are developed in class in form of learn by doing assignments and then these mapping are programmed using SQL Server Integration Services feature in Microsoft's BI stack. In module four the students act as online analytical systems' (OLAP) developers. They learn to create OLAP systems (a.k.a Cube) by using the datamart populated in module 3 as a data source. They build these systems using SQL Server Analysis Services feature in Microsoft's BI stack. In the last module, they act as report developers. They learn to design, build, and deploy reports using the OLAP system they build in module 4. They build these systems using SQL Server Reporting Services feature in Microsoft's BI stack. Once they have conducted the entire BI system development cycle in class with my guidance, they are then assessed on replicating these skills in their homework, quizzes, and group projects. I have been using this LBD model in this class since 2007. I will share my lessons learned, best practices, tips during our panel discussion.

Figure 1. Learning by Doing

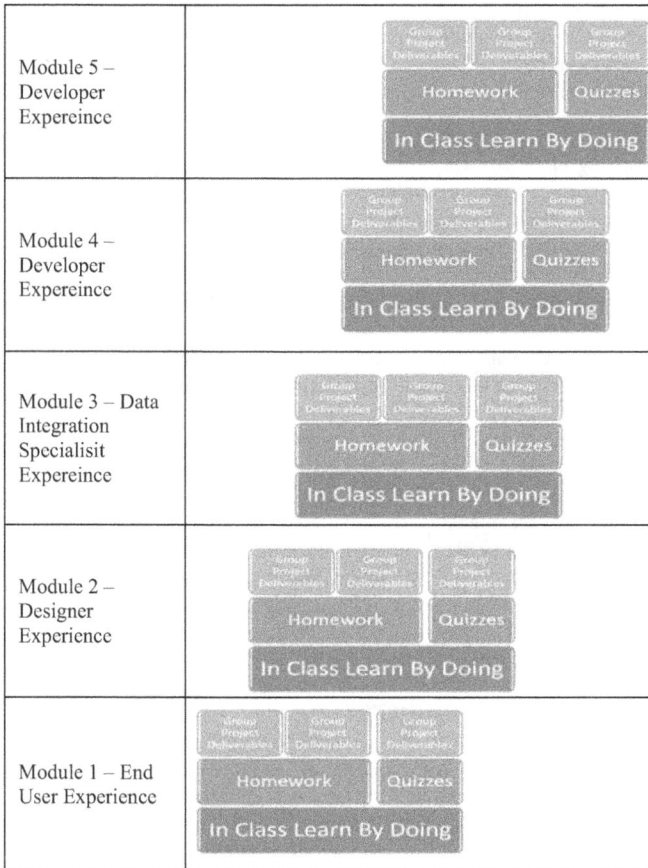

Module 5 – Developer Expereince	Group Project Deliverables / Group Project Deliverables / Group Project Deliverables / Homework / Quizzes / In Class Learn By Doing
Module 4 – Developer Expereince	Group Project Deliverables / Group Project Deliverables / Group Project Deliverables / Homework / Quizzes / In Class Learn By Doing
Module 3 – Data Integration Specialisit Experience	Group Project Deliverables / Group Project Deliverables / Group Project Deliverables / Homework / Quizzes / In Class Learn By Doing
Module 2 – Designer Experience	Group Project Deliverables / Group Project Deliverables / Group Project Deliverables / Homework / Quizzes / In Class Learn By Doing
Module 1 – End User Experience	Group Project Deliverables / Group Project Deliverables / Group Project Deliverables / Homework / Quizzes / In Class Learn By Doing

2.3 Diane Lending

The Flipped Classroom refers to changing the classroom model from a traditional lecture-based classroom followed by homework to a model where content delivery is done at home before an active learning experience in the classroom. Figure 2 contrasts the time lines of the two models. The concept was popularized by two high school chemistry teachers (e.g., Bergmann and Sams, 2008-2009) who found that students learned concepts better when they worked problems in class rather than struggling on them at home. It has been extended through pre-recorded lectures such as the Khan Academy. Research is mixed on whether the technique is successful in all classes or all subjects (Straumsheim, 2013).

I have used the Flipped Classroom combined with Team-Based Learning concepts at the undergraduate level in several classes including Systems Analysis and Design. In this class, I assign reading for each class. The class begins with a short reading quiz (five multiple-choice questions) taken by each student individually and then in small groups. I then spend class time on short case-based activities where students actually do systems analysis and design. This has been successful with exam averages increasing by close to five points with this method. However, it has required a complete redesign of my teaching activities. In the panel, I will share some lessons I have learned with this approach.

In the Management Information Systems class at the MBA level, I use a different type of classroom flipping. Ideally, class time is spent on discussions and cases. However, the students have quite different MIS backgrounds from complete novices to MIS professionals. To cope with this, I record lectures introducing the

technical concepts using PowerPoint, Collaborate, and Blackboard. Students who do not understand the concepts can watch the pre-recorded lectures. To encourage watching the lectures, I have pre-class quizzes on Blackboard that students may repeat an unlimited amount of times. I hope that each student will earn an A on these quizzes.

Figure 2. Timelines for the Traditional Classroom versus the Flipped Classroom

Traditional Classroom		
In-Class	**Content Delivery** Usually done by instructor in lecture format	
Out-of-Class		Student does homework on their own
Flipped Classroom		
In-Class		**Active Learning** • Students work problems with teacher guidance • Group work • Just in time teaching • Project-based learning • Team-based learning • Discussions, collaborative learning, debates
Out-of-Class	**Content Delivery** • Video • Recorded lecture • Reading	

2.4 Christina Outlay

Project-based learning requires two key factors – the project must involve the solution of a problem and the project results in some sort of end product being produced (Helle et al. 2006). I use three types of project-based approaches in the classroom: experiential learning, service learning, and online case-based project exercise. During the panel, I will share key factors to consider when using project-based learning in conjunction with other active-learning approaches. I will also share the benefits and challenges I've identified along the way.

I use project-based, experiential field-learning along with a flipped classroom and collaborative groups in my Information Technology Capstone Course, Information Technology Service Management. During the first six weeks of this course, students learn a framework of best practices for IT operations and other concepts that influence how an IT division operates. Students also learn Scrum agile development methodology. Students complete readings, videos and quizzes outside of class and in-class activities working in teams to practice project-related tasks. The remaining 10 weeks of the class is the project, where students work in Scrum teams for a corporate partner to analyze an operational issue the company is experiencing and develop a proposed solution. The project results in an end product consisting of redesigned operational processes, a long-term operational strategy, project implementation plan and a formal presentation to share recommendations with the corporate partner.

My second course, Introduction to Project Management, incorporates a service-learning project. Service learning projects model the idea that giving something back to the community is an important college outcome, and that working with community partners is good preparation for citizenship, work, and life (Weis, 2000). In addition to traditional lectures, in-class exercises and homework, students work in project teams on a service project for a community partner. Students apply the project management tools and techniques they learn in class to complete their projects and reflect on their experiences during class. Students also have the opportunity to earn community service credit for their project work (community service is a graduate requirement for the College).

My online class, Introduction to Information Systems, consists of essay-based assignments, online discussions, and group collaboration on three course components (an assignment, midterm project and final project). Both the midterm and final are cased-based group projects and require that students apply class learnings to determine the company's strategic objectives and data needs related to those objectives. Based on this analysis, students design and implement a technical solution for the company using Microsoft Access (midterm) or Microsoft Excel (final). By working in virtual groups, students also gain some initial experience (and confidence) collaborating online, which is a valuable skill for anyone working in today's business environment.

2.5 Jeria Quesenberry

I believe the key to education is for students to be fully engaged in the learning process and to be active participants in the classroom, rather than being passive observers. I believe this is particularly critical in the early IT courses where students are exposed to core concepts frequently for the first time. During the panel I will summarize several of the active learning approaches I have employed including: case based analysis, flipped classrooms, global project-based activities, and service-learning projects. During the discussion I will highlight the benefits and challenges I have encountered and share considerations for others who may incorporate these approaches in their teaching.

In my introduction course, the Information Systems Milieux, I built in extensive active-learning approaches. For example, the course includes three major case analysis reports and a series of in-class case critiques. I also limit my lectures to core materials and fundamental concepts, so that the majority of class time is devoted to: class discussions, debates, 'think-pair-share,' 'learning by teaching,' and collaborative learning groups. I found that these activities are more time consuming to prepare than a traditional lecture, but have stronger learning outcomes in that it better engages students in problem solving, discussion and reflection.

I also teach an elective course entitled Contemporary Themes in Global Systems, which includes several project-based activities. The core project is a cultural website usability assessment where small teams of four to six students work on distributed teams to create several written reports and video presentations. Team members are co-located in Pittsburgh (CMU), Qatar (through a partnership with Selma Limam Mansar at CMU-Qatar) and/or Singapore (through a partnership with Benjamin Gan Kok Siew at Singapore Management University). As Ben previously mentioned in his abstract, this project allows the students to experience – firsthand – working around the global clock. The process helps students to build skills in collaboration, negotiation, cross-cultural communication, and project management. At the

end of the semester, the Pittsburgh students again collaborate with Qatar students in a global case competition on disaster relief. This project requires students to analyze cultural considerations from a variety of perspectives and deliver their case recommendations via a written report and video presentation.

I have also been active in several service-learning projects. As Jacoby (1996) states, "service-learning is a form of experiential education in which students engage in activities that address human and community needs together with structured opportunities intentionally designed to promote student learning and development" (p. 5). I currently co-teach a course with several faculty in my Program, including co-panelist Randy Weinberg, entitled Information Systems Applications. This course is a senior capstone project course where teams of students analyze, design and build an information system for a real-world non-profit organization. The course is a full-emersion project based course with limited classroom instruction. I also served for several years as an instructor for the Information Systems in the Community Summer Institute at Carnegie Mellon University, which was an intensive, 6-week, summer service-learning project in information systems for students from partner HBCUs. In both of these courses, I have found that the hands-on / real-world approach helps build students' perceptions of their skills and their exposure to a variety of IT skills (e.g., project management, technical, and teamwork abilities).

2.6 Randy Weinberg

As this panel notes as a main theme, service learning is increasingly common in undergraduate Information Systems and Computer Science curricula. There is a growing body of research reports and literature that document theory, practice and current experience in service learning. Service learning provides students with guided and supervised active-learning opportunities in practical, "real world" situations with community partners outside the classroom. Students frequently report a wide range of positive outcomes, including increased confidence, better communication skills, sharper technical skills, and sense of accomplishment. For a recent collection of articles on service learning in Computer and Information Sciences, see, for example, Nejmeh (2012).

What has been under-investigated are the benefits of the experience for service learning community partners. Recent interesting reports suggest that outcomes for community partners sponsoring Information Systems or Computer Science projects are often less than ideal. In fact, outcomes for community partners may actually be of little or no value, and, in some cases, even harmful as students may deliver unmaintainable, expensive and unreliable solutions (Connolly, 2012).

Panelist Jeria Quesenberry, Information Systems colleagues and I co-teach a senior capstone project course in which teams of students engage in semester length service learning projects with (usually) local, non-profit community partner organizations. Over the years, we have supervised dozens of such engagements and assessed the apparent quality of team process and deliverables. The lasting value our student teams have typically provided for their community partners, however, has generally not been remarkable. Systems solutions that are incomplete, not-quite-functional, not properly deployed, not fully tested or documented, or that meet student needs rather than partner needs are not unusual. Shifting emphasis, we have recently begun to focus on achieving value-added, sustainable community partner outcomes as a key component of the course design and assessment of student achievement.

3. REFERENCES

[1] Bergmann, J. and Sams, A. (2008/2009). "Remixing Chemistry Class." *Learning & Leading with Technology*, December 2008/January 2009, (36:4), 22-27.

[2] Connolly, R. (2012). "Is There Service In Computer Service Learning?" *Proceedings of ACM SIGCSE'12, Association for Computing Machinery,* Raleigh, NC, USA. 337-342.

[3] Helle, L., Tynjälä, P., & Olkinuora, E. (2006). "Project-based Learning in Post-Secondary Education–Theory, Practice and Rubber Sling Shots." *Higher Education*, (51:2), 287-314.

[4] Jacoby, B. (1996). "Service-Learning in Today's Higher Education." In Jacoby, B. (Ed.), *Service-Learning in Higher Education: Concepts and Practices.* San Francisco, California: Jossey-Bass, 3-25.

[5] Nejmeh, B.A. (2012). "Service-Learning in the Computer and Information Sciences: Lessons Learned and Guidance for the Future." In Nejmeh, B.A., (Ed.), *Service-Learning in the Computer and Information Sciences: Practical Applications in Engineering Education*, John Wiley & Sons, Inc., Hoboken, NJ, USA. doi: 10.1002/9781118319130.ch25.

[6] Straumsheim, Carl (2013). "Still in Favor of the Flip." *Inside Higher Ed*, October 30, 2013, http://www.insidehighered.com/news/2013/10/30/despite-new-studies-flipping-classroom-still-enjoys-widespread-support.

[7] Weis, W. L. (2000). "Service-Learning in Business Curricula: Walking the Talk." *National Society for Experiential Education Quarterly*: 11-16.

Corporate Psychopaths: Implications for the IS Workforce

Conrad Shayo
California State University,
San Bernardino
5500 University Parkway
San Bernardino, CA 92407
+1(909)537-5798
cshayo@csusb.edu

Frank Lin
California State University,
San Bernardino
5500 University Parkway
San Bernardino, CA 92407
+1(909)537-5787
flin@csusb.edu

Tapie C.E. Rohm
California State University,
San Bernardino
5500 University Parkway
San Bernardino, CA 92407
+1(909)537-5786
trohm@csusb.edu

Lorne Olfman
Claremont Graduate
University
130 E. 9th St.
Claremont, CA 91711
lorne.olfman@cgu.edu

ABSTRACT

The main purpose of this panel is to raise awareness on the prevalence of corporate psychopathy and draw on preliminary findings on a research in progress to discuss the implications of corporate psychopathy on IT workers. This is an issue that has not received much attention in the Computer and People Research community. The panel will propose measures that IT scholars, educators and practitioners can take to prevent or mitigate the impact of corporate psychopaths.

Categories and Subject Descriptors

K.7.4. Professional Ethics

General Terms

Management, Performance

Keywords

Work Climate, Psychopathy, Morale

1. INTRODUCTION

On September 2005, Elizabeth Millard posited the following question in the CIO Insight Online Magazine: 'Does It Take a Psychopath to Make a Good CIO?'[1]. Psychopaths are people in the general population (believed about 1%) who have a personality disorder that makes them lack conscience or empathy for others [2], [3] [10], [11]. Brain imaging research of individuals with psychopathic behavior indicates brain abnormalities in the corpus callosum, prefrontal cortex, temporal cortex, hippocampus, parahippocampal gyrus, angular gyrus, cingulate, basal ganglia, and amygdala. [4]. Although the term "psychopath" is used to refer to serial killers and disgusting criminals most of whom are in jail for life or on death row, (for example Charles Manson, Ted Bundy, or John Wayne Gacy), most psychopaths are not. They are found everywhere-- in our homes, neighborhoods, workplaces, churches and synagogues. Research indicates that

Permission to make digital or hard copies of all or part of this work for personal or classroom use is granted without fee provided that copies are not made or distributed for profit or commercial advantage and that copies bear this notice and the full citation on the first page. Copyrights for components of this work owned by others than ACM must be honored. Abstracting with credit is permitted. To copy otherwise, or republish, to post on servers or to redistribute to lists, requires prior specific permission and/or a fee. Request permissions from permissions@acm.org.
SIGMIS-CPR'14, May 29–31, 2014, Singapore, Singapore.
Copyright © 2014 ACM 978-1-4503-2625-4/14/05...$15.00.
http://dx.doi.org/10.1145/2599990.2600017

some psychopaths have successful corporate careers [5], [6]. Examples of corporate psychopaths found in the literature include: Ken Lay and Jeff Skilling at Enron, Al Dunlap at Sunbeam Corporation, Bernard Madoff at Bernard L. Madoff Investment Securities LLC and Bernie Ebbers at WorldCom [7]. While corporate psychopaths are highly intelligent, charismatic, and qualified; they are fearless, remorseless, and wired to get anything they want through glibness, superficial charm, conning and manipulation [3], [5], [6]. They are accomplished pathological liars: calculating, shallow, cold, and with a grandiose sense of self-worth. They refuse to take responsibility for their own actions, shamelessly take credit for others' accomplishments, and are incapable of experiencing feelings of others. They ensnare their victims to climb the corporate ladder, and once there, they ruthlessly punish anyone who gets on their way. [3]

2. Panel Topic Areas

Corporate Psychopathy Issues and Preliminary Research Findings: [Conrad Shayo]. IT workers cannot insulate themselves from the impact of corporate psychopaths on their work and future careers. Some of the main issues relate to what the unit of analysis should be, and the type of organizations psychopaths are mostly attracted to: Should IT workers view the psychopathic behavior as emanating from individuals in the organization leadership or the organization as a whole? For example, Milton Friedman takes the view that a corporation can neither be moral or immoral, so the unit of analysis should focus on the individual. Peter Drucker takes the opposite view, that it is, the corporation should be held socially responsible for its actions. Noam Chomsky and Robert Hare think both units of analysis are fine [8]. Moreover, the literature on corporate psychopaths suggests that corporate psychopaths are mainly attracted to some organizations more than others and some positions in the organization than others. The CEO, COO, and CFO positions are mentioned often in the literature [9], but are some corporate psychopaths attracted to the CIO position? The above discussion will be followed by a presentation of preliminary research findings on the impact of corporate psychopathy on IT workers' perceptions of job satisfaction, workforce bullying, excessive workload, employee commitment to the organization, organization commitment to employees, and organizational constraints and support.

Proposed Measures for Dealing with Corporate Psychopathy: [Frank Lin]. It is readily acknowledged that most IT and HR professionals are not trained to identify corporate psychopaths [6], [7]. Psychopaths use their intelligence, qualifications, manipulation and charisma to woo their gullible victims very carefully. They make them feel they are their best friend, and by the time they realize it, they have done their damage [8]. It is up to the non-psychopathic corporate leadership to develop a long term corporate succession strategy that monitors, evaluates, and grooms employees with leadership potential. Some of the issues center on: what happens when the leadership has a critical mass of psychopaths as was the case with Enron? How should organizations prevent the formation of a psychopathic leadership? What role should the Board of Directors or shareholders play? What role should IT researchers and educators play in exposing IS practitioners and students to the existence of psychopathic behavior in organizations? What are the dangers of stigmatizing (false-positive) individuals as psychopaths when in reality they are not? Should there be a voluntary assessment instrument to assess presence of psychopathy in potential leaders?

Preliminary Findings [Tapie Rohm]. The panelists are currently using the Psychopathy Measure–Management Research Version (PM-MR) developed by Clive Boddy to collect the preliminary data that will be presented by Dr. Rohm.

3. Panelists

Conrad Shayo studies and consults in the areas of IT assimilation, performance measurement and end- user computing. He participates as a California Awards for Excellence (CAPE) Examiner evaluating organizations that apply for the Malcolm Baldrige excellence award. He will discuss the most recent literature on corporate psychopathy.

Frank Lin studies and consults in the areas of organizational assessment, business process improvement/redesign, organizational modeling, enterprise architecture, strategic use of information technology, diffusion of information technology in organizations, and global and cultural intelligence. He will discuss some proposed measures for dealing with corporate psychopathy.

Tapie C.E. Rohm studies and consults in the areas of IT security, informatics, IT strategy, and virtual societies. He is the founding president of the International Information Management Association. He will present some preliminary research findings on the impact of corporate psychopathy on IT workers.

4. Panel Moderator and Format

Dr. Lorne Olfman the panel moderator will provide the background on the panel and moderate the panel presentations and deliberations from the audience.

5. ACKNOWLEDGMENTS

Our thanks go to Dr. Clive Boddy for allowing us to use his Psychopathy Measure – Management Research Version Instrument.

6. REFERENCES

[1] Millard, E. (2005, September 28). Does it Take a Psychopath to Make a Good CIO? Retrieved from CIO Insight: http://www.cioinsight.com/c/a/Expert-Voices/Does-it-Take-a-Psychopath-to-Make-a-Good-CIO/ [Accessed 04/16/2014]

[2] Quilty, L.C., Ayearst, L., Chmielewski, M., Pollock, B.g., & Bagby, R.M. (2013). The Psychometric Properties of the Personality Inventory for DSM-5 in an APA DSM-5 Field Trial Sample. *Assessment 20(3)*, 362 –369.

[3] Hare, R. (1999). Without Conscience: The Disturbing World of the Psychopaths Among Us.Guildford Press, New York: NY.

[4] Raine, A., Todd Lencz, T., Taylor,K., Hellige, J.B., Bihrle, S., Lacasse,L., Lee, M., Ishikawa, S., Colletti, P. (2003). "Corpus Callosum Abnormalities in Psychopathic Antisocial Individuals." *JAMA Psychiatry. 60(11) pp.1134-1142*

[5] Boddy, C.R., Ladyshewsky, R.K. (2010). "The Influence of Corporate Psychopaths on Corporate Social Responsibility and Organizational Commitment to Employees." *Journal of Business Ethics*, 97: pp. 1-19.

[6] Strout, M. (2005). *The Sociopath Next Door*. Broadway Books, New York: NY.

[7] Purdue, A. D.(2011, August). *Psychology and Corporate Crime*. (Master's Thesis), Retrieved from Appalachian State University: http://libres.uncg.edu/ir/asu/f/Pardue,%20Angela_2011_Thesis.pdf [Accessed 04/16/2014]

[8] Hare, R. A. (2013, January 13). *The Psychopathic Corporation--A Clinical Diagnosis (PCL-R)*. Retrieved from You Tube: http://www.youtube.com/watch?v=lmUXp_zE14E [Accessed 04/16/2014]

[9] Boddy, C. (2011). The Corporate Psychopaths Theory of the Global Financial Crisis. *Journal of Business Ethics*, (102) pp. 255–259.

[10] Babiak, P. & Hare, R.D. (2006). *Snakes in Suits: When Psychopaths Go to Work*. Harper Collins Publishers, New York:NY.

[11] Hare, R.D. (2011). *Without Conscience: The Disturbing World of the Psychopaths Among Us*. The Guilford Press, Florance, KY.

Collaboration in the Open-source Arena: The WebKit Case

Jose Teixeira
University of Turku
Turku, Finland
jose.teixeira@utu.fi

Tingting Lin
University of Turku
Turku, Finland
tingting.lin@utu.fi

ABSTRACT

In an era of software crisis, the move of firms towards distributed software development teams is being challenged by emerging collaboration issues. On this matter, the open-source phenomenon may shed some light, as successful cases on distributed collaboration in the open-source community have been recurrently reported. In this paper, we explore the collaboration networks in the WebKit open-source project, by mining WebKit's source-code version-control-system data with Social Network Analysis (SNA). Our approach allows us to observe how key events in the mobile-device industry have affected the WebKit collaboration network over time. With our findings, we show the explanation power from network visualizations capturing the collaborative dynamics of a high-networked software project over time; and highlight the power of the open-source *fork* concept as a nexus enabling both features of competition and collaboration. We also reveal the WebKit project as a valuable research site manifesting the novel notion of open-coopetition, where rival firms collaborate with competitors in the open-source community.

Categories and Subject Descriptors
• *Software and its engineering~Open source model* • *Software and its engineering~Programming teams*

General Terms
Management, Economics, Human Factors, Theory

Keywords
Free-software, open-source, distributed software development, software ecosystem, WebKit, coopetition, open-coopetition

INTRODUCTION
In an era of software crisis[1], the move of firms towards geographically-distributed, and often off-shored, software

---

[1] A brief discussion on the software-crisis is provided by Fitzgerald, B. "Software Crisis 2.0." Computer 45.4 (2012): 89-91.

Permission to make digital or hard copies of all or part of this work for personal or classroom use is granted without fee provided that copies are not made or distributed for profit or commercial advantage and that copies bear this notice and the full citation on the first page. Copyrights for components of this work owned by others than ACM must be honored. Abstracting with credit is permitted. To copy otherwise, or republish, to post on servers or to redistribute to lists, requires prior specific permission and/or a fee. Request permissions from permissions@acm.org.

SIGMIS-CPR'14, May 29–31, 2014, Singapore, Singapore.
Copyright is held by the owner/author(s). Publication rights licensed to ACM.
ACM 978-1-4503-2625-4/14/05...$15.00.
http://dx.doi.org/10.1145/2599990.2600009

development teams is being challenged by collaboration issues. On this matter, the open-source phenomenon may shed some light, as successful cases on distributed collaboration in the open-source community have been recurrently reported [1], [2]. While practitioners move with difficulty towards globally distributed software development, there is a lack of research in academia addressing the collaboration dynamics of large-scale distributed software projects[3], [4]. In this paper, we attempt to bridge this gap by exploring the collaboration networks within the WebKit open-source project.

WebKit is an open-source project providing an engine that renders and interprets content from the World Wide Web. Its technology permeates our digital life since it can be found in the most recent computers, tablets and mobile devices sold by Apple, Google, Samsung, Nokia, RIM, HTC, and others. With more than 10 years of history, the WebKit project has brought together volunteers and firm-sponsored software developers that collaborate over the Internet by open and transparent manners while giving up the traditional intellectual property rights.

Previous socio-technological analysis addressing collaboration within large scale open-source software projects tend to adopt either of the two equally unsatisfactory alternatives: (1) providing thick qualitative descriptions of selected cases, thus overlooking the actors, actions and interdependent patterns of the collaborative network [5]–[7]; or (2) reducing figurational complexity to a set of quantitative indicators, thus disfiguring all practical purposes of the phenomena under investigation [8]–[10].

We opted to make our socio-technological analysis, without confining ourselves to one of the aforementioned alternatives, by analyzing how key actors and actions in the mobile-device industry affected the WebKit collaboration network over time. While addressing a previous call[11] for the advancement of methods and techniques to support the visualization of temporal aspects (e.g. pace, sequence) to represent change and evolution in ecosystems[2], we employed Social Network Analysis (SNA) over publicly-available and naturally-occurring open-source data that allowed us to re-construct and visualize the evolution of the WebKit collaboration in a sequence of networks.

The rest of this paper is organized as follows: after we briefly introduce the WebKit project, we review a series of seminal works on open-source software, and previous research addressing the open-source phenomenon by employing SNA methodological approaches. We then elaborate our methodology in details, followed by an illustration of our findings. In the end, we discuss

---

[2] Basole, R. employs the ecosystems term as a complex network of companies interacting with each other, directly and indirectly, to provide a broad array of products and services. Thus the ecosystem metaphor can also be applied in the WebKit project.

the contributions of this paper and conclude with future-oriented remarks.

THE WebKit PROJECT

Within this section we introduce to the readers the WebKit project, giving it central significance to the research context, where we address it as a complex IT artifact that emerges and evolves as function of techno-social processes over time [12].

WebKit is an engine for browsers and other software applications. It renders and interprets content deployed on the World Wide Web where standards like HTML and JavaScript predominate. WebKit is licensed under BSD-style and LGPL licenses, thus it is freely usable for both open source and proprietary applications [13]. WebKit technologies are remarkably ubiquitous as they empower many Internet browsers (such as Apple Safari and Google Chrome) and plenty of mobile devices sold by Apple, Nokia, Samsung, RIM, HTC, Motorola, and others. Moreover, WebKit is embedded on thousands of software applications running on Windows, Mac and Linux operating-systems.

The WebKit project started as a fork of two other open-source projects: the KTML project and the KJS libraries provided by the KDE open-source community. Forking is an essential event shaping open-source communities [2], [14]; it reflects the freedom of allowing anyone to create derivative works for any purpose. In this case Apple, after deciding to enter the Internet browser market, decided to fork the KTML and KJS projects inheriting a valuable code-base for further development in accordance with their own strategy. Since its source-code (i.e. the software technology blueprint) was published by Apple, it has been further developed by non-affiliated open-source developers (i.e. from the KDE community) and others from firms like Apple, Google, Nokia, RIM, Igalia, Intel and Samsung. Since Apple's WebKit debut, the overall project was once again forked in 2010, leading to the creation of the WebKit2 project for a more platform-independent version. More recently, Google announced that it had forked core components of WebKit to be used in future versions of its browsers[3]. Figure 1 illustrates the forking within the WebKit history.

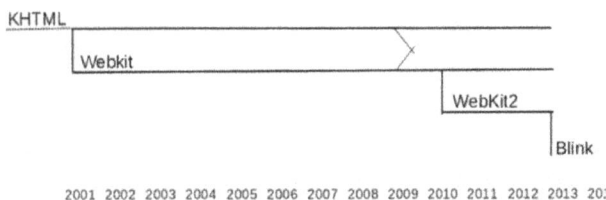

Figure 1: Forks within the WebKit project

Resembling the peer-reviewed mechanisms employed in the academia, the WebKit coding policy distinguishes and empowers different actors, including regular contributors, committers and reviewers. Similar to other open-source communities, the WebKit project is also based on a high level of meritocracy, where software developers are ranked by their prior contributions to the community [2], [15] that are evaluated by their peers within the network.

Even if WebKit has attained a remarkable ubiquity, the project has been rarely addressed by the academia. In this research, we strive to study the collaboration dynamics in the open-source community; WebKit is then an ideal case field given its highly collaborative and networked characteristics.

RELEVANT LITERATURE

The open-source phenomenon has attracted steady attention from multi-disciplinary scholars in the last decades [2], [5], [14], [16]. To illustrate the growing academic relevance of the open-source phenomenon, we observed that many prominent academic outlets, including "Research Policy" ,"IEEE Network", "IEEE Software", "Management Science" and the "Journal of the Association for Information Systems", have recently published special issues on open-source software. Several recent and comprehensive literature reviews have addressed the open-source phenomenon [17]–[20]. And the phenomenon keeps evolving from the earliest purist views focusing on freedom [21], to a newer perspective considering open-source as an alternative and viable business [14], [22].

Few scholars have leveraged the network perspective and the SNA approach to study the open-source phenomenon. However, there are some notable exceptions [8], [10], [23] who have based their network analysis on metadata from public source-code repositories and/or email data in bug-fixing contexts. We also conducted SNA in this research; however, unlike most of the above-mentioned research with cross-sectional analysis of static networks, we adopted a longitudinal view as we are more interested on how the collaboration network evolves over time. Moreover, this research departs from the prior research with a new aim to understand how mobile device vendors collaborate on the open-source arena. Rather than analyzing solely the social network of the WebKit community, we also acknowledged key actors and actions on the higher level of mobile-device industry, seeking to understand how key exogenous events in the industry have affected WebKit and its social network. To sum up, rather than extracting quantitative indicators from the collaborative network by solely looking at IT artifacts[4], we also look at its surrounding industrial environment seeking for understanding on how different happenings on the industry shaped the collaboration network developing the same IT artifacts.

METHODOLOGY

In this section we will elaborate on our research design and methodological details. Without ever leaving our labs, and by looking at naturally-occurring data publicly available on the Internet, our methodology combines the screening of key happening in the mobile devices industry with a computer-based method of SNA.

We started by screening, by ethnographic manners, publicly available data such as company announcements, financial reports and specialized-press that allowed us to review immense online information pertaining to the competitive mobile-devices industry; therefore, we were able to study the insight of the industrial context. After attaining a better understanding of the the competitive dynamics of the mobile-devices industry, we later started extracting and analyzing the social network of the WebKit community leveraging SNA [24], [25], which is an emergent method widely established across disciplines of social sciences in

---

[3]Google announcement of Blink, a WebKit project fork is available at http://blog.chromium.org/2013/04/

[4]In our case WebKit source-code and it's version-control-system

general[25]–[28] and information systems in particular [10], [29], [30] .

We first built the social network matrices with UCINET[31] based on the WebKit project change-log. In the analysis, we focused on the visualization of the collaboration network, which evolves over time, to reveal dynamics among the WebKit software developers. We then attempted to understand the visualized networks with our previously acquired tacit understanding from the competitive mobile-devices industry. The visualization, together with a deeper understanding of the phenomenon under investigation, corresponds to the notion of figuration [32]as pointed out by some prior multi-disciplinary studies [33]–[36]. We provide more details of our data collection and analysis in the following sections.

Data-collection

Our screening of public and natural-occurring data available on the Internet followed the general ethnographic principles that have been extensively established in social sciences and information systems [37], [38]. Specifically, we have reviewed relevant firm's public announcements, publicly available financial reports, news from specialized press and discussions in forums and blogs. Our empirical materials span the time period from September 2006 until April 2013, and all are freely available to the public on the Internet.

After acquiring a deeper understanding from the competitive dynamics of mobile-devices industry, we also conducted SNA which allows us to depict overall pictures of the collaborative dynamics among different developers in the WebKit project. The input data of SNA is based on different source-code versions of the WebKit project. Our last compilation was filed on 3rd April 2013, which comprises ca. 1.4GB. From the version-control change-log documentation[5], we extracted basic information as input for the SNA, including each developer's email address and the time stamp when he/she made a change to a specific file (see Figure 2). We then connect the developers who work on the same file, and construct a network of collaboration activities among all the developers. With the visualization of the collaboration network over time, we aim to understand the evolution of the code-based collaboration with a lens of social structure. We will describe the details of our data analysis in the following section.

Data-analysis

While screening the competitive dynamics of mobile-devices industry we selected key events from the industry regarding open-source software in general and the WebKit project in particular. We started with a chronological approach; however, we went back and forth in the dynamic history of the mobile-devices industry, trying to make sense of our online observations. Our practice-accumulated skills, regarding software development, open-source software and software version control systems, dealing with very specific concepts and terminologies, revealed to be essential for sense-making of the collected ethnographic material. We have identified a set of endogenous and exogenous events that, according to our interpretations, could have impacted the evolutionary dynamics of the WebKit project (see Table 1). These major events give us a more clear history line to understand the evolution of this project, as well as the industrial context in which it is embedded.

Table 1. Key selected events within WebKit

Date	Event
Jun 2001	WebKit started within Apple as a fork of KHTML and KJS open-source projects.
Sep 2006	Apple, forced by the open-source community, published WebKit source-code in a public repository.
Jun 2007	Apple released 1st generation of iPhone
Sep 2008	Google launched Chrome and Android
Jun 2009	Nokia and Intel Announced Strategic Relationship
Feb 2011	Nokia and Microsoft formed a broad strategic partnership. Intel searched for new partners for Meego.
Jul 2012	The patent war broke out between Apple and Samsung, and their hostilities reached climax with the first trial in U.S. $1.049 billion in damages.
Apr 2013	Google announced to fork WebKit's core components, just 1 month after Apple registered WebKit as its trademark.

The qualitative ethnographic efforts, conducted prior to and during our computerized SNA, revealed to be fundamental while analyzing the WebKit social network evolutionary dynamics. To prepare for the SNA, the identified industry-events were used as partitions on the whole period of the project history since 2006[6]. We then applied SNA and constructed the collaboration network of developers in each partitioned time slice. In this way, we are able to assess how the collaboration network has evolved over time in response to the exogenous events in the industry. Specifically, the input of SNA was based on developers' active contributions to the WebKit source-code from 1 September 2006 till 3 April 2013. These contributions were documented in the publicly available WebKit change log produced both by the WebKit committers (i.e. the ones with read-write access to the project repository) and the WebKit reviewers (i.e. the ones with a final word on what stays in or out of the project blueprints). Figure 2 shows a sample of the change log to illustrate how the collaboration network is identified and constructed.

The log was parsed, validated and processed with the Python programming language, tracing back all collaborations in a period of almost 7 years since September 2006. By 3 April 2013, when Google forked the WebKit project to create Blink[39], we could identify 445 nodes and 2169 edges, forming a complex mesh in which 445 software developers have worked together.

---

[5]A book on the practice of version control systems in the open-source community is freely available on the Internet at http://svnbook.red-bean.com/. It might contribute to a better understanding on how our data was collected.

[6]Although the WebKit project started in 2001, in the raw-data we can access, the earliest change on WebKit source-code is only documented in 2006.

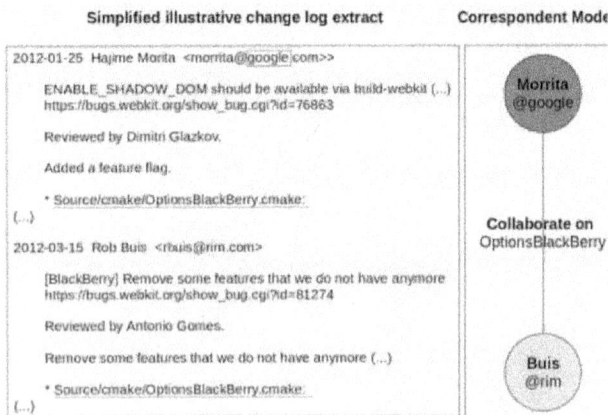

Figure 2: Modeling the WebKit change log

The collaborative network during a certain time slice can be formally defined as:

$$Gt = (V, Av, E)$$

Where:

V = A set of nodes representing the developers contributing to the WebKit open-source software project

E = A set of edges, identifying the connections between two developers if they have worked on the same software source-code file.

Av = A set of nodes-attributes, capturing each developer's company affiliation. This information is extracted from the email address of each developer.

Based on this definition, we used UCINET[40] to build the network matrices. Various numeric network measures have been established in SNA: For example, eigenvector-centrality [41], [42] degree-centrality and betweenness-centrality [25] reveal the importance of a node in a network. Other aspects of a network can also be manifested with important measures such as network-density [24], cluster coefficients [43], strength of ties [44], etc. However, as our SNA goes hand-in-hand with a interpretivist ethnography on the competitive mobile industry, the visualization of network graphs is sufficient to naturally uncover the history line and the dynamics of collaboration in a qualitative and straight-forward way. The visualization of social networks has been widely used by scholars [33]–[36], but few studies have explored the time dimension to observe how networks evolve [45]. We used the software Visone [46] to visualize a sequence of networks according to the established time slices partitioned by the major events, and interpreted the network evolution with understandings generated from the previous collection of rich qualitative material capturing the competitive dynamics of the mobile-devices industry.

For a better understanding on the industry level, we opt to focus on the network of developers from major mobile device vendors involved in the WebKit project. The selection of these major vendors is based on a prior public-report by Bitergia on WebKit collaboration [47], where the 10 most active organizations have been identified on the development of the WebKit project, including Apple, Google, Nokia, Rim, Igalia, Intel, Samsung, Univ. Szeged (Inf), Adobe, and Torchmobile. Therefore, we highlighted these 10 vendors with different colors in the visualized networks, and marked other developers' affiliation as "other" and in gray color. It is worth noticing that most software developers within WebKit are non-affiliated developers without explicit firm-sponsorship; therefore, most of "other" developers are independent contributors.

FINDINGS

In this section, we illustrate our findings with network visualizations showing the evolution of the collaboration network throughout the development progress of WebKit software source-code.

Our visualizations (Figure 3-6) facilitate an intuitive understanding on how key players in the mobile-devices industry collaborate in the open-source arena. The first visualizations (Figure 3-4) capture the early development of the WebKit project; while our last visualizations (Figure 5-6) capture the hyper-collaborative nature of the WebKit project during the last four years, when it started empowering our computers and mobile-devices in a larger scale. Using Visone [46], we also visualized the centrality of each developer by differentiation on node size, i.e. the larger the node is, the more central the represented developer acts in the community. The value of centrality depends on the number of adjacent nodes that a node is connected with. Therefore, the higher a developer's centrality is, the more active he/she is in collaborating with others.

Our first network-visualization, i.e. Figure 3, depicts the collaboration on the WebKit project from 1 September 2006 (i.e. when apple first published WebKit source-code) to 29 June 2007 (i.e. when Apple released the first generation iPhone leading to the emergence of millions of mobile-devices powered by WebKit). From this visualization of early WebKit history, we can observe four developers from Apple who collaborate only among themselves, segregated from others in the WebKit community; while one Apple-affiliated developer acts as a bridge to the rest of WebKit community. Interestingly, the latter Apple developer doesn't have any connection with other four colleagues during this particular period in the project. Although the total number of nodes is relatively small at this early stage, there is no isolates despite the evident segregation between the two sub-networks.

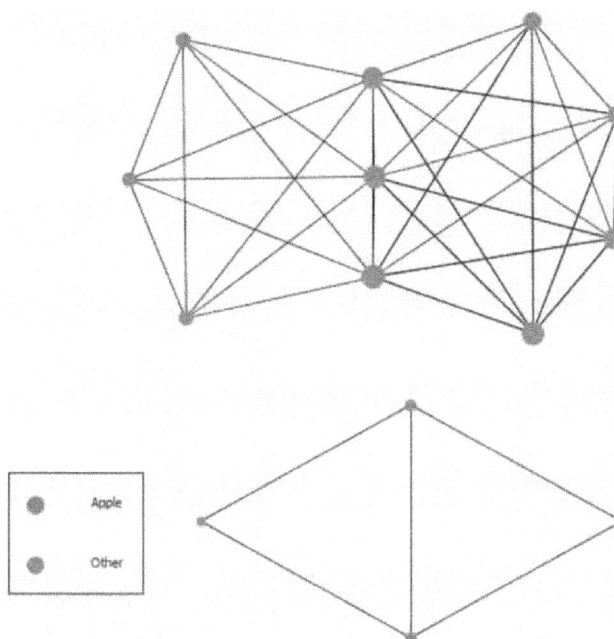

Figure 3: Visualizing the WebKit bootstrap

Our second network visualization, Figure 4, captures a thriving phase of collaboration within the WebKit project from 29 June 2007 (i.e. the release of the first iPhone) to the end of September 2008 (i.e. the month that Google launched Chrome and Android platforms integrating WebKit). Although the number of Apple affiliated developers remains the same, the project has attracted increasing participation among non-affiliated developers. Meanwhile, one developer from Torchmobile emerged in the network. In addition, the density from the network has increased compared to the last visualization in Figure 3.

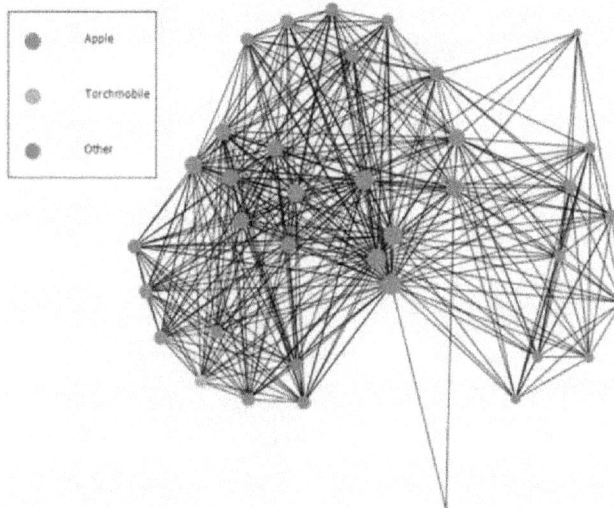

Figure 4: WebKit and KHTML join forces

This eye-opening expansion of the WebKit community and intensified collaboration can be partially explained by the unforking of KDE's KHTML and [48]. It indicates that after years of split development of WebKit and KHTML (though with code exchanges to integrate on both sides), Apple and KHTML developers have decided to increase collaboration and many KHTML developers have become reviewers and submitters for the WebKit source-code repository, and vice versa.

Our third network-visualization, Figure 5, demonstrates the later phase of the WebKit project, starting from the end of September 2008 (i.e. the launch of Chrome and Android) to 3 February 2011 (i.e. when Nokia and Microsoft announced a strategic partnership leaving alone Intel with the Meego platform [49], [50].

During this phase, considering the companies' participation on the

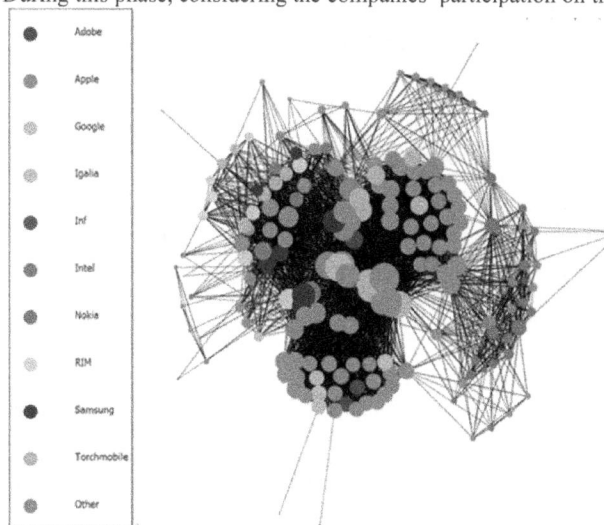

Figure 5: Mass collaboration

WebKit development, Apple has lost its unique central-role, and shares network-centrality with Google, Samsung and Igalia. On the other hand, RIM and Nokia, adopting WebKit within their latest mobile platforms, remains in periphery with observable separation from the most central players.

However, thanks to our previous qualitative ethnographic work we must highlight that this visualization must be interpreted carefully, since Igalia, a Spanish firm specialized on open-source software development services, has been working on the projects during this period. Providing software services to many major firms, Igalia often represents the interests of Nokia and Intel on the aemo and Meego platforms [51]. Therefore, given Igalia's central position in the network, we cannot conclude the peripheral role of Nokia and Intel despite their network position. Nevertheless, the clear separation between Nokia and Intel, who are former partners in the Meego project [52], [53], in the network is consistent with the breakage of cooperation between the two companies, due to the new partnership strategy Nokia adopted at that time.

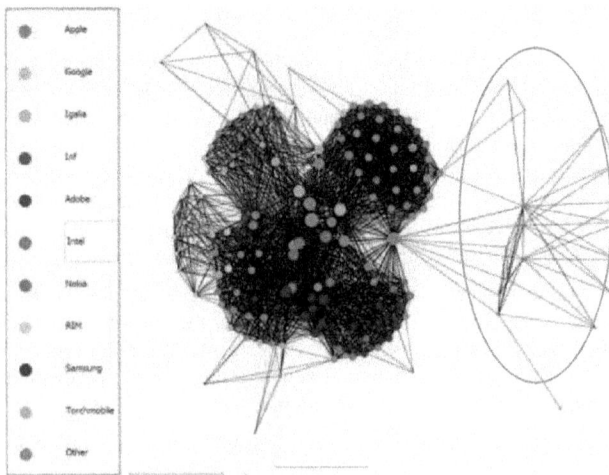

Figure 6: Patent-wars, trademarks and forking

Our last network-visualization, Figure 6, illustrates the latest phase of the WebKit project from the end of 3 February 2011 (i.e. Nokia and Microsoft's announcement of a strategic partnership) to 3 April 2013 (i.e. Google forks the WebKit core creating the Blink project).

Similar to Figure 5, in Figure 6 we can also observe that contributors sponsored by Nokia and Intel are on opposite sides of the network, reflecting the lack of collaboration between those two firms in the WebKit project. This lack of collaboration increased as Nokia became increasingly dependent on Microsoft software to power their devices. Therefore, Nokia become even more peripheral in the open-source community, which is also visible in the visualized network. As compared to Figure 5, here the blue nodes representing Nokia developers have significantly decreased in size and moved further away from the central groups.

Comparing Apple and Samsung's roles in the networks shown in Figure 5 and Figure 6, we also attain interesting findings: Even if Samsung and Apple are involved in expensive patent wars in the courts [54] and stopped collaborating on hardware components [55], their contributions remained strong and central within the WebKit open-source project. However, the distance between the two groups has indeed increased as the rivalry has upgraded since the patent wars in 2012.

Additionally, across all visualizations, non-affiliated developers, who are often volunteers without firm-sponsorship, are more central within the WebKit collaboration network than developers affiliate with the 10 organizations we highlighted according to the previously mentioned Bitergia study [47].

DISCUSSION

Before discussing the contributions and implications of our study, it is important to mention that this research is entirely based on naturally-occurring data available to the public on the Internet. Thanks to WebKit's strict policy for committers and reviewers, our data set was extremely clean, facilitating a smooth data extraction ahead of SNA. Thus, our data cleansing efforts were minimal, contrasting with prior research reporting enormous difficulties in the collecting, cleaning and screening of open-source projects data[8], [10], [23].

Academic contributions

Our findings seem to integrate with a variety of theories on management, cooperation and innovation in networked

communities. Perhaps one of the most interesting ones, that explains features from the evolutionary collaborative dynamics of the WebKit project is a management theory on the paradox of firm investment in open source software [56] stating that in a scenario of pooled R&D development, the firms adopting open source components have four common characteristics:

• there is pre-existing open source code being developed without the intervention of the focal firms;

• the "buy vs. build" decision to use external innovation is made easier because the code was "free";

• the firms were willing to contribute back to the existing projects on an ongoing basis, to assure that the technology continued to meet their respective needs, to maintain absorptive capacity, and to avoid discouraging external innovators;

• the firms could continue to yield returns for internal innovation by combining the internal and external technologies to make a product offering that was not directly available through open source.

In this WebKit case, we can observe that the most active firms contributing to the project exhibited all of the previous mentioned characteristics, while the more peripheral firms failed to meet the third characteristic. This last group of firms were clearly more interested in integrating WebKit into their technological pools without strategically contributing back[7].

Another theoretical contribution that emerged from our approach highlights the power of the open-source *fork* concept as a nexus enabling both features of competition and collaboration. As previously mentioned, *fork* reflects the open-source freedom of allowing anyone to create derivative works. A *fork* divide a community in two, the simple existence of a threat of a *fork* have significant implications within a previously united community. As a form of schism, all developers have the freedom of leaving the community, with a copy of the existing code-base and further develop the project by its own manners. It was argued before that [57] that *fork* serves as an invisible hand of sustainability ensuring that the code-base remains open and best fulfills the needs of the community it lives on. The occurrence of several forks on the initial WebKit code-base (see Figure 1) is better understood with prior work [58] that identifies the need of porting a program to a new hardware or software architecture as a driver of forking[8].

In the WebKit case, *fork* enabled a set of networked collaboration features: The existence of an existing code-base reduced the barriers to entry of firms seeking to integrate Internet-browsing technologies into their digital platforms. The initial WebKit code-base was then forked several times as more and more firms were interested in porting the "program" into heterogeneous hardware/software stacks. On other hand, the threat of a *fork* stimulated a collaborative sense of community [59] and the setup of basic norms and values [60] unifying the community against possible break-up forces. All this in a scenario of pooled R&D where costs and governance are shared within a collaborative community [56].

---

[7]Coincidence or not, firms that played a more central role in the WebKit project such as Google, Apple and Samsung were by 2013 the leaders of the mobile-devices industry. While more more peripheral firms such as RIM and Nokia lost market-share.

[8]I.e Google argued that the complex architectures of WebKit were slowing down the collective pace of innovation when announcing its Blink fork of WebKit.

Even if the initial goal of this research was to study collaboration in the WebKit project, we identified that *fork* also enables a set of competition features: First of all, even if *fork* facilitates the commoditization of technology that can be copied and ported to architecturally different products, in the WebKit case this only concentrated a small effort of the "whole product" offering from many of the involved firms. Firms relying on WebKit source of innovation, kept differentiating both while porting it to their own architectures and in other areas of their computer-based platform/ecosystem. Moreover, firms exhibit competition when recruiting talented open-source developers or when sourcing from open-source service providers[9]. Besides competing for talented labor needed for developing such a large-scale open-source *fork*, firms also compete for abortive capacity[56], [62], technological learning [6] and organizational learning [6], [63]. With the previous mentioned reduced barriers to entry there is an increased risk of free riding [64], innovators must master the open-source community project for better guiding its development according their own interests while being aware that copycats[10] can always *fork* their contributions.

Our research witnessed a peculiar extent of collaboration between rival firms from the evolving network, moreover we recognized *fork* as a nexus enabling both features of competition and collaboration, leading us with the proposition that the open-source community can also be a great arena to observe the phenomenon of coopetition[65], [66]. However, we were not able find published Management or Information Systems literature exploring coopetition features in the open-source arena[11], an area that we will further explore while proposing already a neologism:

Open-coopetition: A portmanteau of cooperative competition in the open-source arena, where R&D is jointly performed by competing firms by open-source manners, giving-up authorship-granted intellectual property rights for maximizing both blueprints transparency and collaborative benefits.

Implications for practice

We shed lights on the potential of visualizing the evolutionary collaborative dynamics in R&D projects, especially for practitioners dealing with large-scale and networked productions. Different stakeholders in large-scale open-source software projects could gain strategic and operational benefits: For software developers, our methods empower them with better understanding on the overall network to improve development processes. For users, adopters and integrators, we can depict the project evolution for thorough assessments of its sustainability and dynamics when reacting to exogenous events. And for investors, clarifying the network dynamics can improve the forecast of product attractiveness and future growth.

We also provided a rich description on how hight-tech giants collaborated with rival-competitors in the WebKit project by open-source manners. Given the current financial success of the high-tech firms with a more central role in WebKit development (i.e. Apple, Google, Samsung), R&D managers are reminded once again for the dangers of ignoring open-source software as an external source of innovation.

CONCLUDING REMARKS AND FUTURE RESEARCH

In this paper, we attempt to provide a better understanding of how key players of mobile-device industry collaborate in the open-source arena, by investigating the development of the WebKit project. We combined an ethnographic approach and network visualization supported by SNA. Our findings show the explanation power of such mixed-methods on the meanings of network dynamics and highlight the power of the open-source *fork* concept as a nexus enabling both features of competition and collaboration.

For future research, we aim to further theorize our findings integrating the notion of open-coopetition, in a quest for better understanding how firms collaborate with competitors in the open-source arena. We will further explore the concept of forking as we will align our research journey with an ongoing development of the WebKit project, assessing how the current WebKit social network will be affected by Google's recent decision to fork the WebKit project.

AKNOWLEDGEMENTS

The idea of this research project surged by pure serendipity at the *Inforte seminar on Big Data and Social Media Analytics* by Sudha Ram and Matti Rossi. The researchers thank the financial support from the *Fundação para a Ciência e a Tecnologia* (grant SFRHBD615612009) and *Liikesivistysrahasto* (grant 3-1815). Acknowledgements also for *Lero - the Irish software engineering research centre* were part of this research was conducted. Special thanks to Jari Salo, Reima Suomi, Sarah Beecham and Gregorio Robles for early comments on manuscripts. A last word to the WebKit developers for developing cool, open and research-friendly technologies.

More methodological details, data, high-resolution visualizations and source-code at http://users.utu.fi/joante/WebKitSNA/.

REFERENCES

[1] A. Bonaccorsi and C. Rossi, "Why open source software can succeed," *Res. Policy*, vol. 32, no. 7, pp. 1243–1258, 2003.

[2] E. Raymond, "The cathedral and the bazaar," *Knowl. Technol. Policy*, vol. 12, no. 3, pp. 23–49, 1999.

[3] B. Sengupta, S. Chandra, and V. Sinha, "A research agenda for distributed software development," in *Proceedings of the 28th international conference on Software engineering*, 2006, pp. 731–740.

[4] M. Paasivaara and C. Lassenius, "Collaboration practices in global inter□organizational software development projects," *Softw. Process Improv. Pr.*, vol. 8, no. 4, pp. 183–199, 2003.

[5] J. Lerner and J. Tirole, "Some simple economics of open source," *J. Ind. Econ.*, vol. 50, no. 2, pp. 197–234, 2002.

[6] A. Bonaccorsi, S. Giannangeli, and C. Rossi, "Entry strategies under competing standards: Hybrid business models in the open source software industry," *Manag. Sci.*, vol. 52, no. 7, pp. 1085–1098, 2006.

[7] S. Mian, J. Teixeira, and E. Koskivaara, "Open-Source Software Implications in the Competitive Mobile Platforms

---

[9] According Agerfalk and Fitzgerald open-source service providers are typically SMEs [61]

[10] Even if copycats term is often used in management to refer to free-riders in the emerging economies, in the open-source world it refers to firms that integrate open-source technologies without contributing back up-stream to its development.

[11] An interesting pharmaceutical article bridging open-source and coopetition by Munos, B. "Can open-source R&D reinvigorate drug research?" Nature Reviews Drug Discovery 5 (2006): , 723-729

Market," in *IFIP Wg 6.11 Conference on E-business, E-services, and E-society, I3E 2011*, 2011, pp. 110–129.

[8] L. Lopez-Fernandez, G. Robles, and J. M. Gonzalez-Barahona, "Applying social network analysis to the information in CVS repositories," 2004.

[9] K. Crowston and J. Howison, "The social structure of free and open source software development," *First Monday*, vol. 10, no. 2–7, 2005.

[10] J. Xu, S. Christley, and G. Madey, *Application of social network analysis to the study of open source software*. Elsevier Press, 2006.

[11] R. C. Basole, "Visualization of interfirm relations in a converging mobile ecosystem," *J. Inf. Technol.*, vol. 24, no. 2, pp. 144–159, 2009.

[12] W. J. Orlikowski and C. S. Iacono, "Research commentary: Desperately seeking the ' it' in it research—a call to theorizing the it artifact," *Inf. Syst. Res.*, vol. 12, no. 2, pp. 121–134, 2001.

[13] WebKit, "The WebKit Open Source Project - WebKit Project Goals." [Online]. Available: http://www.webkit.org/projects/goals.html. [Accessed: 14-Jun-2013].

[14] J. Feller and B. Fitzgerald, *Understanding open source software development*. Addison-Wesley London, 2002.

[15] S. Sharma, V. Sugumaran, and B. Rajagopalan, "A framework for creating hybrid open source software communities," *Inf. Syst. J.*, vol. 12, no. 1, pp. 7–25, 2002.

[16] S. Weber, *The success of open source*, vol. 368. Cambridge Univ Press, 2004.

[17] K.-J. Stol and M. A. Babar, "Reporting empirical research in open source software: the state of practice," in *Open Source Ecosystems: Diverse Communities Interacting*, Springer, 2009, pp. 156–169.

[18] J. Lindman, M. Rossi, and A. Paajanen, "Matching open source software licenses with corresponding business models," *IEEE Softw.*, vol. 28, no. 4, pp. 31–35, 2011.

[19] Ø. Hauge, C. Ayala, and R. Conradi, "Adoption of open source software in software-intensive organizations–A systematic literature review," *Inf. Softw. Technol.*, vol. 52, no. 11, pp. 1133–1154, 2010.

[20] A. Aksulu and M. Wade, "A comprehensive review and synthesis of open source research," *J. Assoc. Inf. Syst.*, vol. 11, no. 11, pp. 576–656, 2010.

[21] R. Stallman, *The GNU manifesto*. 1985.

[22] B. Fitzgerald, "The transformation of open source software," *Mis Q.*, pp. 587–598, 2006.

[23] S. Valverde and R. V. Solé, "Self-organization versus hierarchy in open-source social networks," *Phys. Rev. E*, vol. 76, no. 4, p. 046118, 2007.

[24] J. Scott, *Social network analysis*. SAGE Publications Limited, 2012.

[25] S. Wasserman and K. Faust, *Social network analysis: Methods and applications*, vol. 8. Cambridge university press, 1994.

[26] D. J. Watts, "The ' new' science of networks," *Annu. Rev. Sociol.*, pp. 243–270, 2004.

[27] B. Uzzi, "The sources and consequences of embeddedness for the economic performance of organizations: The network effect," *Am. Sociol. Rev.*, pp. 674–698, 1996.

[28] S. P. Borgatti and P. C. Foster, "The network paradigm in organizational research: A review and typology," *J. Manag.*, vol. 29, no. 6, pp. 991–1013, 2003.

[29] Y. Yoo, K. Lyytinen, and R. J. Boland, "Distributed innovation in classes of networks," in *Hawaii International Conference on System Sciences, Proceedings of the 41st Annual*, 2008, pp. 58–58.

[30] H. Oinas-Kukkonen, K. Lyytinen, and Y. Yoo, "Social networks and information systems: ongoing and future research streams," *J. Assoc. Inf. Syst.*, vol. 11, no. 2, p. 3, 2010.

[31] S. P. Borgatti, M. G. Everett, and L. C. Freeman, "Ucinet for Windows: Software for social network analysis," 2002.

[32] N. Elias, *What is sociology*. Columbia University Press, 1978.

[33] A. Cambrosio, P. Keating, and A. Mogoutov, "Mapping collaborative work and innovation in biomedicine: A computer-assisted analysis of antibody reagent workshops," *Soc. Stud. Sci.*, pp. 325–364, 2004.

[34] W. Glänzel and A. Schubert, "Analysing scientific networks through co-authorship," in *Handbook of quantitative science and technology research*, Springer, 2005, pp. 257–276.

[35] K. Porter, K. B. Whittington, and W. W. Powell, "The institutional embeddedness of high-tech regions: relational foundations of the Boston biotechnology community," *Clust. Networks Innov.*, vol. 261, p. 296, 2005.

[36] B. Å. Lundvall, *National Systems of Innovation: Towards a Theory of Innovation and Interactive Learning*. Anthem Press, 2010.

[37] P. Atkinson, "Rescuing autoethnography," *J. Contemp. Ethnogr.*, vol. 35, no. 4, pp. 400–404, 2006.

[38] M. Myers, "Investigating information systems with ethnographic research," *Commun. AIS*, vol. 2, no. 4es, p. 1, 1999.

[39] "Google sticks a fork in WebKit, announces Blink rendering engine | News | TechRadar." [Online]. Available: http://www.techradar.com/news/internet/web/google-sticks-a-fork-in-webkit-announces-blink-rendering-engine-1142386. [Accessed: 16-Jun-2013].

[40] S. P. Borgatti, M. G. Everett, and L. C. Freeman, "Ucinet for Windows: Software for social network analysis," 2002.

[41] P. Bonacich, "Some unique properties of eigenvector centrality," *Soc. Networks*, vol. 29, no. 4, pp. 555–564, 2007.

[42] B. Ruhnau, "Eigenvector-centrality—a node-centrality?," *Soc. Networks*, vol. 22, no. 4, pp. 357–365, 2000.

[43] R. Albert and A.-L. Barabási, "Statistical mechanics of complex networks," *Rev. Mod. Phys.*, vol. 74, no. 1, p. 47, 2002.

[44] M. S. Granovetter, "The strength of weak ties," *Am. J. Sociol.*, pp. 1360–1380, 1973.

[45] D. Bhattacharya and S. Ram, "Sharing News Articles Using 140 Characters: A Diffusion Analysis on Twitter," in *Advances in Social Networks Analysis and Mining (ASONAM), 2012 IEEE/ACM International Conference on*, 2012, pp. 966–971.

[46] U. Brandes and D. Wagner, "Analysis and visualization of social networks," in *Graph drawing software*, Springer, 2004, pp. 321–340.

[47] Bitergia, "WebKit Report by Bitergia." [Online]. Available: http://bitergia.com/public/reports/webkit/2013_01/. [Accessed: 12-Jun-2013].

[48] T. Unrau, "The unforking of KDE's KHTML and Webkit | Ars Technica." [Online]. Available: http://arstechnica.com/information-technology/2007/07/the-unforking-of-kdes-khtml-and-webkit/. [Accessed: 12-Jun-2013].

[49] PCWorld, "Nokia-Microsoft Deal Hurts Intel Smartphone Chances | PCWorld." [Online]. Available:

http://www.pcworld.com/article/219455/article.html. [Accessed: 13-Jun-2013].

[50] TechRadar, "Intel: MeeGo exists because Microsoft let us down | News | TechRadar." [Online]. Available: http://www.techradar.com/news/computing-components/processors/intel-meego-exists-because-microsoft-let-us-down-684665. [Accessed: 13-Jun-2013].

[51] Igalia, "Igalia: Igalia history." [Online]. Available: http://www.igalia.com/about-us/igalia-history. [Accessed: 13-Jun-2013].

[52] Intel, "Intel and Nokia Merge Software Platforms for Future Computing Devices." [Online]. Available: http://www.intel.com/pressroom/archive/releases/2010/20100215corp.htm. [Accessed: 13-Jun-2013].

[53] Nokia, "Intel and Nokia merge software platforms for future computing devices » Nokia – Press." [Online]. Available: http://press.nokia.com/2010/02/15/intel-and-nokia-merge-software-platforms-for-future-computing-devices/. [Accessed: 13-Jun-2013].

[54] Bloomberg, "Apple Import Ban on Old IPhones Stokes Samsung Patent War - Bloomberg." [Online]. Available: http://www.bloomberg.com/news/2013-06-04/apple-faces-u-s-import-ban-on-some-devices-after-samsung-win.html. [Accessed: 13-Jun-2013].

[55] Korea Times, "Moving from love-hate to hate-hate." [Online]. Available: http://www.koreatimes.co.kr/www/news/tech/2012/10/133_122173.html. [Accessed: 13-Jun-2013].

[56] J. West and S. Gallagher, "Challenges of open innovation: the paradox of firm investment in open□source software," *RD Manag.*, vol. 36, no. 3, pp. 319–331, 2006.

[57] L. Nyman, T. Mikkonen, J. Lindman, and M. Fougère, "Forking: the invisible hand of sustainability in open source software," in *Proceedings of SOS*, 2011, pp. 1–5.

[58] L. Nyman and T. Mikkonen, "To Fork or Not to Fork: Fork Motivations in SourceForge Projects," in *Open Source Systems: Grounding Research*, Springer, 2011, pp. 259–268.

[59] K. Lakhani and R. Wolf, "Why hackers do what they do: Understanding motivation and effort in free/open source software projects," 2003.

[60] M. Bergquist and J. Ljungberg, "The power of gifts: organizing social relationships in open source communities," *Inf. Syst. J.*, vol. 11, no. 4, pp. 305–320, 2001.

[61] P. J. Agerfalk and B. Fitzgerald, "Outsourcing to an unknown workforce: Exploring opensourcing as a global sourcing strategy," *MIS Q.*, vol. 32, no. 2, p. 385, 2008.

[62] W. M. Cohen and D. A. Levinthal, "Absorptive capacity: a new perspective on learning and innovation," *Adm. Sci. Q.*, pp. 128–152, 1990.

[63] C. L. Huntley, "Organizational learning in open-source software projects: an analysis of debugging data," *Eng. Manag. IEEE Trans.*, vol. 50, no. 4, pp. 485–493, 2003.

[64] T. R. Eisenmann, *Managing Proprietary and Shared Platforms: A Life-Cycle View*. Division of Research, Harvard Business School, 2007.

[65] B. J. Nalebuff and A. Brandenburger, *Co-opetition*. HarperCollinsBusiness, 1996.

[66] M. Bengtsson and S. Kock, "" Coopetition" in Business Networks—to Cooperate and Compete Simultaneously," *Ind. Mark. Manag.*, vol. 29, no. 5, pp. 411–426, 2000.

Linking Career Anchors and a Social Cognitive Framework: Developing an Interview Instrument

Patrick Donohue
University of Limerick
Limerick
Ireland
+353 61 208832

patrick.donohue@ul.ie

Norah Power
University of Limerick
Limerick
Ireland
+353 61 202769

norah.power@ul.ie

ABSTRACT

It is not unusual for researchers to struggle in sourcing potential participants for interviews. This is particularly true when it comes to interviewing senior IT personnel. Critical to the success of such interviews is the careful planning and structure of the interview in advance and prudent use of the time allotted. This paper proposes the use of an instrument to complement the interview process, with a view to optimizing the allotted interview time. Such an instrument is presented, tested with interviewees and supported by links to a theoretical framework that is based on social cognitive theory.

Categories and Subject Descriptors

K.7.1 [**Occupations**]:

General Terms

Human Factors, Theory

Keywords

Career anchors, interviews, interview instruments, social cognitive frameworks, social cognitive theory, triadic reciprocal determinism

1. INTRODUCTION

1.1 Interviews in computer personnel research

Interviewing is a long established method for eliciting knowledge and is particularly useful when undertaking qualitative research [1, 2]. Time management and structure are critical when preparing for and undertaking such interviews; every effort should be made to make best use of the time allotted, as interview opportunities may not often arise.

In order for the interview to be meaningful, some form of structure is desirable. Semi-structured interviews are a means to this end [2]; they are semi-structured, insofar as there is an opportunity to deviate from the initial questions when the interviewee is relaying some interesting idea. The interviewer is therefore given an opportunity to elicit meaningful knowledge from the interview that would not have necessarily been the result of asking the planned questions.

If an interview is recorded, it can be typed at a later stage, with a view to deeper analysis and coding [3, 4, 5]. In order to do this it is important for the interviewer to develop a key set of questions that elicit the most meaningful knowledge possible. It is quite common to have difficulty in sourcing interviewees, depending on the nature of the research being undertaken. Therefore, it is critical to have a well-structured interview plan to ensure maximum benefit from the interview.

After a successful interview, it is not unusual to have developed a rapport with the interviewee. Could this be put to good use (time permitting) by complementing the interview with an interview instrument?

1.2 The benefits of interview instruments

Interview instruments are a useful tool in assisting the knowledge elicitation process. They can give the standard interview structure or complement them and in the latter case, give extra meaning and context to the knowledge already acquired. In research being undertaken by the first author, a number of senior IT Financial Services personnel were interviewed. They were asked about their views relating to staff motivation. It was realized that after developing a rapport with the interviewees, an opportunity arose to further complement the interview responses. An interview instrument was one method that was considered, but the challenge was to develop a method that would suit the specific research area. Such an instrument would need to be relevant, meaningful and interesting for the participant.

An approach considered was a card sorting exercise, where statements would be put to the interviewee, with corresponding inverse statements [6]. In order for the exercise to be meaningful, the statements developed would need to have an appropriate context linked to the original interview.

1.3 Developing an interview instrument

The challenge was to develop an instrument that would complement a standard interview and specific to the research being undertaken. This paper proposes an approach in developing such an instrument. As the interviews relate to motivation, an appropriate area of research is examined. A link is subsequently made with social cognitive theory [7, 8] through the use of a social cognitive framework [9] and the instrument is tested with actual interviewees. Further details of the instrument, its purpose and application, will be discussed later when describing the testing of the instrument on actual interviewees.

Permission to make digital or hard copies of all or part of this work for personal or classroom use is granted without fee provided that copies are not made or distributed for profit or commercial advantage and that copies bear this notice and the full citation on the first page. Copyrights for components of this work owned by others than the author(s) must be honored. Abstracting with credit is permitted. To copy otherwise, or republish, to post on servers or to redistribute to lists, requires prior specific permission and/or a fee. Request permissions from permissions@acm.org.
SIGMIS-CPR'14, May 29-31, 2014, Singapore, Singapore.
Copyright is held by the owner/author(s). Publication rights licensed to ACM.
ACM 978-1-4503-2625-4/15/05...$15.00.

2. DEVISING SEMI-STRUCTURED INTERVIEWS

2.1 Interviewing senior IT personnel

Semi-structured interviews [2] are invaluable when applied inasmuch as the interviewer should not deviate too far from the initial research path. Senior personnel in any organization are busy people and it can be very difficult for researchers to source willing volunteers. For example, Feeny *et al*, [10] in their pursuit to analyze the working relationship between CEOs and CIOs, recognize this difficulty.

When an opportunity for an interview arises, it is critical that the structure of the interview makes best use of the allowed time. How can interview questions be meaningful and yet have some structure at a higher level? It is important that at a fundamental level, the interviewer should know the most valuable and pertinent questions that need to be asked.

2.2 Determining the interview questions

The questions need to be broad enough to cover the area being researched, but at the same time specific enough to elicit the required detail of knowledge [9]. It is helpful if the interviewer has an appropriate framework in advance to help in the interview preparation. Such a framework should lend itself to the development of appropriate questions.

2.3 Using an appropriate interview instrument

The interviews being undertaken were related to the motivation of senior IT personnel in the financial services sector. After a number of interviews, it became apparent that an instrument was required that would utilize an established set of career anchors [11, 12, 13]. Such an instrument would need to complement the interview process, with due regard to the time constraints involved. It should help to further clarify knowledge elicited from the interview so far. A good time to use the instrument would be at the end of the standard interview, where hopefully a level of rapport would have been established and the instrument may give clearer context.

Furthermore, it would be useful if the instrument was based on an underlying theory, giving the analysis and results more meaning.

3. SOCIAL COGNITIVE THEORY

3.1 The relevance of Social Cognitive Theory

Social Cognitive Theory is a well-established theory that proposes observing others as a means of knowledge elicitation [7]. It can be the basis for developing frameworks and models for the purposes of practical research application. One such model, as proposed by Compeau, *et al* [14] is used to test hypotheses relating to self-efficacy, expected outcomes and their influence on computer usage. The paper illustrates how a model may be used, based on social cognitive constructs to test the reliability of such hypotheses.

3.2 A Social Cognitive Framework

Downey [9] proposed the use of a social cognitive framework based on the Triadic Reciprocal Determinism model [8] derived from social cognitive theory [7] for the development of interview questions. The Framework illustrates dependencies between three key aspects of how people behave in a particular environment. The social cognitive dependency model illustrated in Figure 1 is derived from this model; it outlines the key components of the

framework from a work context and enumerates the dependencies between them. The main components of the model relate to the person, their behaviors and the environment. This model is applied in a work context.

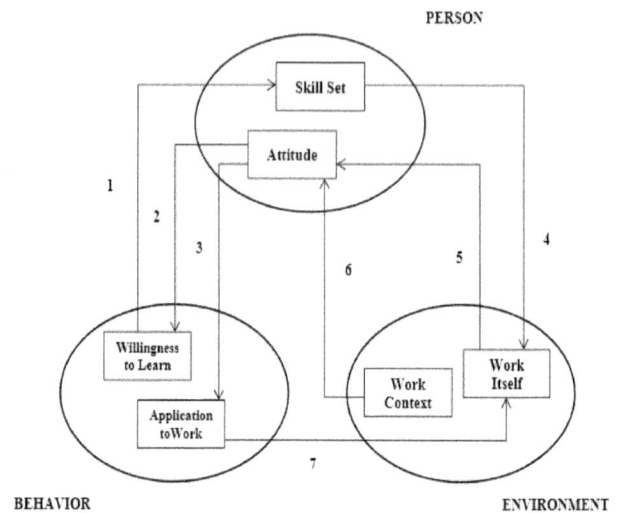

Figure 1. The Social Cognitive Dependency Model derived from Downey [9]

Downey showed how the three main elements of the framework may be used to produce interview questions. A question like "What do you do?" can be derived from the *environment* element; "What skills do you need" can be associated with *person* and "How did you acquire these skills?" may be applied to *behavior*. This approach clearly links interview questions to the framework. These questions are specific and relate to the primary elements of the framework. Table 1 lists the components, their sub-components and examples of their meaning; these may be the starting point for the development of interview questions and/or more specific statements.

It follows that further examination of the model can lead to these specific statements; in particular, questions may be derived from the dependencies between the components.

3.3 Framework observations

Although it may be clear that the model contains three main elements, namely person, behavior and environment, the dependencies between these components, including their sub-components, require deeper analysis. Table 1, as described, lists the components and sub-components of the framework.

The dependencies, as numbered in Figure 1, may be used for the generation of further questions and statements. The following is a narrative description of their meaning:

1. A person acquires a skillset (**person**) the extent and effectiveness of which is based on a willingness to learn (**behavior**).

2. A person's willingness to learn (**behavior**) is governed by a person's attitude (**person**).

3. How one applies oneself to work (**behavior**) is reliant on attitude (**person**).

Table 1. Framework components and sub-components

Component	Sub-component	Can relate to
PERSON	Skill Set	Education
		Training
		Experience
	Attitude	Exploitation of abilities
		Opportunities presented in environment
		Career anchors
BEHAVIOR	Willingness to learn [15]	The need for incentives (Theory X)
		Self-motivation (Theory Y)
	Application to work [15]	The need for incentives (Theory X)
		Self-motivation (Theory Y)
ENVIRONMENT	Work context	Nature of business
	Work itself	Culture, etc.

4. A work scenario (**environment**) requires a particular skillset (**person**).

5. The process of working (**environment**) influences one's attitude (**person**).

6. The work context (**environment**) influences one's attitude (**person**).

7. The effectiveness of work (**environment**) is influenced by how one applies oneself (**behavior**).

The nature of these statements is significant as they may be the basis for developing links to an appropriate interview research area such as motivation.

3.4 Researching motivation

The main purpose of the instrument being described is to assist in the knowledge elicitation of senior IT Financial Services staff, with particular emphasis on motivation. Motivation is an important characteristic in selecting IT staff and their further development, but are there specific motivational factors specific to IT personnel working in this sector? Further to this, do these factors change during a person's career?

An area of research is required to assist in the instrument development process; one established area being that of career anchors [13]. This approach to motivation and subsequent career orientation is well established in the literature [11, 12, 13, 16, 17, 18, 19, 20, 21, 22, 23, 24, 25, 26]. If career anchors are suitable for the development of interview questions and specific statements, can these anchors be linked to the social cognitive framework proposed?

The development of an interview instrument could well be based on specific statements derived from career anchors. Such statements would be directly related to these defined anchors. In order to develop pertinent statements, a set of core career anchors [12, 13, 17] needs to be examined.

4. THE RELEVANCE OF CAREER ANCHORS

4.1 Career anchors and IT personnel

Career anchors are a means of identifying what an individual's belief is of their own personal motivation [13]. Table 2 outlines a set of anchors as identified by Schein and further supplemented by Delong [12]. Each anchor defines a specific aspect of motivation varying from professional status (identity) to the need for a secure, stable working environment. Three of the anchors are described in greater detail.

Technical or functional competence relates to an individual's perception of their ability and their desire to solve technical and functional problems; for example, the ability to program using a specific programming language or the application of a systems design methodology.

Managerial competence, on the other hand, deals with the desire to manage more so than the operational or technical aspects of a job. It is not necessarily important what business or industry is involved.

Security and stability relates to the need for a secure work environment. This may be to do with general job security with a regular income, or more specific to a particular job and its associated responsibilities within in an organization.

The descriptions of the anchors, as outlined in Table 2 are used in this research to develop a set of statements, the context of which is related to IT personnel. These statements can be incorporated into an interview instrument.

Table 2. Career Anchors [17]

Anchor no.	Anchor	Description
1	MANAGERIAL COMPETENCE [13]	The need for problem analysis skills, emotional stability, and interpersonal competence
2	TECHNICAL/FUNCTIONAL COMPETENCE [13]	The challenge of the technical field, functional area or content, managerial process
3	SECURITY/STABILITY [13]	The desire for an organization which provides long-run stability, good benefits, and basic job security
4	CREATIVITY/ENTREPRENEURSHIP [13]	The need to create something on one's own, try new projects
5	AUTONOMY/INDEPENDENCE [13]	The need to be free of constraints to pursue professional or technical/functional competence
6	IDENTITY [12]	The desire for status and prestige from belonging to certain companies or organizations
7	SERVICE [12]	Concern with helping others and seeing changes that result from efforts made
8	VARIETY [12]	The desire for a large number of different types of challenges

Table 3. Examples of project risk constructs [6]

Statement	Opposite statement
Someone on the customer's side has taken clear, committed ownership of the project	Nobody wants to 'own' the project
There seems to be no hidden agenda	The 'real' agenda seems to be hidden
We've experience of this application	The application is new to us
The new system doesn't have to be particularly adaptable to future needs	The new system must be adaptable enough to cope with unknown future needs
The application logic is straightforward	The application logic is complex

5. DEVELOPING AN INTERVIEW INSTRUMENT

5.1 Structuring the instrument

The purpose of the instrument is to provide a complementary means of eliciting knowledge from interviewees. As the interviews are seeking insights into motivation, it is appropriate that the instrument should be based on career anchors.

Moynihan [6, 27] demonstrates how statements and their inverse can be used when developing an interview instrument. He bases this approach on a bi-polar distinction of constructs, as proposed by Bannister and Fransella [26]. After interviewing experienced project managers [6], he elicits a set of constructs relating to project requirements uncertainty. These constructs consist of statements describing risk and their polar opposites. He uses these constructs as the basis for a card sorting exercise, asking the project managers to select which statement for each construct is more accurate for a specific project, indicating whether or not

they made a very big difference (VBD), a big difference (BD) or little or no difference (LND). Table 3 lists five random constructs of the 113 elicited.

This approach may be the basis for the development of interview instrument using career anchors. Index cards can be used for the career anchor statements. Each card (Figure 2.) comprises of a statement, an inverse statement [28] and a scale indicating a level of importance or relevance. The cards are then coded indicating the career anchor type and statement number.

Figure 2 shows the structure of an instrument card. The reference *1) a.* on the card refers to the anchor being used, in this case managerial competence. *(MaCo)*. The card is divided in two; on the left is a statement relating to the particular anchor, with an inverse statement on the right. The interviewees can decide which is the more appropriate statement describing themselves and for the given statement, whether it is of high (H), medium (M) or low (L) importance.

1) a. MaCo	
A	B
Problem analysis skills are important to me in performing a management role	Problem analysis skills are not that important to me in performing a management role
H M L	H M L

Figure 2. An Interview Instrument Card

Table 4. The Instrument Statements

Anchor No.	A (Statement)	B (Inverse statement)
1) a.	Problem analysis skills are important to me in performing a management role	Problem analysis skills are not that important to me in performing a management role
1) b.	I like dealing with high levels of responsibility	I do not particularly like dealing with high levels of responsibility
1) c.	I like dealing with people	Dealing with people is not that important in performing my role
2) a.	I like technical challenges	Technical challenges are not that important to me
2) b.	I like working in a particular business/industry	The business/industry I work in is not that important
2) c.	The content of the work is more important than the managerial process	The managerial process is more important than the work content
3) a.	I like long-term stability	Long-term stability is irrelevant
3) b.	I like the perks	The benefits are not that important
3) c.	I like job stability	Job stability is not that important to me
4) a.	I like to be creative	Creativity is not that important
4) b.	I like the opportunity to try new things	New projects are not that important to me
5) a.	I like to be free to develop my competencies	Autonomy is not that important to me
6) a.	I like the status of the job (IT)	Status means nothing to me
7) a.	I like to see the results of helping people	Seeing the results of helping people is not that important
8) a.	I like many different challenges	I like dealing with challenges individually

5.2 Developing the statements

A collection of statements is needed that can be directly related to career anchors. Table 4 shows a number of these statements and their inverse that may be used for the basis of the interview instrument. Each main number refers to an established anchor as listed in Table 2. The statements can be refined or modified to suit the particular interview context. The list of statements is not exhaustive; each anchor statement may be added to, depending on the interview context.

5.3 Anchor coding

A code is assigned for each of the anchor types. These are then used as identifiers for each of the cards. Figure 2 shows a card developed for a *Managerial Competence* statement. The code is based on the first two letters of each word or four letters if only one word describes the anchor. *Managerial Competence* results in the code *MaCo* being used, whereas *Iden* is used for Identity. The code is completed with the addition of a letter, indicating the bi-polar statements being used (*MaCo(a)*).

6. LINKING THE INSTRUMENT TO A SOCIAL COGNITIVE FRAMEWORK

6.1 Primary components

The relationships among the main components are illustrated in Figure 4. The interview instrument uses coded statements and their polar opposites [28] that are based on established career anchors [12, 13]. The anchors are linked to the appropriate component of the social cognitive framework [9], a framework derived from social cognitive theory [7], through the foundation of the triadic reciprocal determinism model [8].

6.2 Linking career anchors to the framework

A key challenge in developing the instrument is identifying links between the anchors and components of the social cognitive framework. Figure 3 identifies some of the anchors and their corresponding links. The anchor codes, as previously described, are four characters in length, comprising the first two letters of each word, or one word where only one is used to describe the anchor. The framework codes are based on key components and their corresponding relationships, where appropriate. For example, the code *EPwcat* is a relationship between environment and person. The *wc* relates to work context and *at*, attitude. The *EP* segment of the code shows the direction of the relationship, going from environment to person.

The code *Pat* is an example where a link is made between an anchor code and one of the main components of the framework. For example, the anchor code *AuIn(a)* (Autonomy/Independence) links to *Pat* (Person(attitude)).

7. TESTING THE INSTRUMENT

7.1 The interview structure

The interview instrument was introduced to complement on-going research into the motivation of IT staff. The interviewees were senior IT managers in the Financial Services sector, all of whom had significant experience. Six interviews were undertaken during the summer and fall of 2013.

Anchor codes	Map to	Framework codes
TeCo(a)		PEsswi
CrEn(a)		Bapwo
Vari(a)		PBataw
MaCo(a)		
CrEn(b)		Bwile
MaCo(b)		
MaCo(c)		
AuIn(a)		Pat
Serv(a)		
TeCo(b)		
TeCo(c)		
SeSt(a)		EPwcat
SeSt(b)		
SeSt(c)		
Iden(a)		

Figure 3. Coded anchor statements

with associated framework elements

The interviews were part of a longer study into the motivation of senior IT personnel in the Financial Services sector. Each participant was interviewed in their own workplace, all of whom agreed to the card sorting exercise in advance.

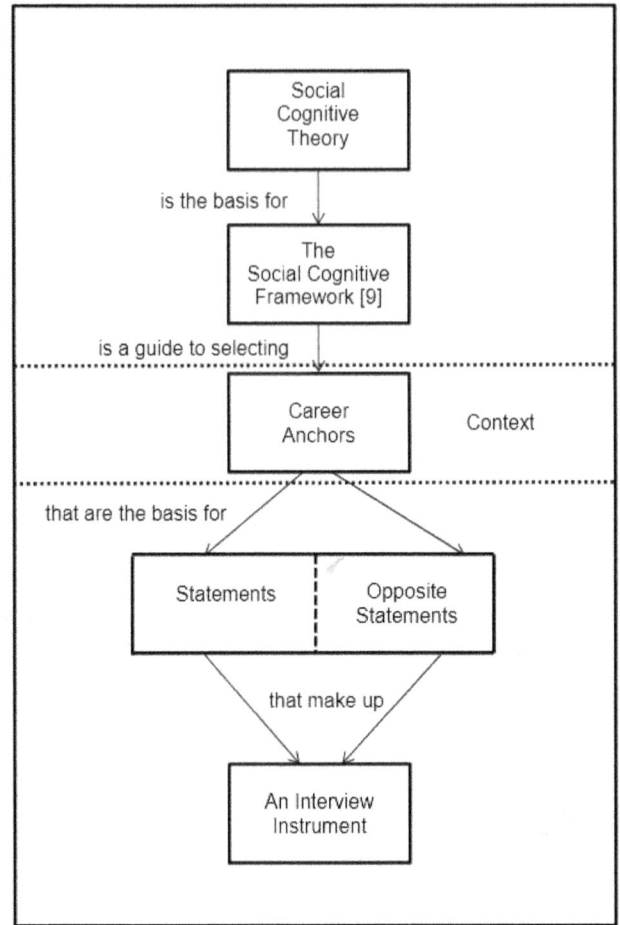

Figure 4. Foundations for developing an interview instrument

After a semi-structured interview was undertaken, each interviewee was asked to partake in a card sorting exercise. It was important for the exercise to be undertaken at the end of the interview for a number of reasons: a rapport had developed between the interviewer and interviewee, the card statements had context and most importantly, the interviewee, on recounting experiences in the interview could be expected to have a clearer memory of attitudes from a number of years ago.

7.2 Using the instrument

On completion of the standard interview, the interviewee was asked whether or not they would be willing to participate in a card sorting exercise. If so, they were given a set of cards and responded by ticking one H/M/L box for one statement or its opposite per card. The statements, as previously listed in Table 4, each related to a specific career anchor. The H/M/L allowed the interviewee to specify whether a statement was of high, medium or low importance. The statements themselves related to the interviewee's current status.

When the card marking was complete, they were asked to sort the cards that were of high importance into order of priority. On completion of the exercise, the interviewee was asked to engage with the process a second time, this time based on when they left high school or started college.

It was found that undertaking this exercise at the end of the interview had a number of advantages, namely the established rapport with the interviewee, the context of the statements and as the interviewee was asked about their past, it would assist in jogging the interviewee's memory. Six interviewees took part in the exercise; they were senior IT personnel in the financial services sector. The response from every participant was extremely favorable, each commenting to the effect that they would be reflecting on the exercise further.

Prior to the interviews, each interviewee stated that their time was limited, however, towards completion of every interview, each participant was willing to extend the allotted time. It is reasonable to assume that the experience was both useful and enjoyable for the participants.

7.3 Relevance of the instrument

The interview instrument exercise was undertaken twice after each interview to establish which anchors were less likely to change (durable) and which were likely to change over time (dynamic). When further used, it is hoped that the results will show trends based on durable and dynamic anchors and also indicating the important aspects of the social cognitive framework when analyzing the responses. It is expected that trends will be identifiable as more participants are interviewed. The traditional interview before the exercise was invaluable in establishing context, particularly when the attitudes expressed related to earlier experience.

The instrument complemented the standard interview favorably, adding further value and context to the initial questions asked.

8. Conclusions

Sourcing suitable research interviewees can be problematic, in particular if the potential interviewees are senior staff. If successful in sourcing a participant, it is critical that the time allotted is used to best effect. A well-structured interview is a key factor in eliciting meaningful and pertinent knowledge from participants.

This paper outlined the approach used in developing an instrument to help interviewees reflect on their career motivation. Career anchors were used to develop instrument statements relating to motivation. A link was made between career anchors and social cognitive theory through the use of a social cognitive framework. The interview instrument has been tested by the first author during actual research interviews, one outcome being the identification of both dynamic and durable career anchors.

The instrument was used at the end of the interview; the rationale being that a rapport would build between the interviewer and interviewee. The response to using the interview instrument was very favorable in each case; this was commented on by the interviewees who were willing to extend the interview length, at their suggestion, beyond the allotted time.

A link between established career anchors and a specific social cognitive framework was proposed. Several links have been identified, but further work is required to make a more robust link between the career anchors of senior IT personnel and social cognitive theory.

9. REFERENCES

[1] King, N., Cassell, C., (Ed), and Symon, G., (Ed). 1994. *The Qualitative Research Interview,* Qualitative Methods in Organizational Research: A Practical Guide, Sage Publishing, 14-36.

[2] Wengraf, T. 2001. *Qualitative Research Interviewing: Biographic Narrative and Semi-Structured Methods,* Middlesex University.

[3] Corbin, J., and Strauss, A. 1990. *Grounded theory method: Procedures, canons, and evaluative procedures,* Qualitative Sociology, 13(1), 3-21.

[4] Corbin, J., & Strauss, A. 2008. *Basics of Qualitative Research,* 3rd edition, Sage Publications.

[5] Glaser, B., & Strauss, A. 1965. *The discovery of grounded theory,* Chicago, Aldine.

[6] Moynihan, T., 2000. Coping with "requirements-uncertainty": the theories-of-action of experienced IS/software project managers, *Journal of Systems and Software,* 53(2), 99–109.

[7] McGregor, D. 1960.*The Human Side of Enterprise,* New York, McGraw-Hill.

[8] Bandura, A. 1986. *Social foundations of thought and action: A social cognitive theory.* Englewood Cliffs, NJ: Prentice-Hall.

[9] Downey, J. 2005. A framework to elicit the skills needed for software development, *Proceedings of the SIGMIS Conference on Computer Personnel Research, CPR '05.* ACM, New York, NY, 122–127.

[10] Feeny, D. F., Edwards, B. R., and Simpson, K. M. 1992. Understanding the CEO/CIO relationship. *MIS quarterly,* 435-448.

[11] DeLong, T.J. 1982a. *The Career orientations of MBA Alumni: A Multidimensional Model,* Katz, R. (Ed) (1982) Career Issues in Human Resource Management, Engle-wood Cliffs, NJ: Prentice-Hall, Inc.

[12] DeLong, T.J. 1982b. Re-examining the Career Anchor Model, *Personnel,* 59(3), 50- 61.

[13] Schein, E.H., 1978. *Career Dynamics: Matching Individual and Organizational Needs,* Addison-Wesley, Reading MA.

[14] Compeau, D., Higgins, C. A., and Huff, S. 1999. Social cognitive theory and individual reactions to computing technology: a longitudinal study. *MIS Quarterly,* 145-158.

[15] Miller, N.E., and Dollard, J. 1941. *Social Learning and Imitation,* New Haven, CT: Yale University Press.

[16] Beecham, S., Baddoo, N., Hall, T., Robinson, H., and Sharp, H. 2008. Motivation in Software Engineering: A systematic literature review, *Information and Software Technology,* 50, 860-878.

[17] Crook, C., Crepeau, R. and McMurtrey, M. 1991. Utilization of the career anchor/career orientation constructs for management of I/S professionals. *Proceedings of the SIGMIS Conference on Computer Personnel Research, CPR '91.* ACM, New York, NY, 12–23.

[18] Hsu, M.K., Chen, H.G., Jiang, J.J. and Klein, G. 2003. Career satisfaction for managerial and technical anchored IS personnel in later career stages, *ACM SIGMIS Database, 34(4),* 64–72.

[19] Lash, P.B. and Sein, M.K., 1995. Career paths in a changing IS environment: a theoretical perspective, *Proceedings of the SIGMIS Conference on Computer Personnel Research, CPR '95.* ACM, New York, NY. 117–130.

[20] Mgaya, K. V., Uzoka, F.E., Kitindi, E.G., and Shemi, A.P. 2009. Examining career orientations of information systems personnel in an emerging economy context, *Proceedings of the SIGMIS Conference on Computer Personnel Research, CPR '09.* ACM, New York, NY, 41-56.

[21] Peterson, J. and Roger, A. 2009. Career Anchor Profiles: An Exploratory Study of Business School Participants in France, *Colloque international sur les indicateurs d'évaluation de la responsabilité sociale et environnementale des entreprises,* 8-10 Juin 2009, Lyon, Université Jean Moulin Lyon 3, France.

[22] Sumner, M., Yager, S. and Franke, D. 2005. Career orientation and organizational commitment of IT personnel, *Proceedings of the SIGMIS Conference on Computer Personnel Research, CPR '05.* ACM, New York, NY, 75-80.

[23] Sumner, M., & Franke, D. 2007. Career orientation and the global IT workforce: research in progress, *Proceedings of the SIGMIS Conference on Computer Personnel Research, CPR '07.* ACM, New York, NY, 213–215.

[24] Thatcher, J.B., Liu, Y. and Stepina, L.P. 2002. The Role of Work Itself: An Empirical Examination of Intrinsic Motivation's Influence on IT Workers' Attitudes and Intentions, *Proceedings of the SIGMIS Conference on Computer Personnel Research, CPR '02.* ACM, New York, NY, 25-33.

[25] Igbaria, M., Greenhaus, J. H., & Parasuraman, S. 1991. Career orientations of MIS employees: an empirical analysis. *MIS Quarterly,* 151-169.

[26] Jiang, J., & Klein, G. 1999. Supervisor Support and Career Anchor Impact on the Career Satisfaction of the Entry-Level information systems professional. *Journal of Management Information Systems,* 16(3), 219-240.

[27] Moynihan, T. 1996. An inventory of personal constructs for information systems project risk researchers, *Journal of Information Technology,* 11(4), 359–371.

[28] Bannister, D., & Fransella, F. 1989. *Inquiring Man: The Psychology of Personal Constructs,* third edition, Routledge, London.

Does Teleworking Negatively Influence IT Professionals? An Empirical Analysis of IT Personnel's Telework-enabled Stress

Christoph Weinert
Centre of Human Resources Information Systems
University of Bamberg, Germany
+49 951 8633918
christoph.weinert@uni-bamberg.de

Christian Maier
Centre of Human Resources Information Systems
University of Bamberg, Germany
+49 951 8633919
christian.maier@uni-bamberg.de

Sven Laumer
Centre of Human Resources Information Systems
University of Bamberg, Germany
+49 951 8632873
sven.laumer@uni-bamberg.de

Tim Weitzel
Centre of Human Resources Information Systems
University of Bamberg, Germany
+49 951 8632871
tim.weitzel@uni-bamberg.de

ABSTRACT

Despite the wide dissemination and acceptance of teleworking in the IT industry, companies like Yahoo!, HP, or Best Buy have stopped their telework programs, which indicates that there might also be some negative side effects in this type of work. In regard to this, our research focuses on one particular negative side of teleworking by focusing on teleworking-induced stress of IT professionals. We theorize that teleworking-induced stressors influence IT personnel's psychological and behavioral strain in the form of exhaustion due to teleworking and discontinuous intention towards teleworking. Results of an empirical online survey with 57 IT professionals validate these dependencies, which gives us the grounds to identify work overload, work-home conflict, information underload, and social isolation as influence factors of exhaustion due to teleworking. Further results reveal that discontinuous intentions towards teleworking is directly influenced by social isolation and exhaustion due to teleworking, whereas the influence of work overload is mediated by exhaustion due to teleworking. Work overload due to telework has the strongest effect on exhaustion due to teleworking, which in turn is the strongest influence factor on the discontinuous intention towards teleworking.

Categories and Subject Descriptors

H.1.2 [Models and principles]: User/Machine Systems; J.4 [SOCIAL AND BEHAVIORAL SCIENCES] Psychology

General Terms: Management, Human Factors

Keywords

teleworking, teleworking exhaustion, discontinuous teleworking intention

Permission to make digital or hard copies of all or part of this work for personal or classroom use is granted without fee provided that copies are not made or distributed for profit or commercial advantage and that copies bear this notice and the full citation on the first page. Copyrights for components of this work owned by others than the author(s) must be honored. Abstracting with credit is permitted. To copy otherwise, or republish, to post on servers or to redistribute to lists, requires prior specific permission and/or a fee. Request permissions from Permissions@acm.org.
SIGMIS-CPR '14, May 29 - 31 2014, Singapore, Singapore.
Copyright is held by the owner/author(s). Publication rights licensed to ACM.
ACM 978-1-4503-2625-4/14/05…$15.00.

1. INTRODUCTION

The rapid improvement of information and communication technologies (ICTs) such as portable computers, reliable broadband communications and cloud computing gives employees the opportunity to work from remote locations in a common and synchronous manner [57]. The type of work enabled by ICTs is known as teleworking [19] and is established to reduce an organizations' expenses [20]. Teleworking becomes an alternative to traditional office work as it improves employees' work-life balance. In 2013, a report of *WorldatWork* indicates that 88 percent of organizations around the world offer their employees the possibility to telework [60]. The European Union and the United States estimate that 12 percent of all employees are teleworkers, and by 2016, this percentage will exceed to over 20 percent [57]. In particular, IT companies provide employees the opportunity to work from home in order to retain them in the war for IT talent [32], for without this option they would have mostly likely left the organization [33].

Nonetheless, despite the wide dissemination and acceptance of teleworking especially in the IT sector, research has identified plenty of telework-specific challenges and dangers. Among others, social isolation and blurring boundaries are some negative side effects of teleworking [11, 38]. For example, Hewlett Packard joined other technology companies like Yahoo! and Best Buy in their decision to stop their telework program [6, 33]. The rationale for this is that organizations aiming to establish a strong corporate culture need all employees in their offices during turbulent times [33].

This example illustrates the diverse negative aspects of teleworking and the need to understand their consequences for individuals in a more detailed manner. In regard to this, we focus on IT teleworkers who are a unique group of IT personnel that work remotely from home and thus away from the main workplace [5, 55]. Due to the temporal and spatial distance to the workplace IT teleworkers work in a completely different environment, which leads to specific challenges (e.g. social isolation) [11]. IT personnel are crucial to companies in order to manage the still growing and expanding usage of information systems (IS) and technology [40]. Therefore, we aim to contribute to this discourse, as we focus on the negative side of IT personnel's telework by analyzing the negative consequences of this particular form of IT work on an individual level. It is therefore particularly important to identify the teleworking-induced stressors and examine how these determine psychological strain in terms of exhaustion as well as behavioral strain in terms of discontinuous intention towards teleworking. In the tradition of Moore [40, 41], Ahuja et al. [1], and Rutner et al. [51], we analyze this situation for IT personnel. Hence, the question of our research is:

How do teleworking-induced stressors influence IT personnel's exhaustion due to teleworking and discontinuous intention towards teleworking?

To answer this research question, we focus on several telework stressors and theorize their influence on psychological and behavioral consequences. Findings from the partial least squares analysis show that the four identified teleworking stressors – work overload, work home conflict, information underload, and social isolation – cause reactions of feeling exhausted due to telework which in turn influences discontinuous intention towards further teleworking.

This research article is organized as follows. First, we present the theoretical background of technostress and teleworking. After this the hypotheses are developed and the methodology is described. The results of the partial least squares model and the post hoc analysis are then presented. Finally, the findings are critically discussed and limitations as well as future research streams are described.

2. THEORETICAL BACKGROUND

2.1 Technology Enabled Stress

The phenomenon of technology enabled stress is explained by the person-environment fit theory [13]. The theory posits that there is a balance between individuals and their environment. People and their environment are in balance when the values and the abilities of the person meet the supplies and demands of the environment. If the person and their environment are not in balance the equilibrium is disrupted, which causes strain. For example, if the supplies of the environment are not fulfilling the values of the person, a misfit could occur, which results in strain. Additionally, the misfit could also occur if the abilities of the person and the demands of the environment are out of balance. The appearance of these perceived misfits occurs through stressors, which eventually lead to strain [2].

Based on the person-environment fit theory, technology enabled stress, is understood as *"any stress experience[d] by end-users of information and communication technologies (ICTs)"* [48, p. 417]. IT stressors are IT-based events or properties of events encountered by individuals, which lead to strain [2, p. 834, 37]. Strain can be distinguished into psychological- and behavioral-strain. Psychological strain is defined as an *"individual's psychological response to the stressors"* [2, p. 834] such as fatigue, tiredness, exhaustion and burn-out. On the other hand behavioral strain acknowledges a reduced productivity, increased turnover and absenteeism as well as poor task performance [56].

In sum, the person-environment fit theory is used as a theoretical lens and the technostress research claims that IT stressors occur due to the use of ICT, which in turn might influence psychological as well as behavioral strain. A technostress model is shown in Figure 1.

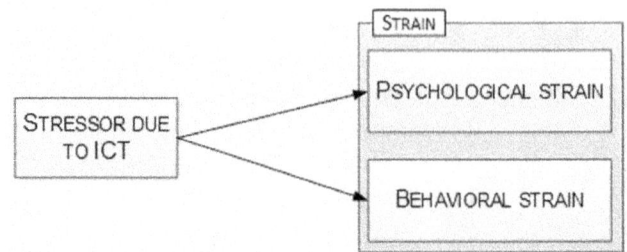

Figure 1: Technostress

2.2 Teleworking

Teleworking, also known as telecommuting, remote work, or virtual work [9, 20], has experienced a high degree of inconsistency and arbitrariness in its perception among academic research [53]. For example, Bélanger and Allport [9] define teleworking as *"working away from the traditional office using computers and telecommunication facilities to maintain a link to the office"* [9, p. 102], whereas other studies perceive telework in a broader way, as any kind of distributed work enabled by information technologies [19]. Shin et al. [53] focus on the location by defining telework as the reduction of commuting distance by working at home. Over the last years, a consensus about telework has grown, making telework seen as remote work involving the use of ICTs (e.g., [30, 55]).

In IS research, teleworking has been examined in relation to productivity and satisfaction [22, 23, 57]. Van der Meulen et al. [57] investigate the distraction level between home and office and its influences on the telework-productivity relationship. Findings demonstrate that distraction gain will increase the positive effects of the telework's productivity. Bélanger et al. [10] investigate the availability of information system and communication technologies as well as the communication patterns of teleworkers and how these influence the perceived productivity, performance, and satisfaction among teleworkers. The analysis shows that technology variables positively influence productivity, performance, and satisfaction of teleworkers, whereby the interaction between the technology variables influences productivity. Igbaria and Guimaraes [29] explore whether turnover intentions and their determinants differ for teleworkers and non-teleworkers. Results show that role conflict and role ambiguity are faced less among teleworkers and that they are more satisfied with their supervisor and are more committed to their organization. Nonetheless, teleworkers are less satisfied with peers and promotion. Boell et al. [11] published a literature review to identify the benefits and weaknesses of teleworking on an organizational as well as an individual level. For the individual, they identify five main advantages: financial benefits, increased work-life balance, spatial mobility, increased work autonomy, productivity, and job satisfaction. On the contrary, they also identify work-life blurring and interruptions as well as the lack of socialization, career and workplace involvement, trust and technical support as disadvantages for the individuals. On the organizational level, five further major advantages of telework are specified, whereas the challenges of telework at the organizational level encompass seven significant constructs.

In psychology research, Mann and Holdsworth [38] focus on psychological consequences and show the mental impact of telework compared to office-based work. Their results indicate a negative emotional impact of teleworking and more mental health symptoms of stress by teleworkers than by office workers. Among others, Mann et al. [38] and Baruch [7] analyze the advantages and disadvantages of teleworking. Mann et al. [38] state that a better balance of home and work life, increased flexibility, reduction in commuting, reduced overheads for employers, increased skill base for employees and increased productivity are advantages of teleworking whereas, social isolation, absenteeism, the blurring of boundaries and the lack of support and career progression are found to be negative results of teleworking. Likewise, Baruch [7] identifies some possible benefits and pitfalls of telework for individuals. He states that telework might lead to improved performance and better productivity, less commuting time, satisfying the need for autonomy, less work related stress and more time with family members. On the contrary, there are some shortcomings due to telework such as fewer opportunities for affiliation, detachment from social interactions, more home-related stress, less influence over people and events at the workplace and fewer career development options.

In sum, teleworking is seen as remote work, which involves the use of ICTs and has been examined in relation to productivity, satisfaction, mental impacts and general advantages and disadvantages. In the following passages we will focus the negative side of teleworking and propose a research model for an investigation of stressors and their consequences associated with the teleworking of IT personnel.

3. HYPOTHESES DEVELOPMENT

Based on literature investigating the negative side of IT work [1, 40] and the negative effects of teleworking in general [7, 26, 52], we focus on the four different telework-induced stressors – work overload, work-home conflict, information underload, and social isolation – and theorize their influence on psychological and behavioral strain. Work overload and work-home conflict are of relevance in the telework context [7, 31, 43], and have consistently been found to influence exhaustion [24]. Information underload and social isolation are particularly relevant for the telework context. For example, social isolation is seen as a key factor of distributed work [17] and information and communication are commonly considered as a key challenge in the telework domain [8], thus they are included to capture the unique nature of teleworkers.

In the following, we develop hypotheses for the influence of these telework stressors and psychological and behavioral strain in terms of exhaustion due to telework and discontinuous intention towards telework. Eventually, the relationship between exhaustion and discontinuous intention towards telework is developed.

In IS research, **work overload** is seen as most the influencing factor for work exhaustion by IT personnel [1, 40]. It is defined as

"the perception that assigned work exceeds an individual's capability or skill level" [2, p. 834]. In the context of teleworking, ICTs which enable telecommuting may encourage employees to continue working at home even after normal work hours [20], which might exceed an employee's capability. Hence, we hypothesize that:

H1: IT personnel's perceived work overload due to telework is positively related to (a) IT personnel's exhaustion due to telework and (b) IT personnel's discontinuous intention towards teleworking.

A **work-home conflict** caused by telecommuting is defined by Greenhaus and Beutell [27] as a *"form of inter-role conflict in which the role pressures from the work and family domains are mutually incompatible in some respect."* [27, p. 72]. A spillover of negative and positive emotions from work to family life and family life to work pattern is observed. Work-home conflict due to teleworking arises from blurring the distinction between the roles of worker and family member [17, 27]. The blurring of boundaries in the context of telecommuting refers to the degree in which either family or work influences the other because they occupy the same place at, potentially, the same time [20]. In addition, the change between traditional work and teleworking leads to a change in roles. For example, commuting has been seen as a useful transition between the roles of work and home and also as a useful break between work and home [38], which is no longer necessary due to telework. Blurring boundaries between work and home has been linked with psychological as well as behavioral strain [1]. For example, Baard and Thomson [3] state that family responsibilities during work hours increase psychological strain among teleworkers. Likewise, Ayyagari et al. [2] show empirical evidence that the work-home conflict affects psychological strain positively. Therefore, we expect that:

H2: IT personnel's perceived work-home conflict due to telework is positively related to (a) IT personnel's exhaustion *due to telework and (b) IT personnel's discontinuous intention towards teleworking.*

Information underload is *"the perception that less than the desired amount of job-related information is being received"* [42, p. 698]. Communication and thus information are commonly considered as a key challenge in the telework domain [8]. Working in traditional office structure makes it easier to develop and maintain strong, positive, and deep ties between employees and coworkers. The disruption of these ties due to teleworking makes it more difficult to transmit information [49]. Furthermore, the spatial distance to colleagues at work might be translated into psychological distance, which might lead to an "out of sight, out of mind" attitude [39] and influences the information transaction [20]. In addition, employees receive information and communicate with colleagues from different physical locations, at different times, and do not work in a shared context as in the traditional office, causing a behavioral strain in the form of productivity and performance possibly decreasing [10]. Additionally, Bélanger and Allport [9] suggest these information and communication difficulties are the cause of further negative consequences, so that we assume that:

H3: IT personnel's perceived information underload due to telework is positively related to (a) IT personnel's exhaustion due to telework and (b) IT personnel's discontinuous intention towards teleworking.

Social isolation is seen as the greatest negative effect of teleworking [54]. Due to the change from traditional office structures to teleworking the social networking and friendship formation suffers because it typically occurs in the workplace. The same changes lead to psychological strain such as a decrease in satisfaction because many employees derive satisfaction from their interaction with coworkers, the act of socializing, and the social support they receive. In addition, gossip is one factor that employees miss most while working at home, which cannot be substituted by the communication trough ICTs [17]. Simpson et al. [54] claim that social isolation might affect one's psychological well-being and Pratt [46] states that people who relied on office networks for social contacts stopped teleworking and returned to the office for "standing around the water cooler or coffeepot", which indicates an impact from social isolation on behavioral strain such as discontinuous intention towards teleworking. Hence, we assume that:

H4: IT personnel's perceived social isolation due to telework is positively related to (a) IT personnel's exhaustion strain due to telework and (b) IT personnel's discontinuous intention towards teleworking.

Moore [40] claims that psychological strain such as work exhaustion among IT personnel is expected to lead to a higher propensity to leave the job. Likewise Ahuja et al. [1] show that work exhaustion and organizational commitment has a statistically significant influence on turnover intention, which represents an instance of behavioral strain. Moreover, Maier et al. [35, 36] show that the perception of IT characteristics influence psychological strain such as job satisfaction which in turn influences behavioral strain such as turnover intention in order to avoid these negative perception reactions. Consequently, we propose that IT employees who feel fatigued, tired, or exhausted due to the characteristic of teleworking show a higher intention to stop teleworking to overcome the negative psychological outcome of telecommuting. Hence, we hypothesize that:

H5: The higher IT personnel's exhaustion due to teleworking the higher IT personnel's discontinuous intention towards teleworking.

All hypotheses are presented in the research model (Figure 2).

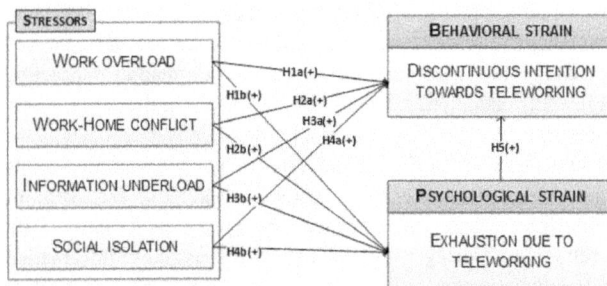

Figure 2: Model of IT personnel's teleworking induced stress

4. RESEARCH METHODOLOGY

In order to validate the research model, we captured data through an online survey. A global carrier portal who works together with our institute for recruiting studies promoted this online questionnaire. As part of one of these studies, the hyperlink to the questionnaire was sent out to the members of the online carrier portal so that we were able to focus on participants who are presently employed. Throughout this mail out, we received 304 responses and based our research on the answers of 57 individuals. We focus on 57 responses because this dataset does not contain missing values, involves only IT personnel and includes the IT personnel who at least partially do telework. For data analysis, SmartPLS [50] and SPSS were used. The demographic characteristics and the extent of their telework usage as well as the amount of colleagues who work at the office are represented in Table 1.

Table 1: Demographics and telework usage

Telework usage		Colleagues in the office		Demographics		
Never	0.0%	None	0.0%	Gender	Female	10.5%
Rarely	31.6%	At least one	19.3%		Male	89.5%
Sometimes	31.6%	Some	26.3%		<19	0.0%
Most of the time	17.5%	An extreme amount	38.6%		19-24	0.0%
Very often	19.3%	All	15.6%	Age	25-34	33.3%
					35-44	28.1%
					45-54	24.6%
					>54	14.0%

In the following we describe the measurement of our research. **Gender** and **age** are specified by the participants by capturing their demographic data. **Telework usage** and **amount of colleagues who work in the office** are captured by asking the participants "How often do you work at home?" and "I work at home and ___ of my colleagues work in the office of my employer". Both constructs were measured by a 5-point Likert scale from *never* to *very often* for telework usage and from *none to all* for the amount of colleagues who work in the office.

Information underload is measured by the scale based on O'Reilly's [42] scale of information underload and **social isolation** is captured by the scale based on Gil-de-Zúñiga [21]. Both constructs were measured on a 5 point Likert scale from *strongly agree* to *strongly disagree*.

Work overload, work-home conflict, and psychological strain due to teleworking are measured by using a scale based on Ayyagari et al. [2]. **Discontinuous intention towards teleworking** is captured by a scale based on the discontinuous usage intention scale by Maier et al. [37]. All four constructs were measured on a 7 point Likert scale from *strongly agree* to *strongly disagree*. All measurement items are displayed in Table 2.

Table 2: Measurement Items

Construct	Items	Loadings
Work overload	Working at home creates a variety of problems, number of requests and complaints in my job, which would not occur without teleworking. (WO-1)	0.886
	I feel rushed through the work at home. (WO-2)	0.962
	I feel pressured by working at home. (WO-3)	0.953
Work-Home conflict	By working at home, boundaries blur between my work and my private life. (WHC-1)	0.895
	By working at home, conflicts arise with my personal responsibilities. (WHC-2)	0.923
	I do not get all the tasks done at home because I need materials from the office of my employer. (WHC-3)	-
Information underload	When I work at home, I receive too little information from my colleagues in the office of my employer. (IU-1)	0.959
	When I work at home, it is difficult to receive relevant information from my colleagues in the office of my employer. (IU-2)	0.957
	During my time at home, the amount of information I receive from my colleagues in the office is very low. (IU-3)	0.905
Social isolation	I feel less integrated in my team at work. (SI-1)	0.920
	I feel poorly informed about the relevant issues from my team at work. (SI-2)	0.876
	It is more difficult for me to use corporate services or utilities at home. (SI-3)	0.829
	I have a lot of contact with my colleagues in the office of my employer.* (SI-4)	-
Exhaustion due to telework	I feel exhausted from working at home. (ET-1)	0.922
	I feel tired from working at home. (ET-2)	0.966
	Working all day at home is a strain for me. (ET-3)	0.953
	I feel burned out from working at home. (ET-4)	0.956
Discontinuous intention towards teleworking	I intend to continue working at home rather than working at the office of my employer.* (DI-1)	-
	My intentions are to continue working at home than working from other locations of my employer.* (DI-2)	-
	If I could, I would like to discontinue my work at home. (DI-3)	1.000
* reverse coded		

5. RESULTS

To present valid results we first test the data sample of the common method bias (CMB) and following to that we present the measurement model. Subsequently, the structural model is described and afterwards a post hoc analysis is conducted.

5.1 Common Method Bias

Perceived and subjective measures are used to capture individuals' responses to a certain situation. A potential issue with subjective measures is the common method bias [44]. To evaluate the extent of CMB, Williams et al. [59] provide an approach to determine the extent by using PLS. Therefore an additional method factor is entered into the PLS model, which contains each indicator of the origin model. In addition, all remaining factors are transformed into single-item constructs. Finally, the ratio of R^2 and path coefficients with the CMB factor to R^2 and path coefficients without the CMB factor are compared. The method factor explains an average R^2 of 0.004 so that a ratio of 1:203 is received. By comparing this ratio with the ratio of prior research using this approach [34], we can state that no signs of CMB influence are observed.

5.2 Measurement Model

All constructs of the measurement model are measured by reflective indicators such that the four aspects of the goodness of fit – content validity, indicator reliability, construct reliability, and discriminant validity – have to be validated [4].

Content Validity. All measurement items we used in the present research originate from prior research, which is described in section 4. These validated and robust measures are applied to the context of teleworking and are displayed in Table 2.

Indicator Reliability. The indicator reliability reflects the relation of the variance of one indicator that comes from the corresponding latent variables. In order to explain at least 50 per cent of the variance of a latent variable by the indicators, values should be more than 0.707 [14]. As shown in Table 2 this condition is fulfilled, except for the items WHC-3, SI-4, DI-1 and DI-2, which have been removed from the model. In addition, a bootstrap method with 5,000 samples is performed and shows significant levels of all loadings of at least 0.001.

Construct Reliability. The construct reliability reflects criteria to determine the quality at the construct level. Therefore, composite reliability (CR) should be higher than 0.7 and average variance extracted (AVE) should be higher than 0.5 [18]. Table 3 displays that the CR as well as AVE criteria are fulfilled.

Discriminant Validity. Discriminant validity describes the extent to which measurement items differ from each other [12]. Discriminant validity is the degree to which a scale measures the variable it is intended to measure, rather than other variables, and it is indicated by low correlations between the measure of interest and the measure of other constructs [18]. It can be demonstrated when the squared root of the AVE for each construct is higher than the correlations between the construct and all other constructs. The square root of the AVE for each construct is located on the diagonal of Table 3 and is higher for all constructs.

Table 3: Measurement Model

Construct	AVE	CR	1	2	3	4	5	6
Work overload	0.873	0.954	0.934					
Work-Home conflict	0.827	0.905	0.866	0.909				
Information underload	0.885	0.959	0.604	0.570	0.941			
Social isolation	0.767	0.908	0.752	0.743	0.599	0.876		
Exhaustion due to teleworking	0.902	0.973	0.812	0.776	0.634	0.715	0.949	
Discontinuous intention towards teleworking	1.000	1.000	0.613	0.566	0.564	0.617	0.741	1.000

Note: All loadings are significant at p<0.001; Square rooted AVE is listed on the diagonal by latent variables correlation

5.3 Structural Model

The coefficient of determination (R^2) and the significance levels of the path coefficients [15] are used to validate the structural model. As displayed in Figure 3, work overload, work-home conflict, information underload, and social isolation explain 72.4 percent of IT personnel's exhaustion due to teleworking. In addition, IT personnel's discontinuous intention towards teleworking is explained to 57.8 percent by work overload, work-home conflict, information underload, social isolation, and exhaustion due to teleworking. The structural equation model shows that all teleworking-induced stressors are statistically significant to exhaustion due to teleworking, whereas only social isolation demonstrated a statistically significant influence on discontinuous intention towards teleworking. Furthermore, the relationship between exhaustion due to teleworking and discontinuous intention towards teleworking is also significant. Results show that H1a, H2a, H3a, H4a, H4b and H5 are supported.

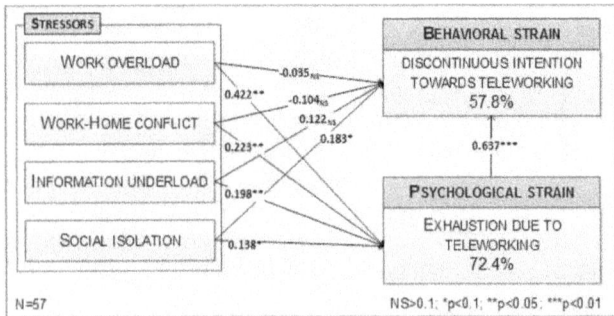

Figure 3: Structural model

5.4 Post-Hoc Analyses

For further specification of the results, we next analyze the effect strength of the independent variables on exhaustion due to teleworking and discontinuous intention towards teleworking and test whether or not psychological strain acts as mediator between stressors and behavioral strain.

5.4.1 Strength of Effect

To determine the strength of effect of the teleworking stressors on the two strain variables the f^2 values are calculated [16], and displayed in Table 4. The main effect on exhaustion due to teleworking is recorded by work overload, whereas exhaustion due to telework indicates the strongest effect on discontinuous intentions towards teleworking. All other effects are low, besides the effect of work overload, work-home conflict, and information underload on discontinuous intention towards teleworking, which do not exist.

Table 4: Strength of Effect

Dependent variables	Independent variables	f^2	Interpretation
Exhaustion due to teleworking	Work overload	0.181	medium
	Work-Home conflict	0.069	low
	Information underload	0.076	low
	Social isolation	0.025	low
Discontinuous intention towards teleworking	Work overload	0.000	non
	Work-Home conflict	0.009	non
	Information underload	0.019	non
	Social isolation	0.031	low
	Exhaustion due to teleworking	0.265	medium

5.4.2 Mediation Effect

The direct effect of the teleworking stressors on the discontinuous intention towards teleworking might be moderated by exhaustion due to teleworking. In order to test the mediation statistically we used a bootstrapping method as suggested by Preacher and Hayes [47].

Table 5: Mediation Effect of Telework-Exhaustion

Independent variables	Mediator	Dependent variables	Indirect effect	Bootstrapping results	
				Lower	Upper
				Bias-corrected confidence interval	
Work overload	Exhaustion due to teleworking	Discontinuous intention towards teleworking	0.33	0.069	0.711
Work-Home conflict			0.15	-0.027	0.517
Information underload			0.20	-0.005	0.702
Social isolation			0.15	-0.059	0.627

Table 5 shows the indirect effects as well as the 95 percent-bias-corrected confidence intervals (1,000 bootstrap resamples) of each independent variable. Results demonstrate that only in the case of work overload the zero is not within the bias-corrected interval, which proves that work overload has an indirect effect on discontinuous intention towards teleworking. In all other cases the zero is within the bias-corrected interval and thus they have no indirect effect through exhaustion due to teleworking on discontinuous intention towards teleworking.

6. DISCUSSION, IMPLICATIONS, AND FUTURE RESEARCH

The research question, how teleworking-induced stressors influence IT personnel's exhaustion due to teleworking and discontinuous intention towards teleworking, is focused in this research article. The research aims to extend the telework literature by showing the negative side effects of an increasingly global work environment among IT personnel. The study hypothesizes that different teleworking-induced stressors influence IT personnel's exhaustion due to telework, which in turn leads to discontinuous intention towards teleworking. The results indicate that all identified teleworking-induced stressors (work overload, work-home conflict, information underload, and social isolation) have a significant influence on IT personnel's exhaustion due to teleworking. This means that the consequences of an increasingly distributed IT workforce influence the employee's psyche negatively with exhaustion as a result. In addition to that, findings of a post-hoc analysis reveal that work overload due to teleworking is the main influencing factor for exhaustion due to teleworking. This exhaustion as well as social isolation caused by teleworking are causes of intentions to stop teleworking and go back to the traditional office structure. As shown in the post hoc analyses, work overload influences the intention to stop teleworking indirectly through exhaustion due to teleworking, which also has the strongest effect on discontinuous intention towards teleworking. These results have several implications which will be discussed in the following paragraphs.

In IS research we extend technostress research (e.g., [2, 48, 56]) by identifying and specifying four teleworking-induced stressors. Beside the renowned ICT-stressors we present specific teleworking stressors, which are highly ICT-enabled and evaluate their influence on psychological and behavioral strain.

In addition, several investigations demonstrate that IT personnel's work stressors in general lead to work exhaustion and turnover intention [40, 51]. Moreover Ahuja et al. [1] focus on the specific stress from IT personnel in the IT consultancy business. We extend these findings by focusing on an additional specific group of IT personnel, the IT teleworkers. They are a unique group of the IT personnel because they work in a totally different environment. They work with temporal and spatial distance to the workplace and depend highly on the usage of ICTs to maintain a link to the office. In the war for talents, teleworking is one opportunity to recruit and retain IT talents without spatial limitations, which makes this group so special. By showing that several stressors related to teleworking increase IT teleworker's exhaustion we extend the findings of general work stress research (e.g. [40],[1, 51]) as well as telework research (e.g. [52]).

Furthermore, we provide evidence that telework-induced stressors and exhaustion due to teleworking determine an intention to stop teleworking. Therefore, we provide evidence for a different scenario by focusing on IT personnel working in a teleworking context and extend the findings of general work stress research (e.g. [40],[1, 51]) as well as telework research in general (e.g. [24, 25]). Hence, with our research we contribute to this stream of research by theorizing and evaluating that stress is related to different aspect of IT personnel's daily work. Following Ahuja et al. [1], Moore [40] and our approach we call for further investigations of IT personnel stress in different contexts to develop a unified theory of stress related to IT work, which especially illustrates the diverse working scenarios of IT personnel.

The empirical investigation of the consequences of major teleworking-induced stressors extends the conceptual view about pitfalls of teleworking (e.g., [7, 11, 38]) by statistical analyzing negative consequences of teleworking among IT personnel.

Findings show that the distributed work of IT personnel enabled by ICT leads to implications for practice. Stressors caused by teleworking increase exhaustion, which in turn leads to the intention to stop working in a teleworking setting. As a result, organizations as well as employees should go back either to traditional work structure or start doing something to avoid stressful stimuli caused by teleworking. Yahoo has decided to stop teleworking, which comes along with diminishing the positive effect teleworking also has. Hence, organizations have to monitor their employees who work at home and provide trainings and other coping mechanisms [58] in order to maintain the huge advantages of IT personnel's teleworking.

For future research, more stressors should be included into the research model. We will investigate how office-induced stressors influences exhaustion and discontinuous intention and then compare these two perspectives. As every empirical research, some issues limit the present research results. First, the model encompasses just a specific choice of the major stressors due to teleworking. There might be more influence factors caused by teleworking, which are not considered within the present research. The measurement items were strongly adapted to the telework context, so strongly that the constructs should be validated again, since we are limited by a single item construct measuring the intention to discontinue teleworking. Also important to mention is the small sample size on account of the IT personnel focus and involving only those in our datasets who contain no missing values and those who have experience in working in a teleworking scenario. Nonetheless, the data sample is validated by the rule of ten [28], though we are aware that our results are limited as discontinuous intention is measured by a single item construct and the data sample contains clearly more males than females, possibly due to heterogeneity of IT personnel [45].

7. CONCLUSION

Based on the IT personnel work stress and telework literature we identified specific telework-induced stressors and hypothesized there influence on psychological and behavioral strain in the form of exhaustion due to teleworking and discontinuous intention towards teleworking. The research model was evaluated by the perceived data of 57 IT professionals. Results demonstrate that all identified teleworking-induced stressors influence exhaustion due to teleworking. Discontinuous intention is directly influenced by social isolation and exhaustion due to teleworking and indirectly by work overload, which illustrates the negative side of IT personnel's teleworking.

8. REFERENCES

[1] Ahuja, M. K., Chudoba, K. M., Kacmar, C. J., McKnight, D. H., and George, J. F. 2007. It Road Warriors: Balancing Work--Family Conflict, Job Autonomy, And Work Overload to Mitigate Turnover Intentions. MIS Quarterly 31, 1, 1–17.

[2] Ayyagari, R., Varun, G., and Russell, P. 2011. Technostress: Technological Antecedents and Implications. MIS Quarterly 35, 4, 831–858.

[3] Baard, N. and Thomas, A. 2010. Teleworking in South Africa: Employee Benefits and Challenges. SA Journal of Human Resource Management 8, 1.

[4] Bagozzi, R. P. 1979. The Role of Measurement in Theory Construction and Hypothesis Testing: Toward a Holistic Model. In Conceptual and Theoretical Developments in Marketing, O. C. Ferrell, S. W. Brown and C. W. Lamb, Eds. Proceedings series - American Marketing Association. American Marketing Association, Chicago, 15–32.

[5] Bailey, D. E. and Kurland, N. B. 2002. A Review of Telework Research: Findings, New Directions, and Lessons for the Study of Modern Work. Journal of Organizational Behavior 23, 4, 383–400.

[6] Ballenstedt, B. 2013. Telework Now Offered by 88 Percent of Organizations. http://www.nextgov.com/cio-briefing/wired-workplace/2013/10/telework-now-offered-88-percent-organizations/72125/?oref=ng-dropdown. Accessed 18 October 2013.

[7] Baruch, Y. 2000. Teleworking: Benefits and Pitfalls as Perceived by Professionals and Managers. New Technology, Work and Employment 15, 1, 34–49.

[8] Bélanger, F. 1999. Communication Patterns in Distributed Work Groups: A Network Analysis. IEEE Transactions on Professional Communication 42, 4, 261.

[9] Bélanger, F. and Allport, C. D. 2008. Collaborative Technologies in Knowledge Telework: An Exploratory Study. Information Systems Journal 18, 1, 101–121.

[10] Bélanger, F., Collins, R. W., and Cheney, P. H. 2001. Technology Requirements and Work Group

Communication for Telecommuters. Information Systems Research 12, 2, 155.

[11] Boell, S. K., Campbell, J., Cecez-Kecmanovic, D., and Cheng, J. E. 2013. The Transformative Nature of Telework: A Review of the Literature. AMCIS 2013 Proceedings.

[12] Campell, D. T. and Fiske, D. W. 1959. Convergent and Discriminant Validation by the Multitrait-multimethod Matrix. Psychological bulletin 56, 2, 81–105.

[13] Caplan, R. D. 1987. Person-environment Fit Theory and Organizations: Commensurate Dimensions, Time Perspectives, and Mechanisms. Journal of Vocational Behavior 31, 3, 248–267.

[14] Carmines, E. G. and Zeller, R. A. 2008. Reliability and Validity Assessment, Sage, Newbury Park, Calif.

[15] Chin, W. W. 1998. The Partial Least Squares Approach for Structural Equation Modeling. In Modern Methods for Business Research, G. A. Marcoulides, Ed. Lawrence Erlbaum.

[16] Cohen, J. 1988. Statistical Power Analysis for the Behavioral Sciences. L. Erlbaum Associates, Hillsdale, N.J.

[17] Ellison, N. B. 1999. Social Impacts: New Perspectives on Telework. Social Science Computer Review 17, 3, 338.

[18] Fornell, C. and Larcker, D. F. 1981. Evaluating Structural Equation Models with Unobservable Variables and Measurement Error. Journal of Marketing Research (JMR) 18, 1, 39–50.

[19] Fritz, M., Higa, K., and Narasimhan, S. 1995. Toward a Telework Taxonomy and Test for Suitability: A Synthesis of the Literature. Group Decision and Negotiation 4, 4, 311-334.

[20] Gajendran, R. S. and Harrison, D. A. 2007. The Good, the Bad, and the Unknown about Telecommuting: Meta-analysis of Psychological Mediators and Individual Consequences. Journal of Applied Psychology 92, 6, 1524–1541.

[21] Gil-de-Zúñiga, H. 2006. Reshaping Digital Inequality in the European Union: How Psychological Barriers Affect Internet Adoption Rates. Webology 3, 4.

[22] Golden, T. 2001. Rightsizing Telework: More Is Not Always Better. AMCIS 2001 Proceedings.

[23] Golden, T. 2002. Toward Reconciling Competing Perspectives on Telework. AMCIS 2002 Proceedings.

[24] Golden, T. 2012. Altering the Effects of Work and Family Conflict on Exhaustion: Telework During Traditional and Nontraditional Work Hours. Journal of Business & Psychology 27, 3, 255–269.

[25] Golden, T. D. 2006. Avoiding Depletion in Virtual Work: Telework and the Intervening Impact of Work Exhaustion on Commitment and Turnover Intentions. Journal of Vocational Behavior 69, 1, 176–187.

[26] Golden, T. D., Veiga, J. F., and Dino, R. N. 2008. The Impact of Professional Isolation on Teleworker Job Performance and Turnover Intentions: Does Time Spent Teleworking, Interacting Face-to-face, or having Access to Communication-enhancing Technology matter? Journal of Applied Psychology 93, 6, 1412.

[27] Greenhaus, J. H. and Beutell, N. J. 1985. Sources of Conflict Between Work and Family Roles. Academy of Management Review 10, 1, 76–88.

[28] Hair, J. F., Ringle, C. M., and Sarstedt, M. 2011. PLS-SEM: Indeed a Silver Bullet. The Journal of Marketing Theory and Practice 19, 2, 139–152.

[29] Igbaria, M. and Guimaraes, T. 1999. Exploring Differences in Employee Turnover Intentions and Its Determinants among Telecommuters and Non-Telecommuters. Journal of Management Information Systems 16, 1, 147–164.

[30] Kerrin, M. and Hone, K. 2001. Job Seekers' perceptions of Teleworking: A Cognitive Mapping Approach. New Technology, Work & Employment 16, 2, 130.

[31] Kossek, E. E., Lautsch, B. A., and Eaton, S. C. 2006. Telecommuting, Control, and Boundary Management: Correlates of Policy Use and Practice, Job Control, and Work–family effectiveness. Journal of Vocational Behavior 68, 2, 347–367.

[32] Laumer, S., Eckhardt, A., and Weitzel, T. 2010. Electronic Human Resources Management in an E-Business Environment. Journal of Electronic Commerce Research 11, 4, 240–250.

[33] Lee, A. 2013. First Yahoo, Now HP Cracks Down on Telecommuting. http://www.cruxialcio.com/first-yahoo-now-hp-cracks-down-telecommuting-2116. Accessed 18 October 2013.

[34] Liang, H., Saraf, N., Hu, Q., and Xue, Y. 2007. Assimilation of Enterprise Systems: The Effect of Institutional Pressures and the Mediating Role of Top Management. MIS Quarterly 31, 1, 59–87.

[35] Maier, C., Laumer, S., Eckhardt, A., and Weitzel, T. 2012. Online Social Networks as a Source and Symbol of Stress: An Empirical Analysis. ICIS 2012 Proceedings.

[36] Maier, C., Laumer, S., Eckhardt, A., and Weitzel, T. 2013. Analyzing the Impact of HRIS Implementations on HR Personnel's Job Satisfaction and Turnover Intention. The Journal of Strategic Information Systems 22, 3, 193–207.

[37] Maier, C., Laumer, S., Eckhardt, A., and Weitzel, T. 2014. Giving Too Much Social Support: Social Overload on Social Networking Sites. Forthcoming in: European Journal of Information Systems.

[38] Mann, S. and Holdsworth, L. 2003. The Psychological Impact of Teleworking: Stress, Emotions and Health. New Technology, Work and Employment 18, 3, 196–211.

[39] McCloskey, D. W. and Igbaria, M. 2003. Does 'Out of Sight' Mean 'Out of Mind'? An Empirical Investigation of the Career Advancement Prospects of Telecommuters. Information Resources Management Journal 16, 2, 19.

[40] Moore, J. E. 2000. One Road to Turnover: An Examination of Work Exhaustion in Technology Professionals. MIS Quarterly 24, 1, 141–168.

[41] Moore, J. E. 2000. Why is this Happening? A Causal Attribution Approach to Work Exhaustion Consequences. Academy of Management Review 25, 2, 335–349.

[42] O'Reilly, C. 1980. Individuals and Information Overload in Organizations: Is More Necessarily Better? The Academy of Management Journal 23, 4, 684–696.

[43] Peters, P. and van der Lippe, T. 2007. The Time-pressure Reducing Potential of Telehomeworking: The Dutch Case. The International Journal of Human Resource Management 18, 3, 430–447.

[44] Podsakoff, P. M., MacKenzie, S. B., Jeong-Yeon Lee, and Podsakoff, N. P. 2003. Common Method Biases in Behavioral Research: A Critical Review of the Literature and Recommended Remedies. Journal of Applied Psychology 88, 5, 879.

[45] Prasad, J., Enns, H. G., and Ferratt, T. W. 2007. One Size Does not Fit All: Managing IT Employees' Employment Arrangements. Human Resource Management 46, 3, 349–372.

[46] Pratt, J. H. 1984. Home Teleworking: A Study of its Pioneers. Technological Forecasting and Social Change 25, 1, 1–14.

[47] Preacher, K. and Hayes, A. 2004. SPSS and SAS Procedures for Estimating Indirect Effects in Simple Mediation Models. Behavior Research Methods 36, 4, 717–731.

[48] Ragu-Nathan, T. S., Tarafdar, M., Ragu-Nathan, B. S., and Tu, Q. 2008. The Consequences of Technostress for End Users in Organizations: Conceptual Development and Empirical Validation. Information Systems Research 19, 4, 417–433.

[49] Rice, R. E. 1992. Task Analyzability, Use of New Media, and Effectiveness: A Multi-site Exploration of Media Richness. Organization Science 3, 4, 475–500.

[50] Ringle, M. C., Wende, S., and Will, A. 2005. SmartPLS: University of Hamburg.

[51] Rutner, P. S., Hardgrave, B. C., and McKnight, D. H. 2008. Emotional Dissonance And The Information Technology Professional. MIS Quarterly 32, 3, 635–652.

[52] Sardeshmukh, S. R., Sharma, D., and Golden, T. D. 2012. Impact of Telework on Exhaustion and Job Engagement: A Job Demands and Job Resources Model. New Technology, Work and Employment 27, 3, 193–207.

[53] Shin, B., El Sawy, O. A., Sheng, O. R. L., and Higa, K. 2000. Telework: Existing Research and Future Directions. Journal of Organizational Computing and Electronic Commerce 10, 2, 85–101.

[54] Simpson, L., Daws, L., Pini, B., and Wood, L. 2001. Beyond the City Limits: An Australian Rural Perspective on Telework. AMCIS 2001 Proceedings.

[55] Sullivan, C. 2003. What's in a Name? Definitions and Conceptualisations of Teleworking and Homeworking. New Technology, Work & Employment 18, 3, 158.

[56] Tarafdar, M., Tu, Q., and Ragu-Nathan, T. S. 2010. Impact of Technostress on End-User Satisfaction and Performance. Journal of Management Information Systems 27, 3, 303–334.

[57] van der Meulen, N., van Baalen, P., and van Heck, E. 2012. Please, Do Not Disturb. Telework, Distractions, and the Productivity of the Knowledge Worker. ICIS 2011 Proceedings.

[58] Weinert, C., Laumer, S., Maier, C., and Weitzel, T. 2013. The Effect of Coping Mechanisms on Technology Induced Stress: Towards a Conceptual Model. AMCIS 2013 Proceedings.

[59] Williams, L. J., Edwards, J. R., and Vandenberg, R. J. 2003. Recent Advances in Causal Modeling Methods for Organizational and Management Research. Journal of Management 29, 6, 903.

[60] WorldatWork. 2013. Survey on Workplace Flexibility 2013. http://www.worldatwork.org/waw/adimLink?id=73898. Accessed 18 October 2013.

The Relationship of Personality Models and Development Tasks in Software Engineering

Manuel Wiesche
Technische Universität München,
Chair for Information Systems
Boltzmannstraße 3,
85748 Garching, Germany
wiesche@in.tum.de

Helmut Krcmar
Technische Universität München,
Chair for Information Systems
Boltzmannstraße 3,
85748 Garching, Germany
krcmar@in.tum.de

ABSTRACT

Understanding the personality of software developers has been an ongoing topic in software engineering research. Software engineering researchers applied different theoretical models to understand software developers' personalities to better predict software developers' performance, orchestrate more effective and motivated teams, and identify the person that fits a certain job best. However, empirical results were found as contradicting, challenging validity, and missing guidance for IT personnel selection. In this research, we explore the current body of knowledge on software developers' personalities by conducting a structured literature review. We provide an overview of the applied psychological models, research designs, contexts, and results. We discuss our findings and suggest promising avenues for further research on software engineering task characteristics and the impact of personality-task fit on software development performance.

Keywords

Software engineering; personality; literature review; disposition; Myers-Briggs Type Indicator (MBTI); five factors model (FFM); job diagnostic survey (JDS); Big 5 personality dimensions.

1. INTRODUCTION

Understanding the personality of software developers has been an ongoing topic in software engineering research (Bartol et al. 1982; Capretz et al. 2010; Cruz et al. 2011; Pocius 1991; Varona et al. 2012). Studies examined the relative stable combination of emotional, motivational, and attitudinal response patterns of an individual to better predict software developers' performance, orchestrate more effective and motivated teams, and identify the person that fits a certain job best (Cruz et al. 2011).

Empirical studies applied different theoretical models from psychology to understand software developers' personalities. Studies applied the Myers-Briggs Type Indicator (MBTI), the Big 5 personality dimensions, and the five factors model (FFM) to understand various dimensions of human aspects of software engineering (Capretz et al. 2010). Researchers found software developers with independent tasks that require creativity as introvert (Lounsbury et al. 2007; Turley et al. 1995), whereas collaboration-intensive tasks such as pair programming or leadership-related tasks require extroversion (Acuña et al. 2006; Wang 2009). The job diagnostic survey (JDS) was applied to understand software engineering tasks characteristics and their effect on turnover (Thatcher et al. 2003) or motivation (Gambill et al. 2000). However, empirical results were found as contradicting (Cruz et al. 2011), lacking validity (Feldt et al. 2008), and missing guidance for IT personnel selection (Shneiderman 1980; Weinberg 1971). While it is widely accepted that software developers' personality affects job satisfaction, the influence of software developers' personality still remains unclear (Hannay et al. 2010; Morris et al. 2010; Salleh et al. 2011; Weinberg 1971).

In addition to these arguments, there are some developments that challenge our understanding of software developers' personalities: Software development trends such as technological change (Gallivan 2004), new methodological paradigms (Aitken et al. 2013), outsourcing (Gopal et al. 2009), distributed teams (Espinosa et al. 2007), open source development (Roberts et al. 2006), developments in task complexity (Varona et al. 2012), globalization, or new business models (ExecutiveBrief 2013) fundamentally change the tasks software developers are confronted with (Snyder et al. 2006).

In this research, we explore the current body of knowledge on software developers' personalities by conducting a structured literature review (Webster et al. 2002). We reviewed and classified relevant literature according to the underlying psychological model, level of analysis, research design, development context, and the outcome of the study. We discuss several observations: Our results provide indicators for a relationship between task-personality fit and software engineering performance. We suggest differentiating task characteristics in software engineering in order to examine the effect of the fit of task characteristics and developer's personality on satisfaction and performance. We observed that most studies focused on individual and team level tasks. We suggest considering the organizational level as well. We outline the challenges in pursuing flexibility and rigor simultaneously and recommend examining personality traits in this context. We suggest carefully reviewing psychological models for appropriateness in software engineering and recommend revisiting the role of autonomy in theoretical models.

Permission to make digital or hard copies of all or part of this work for personal or classroom use is granted without fee provided that copies are not made or distributed for profit or commercial advantage and that copies bear this notice and the full citation on the first page. Copyrights for components of this work owned by others than the author(s) must be honored. Abstracting with credit is permitted. To copy otherwise, or republish, to post on servers or to redistribute to lists, requires prior specific permission and/or a fee. Request permissions from Permissions@acm.org.

SIGMIS-CPR '14, May 29–31 2014, Singapore, Singapore.
Copyright is held by the owner/author(s). Publication rights licensed to ACM.
ACM 978-1-4503-2625-4/14/05…$15.00.
http://dx.doi.org/10.1145/2599990.2600012

In this research, we explore the current body of knowledge on software developers' personalities by conducting a structured literature review (Webster et al. 2002). We reviewed and classified relevant literature according to the underlying psychological model, level of analysis, research design, development context, and the outcome of the study. We discuss several observations: Our results provide indicators for a relationship between task-personality fit and software engineering performance. We suggest differentiating task characteristics in software engineering in order to examine the effect of the fit of task characteristics and developer's personality on satisfaction and performance. We observed that most studies focused on individual and team level tasks. We suggest considering the organizational level as well. We outline the challenges in pursuing flexibility and rigor simultaneously and recommend examining personality traits in this context. We suggest carefully reviewing psychological models for appropriateness in software engineering and recommend revisiting the role of autonomy in theoretical models.

2. METHODS

For this research, we reviewed literature from computer science, information systems, management and psychology. For identifying relevant literature on the personality of software developers, we conducted a structured literature search following the guidelines by Webster and Watson (2002). We identified an initial set of articles and conducted backward and forward searches to identify other relevant articles in the domain of interest. We reviewed all articles and classified them using different criteria.

2.1 Literature search design

We identified key words based on our initial understanding of the research topic and added new key words when we identified additional literature. The final list of key words is summarized in table 1. We combined the key words and searched in title, abstract, key words, and – if possible – full text. We reviewed the top 50 journals as ranked by the Association for Information Systems' MIS Journal ranking[1] and added the conferences *ACM SIG-MIS Computers and People Research (CPR), International Conference on Information Systems (ICIS), Americas Conference on Information Systems (AMCIS), European Conference on Information Systems (ECIS), Hawaii International Conference on System Sciences (HICSS)*, and *Wirtschaftsinformatik (WI)*. We did not limit the time period of our search. However, we could not access several older conference proceedings that were not listed in ACM, IEEE or AIS eLibrary.

We identified potentially relevant publications using the key words in the journals and conferences mentioned above. We pre-screened the publications regarding their relevance for the topic. We reviewed title, abstract, and key words to determine whether the article (a) focused on software developers personality, (b) applied a psychological model or conducted an exploratory analysis to develop an understanding of software developers personality, (c) used empirical data.

---

[1] http://ais.site-ym.com/?JournalRankings, the MIS Journal ranking provides an overview of 9 AIS journal rankings and an average of rank points of each ranking.

Table 1. List of key words used in the literature review.

Key words on personality			
Personality	Disposition	People	Motivation
Big five	Big 5	Five factor model	FFM
PSI	Personal Style Inventory	Satisfaction	
Key words on software engineering			
Software development	Programming	Information system	Software project
Software Engineering			

During the development of our initial sample we applied back- and forward search techniques to identify additional publications relevant for our research inquiry. In the backward search, we reviewed the citations in our initial sample of publications and identified further publications that met the criteria mentioned above. This helped us refine our key words and journal/conference list and increased the list of relevant publications. Similarly, we applied forward search. We reviewed the citations of publications from our initial sample in Google Scholar and thereby identified additional publications that met the criteria mentioned above. The backward and forward searches increased our data set and helped in identifying dissertations, books, and other publications that were not included in our initial list. Our final sample comprises 52 publications.

2.2 Literature analysis

For the analysis of the publications, we followed the guidelines suggested by Webster and Watson (2002) for conducting a concept-centric literature review. We therefore identified several concepts which we used for structuring our analysis. As psychological literature discusses the utility of different psychological tests (e. g., McCrae et al. 1992), we classified different personality tests with the concept of the underlying psychological model. We further included the level of analysis, research design, the software engineering context, the dependent variable, and the outcome of the study.

3. RESULTS

We identified 52 studies that investigate the personality of software developers. The first study was published in 1980, the most recent study was published in 2013. We identified 20 studies applying the MBTI, 11 studies applying the Big 5 model, 8 studies applying the JDS, 5 studies applying the FFM, 1 study applying the 16 personality factors model, 1 study applying the PSI, and 6 studies conducting an exploratory analysis of personality factors. Figure 1 provides an overview of the applied psychological models. In our sample, 32 studies used software developers in their sample, 13 used students from various software engineering classes, 2 used both students and software engineers, 1 study used developers and professors, 3 used managers, and 1 study did not mention details on their sample. Appendix A provides an overview of the found studies. In the following, we summarize the current body of knowledge on software developer personalities grouped by the underlying personality model.

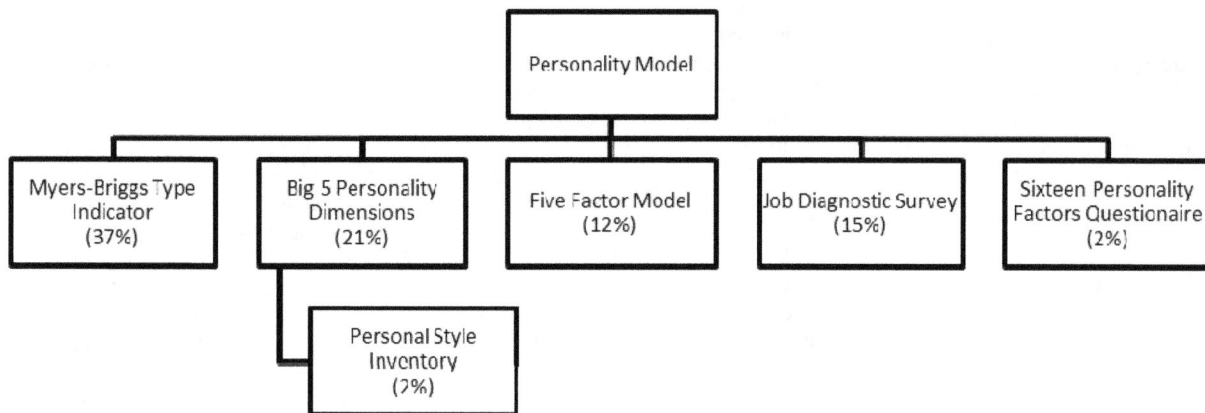

Figure 1. Psychological models applied in the literature.

3.1 Studies applying the Myers-Briggs Type Indicator (MBTI)

The most prominent theoretical model applied in software developer personality research is the Jungian personality dimensions model (Myers et al. 1985). The model presumes that one's personality is based on three dimensions: (1) how people relate to the world, (2) the way information is taken in, and (3) the way information is processed (Kaiser et al. 1982). Thus, the model differentiates the continuum of the people who are drawn to the inner world of ideas (*I - introverts*) to those who are drawn to the outer world of people and things (*E - extroverts*), perception of information is the second continuum ranging from relying on facts and data (*S - sensing*) to conceptualizing using common sense and little data (*N - intuition*), processing information can either be done by using logic and analysis (*T - thinking*) or by using emotion and value judgment (*F - feeling*), and the tendency for taking information in perception (*P - perception*) or processing information (*J - judgement*). This model has been operationalized in the Myers-Briggs Type Indicator (MBTI) measuring each continuum on a complementary scale (Myers et al. 1985).

The earliest application of the MBTI in software engineering was in 1982 (Kaiser et al. 1982), and it has been constantly applied. The MBTI was applied on individuals (Capretz et al. 2010) and groups (Peslak 2006) and with various research methods, including surveys (Gorla et al. 2004), experiments (Peslak 2006), and interviews (White 1984). The model was applied with students (Rutherfoord 2006) and professional developers (Gorla et al. 2004). The majority of the studies examined the effect of the developers' personality on job satisfaction and various forms of individual, team, or project performance. Other studies examined personality antecedents (Yilmaz et al. 2012) or compared personality types between industry and academia (Raza et al. 2012).

The most common personality types are INTJ, ISTJ, ESTP, and ESTJ. Empirical studies identified the ISTJ type as the most prominent among software developers: IS professionals are introverted, highly rational and analytical 'thinkers' rather than 'feelers' (Gorla et al. 2004; Hardiman 1997; Mair et al. 2012; Mourmant et al. 2007; White et al. 1986). While these studies confirmed that introvert types are the most common, there is trend toward other types. Recent research identified extrovert types

such as ESTP and ESTJ as more prominent among software developers in practice (Raza et al. 2012; Shoaib et al. 2009; Yilmaz et al. 2012). Raza et al. (2012) found that software developers in industry are more extrovert than compared to those in academia. In the context of exploratory testing, successful software developers tend to have extrovert personalities as well (Shoaib et al. 2009).

3.2 Studies applying the Big 5 personality dimensions

Another prominent model for assessing personality is the Big Five Personality Dimensions (Big 5) model (Goldberg 1990). The model consists of five personality traits that are universal to the human population. Traits are understood as temporally stable, cross-situational individual differences. The five traits within the Big 5 model are Surgency, Agreeableness, Conscientiousness, Emotional Stability, and Intellect. *Surgency* refers to an individual's orientation towards others. Individuals scoring high on this trait are talkative, bold, assertive and sociable. *Agreeableness* refers to an individual's likability and social conformity. Agreeable individuals get along well with others, are kind, trustworthy, and helpful. *Conscientiousness* refers to an individual's achievement orientation. Conscientious individuals are hard hardworking, organized, and able to complete tasks thoroughly, on time and reliably. *Emotional Stability* refers to an individual being anxious, stressed, volatile, and fearful. Individuals scoring high on this trait experience more negative emotions. *Intellect* refers to an individual's imagination, curiosity, and open-mindedness. Individuals scoring high on intellect are curious and broadminded and appreciate art (Bansal et al. 2010). These traits are understood as a complete description of one's personality. They are stable over a decade-long period in time and across cultures (Zillig et al. 2002).

The Big 5 model has gained prominence in software engineering research in the last 8 years. The model has been applied to both the individual and team level. Researchers using the Big 5 model examined cooperation among software developers. A prominent phenomenon examined was pair programming (e. g., Chao et al. 2006; Hannay et al. 2010; Salleh et al. 2011; Walle et al. 2009). The model has been mainly used to determine the effect of a developer's personality on programming effectiveness. The studies applied different research methods including content analysis, experiments (Hannay et al. 2010; Salleh et al. 2011), and surveys (Chao et al. 2006) and used different samples, i. e., students (Salleh et al. 2011) and professional programmers (Hannay et al. 2010; Walle et al. 2009). However, the studies found contradicting results regarding the effect of personality on performance. Walle et al. (2009) and Salleh at al (2011) suggest that certain personality traits significantly affect performance and satisfaction. Chao et al. (2006) and Hannay et al. (2010) did not find any statistically significant correlation.

3.3 Studies applying the five factors model (FFM)

A slight variation of the Big 5 model is the five factors model (McCrae et al. 1992). While the descriptions of the five traits are similar to the Big 5, the models differ in terms of theoretical basis, causation, and measurement. While the Big 5 assumes that personality traits are so central to social interaction that that labels for all traits are included in the language – the lexical hypothesis – the FFM provides a comprehensive model of causes and contexts (McCrae et al. 1992). Causation is not discussed in the Big 5 model, the FFM assumes biosocial, i. e., genetic and environmental causation. Finally, the Big 5 model comprises a circular measurement model in contrast to the FFM that is based on hierarchical measurement.

The five factors in the FFM are Extraversion, Agreeableness, Conscientiousness, Neuroticism, and Openness to Experience (Wang 2009). *Extraversion* refers to a person's engagement with the external world. Extroverts feel comfortable in social relationships, are enthusiastic, friendly, active and outgoing. *Agreeableness* refers to an individual's way of cooperating with others. *Conscientiousness* refers to how individuals control, regulate, and direct their impulses. *Neuroticism* refers to how an individual experiences negative feelings. Low neuroticism individuals are emotionally stable, appear calm, confident and secure. *Openness to Experience* refers to an individual's imaginative and creative traits (Salleh et al. 2012).

The FFM has been applied in software engineering research as well (Aronson et al. 2006; Salleh et al. 2012; Wang 2009). It has been applied on an individual (Wang 2009) and team (Salleh et al. 2012) level. The topics ranged from new product development (Aronson et al. 2006) to pair programming (Salleh et al. 2012). A set of interrelated experiments with students was run on different dimensions of the model (Salleh et al. 2011; Salleh et al. 2012; Salleh et al. 2009; Salleh et al. 2010) and found that neither Conscientiousness nor Neuroticism affect students' academic performance. Wang et al. (2009) suggest a model that relates personality factors to project manager's leadership behavior and ultimately project success. The authors find Openness, Agreeableness, Conscientious, and Extraversion to affect leadership. Other studies support these findings (Aronson et al. 2006). We observe that FFM studies that were conducted in academic setting (Darcy et al. 2005; Salleh et al. 2012; Salleh et al. 2009; Salleh et al. 2010) did not find significant effects of personality on performance while studies that use data from industry find significant influences of personality on performance (Aronson et al. 2006; Wang 2009).

3.4 Studies applying the job diagnostic survey (JDS)

Another model that is frequently applied for understanding software developers' personality is the job characteristics model (JCM) (Hackman et al. 1975). In contrast to the models introduced above that focus on examining individual differences in the software developers' personality, the JCM examines task characteristics and motivation to affect performance. The model suggests a relationship between the perception of different job characteristics and job outcomes: A more favorable perception of any job characteristic will lead to a better job outcome, such as increased job satisfaction. The JCM has been operationalized by the job diagnostic survey (JDS), measuring *task significance*, defined as the extent to which a job has impact on the lives of people in an organization or society in general; *task identity*, defined as the extent to which a job involves completing a whole identifiable outcome; *skill variety*, defined as the extent to which a job requires the use of different talents; *autonomy*, defined as the extent to which a job provides the employee with discretion to choose how the work is done and to set the schedule for completing the work activities; and *feedback*, defined as the extent to which carrying out the work activities provides the employee with clear information about his or her performance (Hackman et al. 1975; Morris et al. 2010).

The JDS has been applied in different contexts in software engineering research. Several studies applied the JDS to examine the job characteristics of software developers in relation to turnover intention (Thatcher et al. 2003), motivation (Gambill et al. 2000), and job satisfaction (Goldstein et al. 1984). Other studies used the JDS to examine the impact of software on users (Morris et al. 2010), to understand the differences between software developers and others (Couger et al. 1980; Ferratt et al. 1988) and to examine the relationship between contracted and permanent software developers (Ang et al. 2001). While the importance of task characteristics in determining job satisfaction is pointed out (Thatcher et al. 2003), other results suggest that relationships with others influence satisfaction as much as task characteristics (Goldstein et al. 1984). However, the discussion on the usefulness of the JDS for software engineering is ongoing (Ferratt et al. 1988; Polites et al. 2011; Sein et al. 1991).

3.5 Other studies examining software developers' personality

Several studies applied other models or exploratory designs to assess software developers' personality. An early study applied the Sixteen Personality Factors Questionnaire (16PF) to different software engineering jobs and identified significant differences between application programmers, systems analysts, technical programmers, and data processing managers (Moore 1991). Lounsbury et al. (2007) applied the Personal Style Inventory (PSI). The PSI consists of 8 traits, including these of the Big 5 model plus Assertiveness, Image Management, Optimism, Tough-Mindedness, Work Drive, and Customer Service Orientation (Lounsbury et al. 2003). The study found these traits significantly affect job satisfaction. Young et al. (2005) conducted an exploratory study using the concept of repertory grid to identify roles for developing software and examine appropriate personality characteristics for different roles.

Some studies conducted exploratory analyses of certain aspects of personality on software engineering as well. Wynekoop and Walz (2000) conducted a delphi study to identify the most important traits of top performers in software engineering and identify the ability to transfer abstract business problems into technical terms, creativity in problem solving, and good communication skills as the three most important skills. Naqvi et al. (2009) suggest examining the personality requirements for project leaders in order to make effective strategic decisions. Lalsing et al. (2012) conducted a survey among agile development team members and identified a shift from individual task accomplishing to interaction with team members to account for project success in agile software development. Dick et al. (2002) suggest interviewing techniques to identify developers that score high on communication skills, comfort in working with others, confidence in working on a team, and ability to compromise, which constitute an successful software developer for pair programming. Galivan (2004) identifies tolerance of ambiguity, gender, and openness to experience as job satisfaction drivers in technological change situations.

4. DISCUSSION

There are several conclusions that can be drawn from these findings that deem worthwhile for further discussion. We identified several underlying psychological models and will discuss their suitability for the particular context. We identified personality differences depending on the software engineering tasks and suggest further examining tasks to better understand how personality relates with tasks. The ambidexterity of requirements in terms of flexibility and rigor may be assessed to better understand personalities that are able to cope with such situations effectively. Next, the role of personality-task fit in ensuring better project performance is assessed. We discuss the role of autonomy in software engineering personality research and provide insights on identifying the appropriate personality model for studying different software engineering scenarios.

4.1 Understanding task characteristics in software engineering

The identified models can be categorized into two groups: Those that focus on individual personality traits such as the MBTI, FFM, and Big 5 and those that focus on a universal set of task characteristics that together influence job satisfaction such as the JDS. While both groups contribute differently to understanding software developer's personality, our analysis suggests that selecting and managing successful and satisfied software developers is a function of both task characteristics and individual personality.

The JDS assumes a universal set of individual dispositions among every software developer. Since software engineering involves interpersonal relations, reuse of existing work, and methodological guidance, the usability of models like the JDS that assume that job satisfaction is a function of tasks carried out by the employee independently and his/her feelings about the job is only limitedly suitable for assessing software developers personalities. It has been extended with social needs strength to better suit the context of software engineering (Couger et al. 1980). Seeing software engineering as a collaboration-intensive job, Goldstein et al. (1984) introduce team specific requirements. The authors introduce measures for the amount of conflict and ambiguity as a horizontal dimension of team interaction and quality of leadership as vertical dimension of team interaction. However, developments such as new development paradigms (Conboy 2009; Lindvall et al. 2002), user-involvement (Harris et al. 2009), pair programming (e. g., Chao et al. 2006; Salleh et al. 2011) and global virtual collaboration (Sarker et al. 2011) have changed how software developers communicate and interact.

It is important to further understand the relationship between software developers' personalities and different tasks that these developers are confronted with. The topic of task differences has been discussed in literature (e. g., Goldstein 1989; Rehman et al.

2012; Sein et al. 1991). Rehman et al. (2012) for example differentiate analyst, architect, developer, and tester as different software engineering roles. With an enhanced understanding of tasks that are specific to certain software engineering roles, we might be able to provide a more thorough understanding of personality traits that satisfied software developers ought to possess and that consequently affect performance. While existing differentiations are useful steps toward better understanding software engineering tasks they might not be suitable to examine the task-personality relationship that determines successful and satisfying software engineering. Roles like testing were seen as rather un-creative and on an individual level in the past, now turn into exploratory tasks that require extroversion and collaboration (Shoaib et al. 2009).

A promising avenue for further research would be to classify different software engineering tasks according to their requirements in terms of characteristics such as required ability to transfer abstract business problems into technical terms, creativity in problem solving, and good communication skills as the three most important skills (Wynekoop et al. 2000). Using this classification would be helpful in developing taxonomies of software engineering jobs that would help refine software engineering tasks characteristics to match personality traits.

4.2 A new dimension of tasks – the organizational level

Our results reveal that current personality research in software engineering largely focused on individual and team level (e. g., Aronson et al. 2006; Capretz et al. 2010; Peslak 2006; Salleh et al. 2012; Wang 2009). We suggest that organizational requirements affect job satisfaction as well (Abdel-Hamid et al. 1990; Adler et al. 2005; Adler 2005; Chapman et al. 2009). Software engineering team members are confronted with numerous procedural guidelines and expectations to accomplish project goals (Henderson et al. 1992). Such organizational requirements have been found affecting software developer's performance (Abernethy et al. 1997; Basili et al. 1981; Deephouse et al. 2013; Nidumolu et al. 2003). Hardgrave et al. (2003) differentiate factors that influence developer's intentions to follow organizational requirements. They assert that an organizational mandate impacts the degree to which a developer believes that following a methodology has been formally imposed influences the perception of process/behavior control (Hardgrave et al. 2003). Ang and Slaughter (2001) differentiated between permanent and contracted software developers, who work only on one particular project and are often confronted with tasks that are narrow, limited in scope and significance, unchallenging, and lack autonomy. The study found contracted software developers perceive less in-role and extra-role behavior, but perceive a more favorable work environment than permanent software developers.

While these studies outline a more complex relationship between organizational requirements and job satisfaction, we suggest it would be worthwhile to examine the role of organizational requirements in software engineering tasks in detail. A promising avenue for future research would be to further examine how organizational requirements such as formalization (Adler et al. 2005; Adler 2005) or behavior control (Kirsch 1996; Kirsch et al. 2002; Ply et al. 2012) are perceived by different software engineering personalities. The role of the individual has already been considered as important factor for informal control (Chua et al. 2012; Cram et al. 2013; Kirsch et al. 2010).

4.3 Tasks that require flexibility and rigor simultaneously

Building on the observation of organizational requirements of software engineering tasks, another promising avenue for further research might be examining the challenge that software developers are confronted with flexibility and rigor simultaneously (Lee et al. 2006). Consider the example of developing software in a large organization that follows an agile paradigm: the process of following an agile approach such as extreme programming requires constant planning rather than formal planning upfront, reduces the documentation, and minimalist development (Coram et al. 2005). However, the project needs to be embedded in the organizational context, comply with organizational requirements such as development methodologies, and ensure proper documentation (Trimble et al. 2013).

Similar issues are revealed in research on the adoption of agile development paradigms in formalized organizations with high capability maturity levels (Bianco 2011). Considering the example of the Capability Maturity Model (CMM) suggests that many CMM key process areas (KPA) especially on the lower levels are addressed in agile development methodologies. For example the agile practice of user stories establishes a common understanding between customer and developer and thus fulfills the CMM requirements management KPA (Paulk 2001). As the customer is continuously involved in developing and prioritizing user stories a common understanding is established. However, there are certain CMM requirements that are violated in agile practices. Especially on higher levels, CMM recommends quantifying the software quality. Therefore, formal reviews are conducted on a regular basis. In agile development methodologies, peer reviews serve similar purposes. The formal character of quality control in CMM has different effects than the peer pressure applied in peer control (Sewell 1998; Stewart et al. 2012). Similarly, the short-term problem solving in customer-feedback cycles in agile sprints contradicts CMM's goal of organizational learning through long-term documentation outside of the produced code (Rus et al. 2002) would be promising starting points.

It would be worthwhile to examine the personality of software developers, who succeed in this ambidextrous situation of flexibility and rigor (Lee et al. 2006). Examining software engineering teams in large organizations that successfully apply agile principles (Trimble et al. 2013), understand how organizations overcome challenges in adopting agile methodologies (Cohn et al. 2003), or understand the application of frameworks such as the People-Capability Maturity Model (Hunter 1998).

4.4 Personality may account for project control inefficiencies

Our review reveals heterogeneous findings regarding the impact of personality on performance. Several studies provide empirical evidence that personality-task fit enhances performance in terms of productivity and quality (Da Cunha et al. 2007; Gorla et al. 2004; Kaiser et al. 1982; Omar et al. 2010). However, other studies question the importance of personality in software engineering performance (Chao et al. 2006; Hannay et al. 2010; Rehman et al. 2012; Salleh et al. 2012; Salleh et al. 2010). Meta studies in psychology (Hurtz et al. 2000) suggest a relationship between personality and contextual performance. We suggest

examining the relationship between personality traits and software engineering performance more closely. Existing research on software engineering project risks and control mechanisms (Kirsch 1996; Kirsch et al. 2002) has predominantly focused on the organizational, team, and individual characteristics that influence the type of control that is applied in certain situations (Kirsch 1996). Existing research suggests that each type of control represents a distinct approach to influencing the behavior of organizational actors (Cram et al. 2013; Kirsch 1997; Ouchi 1979). The monitoring of organization actors (behavioral control) is applied when management has high knowledge of the transformation process. In situations where management is able to measure output, certain goals or outputs are defined (outcome control). When management has little knowledge of the transformation process and no ability to measure output, social norms (clan control) or empowerment of the organizational actors (self-control) can be applied.

In organization literature, such configurations are referred to as 'task–tool network' (Argote 2012; Argote et al. 2000; McGrath et al. 2002). It specifies which tools are used to perform which tasks. This literature suggests examining the 'member–task–tool network' as well. It specifies which members perform which tasks with which tools. In the context of software engineering, this seems to be promising as well: The results of this review outline software developer's individual differences and their effect on satisfaction. These findings suggest that different kinds of people are attracted or reflected by different task-tool configurations (Boss et al. 2009; Ply et al. 2012). While some studies find software developers value autonomy (Goldstein et al. 1984; Lee et al. 2010; Seaman et al. 1997), others find organizational design as enabling and appreciated (Adler et al. 2005; Adler 2005; Hardgrave et al. 2003; Ply et al. 2012; Riemenschneider et al. 2002). Further examining the relationship of personality and task might enhance our understanding of how controls in software engineering projects assure project success.

4.5 Revisiting the role of autonomy in software engineering personality research

Our results reveal that the applied models suggest that autonomy is among the main factors driving software developer's job satisfaction (e. g., Gorla et al. 2004; Hannay et al. 2010; Kaiser et al. 1982; Morris et al. 2010). The underlying theoretical models argue that the degree to which the work requirements provide substantial freedom, independence, and discretion to the individual in work scheduling and procedure selection affects job satisfaction. But empirical research found that situations with less autonomy are still fulfilling and delightful for software developers (Adler et al. 2005; Ang et al. 2001; Ply et al. 2012; Santana et al. 1995). It appears that in borrowing from psychological concepts that focus strongly on the individual itself, existing theoretical models have omitted organizational procedures such as methodologies or toolkits that support software developers in the work they are doing.

4.6 Identifying the appropriate personality model

Our review identified the MBTI as the most popular model to examine software developer personalities. However, the MBTI has been recognized as inconclusive by psychology research and may bias the conclusions drawn from the results (Furnham 1996). The MBTI operationalizes the Jungian psychodynamic type theory insufficiently in terms of construct validity and reliability (Boyle 1995). Other studies suggest that instead of measuring "truly dichotomous preferences or qualitatively distinct types, […] the instrument measures four relatively independent dimensions" and question the interpretation of the Judging – Perceiving index (McCrae et al. 1989). Instead of developing creative experiment designs that are close to MBTI (Yilmaz et al. 2012), future research should consider the state of the art in personality research in psychology (Oswald et al. 2011) and use models that are better suitable. Further, software developer personality research should differentiate more carefully between the models Big 5 and FFM as they differ in certain characteristics (McCrae et al. 1992; Zillig et al. 2002).

However, there are several limitations that have to be taken into account. First, it should be considered that this review might have missed relevant work. Furthermore, the quality of the studies used for this review differed. For example, some studies did not provide all relevant information on their sample. In four studies, we could not identify the country, in which the study was conducted, which might account for several cultural differences in personalities (Hofstede 1984). While this review is based on a qualitative analysis, a meta-analysis using a quantitative approach on the data could have yielded further details as well (Hunter et al. 2004). Our analysis might over-emphasize conclusions that are had only weak effects in the original study that could have been addressed more accurately in a meta-analysis. Even though meta-analytic reviews are popular on personality topics (Barrick et al. 1991), we argue that the heterogeneity of personality models and dependent variables prohibit a high-quality meta-analysis on this broad topic. We further found several studies that did not provide detailed information on their analysis. Several methodological issues occurred in the studies at hand. The low sample size, non-reliable operationalization and outdated statistical methods may limit the conclusions that can be drawn from the empirical results reported.

5. CONCLUSION

In this research, we reviewed the current body of knowledge on software developers' personalities by conducting a structured literature review. We provided an overview of the prominent psychological models, research designs, contexts, and results. We discuss indicators for a relationship between task-personality fit and software engineering performance. We suggest differentiating task characteristics in software engineering in order to examine the effect of the fit of task characteristics and developer's personality on satisfaction and performance. We observed that most studies focused on individual and team level tasks and suggest considering the organizational level as well. We outline the challenges in pursuing flexibility and rigor simultaneously and recommend examining personality traits in this context as well. We suggest carefully reviewing psychological models for appropriateness in software engineering and recommend revisiting the role of autonomy in theoretical models.

6. ACKNOWLEDGMENTS

We thank SAP AG for funding this project as part of the collaborative research center, Center for Very Large Business Applications (CVLBA).

APPENDIX

Appendix A: Overview of Studies identified in the literature review.

Study	Sample size	Country	Model	Research design
(Couger et al. 1980)	2550 (d)	USA	JDS	Survey
(Kaiser et al. 1982)	38 (d)	USA	MBTI	Survey
(Goldstein et al. 1984)	118 (d)	USA	JDS	Survey
(White 1984)	20 (d)	USA	MBTI	Mixed methods
(White et al. 1986)	68 (d)	USA	MBTI	Survey
(Ferratt et al. 1988)	1005 (d)	-	JDS	Survey
(Sein et al. 1991)	170 (d)	USA	JDS	Survey
(Moore 1991)	113 (d)	USA	16PF	Survey
(Turley et al. 1995)	129 (d)	USA	MBTI	Survey
(Hardiman 1997)	60 (d)	USA	MBTI	Survey
(Bradley et al. 1997)	2 (d teams)	USA	MBTI	Survey
(Buchanan 1998)	610 (s)	USA	Big5	Experiment
(Gambill et al. 2000)	117 (d)	USA	JDS	Survey
(Wynekoop et al. 2000)	50 (d)	USA	-	Delphi study
(Ang et al. 2001)	75 (d)	SGP	JDS	Survey
(Dick et al. 2002)	6 (d)	CDN	-	Exploration
(Thatcher et al. 2003)	193 (d)	-	JDS	Survey

(Capretz 2003)	100 (d, s)	-	MBTI	Survey
(Gorla et al. 2004)	92 (d)	CHN	MBTI	Survey
(Gallivan 2004)	30 (d)	USA	-	Mixed methods
(Katira et al. 2004)	564 (s)	USA	MBTI	Experiment
(Darcy et al. 2005)	29 (s)	USA	Big5	Experiment
(Karn et al. 2005)	-	GB	MBTI	Ethnography
(Peslak 2006)	55 (s)	USA	MBTI	Experiment
(Chao et al. 2006)	60 (d), 68 (s)	USA	Big5	Experiment
(Aronson et al. 2006)	143 (d)	USA	FFM	Survey
(Liu et al. 2006)	218 (d)	RC	Big5	Survey
(Rutherfoord 2006)	22 (s)	USA	MBTI	Experiment
(Young et al. 2005)	6 (d)	GB	-	Survey
(Mourmant et al. 2007)	1471 (d)	F	MBTI	Survey
(Da Cunha et al. 2007)	64 (s)	-	MBTI	Experiment
(Lounsbury et al. 2007)	1059 (d)	USA	PSI	Survey
(Feldt et al. 2008)	47 (d)	S	Big5	Survey
(Derro et al. 2009)	38 (d)	USA	MBTI	Observation
(Salleh et al. 2009)	54 (s)	NZ	FFM	Experiment
(Walle et al. 2009)	44 (d)	S, N	Big5	Observation
(Naqvi et al. 2009)	104 (m)	PK	-	Survey
(Wang 2009)	50 (m)	CHN	FFM	Survey
(Shoaib et al. 2009)	71 (s)	PK	MBTI	Experiment
(Bell et al. 2010)	128 (s)	E	Big5	Experiment
(Salleh et al. 2010)	453 (s)	NZ	FFM	Experiment
(Hannay et al. 2010)	196 (d)	S, N, GB	Big5	Experiment
(Omar et al. 2010)	78 (s)	MAL	MBTI	Experiment
(Morris et al. 2010)	2794 (d)	USA	JDS	Survey
(Salleh et al. 2011)	137 (s)	NZ	Big5	Experiment
(Ülke et al. 2011)	189 (d)	TR	Big5	Survey
(Salleh et al. 2012)	594 (s)	NZ	FFM	Experiment
(Mair et al. 2012)	5 (m)	GB	Big5	Survey
(Raza et al. 2012)	52 (d), 18 (p)	PK	MBTI	Survey
(Lalsing et al. 2012)	3 (d teams)	GB	-	Survey
(Karapıçak et al. 2013)	12 (d)	TR	MBTI	Survey
(Yilmaz 2013)	63 (d)	IRL	MBTI	Experiment

"-" – not mentioned in the study; d – developers, s – students, m – managers, p - professors

7. REFERENCES

1. Abdel-Hamid, T., and Madnick, S. "The elusive silver lining: How we fail to learn from software development failures," Sloan Management Review (32:1) 1990, pp 39-48.

2. Abernethy, M. A., and Brownell, P. "Management control systems in research and development organizations: the role of accounting, behavior and personnel controls," Accounting, Organizations and Society (22:3) 1997, pp 233-248.

3. Acuña, S. T., Juristo, N., and Moreno, A. M. "Emphasizing Human Capabilities in Software Development," IEEE Software (23:2) 2006, pp 94-101.

4. Adler, P., McGarry, F., Irion-Talbot, W., and Binney, D. "Enabling Process Discipline: Lessons from the Journey to CMM Level 5," MIS Quarterly Executive (4:1) 2005, pp 215-227.

5. Adler, P. S. "The Evolving Object of Software Development," Organization Studies (12:3) 2005, pp 401-435.

6. Aitken, A., and Ilango, V. "A Comparative Analysis of Traditional Software Engineering and Agile Software Development," Hawaii International Conference on System Sciences, Maui, HI, 2013, pp. 4751-4760.

7. Ang, S., and Slaughter, S. A. "Work Outcomes and Job Design for Contract versus Permanent Information Systems Professionals on Software Development Teams," MIS Quarterly (25:3) 2001, pp 321-350.

8. Argote, L. Organizational Learning: Creating, Retaining and Transferring Knowledge Springer, New York, 2012.

9. Argote, L., and Ingram, P. "Knowledge transfer: A basis for competitive advantage in firms," Organizational Behavior and Human Decision Processes (82:1) 2000, pp 150-169.

10. Aronson, Z. H., Reilly, R. R., and Lynn, G. S. "The impact of leader personality on new product development teamwork and performance: The moderating role of uncertainty," Journal of Engineering and Technology Management (23:3) 2006, pp 221-247.

11. Bansal, G., Zahedi, F., and Gefen, D. "The impact of personal dispositions on information sensitivity, privacy concern and trust in disclosing health information online," Decision Support Systems (49:2) 2010, pp 138-150.

12. Barrick, M. R., and Mount, M. K. "The Big Five Personality Dimensions and Job Performance: a Meta-Analysis," Personnel Psychology (44:1) 1991, pp 1-26.

13. Bartol, K. M., and Martin, D. C. "Managing Information Systems Personnel: A Review of the Literature and Managerial Implications," MIS Quarterly (6:4) 1982, pp 49-70.

14. Basili, V., and Reiter, R. "A controlled experiment quantitatively comparing software development approaches," Transactions on Software Engineering (SE-7:3) 1981, pp 299-320.

15. Bell, D., Hall, T., Hannay, J. E., Acuna, S. T., and Pfahl, D. "Software Engineering Group Work – Personality, Patterns and Performance," SIGMIS Annual Conference on Computer Personnel Research, Vancouver, 2010, pp. 43-47.

16. Bianco, C. "Agile and SPICE Capability Levels," in: Software Process Improvement and Capability Determination, R. O'Connor, T. Rout, F. McCaffery and A. Dorling (eds.), Springer Berlin Heidelberg, 2011, pp. 181-185.

17. Boss, S. R., Kirsch, L. J., Angermeier, I., Shingler, R. a., and Boss, R. W. "If someone is watching, I'll do what I'm asked: mandatoriness, control, and information security," European Journal of Information Systems (18:2) 2009, pp 151-164.

18. Boyle, G. J. "Myers-Briggs Type Indicator (MBTI): Some Psychometric Limitations," Australian Psychologist (30:1) 1995, pp 71-74.

19. Bradley, J. H., and Hebert, F. J. "The effect of personality type on team performance," Journal of Management Development (16:5) 1997, pp 337-353.

20. Buchanan, L. B. "The impact of big five personality characteristics on group cohesion and creative task performance," Virginia Polytechnic Institute and State University, Blacksburg, VI, 1998.

21. Capretz, L. F. "Personality types in software engineering," International Journal of Human-Computer Studies (58:2) 2003, pp 207-214.

22. Capretz, L. F., and Ahmed, F. "Making Sense of Software Development and Personality Types," IT Professional (12:1) 2010, pp 6-13.

23. Chao, J., and Atli, G. "Critical Personality Traits in Successful Pair Programming," Agile Conference, Ieee, Minneapolis, 2006, pp. 89-93.

24. Chapman, C. S., and Kihn, L.-A. "Information system integration, enabling control and performance," Accounting, Organizations and Society (34) 2009, pp 151–169.

25. Chua, C. E. H., Lim, W.-K., Soh, C., and Sia, S. K. "Enacting Clan Control in Complex IT Projects: A Social Capital Perspective," MIS Quarterly (36:2) 2012, pp 577-600.

26. Cohn, M., and Ford, D. "Introducing an agile process to an organization," Computer (36:6) 2003, pp 74-78.

27. Conboy, K. "Agility from First Principles: Reconstructing the Concept of Agility in Information Systems Development," Information Systems Research (20:3) 2009, pp 329-354.

28. Coram, M., and Bohner, S. "The impact of agile methods on software project management," Engineering of Computer-Based Systems, 2005. ECBS'05. 12th IEEE International Conference and Workshops on the, IEEE, 2005, pp. 363-370.

29. Couger, J. D., and Zawacki, R. A. Motivating and managing computer personnel John Wiley & Sons, Inc., 1980.

30. Cram, W. A., and Brohman, M. K. "Controlling information systems development: a new typology for an evolving field," Information Systems Journal (23:2) 2013, pp 137–154.

31. Cruz, S. S. J. O., Silva, F. Q. B., Monteiro, C. V. F., Santos, P., and Rossilei, I. "Personality in Software Engineering: preliminary findings from a systematic literature review," Conference on Evaluation & Assessment in Software Engineering, Durham, 2011, pp. 1-10.

32. Da Cunha, A. D., and Greathead, D. "Does personality matter?: an analysis of code-review ability," Communications of the ACM (50:5) 2007, pp 109-112.

33. Darcy, D. P., Ma, M. J., and Smith, R. H. "Exploring Individual Characteristics and Programming Performance: Implications for Programmer Selection," Hawaii International Conference on System Sciences, Big Island, Hawaii, 2005.

34. Deephouse, C., Mukhopadhyay, T., Goldenson, D. R., and Kellner, M. I. "Processes and Software Project Performance," Journal of Management Information Systems (12:3) 2013, pp 187-205.

35. Derro, M. E., and Williams, C. R. "Behavioral competencies of highly regarded systems engineers at NASA," 2009 IEEE Aerospace conference, IEEE, Big Sky, MT, 2009, pp. 1-17.

36. Dick, A. J., and Zarnett, B. "Paired Programming & Personality Traits," 3rd International Conference on eXtreme Programming and Agile Processes in Software Engineering, Alghero, Italy, 2002, pp. 82-85.

37. Espinosa, J. A., Slaughter, S. A., Kraut, R. E., and Herbsleb, J. D. "Familiarity, complexity, and team performance in geographically distributed software development," Organization Science (18:4) 2007, pp 613-630.

38. ExecutiveBrief "The 2013 Software Development Trends," SoftServe, Fort Myers, FL.

39. Feldt, R., Torkar, R., Angelis, L., and Samuelsson, M. "Towards Individualized Software Engineering: Empirical Studies Should Collect Psychometrics," international workshop on cooperative and human aspects of software engineering, Leipzig, 2008, pp. 49-52.

40. Ferratt, B. T. W., and Short, L. E. "Are Information Systems People Different: An Investigation of How They Are and Should be Managed," MIS Quarterly (12:3) 1988, pp 427-444.

41. Furnham, A. "The big five versus the big four: the relationship between the Myers-Briggs Type Indicator (MBTI) and NEO-PI five factor model of personality," Personality and Individual Differences (21:2) 1996, pp 303-307.

42. Gallivan, M. J. "Examining IT professionals' adaptation to technological change: the influence of gender and personal attributes," ACM SIGMIS Database (35:3) 2004, pp 28-49.

43. Gambill, S. E., Clark, W. J., and Wilkes, R. B. "Toward a holistic model of task design for IS professionals," Information & Management (37:5) 2000, pp 217-228.

44. Goldberg, L. R. "An alternative" description of personality": the big-five factor structure," Journal of Personality and Social Psychology (59:6) 1990, p 1216.

45. Goldstein, D. K. "The Effects of Task Differences on the Work Satisfaction, Job Characteristics, and Role Perceptions of Programmer/Analysts," Journal of Management Information Systems (6:1) 1989, pp 41-58.

46. Goldstein, D. K., and Rockart, J. F. "An Examination of Work-Related Correlates of Job Satisfaction in Programmer/Analysts," MIS Quarterly (8:2) 1984, pp 103-115.

47. Gopal, A., and Gosain, S. "The Role of Organizational Controls and Boundary Spanning in Software Development Outsourcing: Implications for Project Performance," Information Systems Research (21:4) 2009, pp 960-982.

48. Gorla, N., and Lam, Y. W. "Who Should Work with Whom?," Communications of the ACM (47:6) 2004, pp 79-82.

49. Hackman, J. R., and Oldham, G. R. "Development of the job diagnostic survey," Journal of Applied Psychology (60:2) 1975, pp 159-170.

50. Hannay, J. E., Arisholm, E., Engvik, H., and Sjøberg, D. I. K. "Effects of Personality on Pair Programming," Transactions on Software Engineering (36:1) 2010, pp 61-80.

51. Hardgrave, B. C., Davis, F. D., Riemenschneider, C. K., and Bradberry, K. "Determinants of Software Investigating to Follow Developers ' Intentions Methodologies in Information," Journal of Management Information Systems (20:1) 2003, pp 123-151.

52. Hardiman, L. T. "Personality Types and Software Engineers," Computer (30:10) 1997, pp 10-10.

53. Harris, M. A., and Weistroffer, H. R. "A new look at the relationship between user involvement in systems development and system success," Communications of the Association for Information Systems (24:1) 2009, p 42.

54. Henderson, J. C., and Lee, S. "Managing I/S Design Teams: A Control Theories Perspective," Management Science (38:6) 1992, pp 757-777.

55. Hofstede, G. H. Culture's consequences: International differences in work-related values Sage Publications, Beverly Hills, CA, 1984.

56. Hunter, J. E., and Schmidt, F. L. Methods of meta-analysis: Correcting error and bias in research findings Sage, Thousand Oaks, CA, 2004.

57. Hunter, M. G. "Managing information systems professionals: implementing a skill assessment process," ACM SIGCPR Computers & People Research Conference, ACM, 1998, pp. 19-27.

58. Hurtz, G. M., and Donovan, J. J. "Personality and job performance: The Big Five revisited," Journal of Applied Psychology (85:6) 2000, p 869.

59. Kaiser, K. M., and Bostrom, R. P. "Personality Characteristics of MIS Project Teams: An Empirical Study and Action-Research Design," MIS Quarterly (6:4) 1982, pp 43-60.

60. Karapıçak, Ç. M., and Demirörs, O. "A Case Study on the Need to Consider Personality Types for Software Team Formation," in: Software Process Improvement and Capability Determination, Springer, 2013, pp. 120-129.

61. Karn, J. S., and Cowling, A. J. "A Study of the Effect of Disruptions on the Performance of Software Engineering Teams," International Symposium on Empirical Software Engineering, Noosa Heads, 2005, pp. 417-425.

62. Katira, N., Williams, L., Wiebe, E., Miller, C., Balik, S., and Gehringer, E. "On understanding compatibility of student pair programmers," ACM SIGCSE Bulletin, ACM, 2004, pp. 7-11.

63. Kirsch, L. J. "The Management of Complex Tasks in Organizations: Controlling the Systems Development Process," Organization Science (7:1) 1996, pp 1-21.

64. Kirsch, L. J. "Portfolios of Control Modes and IS Project Management," Information Systems Research (8:3) 1997, pp 215-239.

65. Kirsch, L. J., Ko, D. G., and Haney, M. H. "Investigating the Antecedents of Team-Based Clan Control: Adding Social Capital as a Predictor," Organization Science (21:2) 2010, pp 469-489.

66. Kirsch, L. J., Sambamurthy, V., Ko, D.-G., and Purvis, R. L. "Controlling Information Systems Development Projects: The View from the Client," Management Science (48:4) 2002, pp 484-498.

67. Lalsing, V., Kishnah, S., and Pudaruth, S. "People Factory in Agile Software Development and Project Management," International Journal of Software Engineering & Applications (3:1) 2012, pp 117-137.

68. Lee, G., DeLone, W., and Espinosa, J. A. "Ambidextrous coping strategies in globally distributed software development projects," Communications of the ACM (49:10) 2006, pp 35-40.

69. Lee, G., and Xia, W. "Towards Agile: An Integrated Analysis of Quantitative and Qualitative Field Data on Software Development Agility," MIS Quarterly (34:1) 2010, pp 87-114.

70. Lindvall, M., Basili, V., Boehm, B., Costa, P., Dangle, K., Shull, F., Tesoriero, R., Williams, L., and Zelkowitz, M. "Empirical Findings in Agile Methods An Experience Base for Software Engineering," D. Wells and L. Williams (eds.), Springer Berlin Heidelberg, 2002, pp. 197-207.

71. Liu, P.-C., and Chou, H.-W. "The Effects of Personal Characteristics, Stress Coping Styles, Job Self-efficacy on IT Professionals' Burnout," Fourth Workshop on Knowledge Economy and Electronic Eommerce, 2006.

72. Lounsbury, J. W., Loveland, J. M., Sundstrom, E. D., Gibson, L. W., Drost, A. W., and Hamrick, F. L. "An investigation of personality traits in relation to career satisfaction," Journal of Career Assessment (11:3) 2003, pp 287-307.

73. Lounsbury, J. W., Moffitt, L., Gibson, L. W., Drost, A. W., and Stevens, M. "An investigation of personality traits in relation to job and career satisfaction of information technology professionals," Journal of Information Technology (22:2) 2007, pp 174-183.

74. Mair, C., Martincova, M., and Shepperd, M. "An Empirical Study of Software Project Managers Using a Case-Based Reasoner," Hawaii International Conference on System Sciences, Ieee, Maui, Hawaii, 2012, pp. 1030-1039.

75. McCrae, R. R., and Costa, P. T. "Reinterpreting the Myers-Briggs Type Indicator From the Perspective of the Five-Factor Model of Personality," Journal of Personality (57:1) 1989, pp 17-40.

76. McCrae, R. R., and John, O. P. "An introduction to the five-factor model and its applications," Journal of Personality (60:2) 1992, pp 175-215.

77. McGrath, J. E., and Argote, L. "Group processes in organizational contexts," in: Blackwell handbook of social psychology: Group processes, M.A. Hogg and R.S. Tindale (eds.), Wiley-Blackwell, 2002, pp. 603-627.

78. Moore, J. E. "Personality Characteristics of Information Systems Professionals," ACM SIGMIS Computers & People Research Conference, Athens, Georgia, 1991, pp. 140-155.

79. Morris, M., and Venkatesh, V. "Job characteristics and job satisfaction: understanding the role of enterprise resource planning system implementation," MIS Quarterly (34:1) 2010, pp 143-161.

80. Mourmant, G., and Gallivan, M. "How Personality Type Influences Decision Paths in the Unfolding Model of Voluntary Job Turnover: An Application to IS Professionals," ACM SIGMIS Computers & People Research Conference, St. Louis, 2007, pp. 134-143.

81. Myers, I. B., McCaulley, M. H., and Most, R. Manual: A guide to the development and use of the Myers-Briggs Type Indicator Consulting Psychologists Press, Palo Alto, CA, 1985.

82. Naqvi, I., Rehman, K. U., and Butt, B. Z. "Precautions in Team Leader's Selection: Impact on Business Success," International Conference on Education Technology and Computer, Ieee, Singapure, 2009, pp. 269-274.

83. Nidumolu, S. R., and Subramani, M. R. "The matrix of control: Combining process and structure approaches to managing software development," Journal of Management Information Systems (20:3) 2003, pp 159-196.

84. Omar, M., and Syed-Abdullah, S.-L. "Identifying Effective Software Engineering (SE) Team Personality Types Composition using Rough Set Approach," International Symposium in Information Technology, Kuala Lumpur, Malaysia, 2010, pp. 1499-1503.

85. Oswald, F. L., and Hough, L. M. "Personality and its assessment in organizations: Theoretical and empirical developments," in: APA handbook of industrial and organizational psychology, S. Zedeck (ed.), American Psychological Association, Washington, DC, 2011, pp. 153-184.

86. Ouchi, W. G. "A Conceptual Framework for the Design of Organizational Control Mechanisms," Management Science (25:9) 1979, pp 833-848.

87. Paulk, M. C. "Extreme programming from a CMM perspective," Software, IEEE (18:6) 2001, pp 19-26.

88. Peslak, A. R. "The Impact of Personality on Information Technology Team Projects," ACM SIGMIS Computers & People Research Conference, Claremont, 2006, pp. 273-279.

89. Ply, J. K., Moore, J. E., Williams, C. K., and Thatcher, J. B. "IS Employee Attitude and Perceptions at Varying Levels of Software Process Maturity," MIS Quarterly (36:2) 2012, pp 601-624.

90. Pocius, K. E. "Personality factors in human-computer interaction: A review of the literature," Computers in Human Behavior (7:3) 1991, pp 103-135.

91. Polites, G. L., Roberts, N., and Thatcher, J. "Conceptualizing models using multidimensional constructs: a review and

guidelines for their use," European Journal of Information Systems (21:1) 2011, pp 22-48.

92. Raza, A., and Capretz, L. F. "Do Personality Profiles Differ in the Pakistani Software Industry and Academia–A Study," International Journal of Software Engineering (3:4) 2012, pp 60-66.

93. Rehman, M., Mahmood, A. K., Salleh, R., and Amin, A. "Mapping Job Requirements of Software Engineers to Big Five Personality Traits," Conference on Computer & Information Science, Venice, 2012, pp. 1115-1122.

94. Riemenschneider, C. K., Hardgrave, B. C., and Davis, F. D. "Explaining Software Developer Acceptance of Methodologies: A Comparison of Five Theoretical Models," Transactions on Software Engineering (28:12) 2002, pp 1135-1145.

95. Roberts, J. A., Hann, I.-H., and Slaughter, S. A. "Understanding the motivations, participation, and performance of open source software developers: A longitudinal study of the Apache projects," Management Science (52:7) 2006, pp 984-999.

96. Rus, I., and Lindvall, M. "Knowledge management in software engineering," Software, IEEE (19:3) 2002, pp 26-38.

97. Rutherfoord, R. H. "Using personality inventories to form teams for class projects: a case study," Proceedings of the 7th conference on Information technology education, ACM, 2006, pp. 9-14.

98. Salleh, N., Mendes, E., and Grundy, J. "The effects of openness to experience on pair programming in a higher education context," Conference on Software Engineering Education and Training (CSEE&T), Ieee, Waikiki, 2011, pp. 149-158.

99. Salleh, N., Mendes, E., and Grundy, J. "Investigating the effects of personality traits on pair programming in a higher education setting through a family of experiments," Empirical Software Engineering:December) 2012.

100. Salleh, N., Mendes, E., Grundy, J., and Burch, G. S. J. "An empirical study of the effects of personality in pair programming using the five-factor model," International Symposium on Empirical Software Engineering and Measurement, Ieee, Lake Buena Vista, 2009, pp. 214-225.

101. Salleh, N., Mendes, E., Grundy, J., and Burch, G. S. J. "An empirical study of the effects of conscientiousness in pair programming using the five-factor personality model," International Conference on Software Engineering, ACM Press, Cape Town, 2010, pp. 577-577.

102. Santana, M., and Robey, D. "Perceptions of Control During Systems Development: Effects on Job Satisfaction of Systems Professionals," Computer Personnel (16:1) 1995, pp 20-34.

103. Sarker, S., Ahuja, M., Sarker, S., and Kirkeby, S. "The role of communication and trust in global virtual teams: a social network perspective," Journal of Management Information Systems (28:1) 2011, pp 273-310.

104. Seaman, C. B., and Basili, V. R. "Communication and organization in software development: An empirical study," IBM Systems Journal (36:4) 1997, pp 550-563.

105. Sein, M. K., and Bostrom, R. P. "A psychometric study of the job characteristics scale of the job diagnostic survey in an MIS setting," ACM SIGMIS Computers & People Research Conference, ACM, New York, NY, 1991, pp. 96-110.

106. Sewell, G. "The Discipline of Teams: The Control of Team-Based Industrial Work Through Electronic and Peer Surveillance," Administrative Science Quarterly (43:2) 1998, pp 397-428.

107. Shneiderman, B. Software psychology: Human factors in computer and information systems Winthrop Publishers, 1980.

108. Shoaib, L., Nadeem, A., and Akbar, A. "An empirical evaluation of the influence of human personality on exploratory software testing," Ieee, Islamabad, 2009, pp. 1-6.

109. Snyder, L. A., Rupp, D. E., and Thornton, G. C. "Personnel selection of information technology workers: The people, the jobs, and issues for human resource management," Research in personnel and human resources management (25) 2006, pp 305-376.

110. Stewart, G. L., Courtright, S. H., and Barrick, M. R. "Peer-based control in self-managing teams: linking rational and normative influence with individual and group performance," The Journal of applied psychology (97:2) 2012, pp 435-447.

111. Thatcher, J. B., Stepina, L., and Boyle, R. J. "Turnover of Information Technology Workers: Examining Empirically the Influence of Attitudes, Job Characteristics, and External Markets," Journal of Management Information Systems (19:3) 2003, pp 231-261.

112. Trimble, J., and Webster, C. "From Traditional, to Lean, to Agile Development: Finding the Optimal Software Engineering Cycle," Hawaii International Conference on System Sciences, 2013, pp. 4826-4833.

113. Turley, R. T., and Bieman, J. M. "Competencies of Exceptional and Non-Exceptional Software Engineers," The Journal of Systems and Software (28:1) 1995, pp 19-38.

114. Ülke, H. E., and Bilgiç, R. "Investigating the Role of the Big Five on the Social Loafing of Information Technology Workers," International Journal of Selection and Assessment (19:3) 2011, pp 301-312.

115. Varona, D., Capretz, L. F., Piñero, Y., and Raza, A. "Evolution of software engineers' personality profile," ACM SIGSOFT Software Engineering Notes (37:1) 2012.

116. Walle, T., and Hannay, J. E. "Personality and the nature of collaboration in pair programming," International Symposium on Empirical Software Engineering and Measurement, Ieee, Lake Buena Vista, 2009, pp. 203-213.

117. Wang, Y. "Building the linkage between project managers' personality and success of software projects," 2009 3rd International Symposium on Empirical Software Engineering and Measurement) 2009, pp 410-413.

118. Webster, J., and Watson, R. T. "Analyzing the past to prepare for the future: Writing a literature review," MIS Quarterly (26:2) 2002, pp 13-23.

119. Weinberg, G. M. The psychology of computer programming Van Nostrand Reinhold New York, 1971.

120. White, K. B. "MIS Project Teams: An Investigation of Cognitive Style Implications," MIS Quarterly (8:2) 1984, pp 95-101.

121. White, K. B., and Leifer, R. "Systems Development Success: Project Participants Introduction," MIS Quarterly (10:3) 1986, pp 215-223.

122. Wynekoop, J. L., and Walz, D. B. "Investigating traits of top performing software developers," Information Technology & People (13:3) 2000, pp 186-195.

123. Yilmaz, M. "A Software Process Engineering Approach to Understanding Software Productivity and Team Personality Characteristics: An Empirical Investigation," Dublin City University, 2013.

124. Yilmaz, M., and Oconnor, R. V. "Towards the Understanding and Classification of the Personality Traits of Software Development Practitioners: Situational Context Cards Approach," 2012 38th Euromicro Conference on Software Engineering and Advanced Applications) 2012, pp 400-405.

125. Young, S. M., Edwards, H. M., McDonald, S., and Thompson, J. B. "Personality characteristics in an XP team: a repertory grid study," ACM SIGSOFT Software Engineering Notes, ACM, 2005, pp. 1-7.

126. Zillig, L. M. P., Hemenover, S. H., and Dienstbier, R. A. "What do we assess when we assess a Big 5 trait? A content analysis of the affective, behavioral, and cognitive processes represented in Big 5 personality inventories," Personality and Social Psychology Bulletin (28:6) 2002, pp 847-858.

Systems Thinking during Systems Analysis and Design

Thomas W. Ferratt
University of Dayton
School of Business Administration
Dayton, OH 45469-2130
937-229-2728
ferratt@udayton.edu

ABSTRACT

A number of academicians and practitioners have called for more systems thinking. In this subjective essay I examine elements of systems thinking that are and are not likely to be taught in the education of systems analysts. My purpose is to understand the elements of systems thinking that potential systems analysts learn. Since no definitive model of systems thinking exists, I first summarize the elements of systems thinking in five alternative models of systems thinking extant in the literature – general systems approach and complexity theory, cybernetics, system dynamics, soft system methodology, and critical systems theory and multimethodology – and then examine which of those elements are included in Systems Analysis and Design textbooks. The findings indicate that what is likely to be taught is an approach to understanding and designing an information system that decomposes the system into component parts that interrelate through processing input data into outputs. This reductionist approach also includes an understanding of the information system's boundary, which determines system scope. What is unlikely to be taught, besides the five alternative models of systems thinking, are the general system concepts of synergism, negative entropy, dynamic equilibrium, internal elaboration, multiple goal-seeking, and equifinality of open systems. With this foundation I encourage IS faculty to engage in a continuing dialog on what elements of systems thinking potential systems analysts should learn.

Categories and Subject Descriptors

K.3.2 [**Computers and Education**]: Computer and Information Science Education – *Curriculum, Information systems education*
K.6.1 [**Management of Computing and Information Systems**]: People and Project Management – *Systems Analysis and Design*

General Terms

Management

Keywords

Systems Analysts, Systems Approach, General Systems Theory

Permission to make digital or hard copies of all or part of this work for personal or classroom use is granted without fee provided that copies are not made or distributed for profit or commercial advantage and that copies bear this notice and the full citation on the first page. Copyrights for components of this work owned by others than ACM must be honored. Abstracting with credit is permitted. To copy otherwise, or republish, to post on servers or to redistribute to lists, requires prior specific permission and/or a fee. Request permissions from Permissions@acm.org.

SIGMIS-CPR '14, May 29 - 31 2014, Singapore, Singapore
Copyright 2014 ACM 978-1-4503-2625-4/14/05...$15.00.
http://dx.doi.org/10.1145/2599990.2600013

1. INTRODUCTION

A number of academicians and practitioners have called for more systems thinking. For example, Alter (2004) calls for more systems thinking by business professionals, which includes systems analysts and those they serve. Atwater and Pittman (2006) and Waddock and Lozano (2013) call for more systems thinking by business students in general and, by extension, graduates of business programs, including not only systems analysts but also those they serve. Kim and Senge (1994) and Senge et al. (2007) have called for more systems thinking by managers to work more effectively within organizations and collaborate more successfully on complex sustainability issues across organizations. Capra (2009) basically calls for educating everyone to think systemically for humanity to survive.

What is this "systems thinking" that we should have more of? In the information systems (IS) teaching domain, where faculty develop students to become systems analysts, systems thinking is an approach that systems analysts may use when they engage in systems analysis and design. That approach involves understanding and using concepts from general systems theory (e.g., Kast and Rosenzweig, 1972), including (among others) the idea that a system consists of interacting subsystems, a system with its subsystems exists within a larger environment, and systems seek multiple goals. Mingers and White (2010) describe the systems approach as viewing a situation holistically as a set of diverse interacting elements within an environment, recognizing that the interactions between subsystems are more important than the subsystems themselves in determining the behavior of the system, recognizing a hierarchy of levels of systems and the consequent ideas of properties emerging at different levels with mutual causality both within and between levels, and accepting, especially in social systems, that people will act in accordance with differing goals.

Two implications of these calls for more systems thinking are that (1) systems thinking is not being used enough in practice and (2) more systems thinking would lead to better outcomes for those who use it. Those who have called for more systems thinking have offered support for these implications. Rather than re-stating that support, I focus on examining systems thinking in a domain where IS faculty have some influence.

Specifically, in this subjective essay I examine elements of systems thinking that are and are not likely to be taught in the education of systems analysts, i.e., business professionals whose education ostensibly should include elements of systems thinking. For more systems thinking to occur, systems thinking should be taught and learned by those who would then practice it. The standard curriculum for teaching systems analysts includes a Systems Analysis and Design course (Topi et al. 2010), where at least some elements of systems thinking are surely taught. However, the title of Alter's (2004) paper, "Desperately Seeking Systems Thinking in the Information Systems Discipline," raises the question, "What elements of systems thinking are and are not taught in this core course in the IS curriculum?"

My purpose is to understand what elements of systems thinking potential systems analysts learn. This paper establishes a starting point for that understanding by examining what students learn through textbooks used in the core Systems Analysis and Design course. After reviewing the findings below, I would encourage IS faculty to engage in a continuing dialog on what elements of systems thinking potential systems analysts should learn. Much dialog has already occurred, at least implicitly, in determining the content of the textbooks used to teach the core Systems Analysis and Design course. The texts examined below represent the results of this collective dialog among publishers, authors, and IS educators who adopt published texts. The resulting texts are an unobtrusive record of the dialog, specifying the core of what should be taught, including systems thinking, in the education of systems analysts.

A reasonable assumption is that those elements of systems thinking included in Systems Analysis and Design textbooks are more likely to be taught and learned, whereas those not included are less likely to be taught and learned. Thus, Systems Analysis and Design textbooks serve as an important source of data for answering the question driving this work.

Prior to examining such texts, however, it is essential to have a list of elements of systems thinking that could be taught to identify the elements that are included in the texts. A commonly agreed upon definition of systems thinking would help identify a definitive list of elements of systems thinking. Unfortunately, such a definition does not exist. Cabrera et al. (2008) consider a wide body of systems thinking literature and state, "There are many ways to think about systems thinking." They propose that systems thinking is conceptual and is a more formal, abstract, and structured cognitive endeavor than an ad hoc, informal process of thinking about systems. However, they recognize that the distinction between "systems thinking" and "thinking about systems" is a controversial distinction in the systems science community. I do not attempt to make this distinction here. Rather, I recognize that alternative models of systems thinking exist and accept them as legitimate sources for identifying the elements of systems thinking.

To reflect the varieties of systems thinking that have emerged over time, I use Mingers and White's (2010) organization of the literature into five streams: (1) general systems approach and complexity theory, (2) cybernetics, (3) system dynamics, (4) soft systems and problem structuring methods (PSMs), and (5) critical systems and multimethodology. Initially, I summarize the elements of systems thinking in each stream. The elements of systems thinking that emerge from looking at these various streams may not include all elements of systems thinking, but they provide a reasonable foundation for answering the question driving this work.

After identifying the list of elements of systems thinking that could be taught, I examine the elements of systems thinking that are included in Systems Analysis and Design textbooks. The results of this examination help us understand the elements of systems thinking that potential systems analysts learn. They set the stage for a continuing dialog on what elements of systems thinking systems analysts should learn.

2. ELEMENTS OF SYSTEMS THINKING

Table 1 summarizes the elements of systems thinking in each of Mingers and White's (2010) five streams of the systems thinking literature. Systems analysts are expected to use their knowledge and skills to analyze and design information systems that will improve a situation. All five of these streams represent alternative systems thinking approaches that systems analysts might use to improve a situation. Thus, each of the five alternatives represents an intervention strategy. The elements of the summaries include steps that may be taken in an intervention. Early steps in an intervention involve studying the situation, e.g., study the flow of information, whereas later steps involve making changes, e.g., change the flow of information. A shorthand version is used to include both the early and later steps, e.g., study (or change) the information flow – see cybernetics in Table 1. Since systems concepts from the general systems approach form the foundation for other alternative models of systems thinking, key concepts of general systems theory are included as elements for this first model of systems thinking. Where I thought Mingers and White's (2010) summary would benefit from elaboration, I used works of other authors to develop the summary presented in Table 1.

Table 1. Summary of Elements of Systems Thinking for Alternative Models of Systems Thinking

Alternative Models of Systems Thinking (Mingers and White 2010)	Elements of Systems Thinking
1. General systems approach and complexity theory	The Systems Approach (Mingers and White 2010) • View the situation holistically, as opposed to reductionistically, as a set of diverse interacting elements within an environment • Recognize that the relationships or interactions between elements are more important than the elements themselves in determining the behavior of the system • Recognize a hierarchy of levels of systems and the consequent ideas of properties emerging at different levels, and mutual causality both within and between levels • Accept, especially in social systems, that people will act in accordance with differing purposes or rationalities

Alternative Models of Systems Thinking (Mingers and White 2010)	Elements of Systems Thinking

	Key Concepts of General Systems Theory (Kast and Rosenzweig 1972)
	
	• Subsystems or Components with Interrelationships
	• Holism, Synergism, Organicism, and Gestalt
	• Open Systems View
	• Input-Transformation-Output Model
	• System Boundaries
	• Negative Entropy
	• Steady State, Dynamic Equilibrium, and Homeostasis
	• Feedback
	• Hierarchy
	• Internal Elaboration
	• Multiple Goal-Seeking
	• Equifinality of Open Systems
	Complexity Theory (Mingers and White 2010)
	
	• Chaos and complexity
	    o contrast with traditional assumptions of stability, equilibrium, linear change, cyclicality, robustness, and simple models generating simple behavior (and vice versa)
	    o emphasize instability, far-from equilibrium, sudden change, sensitivity to initial conditions, and complex behavior from simple models (and vice versa)
	• Chaos and complexity effects can be generated within the traditional systems thinking framework as resulting from
	    o particular patterns of, especially positive, feedback loops and
	    o networks of interactions between large numbers of relatively simple units.

2. Cybernetics	Overview (Ashby 1956) • Study (or change) the flow of information through a system • Develop an understanding of (or change) the way in which that information is used by the system as a means of controlling itself A Feedback Loop (grounded in general systems theory) (Green and Welsh 1988), in conjunction with the Law of Requisite Variety (Ashby [and Goldstein] 2011) or Internal Elaboration (Kast and Rosenzweig 1972), includes these steps that must be understood (or changed): • Use standards of performance • Measure system performance • Compare that performance to standards • Feed back information about unwanted variances in the system • Modify the system's comportment o Complexity (or variety) in a system's environment requires complexity (or requisite variety or internal elaboration) in the system to adapt, i.e., modify the system's comportment to achieve equilibrium or maintain control

3. System dynamics	System Dynamics Steps (Forrester 1994)*
	
	• Describe the system (Sweeney and Sterman 2000)
	    o understand how the behavior of a system arises from the interaction of its agents over time (i.e., dynamic complexity)
	    o discover and represent feedback processes (both positive and negative) hypothesized to underlie observed patterns of system behavior
	    o identify stock (or level) and flow (or rate) relationships
	    o recognize delays and understand their impact
	    o identify nonlinearities
	    o recognize and challenge the boundaries of mental (and formal) models**
	• Convert the description to level and rate equations
	• Simulate the model
	• Design alternative policies and structures
	• Educate and debate
	• Implement changes in policies and structure

Alternative Models of Systems Thinking (Mingers and White 2010)	Elements of Systems Thinking
	* Forrester (1994) notes that causal loop diagrams may be used to create an overall impression of the system after identifying the variables that affect system levels or stocks (e.g., number of items of a specific product in inventory at a point in time) and rates or flows (e.g., number of items of a specific product added to inventory over some time period) that cause those levels to change. ** "[O]ne of the most important features of boundaries in relation to system dynamics is that they mask the unintended consequences of actions," which result from acting locally without thinking globally, i.e., across subsystem boundaries (Wolstenholme 2004). Many analysts over many years have followed the steps to describe a system, resulting in a limited set of generic structures, i.e., system archetypes, which are "responsible for generic patterns of behaviour over time, particularly counter-intuitive behaviour. Such 'structures' consist of intended actions and unintended reactions and recognise delays in reaction times" (Wolstenholme 2003).

4. Soft systems and problem structuring methods (PSMs)	Soft System Methodology (SSM), a framework for thinking about, making sense of, and finding ways of improving real-world situations that are perceived as problematical (Checkland and Haynes 1994, Checkland and Poulter 2006, Zexian and Xuhui 2010)
	
	• Engage in a dynamic process of inquiry, based on system ideas, about a real-world problematic situation, which involves people with a diversity of interests and worldviews
	  o Find out about the situation
	  o Explore the situation by developing models of the perceived purposeful (or human) activity system in the situation based on participants' worldviews
	  o Discuss and debate the situation based on the models
	  o Take action to improve the situation
	• Reflect critically on the process of inquiry
	Systems Thinking Elements Embedded in SSM (Checkland and Scholes 1990, Zexian and Xuhui 2010)
	
	• System thinking takes seriously the idea of a whole entity which may exhibit properties as a single whole ('emergence properties'), properties which have no meaning in terms of the parts of the whole.
	• To do systems thinking is to set some constructed abstract wholes against the perceived real world in order to learn about it.
	• Within system thinking there are two complementary traditions. The 'hard' tradition takes the world to be systemic; the 'soft' tradition creates the process of enquiry as a system.
	• SSM is a systemic process of enquiry which happens to make use of system models. It thus subsumes the hard approach, which is a special case of it.
	• To make the above clear it would be better to use the word 'holon' for the constructed abstract wholes, conceding the word 'system' to everyday language and not trying to use it as a technical term.
	• SSM uses a particular kind of holon, namely the so-called 'human activity system'. This is a set of activities so connected as to make a purposeful whole, constructed to meet the requirement of the core system image (emergence properties, layered structure, process of communication and control)
	• In examining real-world situations characterized by purposeful action, there will never be only one relevant holon, It is necessary to create several models of human activity systems and to debate and so learn their relevance to real life

5. Critical systems and multimethodology	Critical Systems Thinking (Mingers and White 2010) • Use different systems theories, methodologies, and methods together in an intervention, e.g., addressing both the quantitative and qualitative aspects of a complex situation with both hard and soft methodologies, which can better address the different phases of an intervention • Address questions about how the boundaries of the project are drawn, since some actors will be included and their viewpoints recognized, while others will be excluded and thus not be able to influence the project based on the boundaries drawn

3. SYSTEMS THINKING IN COMMONLY USED SYSTEMS ANALYSIS AND ESIGN TEXTBOOKS

The textbooks examined for the elements of systems thinking are listed in Table 2. Having taught the core Systems Analysis and Design course, I have some familiarity with textbooks published for this course. I developed an initial list of textbooks through using this familiarity and reviewing various sources of published textbooks, such as publisher websites, library catalogs, and amazon.com. In working with colleagues examining another topic (see Salisbury, Ferratt, and Wynn 2013), we also contacted authors and publishers on the initial list to obtain their inputs as we developed the list in this table. Although other textbooks may be used, these represent a reasonable sample of commonly used textbooks.

The review of textbooks consisted of reviewing the indices and tables of contents for words or phrases representing the elements of systems thinking listed in Table 1. In addition, it involved reviewing the content of referenced pages to understand meaning. It also involved considering material on diagrams, particularly for representing information requirements or the design of the system structure since I expected a number of general systems concepts (e.g., system boundaries, inputs-transformation-outputs, subsystems and their interrelationships) to be at least implicitly embedded in the exposition of diagrams in systems analysis and design.

Table 2 – Commonly Used Systems Analysis and Design Textbooks

Dennis, A., Haley Wixom, B., and Roth, R. M. (2012). *Systems analysis and design*, 5th ed., Hoboken, NJ: John Wiley.
Dennis, A., Haley Wixom, B., and Tegarden, D. (2012). *Systems analysis and design with UML version 2.0: An object-oriented approach*, 4th ed., Hoboken, NJ: John Wiley.
Hoffer, J. A., George, J. F., and Valacich, J. S. (2014). Modern systems analysis and design, 7th ed., Upper Saddle River, N.J.: Pearson Prentice Hall.
Kendall, K. E. and Kendall, J. E. (2014). Systems analysis and design, 9th ed., Upper Saddle River, N.J.: Pearson Education, Inc.
Rosenblatt, H. J. (2014). Systems analysis and design, 10th ed., Boston: Course Technology Cengage Learning.
Satzinger, J. W., Jackson, R. B. and Burd, S. D. (2012). *Systems analysis and design in a changing world*, 6th ed., Boston, MA: Course Technology/Cengage Learning.
Valacich, J. S., George, J. F. and Hoffer, J. A. (2012). *Essentials of Systems Analysis & Design*, 5th ed., Upper Saddle River, N.J.: Pearson Prentice Hall.
Whitten, J. L., and Bentley, L. D., with contributions by Gary Randolph (2007). *Systems analysis and design methods*, 7th ed., Boston: McGraw-Hill/Irwin.

4. RESULTS

Only one textbook (Valacich et al. 2012) has "systems thinking" in its index. It describes systems thinking as "the ability to see organizations and information systems as systems." The only other description of systems thinking in this textbook states, "Systems thinking provides a framework from which to see the important relationships among information systems, the organizations they exist in, and the environment in which the organizations themselves exist."

Only three of the eight textbooks devote a few pages (viz., three to five) to a description of a system (Kendall and Kendall 2014, pp. 20-23; Valacich et al. 2012, pp. 6-10; Whitten and Bentley 2007, pp. 6, 321-324). Looking across these descriptions, only a few of the general systems concepts emerge:

- Subsystems or Components with Interrelationships
- Open Systems View
- Input-Transformation-Output Model
- System Boundaries

None of the texts refers explicitly to any of the five alternative models of systems thinking in Table 1. The model with the most frequently discussed elements is the general systems approach. As in the textbooks with a description of a system, only a few of the general systems concepts are discussed across the set of textbooks. For textbooks that do not describe a system in general, *subsystems or components and their interrelationships* appear in discussions of software, data entities, objects, and user interactions. Elements of the *input-transformation-output model* are widely discussed across textbooks but limited in scope to discussions of the data needed for the information system, the processes, programs, or methods for transforming data, and results generated from the information system. Besides appearing in discussions of information requirements, elements of the input-transformation-output model also appear in discussions of the design of forms, reports, and user interfaces. *System boundaries* are also widely discussed across textbooks. They are typically discussed in the context of use case diagrams to delineate the scope of an information system. When *feedback* is discussed, it is usually in the context of user interaction with an information system, with the information system providing some information to the user in response to some user action, e.g., clicking sounds when keys are pressed or a status bar showing remaining processing time after the user initiates a command. The only other general systems concept discussed is the *hierarchy* of subsystems, which appears implicitly in most textbooks since the discussions focus on decomposition of data flow diagrams or programs rather than the hierarchy of subsystems. These discussions adopt a reductionist approach to dividing a system into its component parts to understand or design the system. What does not appear in these discussions is recognition of emergent properties or synergies that occur with the interactions of components at any given level of the hierarchy.

Besides some aspects of the general systems approach, the only other alternative model of systems thinking that is implicitly present in Systems Analysis and Design textbooks is cybernetics, which occurs in two textbooks (Kendall and Kendall 2014; Whitten and Bentley 2007). Kendall and Kendall (2014) state, "Feedback is one form of system control." They include a figure that "shows how system outputs are used as feedback that compares performance with goals." They also note that the "ideal system...self-corrects or self-regulates." Whitten and Bentley (2007) state, "Because the environment is always changing, well-designed systems have a feedback and control loop to allow the system to adapt itself to changing conditions."

5. DISCUSSION

This review of Systems Analysis and Design textbooks finds that, if Alter (2004) is still searching for systems thinking in the IS discipline, he will discover that systems thinking is not directly discussed in most of those textbooks. Only a limited set of systems thinking elements are likely to be taught in the core Systems Analysis and Design course in the standard IS curriculum. The most widely found elements include the following general systems concepts:

- Subsystems or Components with Interrelationships
- Input-Transformation-Output Model
- System Boundaries
- Hierarchy (with the focus on decomposition, i.e., reductionism, rather than synergy)

Of MIngers and White's (2010) five alternative approaches to systems thinking, only this limited set of concepts underlying the general systems approach and the other alternative approaches is likely to be taught. The remaining general systems concepts, including the following that are not presented in the textbooks reviewed, are not likely to be taught:

- Holism, Synergism, Organicism, and Gestalt
- Negative Entropy
- Steady State, Dynamic Equilibrium, and Homeostasis
- Internal Elaboration
- Multiple Goal-Seeking
- Equifinality of Open Systems

Two other concepts, *open systems view* and *feedback*, are presented rarely or in a limited context.

None of the alternative models of systems thinking is likely to be taught. The textbooks reviewed do not discuss the general systems approach (let alone complexity theory), cybernetics, system dynamics, soft system methodology, or critical systems theory and multimethodology as intervention strategies for improving a situation. A follow-up review of the textbooks reveals that they all include steps for conducting systems analysis and design. An example of these steps is the systems development life cycle presented by Hoffer et al. (2014), which entails planning, analysis, design, implementation, and maintenance to develop and support information systems. These steps for conducting systems analysis and design represent an intervention strategy for improving a situation, but the limited elements of systems thinking included in these textbooks means that they do not represent any one of the five alternative approaches to systems thinking summarized in Table 1. Rather, they represent a reductionist approach to understanding and designing an information system. The approaches taught in these textbooks decompose an information system into component parts that interrelate through processing input data into outputs. The scope of the component parts included in the information system is determined by the information system's boundary.

5.1 Limitations

Examining the content of textbooks commonly used in the core Systems Analysis and Design course of a standard IS curriculum does not necessarily identify the alternative models of systems thinking and the elements of those models that are actually taught and learned in that course. As noted previously, though, the elements of systems thinking included in Systems Analysis and Design textbooks are more likely to be taught and learned than those that are excluded. Faculty teaching Systems Analysis and Design, students who have taken the course, employers of students who have taken the course, or those working on systems and analysis design projects with graduates of this course could be observed or surveyed to provide alternative evidence regarding what is taught and learned.

What is taught and learned in a college course is not necessarily what is practiced. Calls for more systems thinking in practice are not necessarily satisfied by those graduating from a Systems Analysis and Design course. Is the limited systems thinking found in the textbooks reviewed actually used in practice, or does it provide a foundation for those completing a course where these textbooks are used to learn a more robust set of system thinking elements to be used in practice? Other evidence is needed to provide insights for answering this question.

5.2 Future Directions

My purpose in this essay is to understand the elements of systems thinking that potential systems analysts learn, but I hope that the results encourage IS faculty to engage in a continuing dialog on the elements of systems thinking that potential systems analysts should learn. Two questions provide a starting point for continuation of the dialog that has already occurred, as noted previously, among textbook authors, publishers, and faculty teaching the Systems Analysis and Design course:

1. Is the limited systems thinking found in Systems Analysis and Design textbooks adequate for teaching potential system analysts?
2. What would the value be of including additional elements of systems thinking?

Another direction for the future is to engage not only IS faculty but also employers of graduates of IS programs in this dialog.

6. CONCLUSION

This subjective essay addresses the question, "What elements of systems thinking are and are not taught in the core Systems Analysis and Design course in a standard IS curriculum?" A review of eight commonly used Systems Analysis and Design textbooks suggests that the systems thinking that is taught is likely to be limited. Of five alternative models of systems thinking considered in the review of the textbooks – general systems approach and complexity theory, cybernetics, system dynamics, soft system methodology, and critical systems theory and multimethodology – none is found. What is likely to be taught is an approach to understanding and designing an information system that decomposes the system into component parts that interrelate through processing input data into outputs. That approach also includes an understanding of the information system's boundary, which limits the component parts, or scope, of the system. What is unlikely to be taught, besides alternative models of systems thinking, are the general system concepts of synergism, negative entropy, dynamic equilibrium, internal elaboration, multiple goal-seeking, and equifinality of open systems.

Through this essay I encourage IS faculty to engage in a continuing dialog regarding the elements of systems thinking that should be taught to prospective systems analysts. The implicit dialog among authors, publishers, and faculty teaching the Systems Analysis and Design course suggests that the limited systems thinking found in these texts is adequate for graduates of IS programs. This finding sets the stage for additional discussion. I encourage others to join the dialog.

7. REFERENCES

[1] Alter, S. 2004. Desperately seeking systems thinking in the information systems discipline. In *Proceedings of the 25th International Conference on Information Systems* (Washington, D.C., Dec. 12 – 15, 2004). Paper 61. DOI= http://aisel.aisnet.org/icis2004/61.

[2] Ashby, W. R. 1956. *Introduction to Cybernetics*. Methuen, London, UK.

[3] Ashby, W. R. (with an introduction by Jeffrey Goldstein). 2011. Variety, constraint, and the law of requisite variety. *Emergence: Complexity & Organization* 13, 1/2, 190-207.

[4] Atwater, J. B. and Pittman, P. H. 2006. Facilitating systemic thinking in business classes. *Decision Sciences Journal of Innovative Education* 4, 2, 273-292.

[5] Cabrera, D., Colosic, L., and Lobdell, C. 2008. Systems thinking. *Evaluation and Program Planning* 31, 299-310.

[6] Capra, F. 2009. The New facts of life: Connecting the dots on food, health, and the environment. *Public Library Quarterly* 28, 3, 242-248.

[7] Checkland, P. and Haynes, M. G. 1994. Varieties of systems thinking: The case of soft systems methodology. *System Dynamics Review* 10, 189-197.

[8] Checkland, P. B. and Poulter, J. 2006. Learning for Action: A Short Definitive Account of Soft Systems Methodology and Its Use for Practitioners, Teachers and Students. Wiley, Chichester.

[9] Checkland, P. B. and Scholes, J. 1990. *Soft Systems Methodology in Action*. Wiley, Chichester.

[10] Dennis, A., Haley Wixom, B., and Roth, R. M. 2012. *Systems Analysis and Design, 5th ed.* John Wiley, Hoboken, NJ.

[11] Dennis, A., Haley Wixom, B., and Tegarden, D. 2012. Systems Analysis and Design with UML Version 2.0: An Object-Oriented Approach, 4th ed. John Wiley, Hoboken, NJ.

[12] Forrester, J. W. 1994. System dynamics, systems thinking, and soft OR. *System Dynamics Review* 10, 2-3, 245-256.

[13] Green, S. G. and Welsh, M. A. 1988. Cybernetics and dependence – Reframing the control concept. *Academy of Management Review* 13, 2, 287-301.

[14] Hoffer, J. A., George, J. F., and Valacich, J. S. 2011. *Modern Systems Analysis and Design, 6th ed.* Pearson Prentice Hall, Upper Saddle River, NJ.

[15] Hoffer, J. A., George, J. F., and Valacich, J. S. 2014. *Modern Systems Analysis and Design, 7th ed.* Pearson Prentice Hall, Upper Saddle River, NJ.

[16] Kast, F. E. and Rosenzweig, J. E. 1972. General system theory: Applications for organization and management. *Academy of Management Journal* 15, 4 (Dec. 1972), 447-465.

[17] Kendall, K. E. and Kendall, J. E. 2014. *Systems Analysis and Design*, 9th ed. Pearson Education, Inc., Upper Saddle River, NJ.

[18] Kim, D. H. and Senge, P. M. 1994. Putting systems thinking into practice. *System Dynamics Review* 10, 2/3, 277-290.

[19] Mingers, J. and White, L. 2010. A review of the recent contribution of systems thinking to operational research and management science. *European Journal of Operational Research*, 207, 3, 1147-1161.

[20] Rosenblatt, H. J. 2014. *Systems Analysis and Design, 9th ed.* Course Technology Cengage Learning, Boston, MA.

[21] Salisbury, W.. D., Ferratt, T. W., and Wynn, D. E. 2013. Systems analysis and design in the connected age: Considering the role of information security throughout the SDLC. In *Proceeding of the Administrative Sciences Association of Canada* (Calagary), 34, 5, 8-13.

[22] Satzinger, J. W., Jackson, R. B. and Burd, S. D. 2012. *Systems Analysis and Design in a Changing World, 6th ed.* Course Technology/Cengage Learning, Boston, MA.

[23] Senge, P. M., Lichtenstein, B. B., Kaeufer, K., Bradbury, H., and Carroll, J. 2007. Collaborating for systemic change. *MIT Sloan Management Review* 48, 2, 44-53.

[24] Sweeney, L. B. and Sterman, J. D. 2000. Bathtub dynamics: Initial results of a systems thinking inventory. *System Dynamics Review* 16, 4, 249-286.

[25] Topi, H., Valacich, J. S., Wright, R. T., Kaiser, K., Nunamaker Jr., J. F., Sipior, J. C., and De Vreede, G. J. 2010. IS 2010: Curriculum guidelines for undergraduate degree programs in information systems. *Communications of Association for Information Systems* 26, 18, 359-428.

[26] Valacich, J. S., George, J. F., and Hoffer, J. A. 2012. *Essentials of Systems Analysis & Design, 5th ed.* Pearson Prentice Hall, Upper Saddle River, NJ.

[27] Waddock, S. and Lozano, J. M. 2013. Developing more holistic management education: Lessons learned from two programs. *Academy of Management Learning & Education* 12, 2, pp. 265-284.

[28] Whitten, J. L. and Bentley, L. D., with contributions by Gary Randolph 2007. *Systems Analysis and Design Methods, 7th ed.* McGraw-Hill/Irwin, Boston, MA.

[29] Wolstenholme, E. F. 2004. Using generic system archetypes to support thinking and modeling. *System Dynamics Review* 20, 4, 341-356.

[30] Wolstenholme, E. F. 2003. Towards the definition and use of a core set of archetypal structures in system dynamics. *System Dynamics Review* 19, 1, 7-26.

[31] Zexian, Y. and Xuhui, Y. 2010. A revolution in the field of systems thinking – A Review of Checkland's system thinking, *Systems Research & Behavioral Science* 27, 2, 140-155

Using Professional Consultants to Mentor CIS Students on a Simulated Consulting Project

Thomas W. Dillon
James Madison University
Computer Information Systems
Harrisonburg, VA 22807
1-540-568-3015

dillontw@jmu.edu

Diane Lending
James Madison University
Computer Information Systems
Harrisonburg, VA 22807
1-540-568-3480

lendindc@jmu.edu

ABSTRACT

Students who graduate from the Computer Information Systems major at James Madison University tend to be hired by consulting firms. In support of this, our program has developed an IT Consulting class. This class is team taught by members of the consulting firms that hire our students and a faculty member. The consulting firms also serve as mentors to the students in the class as student teams respond to a simulated Request for Proposal. This paper describes our class and the mentoring role taken by the consultants. We describe outcomes of this mentoring relationship from both the consultants' and the students' perspective.

Categories and Subject Descriptors

K.3.2 [Computers and Education]: Computer and Information Science Education – Curriculum, Information systems education K.6.1 [Management of Computing and Information Systems]: People and Project Management – Staffing K.7.1 [The Computing Profession]: Occupations

General Terms

Management

Keywords

Mentorship, IT Consulting, IS Curriculum.

1. INTRODUCTION

The Information Technology (IT) field has migrated from the use of internal employees to the extensive use of external consultants. The Computer Information Systems (CIS) program at James Madison University (JMU) will graduate almost 150 CIS majors this year. Traditionally, more than 70% of JMU CIS majors will enter the field of Information Technology (IT) consulting, most in Washington, D.C. and its suburbs, and most will enter the "Federal" division of the firm they join. These IT consulting firms recruit CIS majors and minors through the University-sponsored career center. In addition, the CIS program at JMU maintains a relationship with many of the IT consulting firms that hire our alumni. Representatives from these IT consulting firms act as guest speakers in CIS program classes, provide support for the large and successful Association of Information Technology

Permission to make digital or hard copies of all or part of this work for personal or classroom use is granted without fee provided that copies are not made or distributed for profit or commercial advantage and that copies bear this notice and the full citation on the first page. Copyrights for components of this work owned by others than ACM must be honored. Abstracting with credit is permitted. To copy otherwise, or republish, to post on servers or to redistribute to lists, requires prior specific permission and/or a fee. Request permissions from permissions@acm.org.
SIGMIS-CPR'14, May 29–31, 2014, Singapore, Singapore.
Copyright © 2014 ACM 978-1-4503-2625-4/14/05...$15.00.
http://dx.doi.org/10.1145/2599990.2600014

Professionals (AITP) Student Chapter, and serve as members of the CIS program Executive Advisory Council.

Having existing relationships with many IT consulting firms, and in the spirit of collaboration, a group of CIS alumni met in 1996 with the CIS program leadership and discussed the possibility of introducing a new innovative "IT consulting" course. The goal of the new IT Consulting course would be twofold: to prepare the students to be top performers when entering a career in IT consulting and to allow the consulting firms to mentor students that were interested in pursuing consulting as a career.

Joshi, et al. [6] examined the necessary attributes essential to be an excellent IT consultant, which they related to being a top performer in an IT role. Joshi, et al. [6] gathered input from members of a consulting firm at differing levels and found that the stakeholders thought it importance that an entry-level top-performer have the ability to deliver, be committed, be cooperative, and be analytical. In addition, they also found it important that entry-level top performers be quick learners and able to manage relationships [6]. In another study, students in a consulting class suggested that negotiating skills, communications skills, and teamwork were critical for success when participating on a consulting project [7].

There is extensive literature for teaching, learning, and career development that supports the role of mentoring in education and career development [8, 9]. The mentor role often transcends the more tradition interaction of teacher and advisor, and promotes the formation of professional identity and socialization within the career field [11, 9]. In addition, research finds that a mentoring relationship is more collaborative than that of traditional teacher or advisor. Mentorship focuses on student learning based on experience and role modeling from a more skilled and experienced professional that is familiar with the discipline and the culture [9].

Corporate recruiters want newly hired consultants that are broadly prepared for the numerous responsibilities they will face in the modern workplace along with an understanding of consulting culture and the career field. This comprises some knowledge and comfort with business analysis, exposure to real-world case studies, and development in their communication, presentation, and interpersonal skills [5]. Our IT Consulting class is designed to fulfill this need. And the use of professional consultants, acting as mentors, is designed to not only provide the identity and cultural preparation sought, but to also provide the outcomes of successful mentorship behavior and mentorship quality (coaching, real-world insights, skill building, development activities, networking, and business contacts) [4, 1].

The role of industry mentoring in the classroom with a simulated project has not been studied fully [10]. Research does show that mentoring can extend and enhance the educational experience by providing connections to the practical world and organizational culture. The mentoring role model provides students with experience, knowledge, wisdom, skills and influence that supports and promotes career development through the mentor/mentee relationship [10,4]. Future research needs to provide a careful definition of mentoring and clarify the concepts of mentoring and to differentiate mentoring from the concepts of training, socialization and friendship in the workplace [2].

In this paper we explain the structure of our IT Consulting class, assess the quality of the mentoring activity and determine if our IT Consulting elective prepares our CIS program graduates for the responsibilities of the modern consulting workplace. Measures of most interest are mentoring behavior, mentorship quality, program characteristics, interaction frequency, and outcome of the relationship [3, 4, 1].

2. COURSE DESCRIPTION: IT CONSULTING WITH A SIMULATED PROJECT

2.1 Course Objectives

The course objectives, presented in Table 1, were developed collaboratively with faculty and consulting firm representation. The course was piloted in the Fall of 1998. Though periodic changes have been made in the delivery of the course in the last 15 years, the objectives have remained basically the same.

Table 1. Course Objectives

1. To develop professionalism in a student.
2. To understand the consulting life cycle.
3. To be able to develop a response to a request for proposal (RFP), Including
   a. Developing References
   b. Developing a project plan
   c. Developing a Staffing plan
   d. Developing a Costing plan
   e. Developing a Technical solution
4. To understand the principle behind and the processes used in Project Management
5. To understand the structure and organization of project teams and to develop good teamwork habits.
6. To identify opportunities for consulting business.
7. To understand the moral and ethical dilemmas for consultants and be able to use sound principles to resolve these dilemmas.
8. To develop the skills necessary to work in large teams and use project management principles to manage the teams.
9. To be able to present a project proposal, project plan, and project design to a prospective client.
10. To develop and use status reports.

2.2 Mentor Firms

Each year, IT Consulting Firms volunteer to participate in the class. This role is highly sought after, but we limit participation to between eight and twelve IT Consulting firms, or Mentor Firms, depending on the number of students we expect to accept into the course. The role of the Mentor Firm is twofold. First, as the name implies, Mentor Firms mentor a team of 3 students in the consulting project during the first half of the semester. During this time the Mentor Firm assists with the project and provides mentor activities (coaching, networking, skill building, etc.). Second, each Mentor Firm provides a class presentation on a consulting topic. Participating Mentor Firms over the last 10 years are presented in the Table 2.

Table 2: Firms that have participated in the last 10 years

Accenture
Acuity
Advanced Technology Systems (ATS)
American Management Systems (CGI-AMS)
Andersen Consulting
Arthur Andersen
Baker Tilley
BluePrint IT
Booz·Allen Hamilton
Broughton Systems
Business Impact Systems (BIS)
CGI
Computer Sciences Corporation (CSC)
CORE Consulting
Deloitte
Dynamics Research Corporation (DRC)
Electronic Data Systems (EDS)
Ernst & Young
High Performance Technologies (HPTi)
IBM
J. D. Edwards
KPMG
PEC
PricewaterhouseCoopers
Protiviti

The CIS program obtains a commitment from each Mentor Firm that they will provide mentorship for a three-student consulting team during the consulting project. Mentor Firms traditionally supply at least two mentors and a few subject matter experts. The mentors are normally a junior and a more senior consultant. Each mentor firm advises the student consulting team, coordinates communication, answers regular questions and identifies subject matter needs. The subject matter experts are often experienced at consulting projects. For example, the consulting project for the last 13 years has been to write a proposal in response to a federal Request For Proposals (RFP). So subject matter experts are often proposal writers, proposal pricing experts, or technical solution analysts.

There is a 1-hour training session for Mentor Firms. In this session, the goals and objective of the class are reviewed, priorities for the Mentor Firms are established, and successful mentoring activities are discussed between the mentors. A small handout is provided along with contact information.

Each Mentor Firm provides one or more class presentations on topics from the syllabus. Topics are negotiated between the course instructor and the Mentor Firm. The class presenters may be the same consultants that serve as mentors, or the Mentor Firm may provide a subject matter expert to deliver the class presentation. For example, a firm vice president responsible for evaluating all proposals completed by the firm has repeatedly served as the presenter when the topic is "writing the technical approach." This subject matter expert is a professional presenter and a master at writing the technical approach. His expertise exceeds that of the standard mentor. A complete list of topics presented in the consulting class is listed in Table 3.

Table 3: Topics Presented by Mentor Firms

| Consulting Life Cycle |
| Role of the Consultant |
| Proposal Writing |
| Writing the Technical Approach |
| Writing the Management Approach |
| Team Building |
| Project Management |
| Business Ethics |
| Research (Gartner Group) |
| Interpersonal Communication |
| Making Presentations |
| Business Process Redesign |
| Business Continuity |
| Risk Management |
| Change Management |
| System Security |
| Buy - vs – Build |
| Outsourcing and Partnering |
| Issues Management and Tracking |
| Incident Reporting |
| Help Desk Development |
| User Training |
| Statement of Work |
| Pricing/Costing a Proposal |
| JAD Facilitation |
| Understanding Client Cultures |

2.3 Deliverables

There are two large graded deliverables for the course. The first is a proposal in response to the RFP. The second is an implementation plan that incorporates content from a selection of required courses in the CIS major.

The proposal is a simulated activity, but we try to be as real-world as possible, so the RFP is captured from the FedBizOpps.Gov website. FedBizOpps is a government supported website that lists most services or equipment that the federal government needs to acquire. For our IT Consulting class we search for IT services that our students can provide. In recent years our students have written proposals to deliver a variety of services, including Court Services and Offender Supervision Agency - IT Security Program, Export-Import Bank - Business Intelligence Reporting System, FEMA Crisis Management System (COTS), and Business System Replacement for the Library of Congress (COTS). To add to the realism of the project, the judges for the proposal project are drawn from the federal sector. Two alumni that serve in senior roles review the proposals and score the projects as if actually submitted. To balance the real-world with the classroom, the course instructor also evaluates the proposal projects.

The second deliverable is an implementation plan for the proposed system. The second deliverable traditionally includes the implementation of topics that are woven through the CIS program curriculum. For example, in 2013 student teams prepared a requirements gathering and determination plan, an enterprise architecture, a detailed business process of 10 tasks, a business continuity plan and a risk management plan. All of these topics are in the junior year of the CIS major/minor curriculum, so this simulation also serves as a content integrating activity for the students that enroll.

3. STUDENT SELECTION AND ENROLLMENT

The IT Consulting class provides many post-graduation employment opportunities for the students that enroll and participate. For this reason, admission to the class is selective. The course is taught to students in the first semester of their senior year. In the spring of the students' junior year, students wishing to enroll in the class prepare an application packet that contains a written statement, a resume, and their academic record. A team of faculty members review each applicant and select the strongest candidates. Approximately 60% of those that apply are admitted.

There is a 75-minute educational session for student teams prior to being introduced to the mentor firms. Goals and objective of the class are reviewed, priorities for the student interaction and proposal project are established, and successful team activities are discussed with the students. A small handout is provided along with contact information.

4. ASSESSING THE QUALITY OF THE MENTORING ACTIVITY

Following in the research of D'Abate and Eddy [6], we chose to assess the quality of our mentoring activity by examining five factors: participant matching, participant preparation, participant interaction, the outcomes of mentoring by the professional consultants, and guidance activities provided for the completing of the proposal project. We used five-point Likert-type scale to measure the responses, ranging from 1 (strongly disagree) to 5 (strongly agree). Student teams and Mentor Firms were surveyed. The data is presented below. There were twelve respondents from each sample.

Participant Matching was a two-item scale design to measure satisfaction with the matching process. "I am satisfied with the student team I was matched with" and "The members of my student team and I got along well" were the two items.

Participant Preparation was a three-item scale designed to measure if the one-hour training was enough preparation. The items were, "The goals and objectives of the mentoring program were communicated well," "I know what was required of me before I signed on to participate as a mentor," and "The orientation session at the beginning of the program prepared me for my role as a mentor."

Participant Interaction was assessed with a five-item scale to measure satisfaction with interactions. Items included were, "We developed an action plan," "we set goals for the relationship," " I shared my own experiences with my student team," "We tracked progress toward the goals we set for completing the proposal," and "We had open, honest and confidential communications."

The outcomes of mentoring by the professional consultants were gathered with a ten-item scale. The items were began with I and were followed by: " provided real-world insights," "was a successful coach," "assisted in skill building," "provided development opportunities," "provided networking tips," "provided business contacts," "participated in learning experiences," "developed action plans," "participated in follow-up discussions," and "provided job-finding skills. "

And finally, the assessment of the guidance for the project activities (completing of the proposal project) included the following four-items: "I successfully communicated," "I responded to questions and problems in a timely manner," "I supported my student team with knowledgeable responses," and "I prepared my student team for their role in the project."

The mean scores for each item in the factor were combined to report the results by each of the five factors.

Table 4: Mean Values of Each Factor

Factor	Mentor Firm	Student Team
Participant Matching	4.68	3.70
Participant Preparation	4.52	3.33
Participant Interaction	4.25	3.20
Outcomes of mentoring	4.03	3.15
Assessment of guidance for the project	4.30	3.23

5. DISCUSSION OF RESULTS

We hoped to determine if our IT Consulting elective prepared our CIS program graduates for the responsibilities of the modern consulting workplace. The outcomes of our survey contained a positive result. Both mentor firms and members of the student teams identified all the factors in the survey with "agree" or "strongly agree." The factors that receive the lowest scores, participant interaction, outcome mentoring, and assessment of the guidance for the project, are discussed.

The participant interaction between mentor firm and student team was about seven weeks long. The members of the mentor firm reside in the Washington D.C. suburbs and the students live approximately two hours away in our college town. Most communication was via email, conference call, or abbreviated visit. This limited time frame and distance may not have allowed the mentor firm to engage with the student team and provide for the sharing and open commination we had hoped. To overcome this limitation we are considering the requirement of at least one visit by the student team to the mentor firms' work location.

The outcomes of the mentoring factor included items such as coaching, skill building, networking, and providing job-finding skills. Again, the length of our interaction is only seven week long. Many of these activities may not be able to happen in such

an abbreviated time frame. We are considering extending the mentoring activity into the second deliverable, but with less project completion responsibilities. This extending time period would then allow for continued interaction between mentor firm and student team, which would hopefully create opportunities for networking, coaching, sharing of real-world insights, and follow-up discussion about skill building and participating in learning experience.

And finally, the assessment of guidance of the mentor firm to the student team was insightful. Though a small sample, it is clear that the student teams expect to have more guidance than is provided by the mentor firms. Discussion with students after the survey allowed us to better understand this factor, and it appears to center on "expectation." The students expect the mentor firm to provide more. They expect more guidance, more time, and more communication. Plans are being made to alter the 75-minute educational session for student teams prior to being introduced to the mentor firms. In addition, a "Being Mentored" handbook is being developed that will clearly present expectations for both mentor firms and student teams.

One caveat in using these results is that the student participants are selected by the faculty members on the basis of being our strongest students. It cannot be assumed that the results with all students would be similar.

6. CONCLUSION

In this paper we explain the structure of our unique IT Consulting class, assess the quality of the mentoring activity and determine if our IT Consulting elective prepares our CIS program graduates for the responsibilities of the consulting environment they will soon inhabit. The results support our hopes that we have begun to meet our goals, but we feel that there are changes that may need to be made to meet all of the goals we have set for the class. These changes will focus on extending the time that the mentor firm and student team interact, allowing for the establishment of mentor/mentee relationships, and providing for coaching, sharing, and network opportunities.

7. REFERENCES

[1] Allen T.D., Eby, L.T. & Lentz, E. (2006). Mentoring behaviors and mentoring quality associated with formal mentoring programs: Closing the gap between research and practice. Journal of Applied Psychology, 91(3), 567-578.

[2] Bozeman, B. & Feeney, M.K. (2007) Towards a useful theory of mentoring a conceptual analysis and critique. Administration & Society, 39(6), 719-739.

[3] D'Abate, C. (2010). Developmental interactions for business students: Do they make a difference, Journal of Leadership & Organizational Studies, 17(2), 143-155.

[4] D'Abate, C.P. & Eddy, E.R. (2008). Mentoring as a learning tool: Enhancing the effectiveness of an undergraduate business mentoring program. Mentoring& Tutoring: Partnership in Learning, 16(4), 363-378.

[5] Heim, G., Meile, L., Tease, J., Glass, J., & Laher, S. (2005). Experiential learning in a management information systems course: simulating IT consulting and CRM system procurement, Communications of the Association for Information Systems, 15(25), 428-463.

[6] Joshi, K. D., Kuhn, K.M. and Niederman, F. (2010) "Excellence in IT Consulting: Integrating Multiple Stakeholders' Perceptions of Top Performers," IEEE Transactions on Engineering Management, 57(4), pp. 589-606.

[7] Komarjaya, J., Huifang, L, and Bock, G.-W. (2004). "Consulting from students' perspective," Consulting to Management, 15(2), pp. 29-33.

[8] McAllister, C.A., Ahmedani, B.K., Harold, R.D., & Cramer, E.P. (2009) Targeted mentoring: Evaluation of a program. Journal of Social Work Education, 45(1), 89-104.

[9] Santora, K.A., Mason, E.J., & Sheahan, T.C. (2013) A model for progressive mentoring in science and engineering education and research. Innovation in Higher Education, 38(5), 427-440.

[10] Weterman, L. Weterman, F. & Hogan, T. (2011) Simulation and industry mentors as a pathway to learning 'near world' project management. 8th Project Management Australia Conference, Sydney, Australia, August.

[11] Zelditch, M. (1990) Mentor roles. Proceedings of the 32nd annual meeting of the Western Association of Graduate Schools, Keynote address, Tempe, Arizona, March, p. 11.

The Four 'W's of Face-to-Face – Suggesting an Enriched Perspective on Nearshoring Relationship Management

Alexander von Stetten
University of Bamberg
An der Weberei 5
96047 Bamberg, Germany
+49 (0) 951 863 2879
alexander.von-stetten@uni-bamberg.de

Daniel Beimborn
Frankfurt School of Finance & Management
Sonnemannstr. 9-11
60314 Frankfurt, Germany
+49 (0) 69 154008 746
d.beimborn@fs.de

Tim Weitzel
University of Bamberg
An der Weberei 5
96047 Bamberg, Germany
+49 (0) 951 863 2871
tim.weitzel@uni-bamberg.de

ABSTRACT

Outsourcing relationships usually benefit from face-to-face (F2F) meetings between client and vendor staff in various manners, for instance, by fostering trust, mutual understanding, and knowledge transfer. While being an expensive and often not frequently used measure in IT offshoring to far-distant countries, frequent F2F meetings are especially attractive in nearshore settings where geographic distance is small; thus establishing distinctive F2F patterns becomes an important criterion for managing a healthy nearshore outsourcing relationship. This paper proposes four 'W's that help both research and practitioners to think about F2F meetings in a structured way and to develop F2F strategies for achieving an effective outsourcing relationship. These 'W's represent different dimensions of F2F in terms of participants ('Who'), location ('Where'), time ('When'), and motives for meeting F2F ('Why'). We apply the four 'W's in a descriptive case analysis of three nearshore IS outsourcing arrangements between Western European clients and Eastern European vendors. This analysis provides evidence for the applicability and value of using the four 'W's, which will support future research on inter-firm collaboration regarding the identification of effective F2F patterns.

Categories and Subject Descriptors

H.0 [**Information Systems**]: General

General Terms

Management, Human Factors.

Keywords

Face-to-face meetings; nearshore outsourcing; Western European/Eastern European nearshore cluster; descriptive case studies.

Permission to make digital or hard copies of all or part of this work for personal or classroom use is granted without fee provided that copies are not made or distributed for profit or commercial advantage and that copies bear this notice and the full citation on the first page. Copyrights for components of this work owned by others than ACM must be honored. Abstracting with credit is permitted. To copy otherwise, or republish, to post on servers or to redistribute to lists, requires prior specific permission and/or a fee. Request permissions from Permissions@acm.org.

SIGMIS-CPR '14, May 29–31, 2014, Singapore, Singapore.
Copyright 2014 ACM 978-1-4503-2625-4/14/05...$15.00.
http://dx.doi.org/10.1145/2599990.2600015

1. INTRODUCTION

The major importance of face-to-face (F2F) meetings for relationship building [e.g., 13, 30], knowledge transfer [e.g., 10, 15], and overcoming cultural differences [e.g., 13, 34] in IT offshoring relationships has been frequently stressed in the literature. Despite its mostly undisputed relevance, budget for meeting F2F in offshore settings is usually limited due to cost reasons [10, 35]. By contrast, those costs and efforts of travel are considerably lower in so called nearshore settings [23], in which activities are sourced *"[...] to a foreign, lower-wage country that is relatively close in distance or time zone (or both)"* [5, p. 44]. The possibility to jump on a plane and talk about an issue F2F within a couple of hours makes nearshore destinations particularly attractive for outsourcing of complex or critical work [9].

This paper dwells on the perceived attractiveness of F2F meetings in nearshore relationships by thoroughly analyzing their specific configuration and role in such settings. Thereby, we intend to shed light on emergent F2F patterns comprising the four elements *participants* (Who), *location* (Where), *time* (When, how often, and how long), and *motives* for meeting F2F (Why) – referred to as the four 'W's in the following. While some research has already considered some of these dimensions in a combined mode [2, 24, 26], the literature on distributed work, so far, lacks a holistic and multidimensional view of F2F patterns considering participants, location, time, and motives for F2F meetings. Thus, we address the following research question:

> *How can F2F meetings be captured in a structured way in order to examine more precisely their role and impact on nearshoring performance?*

By answering this question, we also contribute to the literature on IT nearshoring, which is still under-researched [1] though being a strong and increasing outsourcing trend [28].

The remainder of this paper is organized as follows: First, we present extant literature on F2F meetings in distributed settings. Then, we introduce the concept of the four 'W's of F2F meetings and briefly describe our case research methodology before we turn to detailed case descriptions and analyses of F2F patterns.

2. F2F MEETINGS IN DISTRIBUTED SETTINGS

A great deal of existing research stresses that F2F meetings are an important ingredient of successful collaboration in distributed settings. While Rai et al. [29] showed a direct positive impact of client visits to the vendor site on offshore IS project success, large parts of the existing literature dealing with this issue rather indicate an indirect effect of F2F contact on collaboration success, for example, by facilitating knowledge sharing or by fostering the creation of social ties between remote colleagues [20].

Basically, F2F meetings drive the build-up of strong interpersonal relationships between remote partners [24, 26]. Visiting the other side helps building social capital in offshore IS outsourcing relationships, which in turn facilitates knowledge transfer between client and vendor [13, 34]. The major importance of F2F contact for establishing trust [14, 37] and rapport [13, 20] in distributed settings has been stated frequently, as well. With respect to establishing trust and strong interpersonal ties, scholars also emphasized the particular importance of social events outside the work hours, such as having dinner together or a joint party at the end of a release cycle [17, 36].

Elaborating on the specific aspect of knowledge transfer, Dibbern et al. [10] emphasized the need of F2F contact between client and vendor staff in offshoring relationships if very client-specific knowledge is required on the vendor side. Heeks et al. [15] took the same line, arguing that F2F meetings are more effective for sharing informal information than electronically mediated communication. Besides relationship building and knowledge sharing, bridging cultural boundaries respectively developing a mutual cultural understanding was identified as another benefit of F2F contact in globally distributed settings [13, 34]. Other facets in distributed work environments that are supported by F2F meetings include clarifying complex issues, ambiguities, or previous miscommunication [10, 37], negotiating the meaning of work and setting up communication procedures [26], working out implementation details, and making major decisions [24].

With regard to the interplay between F2F vs. electronic communication, some researchers pointed out that the need for F2F contact rises already in the beginning of a collaboration because electronically mediated communication becomes much more effective and informal after the partners have met F2F [26, 33]; similarly, early F2F meetings help to integrate the offshoring partners' structures and processes [16] and increase both parties' staff's identification with the arrangement [11, 12]. However, F2F contact is not only important in the beginning of a cooperation but also considered relevant at critical points in the project lifecycle [9], like, for example, during the requirements specification phase [3, 4] or when certain project milestones are reached [2]. Moreover, F2F meetings should happen regularly because team identification or trust between the dispersed counterparts vanish over time. Consequently, ongoing investments in F2F meetings are required to renew interpersonal ties and sustain the obtained benefits [26, 27].

Although the value of F2F meetings in distributed settings is beyond debate, visits are associated with some drawbacks, as well. First of all, meeting F2F is usually quite costly, especially if the collaborating parties are located far away from each other [10, 33] and if not only the project manager(s) but a larger number of team members participate in the business trip. Moreover, language and cultural differences might serve as communication barriers. When meeting F2F, team members have to understand and contribute in real-time which can be difficult for non-native speakers who are not fluent in the chosen project language and thus prefer written communication [2, 26, 31]. Inconveniences may also arise from cultural differences, for instance, if Indian developers state their opinion or voice criticism, if at all, only via email but not in F2F meetings due to their obedience to authority [21].

Summarizing, the literature shows that some research has dealt with effects of F2F meetings on distributed work. However, research exclusively addressing this phenomenon and providing a structured analysis of F2F patterns in distributed settings is largely absent. To fill this gap, we conducted three descriptive case studies focusing on the concept of the four 'W's of F2F meetings which is introduced in the following.

3. THE FOUR 'W'S OF FACE-TO-FACE

As outlined above, the literature provides rich insights with regard to the motives for F2F meetings ('Why') and with regard to the point of time such meetings should take place ('When') in distributed team settings. By contrast, research has hardly addressed the questions *where* F2F meetings should happen and *who* should participate in them, yet. In this paper, we argue that all four dimensions ('Why', 'When', 'Where', and 'Who') – the four 'W's – should be thoroughly considered in a combined manner to tap into the full potential of F2F meetings:

'Why': This dimension comprises the explicit motives for meeting F2F. Such motives may include, for instance, project kick-offs, knowledge exchange (e.g., trainings, workshops, pair programming), or socializing reasons (e.g., a teambuilding event).

'When': Depending on the 'Why', this dimension refers to the questions when, how long, and how often a F2F meeting should happen. For example, a new vendor team member would initially always have to visit the client for two weeks (for knowledge transfer reasons).

'Where': The third 'W' of F2F points to the location where the F2F meeting should take place. Meetings can happen at the client's site, the vendor's site, or, in case of regular meetings, in an alternating mode. Meeting at different places allows for the involvement of more project members on that particular side and can have different benefits.

'Who': The 'Who'-dimension deals with the question who should participate in a F2F meeting. For instance, client and vendor could ponder if it is beneficial to include (all or most of the) vendor developers in a kickoff meeting or if it is sufficient to let only the project manager (PM) and the technical team lead participate. The potential range of 'Who' reaches from executives via account/vendor managers, PMs, and technical team leads to each single developer, tester, or administrator directly or indirectly involved in the project. Further, it could also involve the end-users who eventually receive the IT service provided or who use the software developed by the vendor.

Analyzing F2F meetings along these four 'W's yields in a holistic and multidimensional view of such meetings and will enrich our understanding of the effects of F2F and thus also allow for more precise practitioner advices about setting up F2F patterns. To provide empirical evidence for this claim, we present three descriptive case studies in IS nearshore settings and analyze them along the four 'W's.

4. APPROACH

The role of F2F meetings in IT nearshoring relationships constitutes a contemporary, real-life phenomenon being under-researched which clearly calls out for a qualitative research design according to Yin [40]. This research is part of an ongoing larger case study series on relationship management in IT nearshoring in which more than 20 cases were selected from the Western European/Eastern European nearshore cluster[1]. From this sample, we chose three cases providing rich information on the role of F2F meetings which thus are best suited to do a first descriptive analysis of the dimensions of F2F patterns.

When creating the interview guideline, we drew on constructs relevant in the encompassing research area of relationship management in distributed work scenarios (e.g., trust, mutual understanding, knowledge transfer). Overall, we conducted 23 semi-structured interviews (4 of them via Skype and 19 onsite) both on the vendor and on the client side and on all relevant hierarchy levels (cf. Table 1). Both authors acted as interviewers in all 23 interviews. All interviews were recorded and fully transcribed. The subsequent coding was done following the guidelines of Corbin and Strauss [8]: first, all interview passages associated with F2F contact were identified. These passages were then grouped into higher level categories being specific types of F2F meetings/contact (e.g., kickoff-meeting, management meeting etc.). Then, concepts (e.g., working side by side, socializing outside the workplace, knowledge sharing, trust etc.) were drawn from those categories and finally linked to each other. This procedure finally resulted in a total number of 207 codings. The coding was done by the first author and verified by the second author; both authors intensely discussed all final codes and checked them with regard to their reliability. The coding was done using the software MAXQDA.

5. CASE ANALYSIS

Table 1 provides some basic information about the cases and interviewees. Subsequently, the three cases are described in detail, including an overview of the F2F patterns established.

5.1 Relationship 1

5.1.1 Case Description

Client 1 is a German software development company currently employing about 80 persons. Their main product is a manufacturing execution system (MES) which is used by major German automotive producers. Having been a subsidiary of a larger German IT firm until 2010, Client 1 was forced by its parent company to outsource parts of their software production to an Indian vendor in 2004 due to cost reasons. Collaboration with the Indian vendor was highly problematic because of language issues, cultural differences, and a lack of personal contact due to low travel budgets. Consequently, Client 1 replaced the Indian vendor by a nearshore provider in 2007. Besides the common selection criteria (labor cost arbitrage; high expertise; sufficiently large workforce), the new vendor should be located in a country which is closer in culture and geographical distance (less than three flight hours). Moreover, the new vendor was expected to provide solely team members with sufficient German language skills. Finally, Vendor 1 from Belarus was selected. Collaboration with Vendor 1 early turned out to be much more successful than with the previous Indian vendor. At the end of 2012, 21 employees of Vendor 1 worked exclusively for Client 1, all of them having good or very good German language skills. Vendor staff cooperates closely with their client colleagues in a distributed team which is organized as a mirror interface setup [32], including all roles on both sides (PM, developers, quality assurance (QA), support and maintenance). Client 1 is very satisfied with the services provided by Vendor 1. Both sides refer to their relationship as being very open and trustful.

Table 1. Case overview

	Relationship 1	Relationship 2	Relationship 3
Outsourcing object (service provided)	Further development of and support and maintenance for a manufacturing execution system (MES) (4 releases per year)	Further development of an e-banking system (2 releases per year)	Business intelligence (BI) services (programming and generation of reports)
Begin of cooperation	2007	2005	2008
Client: location, industry, size (employees)	Germany, software, 80	Switzerland, software, 200	Germany, telco, >5,000
Vendor: location, size (employees)	Belarus, > 600	Serbia, 140	Belarus, > 1,000
Team size (on vendor side)	21 team members	17 team members	30 team members
Interviews on vendor side	3 (1 project manager (PM), 1 developer, 1 quality assurance engineer/tester)	6 (1 technical team lead, 4 senior developers, 1 developer)	7 (1 account manager, 2 PMs, 1 technical team lead, 3 database developers)
Interviews on client side	2 (1 executive, 1 PM)	2 interviews (1 executive, 1 PM)	3 interviews (head of BI projects, 2 PMs)

---

[1] In this cluster, firms from Western Europe (Germany, Switzerland, Benelux countries etc.) outsource typically to providers in Eastern Europe (Poland, Russia, Belarus, Hungary, Balkan countries etc.).

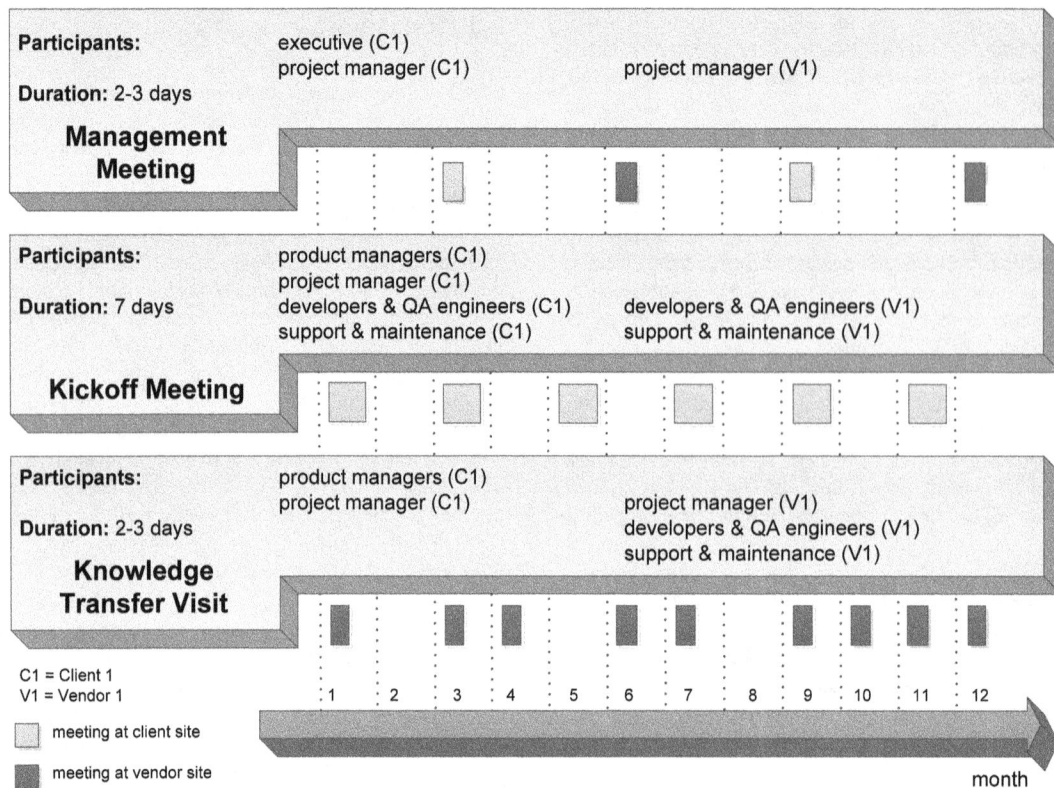

Figure 1: F2F meetings in Relationship 1

5.1.2 F2F Patterns

Client 1 follows a dedicated F2F strategy and the outsourcing relationship is characterized by frequent regular F2F contact between client and vendor team members. As outlined in Figure 1, this F2F strategy consists of three different types of regular F2F meetings:

- Every three months, at the end of each release cycle, a management meeting takes place alternately at the client site in Germany or at the vendor site in Belarus, lasting 2 to 3 days. Participants are the two PMs from both sides and the Client 1 executive who is responsible for the nearshoring relationship. The management meeting is motivated mainly by two reasons: first, the completed release is analyzed and discussed with regard to performance aspects and other emergent issues. Second, participants take this opportunity to socialize with the team. For that purpose, a team event is organized. In Belarus, the whole vendor team working for Client 1 is invited to a joint dinner or outing at every management meeting. When the meeting takes place at the client site in Germany, those client team members working most closely together with the vendor take also part in the team event, together with the managers.

- The second type of F2F contact consists of regular kickoff meetings (5-6 times per year) happening at the beginning of a release cycle as well as before particularly large or complex modules or functionalities are implemented within a release cycle. Kickoff meetings take always place on the client side in Germany and usually last around 7 days. They are attended by the client PM, the product managers responsible for those modules within the MES to be modified or extended, and by all developers, QA engineers (QA = quality assurance), and support and maintenance team members from both sides who

are considered to be needed. In a kickoff meeting, all planned changes and extensions in the MES are discussed so that all concerned team members get and share the same picture before starting implementation. Besides, in-depth introductions to specific software modules are provided to vendor staff on demand by the client product managers. Knowledge transfer between both sides is further fostered by client and vendor staff sitting side by side in the same office and doing their regular work in between the actual meeting phases so that vendor team members can ask their German colleagues anytime anything they need to know. Finally, attention is also paid to the team aspect. Vendor team members normally stay not only for 5 working days but also for the weekend because the client organizes a full-day outing almost every time.

- Third, the client PM visits the vendor site up to 10 times per year (each time for 2 or 3 days) for knowledge transfer reasons. In doing so, he is accompanied 2 to 3 times per year by dedicated product managers if a product training is demanded by the vendor or deemed necessary by the client. Besides knowledge transfer, the client PM's main motive for these visits is maintaining personal contact. During his stay, he ensures to sit very close to the vendor team members, sharing the same office space, to be able to answer upcoming questions immediately while doing his regular daily work. From time to time, he might also work closely together with the vendor staff on some specific topics. During those visits, he always invites some vendor team members to dinner at one evening to maintain interpersonal relationships apart from every-day work.

180

5.2 Relationship 2

5.2.1 Case Description

In 2005, Client 2, a Swiss software company developing and distributing an e-banking system as its core product, decided to outsource some of its software development activities to achieve a more flexible cost structure and because of a shortage of skilled IT workers on the Swiss labor market. Vendor 2, a Serbian company, was selected because: (1) Client 2 concentrated on nearshore vendors because they feared cross-cultural problems when collaborating with Asian vendors; (2) Vendor 2 runs an office in the same Swiss city in which Client 2 is located; (3) members of the executive boards of both companies were in contact and had known each other before. Having started in 2005, the outsourcing relationship between Client 2 and Vendor 2 lasts until today. By the end of 2012, 17 vendor employees, all of them developers including a technical team lead, worked for Client 2 in a distributed team setting. Project management and QA are carried out by the client firm which employs several developers, as well. Overall, the development work is done equally by client and vendor team members who closely collaborate. The interaction structure among vendor and client people is assembled as a full density network [32]: all vendor team members communicate with everyone at the client side if necessary. Both sides refer to the relationship as being very open and the client rates the vendor performance to be very high.

5.2.2 F2F Patterns

As presented in Figure 2, four types of F2F meetings exist in this relationship.

- First, senior managers of Client 2 visit the vendor once per year. Participants from the client side include the chief technology officer (CTO), who is the executive being responsible for the relationship with Vendor 2, one or two other alternating members of the executive board, and the PM. While during those visits, which last 2 to 3 days, some general aspects regarding the outsourcing relationship (e.g., performance measures, future plans, other emergent issues) are discussed between the client representatives, the vendor's chief executive officer (CEO) and his responsible resource manager, the main motive for these visits is meeting all vendor team members. Within a presentation to the whole nearshore team, the client provides an overview about important events in the relationship since the last management visit and shows the future roadmap and plans. Not only concentrating on the outsourcing relationship itself, this presentation comprises some general information about the client and its development, too. Moreover, all nearshore team members are given some small presents (e.g., beach towels, t-shirts, notebook bags) and the whole team is invited to dinner on one evening.

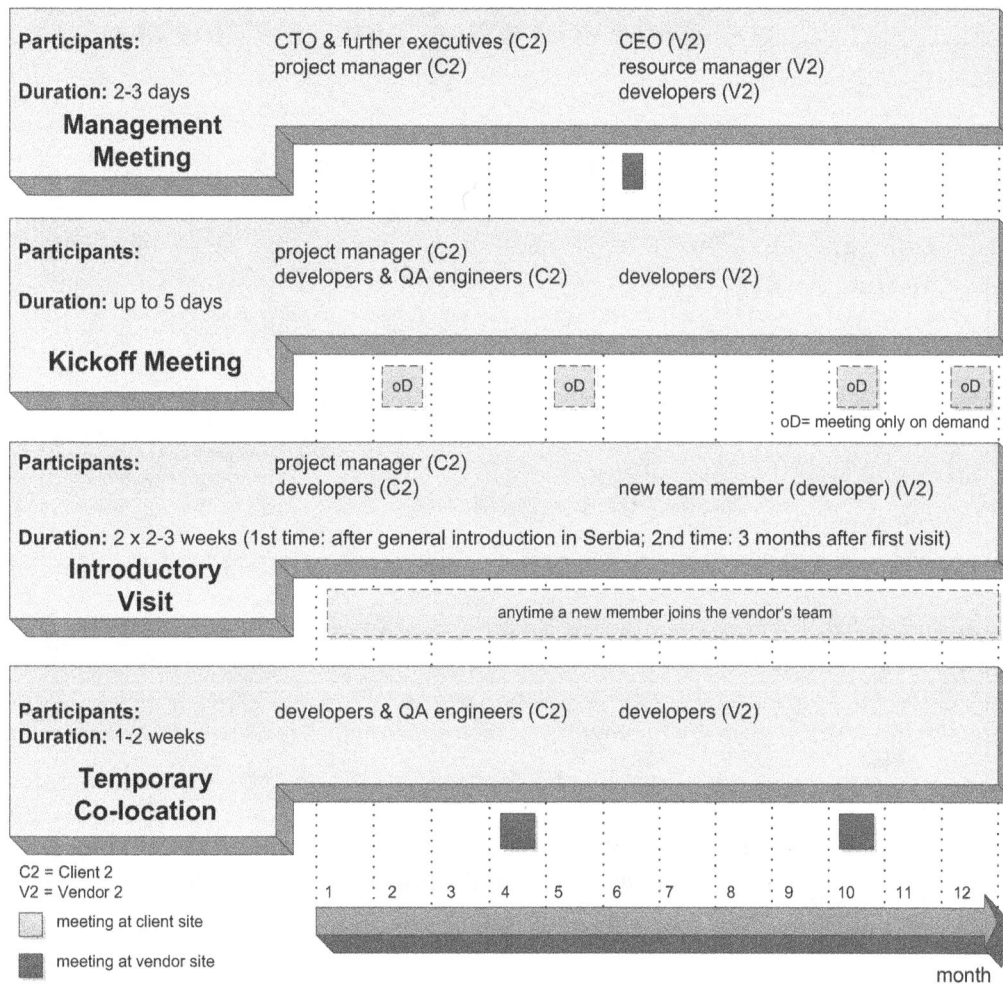

Figure 2: F2F meetings in Relationship 2

- Kickoff meetings represent a second type of F2F contact. Such meetings happen irregularly on demand. If major or complex extensions or changes are planned to be implemented, certain vendor developers are invited to Switzerland to participate in a kickoff meeting with the PM and client colleagues (developers and QA engineers) to talk about the following steps and to discuss emergent issues and possible difficulties. Lasting up to 5 days, such meetings usually also include at least one joint dinner to maintain interpersonal relationships, even though kickoff meetings do not focus on this aspect. While there have been five such kickoff meetings in 2011, there has been none in 2012, reflecting their irregular nature.

- In the first four weeks after having joined the vendor team, every new developer is given a basic introduction by her/his Serbian senior developer colleagues to get some knowledge about the e-banking system, the technology used, and the collaboration in general. After this initial training, s/he is invited to Switzerland for 2 to 3 weeks to have several profound trainings on system/business and architectural/technical knowledge held by the client PM and his senior developers.

Subsequently, the new developer returns to Serbia and starts working on the project. About three months later, s/he travels to Switzerland again to collaborate as closely as possible with the client developers for another 2 to 3 weeks. During this phase, s/he sits right next to the client developers to be able to ask all kinds of questions and get them answered instantly. Beside knowledge transfer, this introduction procedure is also supposed to allow getting to know the client colleagues in person and to establish personal bonds.

- Lastly, 2 to 4 alternating client developers are visiting the vendor site up to two times per year for 1 to 2 weeks. During this short co-location phase, they are doing their normal daily work while sitting in the same office as their vendor colleagues. This measure targets on maintaining interpersonal ties as well as the client developers' respect for their vendor colleagues by realizing their expertise and professionalism onsite in daily work. During their visits, client developers are invited to dinner by their vendor colleagues at least once.

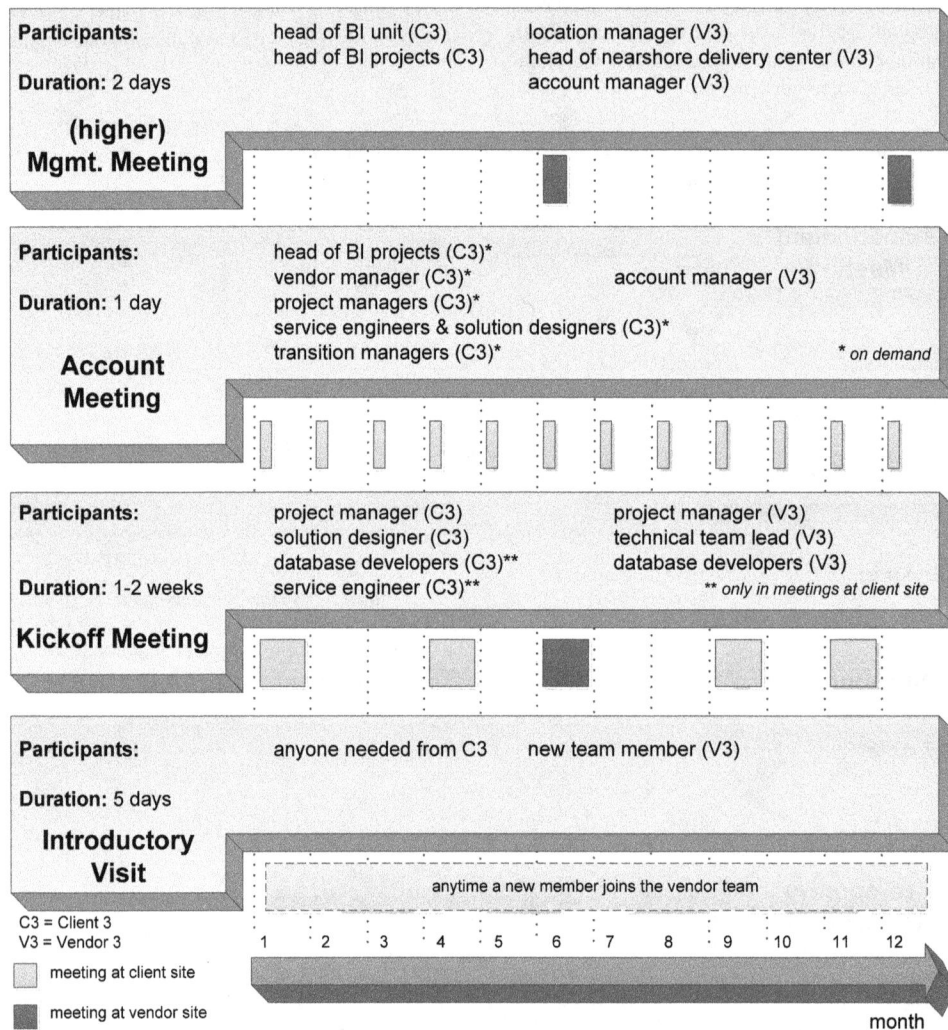

Figure 3: F2F meetings in Relationship 3

5.3 Relationship 3

5.3.1 Case Description

Client 3 is a large German telecommunications firm. In 2008, it decided to cut costs in its business intelligence unit (BIU) which serves as a company internal service provider for the other departments. The significant number of German onsite freelancers and permanently employed contractors within the BIU should be reduced significantly and replaced by one single vendor. Criteria for selecting the vendor were the following: (1) the vendor should be located in a country which is close in culture, time zone, and geographic distance, and (2) it should be able to guarantee the whole team exhibiting good German skills. Eventually, Vendor 3 from Belarus was selected. Quite immediately after the beginning of the cooperation, Client 3 realized that Vendor 3 would not be able to provide an entirely German speaking team. However, it was decided to proceed with the relationship and to switch the whole communication – including the client-internal requirements and specification process – as well as the entire documentation from German to English. Despite the vendor's unfulfilled promise, the collaboration developed positively. By the end of 2012, 30 vendor team members were working for Client 3 in 4 sub-teams that have mirrored counterparts on the client side. Each sub-team consists of 2 PMs, and several database developers as well as QA engineers from both sides. The mirrored parts (client and vendor side) of the respective sub-teams are closely working (virtually) together. The outsourcing relationship is characterized by high levels of trust and openness and Client 3 is satisfied with the services that are provided by Vendor 3.

5.3.2 F2F Patterns

F2F contact between Client 3 and Vendor 3 is organized in four different ways (cf. Figure 3):

- Once or twice per year, there is a (higher) management meeting in Belarus attended by the head of the BIU, the head of BI projects (client side), the location manager, the head of the nearshore delivery center, and the account manager responsible for Client 3 (vendor side). This meeting aims at discussing general matters regarding the collaboration and at maintaining personal contacts between the managers. Moreover, the client managers use this opportunity to see and talk personally to all nearshore team members and to give them some small presents. The entire visit usually takes 2 days.

- The vendor account manager for Client 3, whose home base is the vendor's office in Germany, visits the client at least monthly to talk to everybody who wants/needs a conversation (including top management, transition managers, service engineers, solution designers[2]). Through these visits, client people can discuss all emergent topics and issues regarding the entire outsourcing relationship with the account manager personally onsite.

- Client and vendor staff meet F2F within kickoff sessions which take place 4 to 5 times a year when larger projects are about to start. These meetings are usually held at the client site in

Germany. However, Client 3 tries to ensure that at least one kickoff meeting per year takes place at the vendor site in Belarus, as well. Depending on the particular project, these meetings are attended by the respective PMs from both sides, the responsible solution designer (Client 3), the respective technical team lead (Vendor 3), and certain database developers (Vendor 3). If the meeting takes place at the client site in Germany, the responsible service engineer as well as some database developers from the client side will participate in the meeting, too. Onsite visits for kickoff meetings usually last between 1 and 2 weeks. Besides discussing the upcoming project, relationship building is emphasized during these visits. Team members from both sides maintain their relationships not only by working together onsite but also through joint dinners and weekend getaways. Client 3 tries to ensure that at least one joint dinner and sometimes a weekend outing is organized.

- Eventually, the client aims at introducing every new vendor team member to the client team in Germany shortly after s/he has joined the project, which, however, cannot be realized in every case due to cost reasons. During such introductory visits, which usually last for five days, the new vendor team member is given some basic trainings on technical and business knowledge. However, trainings are not the main purpose of these visits because new vendor team members are already trained intensely by their experienced senior colleagues at the vendor site in Belarus. Rather, such introductory meetings aim at getting to know all client team members in person with whom the new vendor employee will collaborate in the future.

Table 2 gives a cross-case summary about the extracted F2F patterns.

---

[2] The transition manager manages the project lifecycle for a certain project; the solution designer provides the vendor with a solution proposal for the business requirement; the service engineer takes over responsibility for the solution that had been developed by vendor staff.

Table 2. Cross-case summary

Case	F2F pattern	Top management V	Top management C	Account/vendor mgmt V	Account/vendor mgmt C	Project manager (PM) V	Project manager (PM) C	Staff[3] V	Staff[3] C	Vendor site	Alternating	Client site	When? (duration)	Why?
Rel. 1	Management meeting		X			X	X	(X)	(X)		X		4 p.a. (2-3 days)	• Review of last release • (X): Socializing (joint dinner)
	Kickoff meeting						X[4]	X	X			X	5-6 p.a. (1 week)	• Introduction and discussion of the next release and new development tasks • Module/Product trainings • Collocated working • Socializing (weekend outing)
	Client PM visit					X	X[4]	X		X			up to 10 p.a. (2-3 days)	• Knowledge transfer on demand • Collocated working • Socializing (joint dinner)
Rel. 2	Management visit	X	X			X[5]		(X)		X			1 p.a. (2-3 days)	• Information about/discussion of strategic/planning topics • (X): Socializing (small presents, joint dinner)
	Kickoff meeting						X	X	X			X	on demand (up to 5 days)	• Project discussions in case of larger or particularly complex projects • Socializing (joint dinner)
	Introductory visit						X	X	X			X	on demand (2x 2-3 weeks)	• Knowledge transfer • Creation of interpersonal bonds
	Client developers visit							X	X	X			2 p.a. (1-2 weeks)	• Collocated working • Socializing (joint dinner)
Rel.3	Management meeting	X	X	X				(X)		X			1-2 p.a. (2 days)	• Information about and discussion of strategic/planning topics • (X): Socializing (chatting with all nearshore team members, small presents)
	Account manager visit		X	X	X		X		X			X	12 p.a. (1 day)	• Discussion of emergent topics and issues
	Kickoff meeting					X	X	X[6]	X[6]		(X[7])	X	4-5 p.a. (1-2 weeks)	• Project discussions in case of larger or particularly complex projects • Socializing (joint dinner, weekend outings)
	Introductory visit						X	X	X			X	on demand (5 days)	• Creation of interpersonal bonds • Knowledge transfer

---

3 Staff includes all operational resources like developers, testers etc.
4 Also including product managers (managers who are responsible for the particular software module to be further developed).
5 Relationship 2 has no vendor-side PM; the resource manager is involved instead.
6 Always the technical team lead and some selected developers from the vendor side and the solution designer from the client site; if the meeting takes place at the client side, the service engineer and some selected developers (client side) participate, as well.
7 At least one of the 4-5 kickoff meetings per anno usually takes place at the vendor site.

6. EXEMPLARY ANALYSIS OF EFFECTS OF F2F PATTERNS

The previous descriptive analysis of the three case studies gave evidence about dedicated F2F strategies established by the parties involved. In the following, we present some exemplary insights into the *effects* of configuring a F2F strategy along the dimensions of *'Who'*, *'Where'*, *'When'*, and *'Why'*. In our future research, we will analyze all cases of the ongoing larger case study series along this scheme in order to come up with a more detailed understanding of F2F which can also directly inform practitioners who are shaping their outsourcing relationship management strategy.

According to the literature, meeting F2F generally helps to create inter-personal relationships and thus social capital across the client-vendor-boundary which in turn increases the quality of communication, collaboration, and knowledge transfer. The following diagram visualizes the different arguments drawn from the literature which are summarized below.

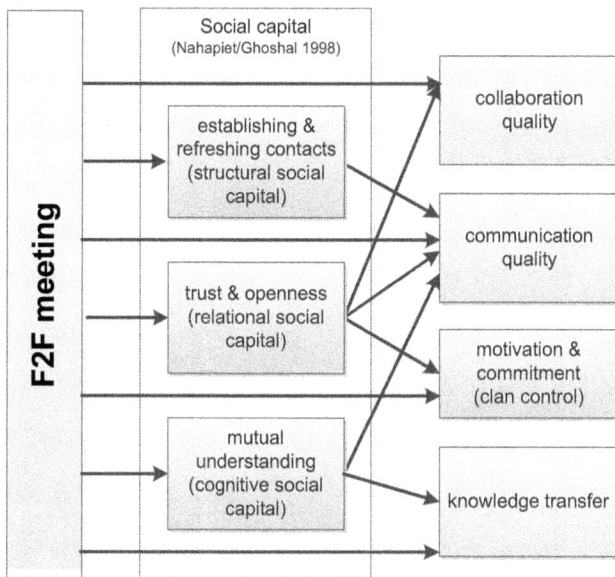

Figure 4: Effects of F2F meetings.

First, F2F has a direct positive impact on communication quality and collaboration quality since colocation during working together leads to more intense and richer communication [29]. However, this direct effect is only apparent during the F2F period and it appears primarily at the operational level (collaboration of software developers, testers etc.). The more sustainable effect of F2F on communication and collaboration quality happens via the creation of social capital [25]. If people from both sides know each other in person, they establish bonds and loose shyness to call the other person. Thus, F2F periods help to create interpersonal ties (structural dimension of social capital) and trust (relational dimension of social capital) which leads people to be more open and to interact more informal in subsequent (remote) communication [14, 37]. Further, F2F also fosters the mutual understanding between client and vendor (cognitive dimension of social capital) which in turn drives communication quality and knowledge transfer [13, 34]. Again, knowledge transfer is also directly affected during F2F phases since the transfer of tacit knowledge is easier F2F than via remote communication or by

codification. Finally, F2F contact helps to establish modes of informal control: social bonding and relationship building create 'clans' among vendor and client staff which leads to the vendor staff being more motivated and committed to deliver high quality services [19]. This happens again directly and via the creation of social capital [7].

This paper contributes to the literature by suggesting to look at F2F contact in a more differentiated way. The effects of F2F are contingent on the different possible configurations of F2F patterns along the four 'W's of F2F introduced in this paper. In the following, we turn our focus around and provide some exemplary analysis regarding the question which F2F effects result from which F2F configuration. Table 3 summarizes these results and provides code examples for the different reasonings.

The exemplary results show that explicitly looking at the four dimensions of F2F is important to understand the impact of F2F meetings and to draw prescriptive suggestions for practitioners. For instance, the creation of mutual understanding mainly depends on the *'Where'* and *'Who'* of F2F. Obviously, it is important for vendor staff to get an impression of how work is done on the client side and of how end-users are actually using the software to be (further) developed etc.; indeed, this kind of mutual understanding is primarily created through F2F on the client side, involving vendor staff (and not only PMs as multipliers or boundary spanners). In turn, we can argue that the client visiting the vendor (which is usually cheaper) for providing trainings to the vendor staff might not be sufficient, particularly for more complex or innovative projects where a high level of mutual understanding and shared knowledge is needed [38]. As another example, the *'When'* of F2F seems to be important for maintaining the very basic social infrastructure of collaboration: The structural dimension of social capital depends on not only having met once; instead, personal contacts need to be refreshed by F2F meetings; here, the *'Where'* aspect is less relevant but the question of *'When'* (or: *'How often'*) needs to be taken into account. As a last example, the importance of collocated working during critical phases of more complex projects is prevalent. This direct effect of F2F on communication quality is straightforward but often too little taken into account by outsourcing managers, who overvalue the costs of temporary colocation compared to project success/failure. In this case, the *'Where'* is less important while the *'Who'* and *'When'* are critical questions to be considered.

Table 3. Case-based mapping of F2F effects and F2F configurations

F2F effect	Who? Vendor side	Who? Client side	Where?	When?	Why?	Reasoning	Exemplary quotes
Direct effect of F2F on communication quality (*during* F2F phase)	PM, staff	PM, staff	On any side	Particularly in complex or difficult phases of the project	Collocated working	F2F communication is richer and being collocated creates more attention among communication partners.	*"When we are working onsite in Germany and have a question, we can directly ask any of our client colleagues and get an answer immediately. When we work from Belarus, we have sometimes to wait for some hours until our email is replied or until the client colleague is available in Skype"* (developer, Vendor 3). *"In Germany, I discussed all ideas with my client colleagues F2F. That was much more effective than via Skype, also because you can use a whiteboard to draw something."* (developer, Vendor 3).
Indirect *sustainable*[8] effect on communication quality via **structural** social capital	Staff	Staff	Alternating on both sides (for easier involvement of all team members)	1-2 p.a. and for new team members	Any	F2F meetings are important to *establish* interpersonal contacts and to get to know the remote colleagues as well as to *refresh* existing contacts that have weakened over time; this drives communication quality.	*"[F2F contact] is very important to know who you are speaking to [...]. That's really important. [...] It intensifies communication"* (senior developer, Vendor 2) *It's necessary to know which characters are working together in such a team. [...] It's always amazing how things change after having met F2F for the first time. When I joined this project, I only had my daily conference calls with the remote colleagues in the first 4 weeks. But then, I travelled to Belarus. There, I had the chance to link voices to faces. Afterwards, daily conference calls were substantially different. It really was a quantum leap regarding how much better communication was after our first F2F contact"* (PM, Client 3). *"Onsite visits also help to keep contact with my client colleagues. It helps them to keep me better in mind. That's important"* (QA engineer, Vendor 1).
Indirect *sustainable*[8] effect on communication quality via **relational** social capital	All, but mainly PM and staff	All, but mainly PM and staff	Alternating on both sides (for easier involvement of all team members)	2-4 p.a.	Socializing, collocated working	F2F meetings, particularly off-work events such as joint dinners or outings, lead to trust and openness among team members, which in turn increase communication quality.	*"If you go out with the vendor colleagues to have a drink, likelihood to establish close contacts is much higher than having communication only by phone. Sometimes, I have great conversations with colleagues from Belarus about soccer etc. A pleasant side effect is that I can approach these guys confidentially anytime if I have a problem during my work and they will help me to sort it out [even if they wouldn't have to]"* (PM, Client 3). *"People need F2F contact for building trust"* (senior developer, Vendor 2). *"You develop something like a bond of trust to another person after you met personally. It's basically a different relation afterwards"* (PM Client 3) *"Confidence-building measures like team excursions help to reduce distance between the team members. After such events, people are more open to each other"* (executive, Client 1).

---

[8] Compared to the direct effect, the indirect effect is more sustainable because it lasts longer than the actual F2F phase.

F2F effect	Who?		Where?	When?	Why?	Reasoning	Exemplary quotes
	Vendor side	Client side					
Indirect *sustainable*[8] effect on communication quality via **cognitive** social capital	Staff	PM, staff	On client side	Initially and when launching new projects	Visits of client site, collocated working, project meetings	F2F meetings on the client side help vendor staff to create a mutual understanding (getting more back-ground information, understanding how remote colleagues work and how end-users actually use the software developed etc.).	*"After having met a client colleague personally, communication via Skype works better. Then, it's easier to understand each other because you might get an idea of what the other one thinks. [...] Also, misunderstandings are less common when you got to know someone in person before"* (senior developer, Vendor 2). *"People pick up more background information when communicating F2F"* (account manager, Vendor 3). *"I think our nearshore colleagues get a better understanding with regard to critical project phases when they are here in our office. It's basically about a better understanding of how critical a current project or task is"* (PM, Client 2). *"Once, we visited [Client 1's end-customer]. There, I saw for the first time how the system is really used within the production of automobiles. It was a great experience and very helpful. They showed us everything. From that point, I better understood the effect of my work respectively code. Since then, I better understand why it is important to implement something this or that way"* (developer, Vendor 1).
	Staff	Staff	On vendor side	Initially	Visits of vendor site	F2F meetings on the vendor side help the client staff to learn about the contribution and work practices of their vendor colleagues.	*"When our developers visit the vendor in Serbia and see the whole nearshore team, their respect for the vendor and their understanding increase. Already realizing the size of the nearshore team and how concentrated they work there contributes to a completely different understanding compared to only communicating by Skype or chat"* (executive, Client 2).
Direct effect of F2F on knowledge transfer	Staff	Staff	On any side	Initially and when launching new projects	Trainings	Onsite visits are commonly used to provide trainings for vendor staff. Besides general company presen-tations and introductions to the software systems the vendor staff works on, vendor team members are given an understanding of how the respective system is used by the actual end-users and they are in-tensely trained on, e.g., specific system modules/products, system architecture, or technical tools like compilers or application servers.	*"The last time I was in Germany, we participated in several product trainings given by the product managers. The client colleagues participated in these trainings, as well. I learned a lot of new things. This really helped me when working on my last task. Without these trainings it would have taken me longer to work on this requirement because the code was really complicated and I had never worked on this product before and therefore had no clue of how it works"* (developer, Vendor 1).

F2F effect	Who?		Where?	When?	Why?	Reasoning	Exemplary quotes
	Vendor side	Client side					
Direct effect of F2F on knowledge transfer (cont.)	Staff	Staff	On any side	Initially and occasionally in certain project phases	Collocated working	Knowledge transfer does not merely take place via dedicated trainings but also by client and vendor staff working side by side in the same office.	"[The client colleagues] don't only visit us to give trainings but also just do their regular work here at our office, sitting right next to us, so that we can directly ask them questions if we have any issues. That's actually knowledge transfer, as well. The German colleagues just answer our questions, completely independent from any trainings" (QA engineer, Vendor 1). "Shortly after I joined the team, I stayed for some days at the client's office and worked closely together with my German colleagues on the same tasks. For me personally, that was actually the most effective way to transfer knowledge between us" (PM, Vendor 1).
Indirect effect on collaboration quality via **relational** social capital	Staff	Staff	On any side	Regularly (2-3 p.a.)	Meetings, socializing, collocated working	The collaboration benefits from F2F meetings because trust and openness between client and vendor colleagues increase after they met in person and refreshed their contacts; however, this positive effect vanishes after some time, calling for regular F2F meetings.	"Personal meetings with our Swiss colleagues, though happening not very often, are very important in my opinion. Our relationship gets more trustful after such meetings, no matter if we visit them or if they come to Serbia. After such meetings, [...] conflicts do almost not exist anymore for some time because our relationship is very open, then. However, this condition doesn't persist too long. That's why I would like to have a F2F meeting every 4 months or so" (team lead, Vendor 2).
Direct effect of F2F on motivation & commitment (i.e., informal modes of control [18])	Staff	Staff, PM	On client side	Occasional	Any	Occasional trips to the client function as an incentive for vendor staff (though not openly promoted as such) and thus have a motivating effect (direct effect "F2F → motivation") which can be rooted in the desire (1) to visit another country (for various reasons) and/or (2) to meet the client colleagues in person.	"Colleagues working for other clients would like to join our team because of the opportunity to travel to Germany from time to time" (PM, Client 3). "Actually, it's very interesting for us to work with another country, another culture, to see or to communicate with people in Germany. Even if you have trips just from Monday to Friday not including the weekends, it's nevertheless a kind of motivation for our developers" (PM, Vendor 3). "Events like joint dinners or excursions are motivating with regard to further cooperation. [...] I'm more committed to [Client 1] because these events reflect the effort they put into our relationship" (QA engineer, Vendor 1).
	Staff	Top Mgmt.	On vendor side	Occasional	Any	Client visits to the vendor site are motivating for vendor staff because they show the client's commitment.	"Once, he [executive of Client 2] showed up with 17 beach towels. I mean, it's not about the beach towels but about the fact that he brought a very large suitcase all the way to us. That's nice. That's one of the things making us loving to work for them" (senior developer, Vendor 2).
Indirect effect of F2F on motivation and commitment via **relational** social capital	PM, Staff	PM	On any side	Occasional	Socializing	F2F contact during social events outside work increases trust and social bonds between people working together which in turn creates higher commitment among vendor staff.	"Activities outside work like having dinner together are absolutely useful. They give you the chance to get to know the client colleagues even better resulting in stronger personal bonds and more confidence. [...] People might do their work even better than they could if they really know and trust each other. I can only speak for myself but I have some client colleagues for whom I would stay some more hours at work if necessary" (PM, Vendor 3).

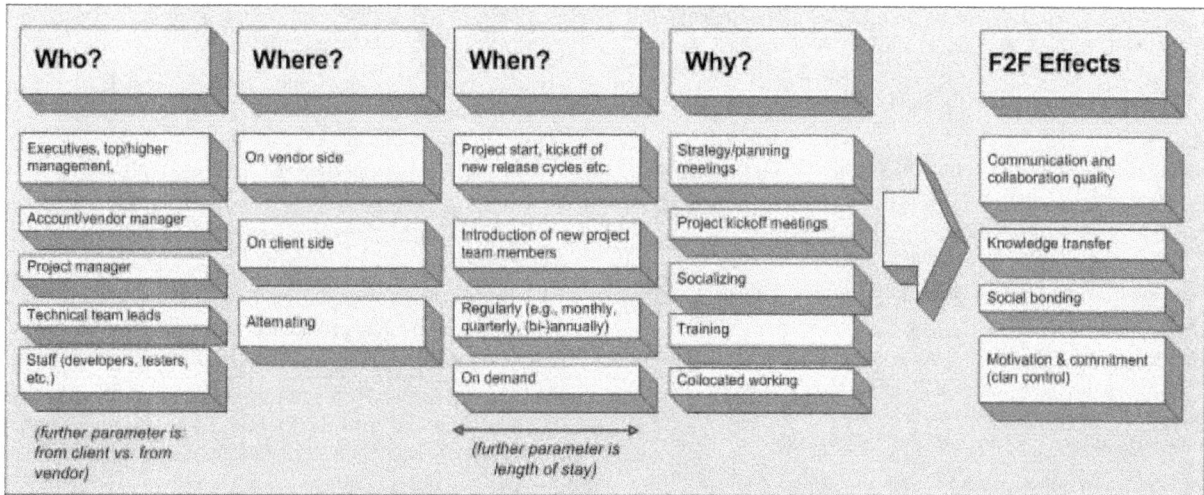

Figure 5: Building blocks of a F2F strategy along the four 'W's

7. DISCUSSION

As pointed out by the application of the four 'W's for describing F2F patterns and by the exemplary analysis of the relationship between F2F configuration and F2F outcomes, this lens shows to be promising for leading to a better understanding of F2F. In the following, we highlight potential implications for research and practitioners resulting from this approach.

7.1 Implications for Research

Our work informs research on outsourcing relationship management with a focus on F2F by providing a concept for a richer F2F conceptualization. In doing so, we are the first after Oshri et al. [26] who explicitly elaborate on F2F meetings as a management action in distributed settings. Moreover, we show that social capital, which has already been used quite frequently in the literature on outsourcing relationship management [e.g., 6, 22, 34], is also suitable for analyzing the particular effects of F2F meetings on outsourcing performance. We also add to research on the strong and increasing outsourcing trend of IT nearshoring [28, 39] which is still under-researched and not well understood, compared to traditional offshore phenomena [1]. Since F2F is one of the few components of outsourcing that significantly differ in nearshoring contexts compared to offshoring, our research can make a decisive contribution to IT nearshoring research.

7.2 Implications for Practice

Although being only a first descriptive study, our results hint at interesting and helpful conclusions for practitioners. The detailed analysis of the F2F patterns observed allows an explicit and combined consideration of the 'Who', 'Where', 'When', and 'Why' of F2F. Depending on the specific requirements and characteristics of the project, the partners have to compose a F2F strategy that supports the collaboration as good as possible. As the analyses showed, different configurations have different effects. For example, there are differences in motivational side effects depending on where the F2F meeting takes place and who is involved. Thus, an important implication of our work is to sensitize practitioners for the differential impact of such configurational F2F options. Figure 5 provides the building bricks of a 'construction kit' for configuring F2F.

8. CONCLUSION

This research provides rich insights on the role of F2F contact in nearshoring relationships. As our main contribution, we highlight and apply the dimensions of 'Who', 'Where', 'When', and 'Why' for describing F2F patterns in a more precise and structured manner than previous works have done. In our case analysis, we show that each of these dimensions has its own explanatory value and that research on relationship management should look at the configurations of F2F meetings along these four dimensions. In our further research, we will proceed with further cases to do a contingency analysis showing under which circumstances which configuration of a F2F strategy (i.e., combinations of building blocks given in Figure 5) is most effective. Future research should also analyze F2F strategies by using a transaction cost lens to take the downside of F2F (i.e., cost) into account and to help answering the question how much investment in F2F contact is efficient with regard to the overall relationship performance. Overall, this will support practitioners in shaping both effective and efficient F2F strategies for their outsourcing arrangements.

9. REFERENCES

[1] Abbott, P.Y. and Jones, M.R. 2012. Everywhere and nowhere: nearshore software development in the context of globalisation. European Journal of Information Systems 21, 5, 529-551.

[2] Carmel, E. 1999. Global Software Teams: Collaborating Across Borders and Time Zones. Prentice Hall, Upper Saddle River, NJ.

[3] Carmel, E. and Nicholson, B. 2005. Small firms and offshore software outsourcing: high transaction costs and their mitigation. Journal of Global Information Management 13, 3, 33-54.

[4] Carmel, E. 2006. Building your information systems from the other side of the world: how Infosys manages time zone differences. MIS Quarterly Executive 5, 1, 43-53.

[5] Carmel, E. and Abbott, P. 2007. Why 'nearshore' means that distance matters. Communications of the ACM 50, 10, 40-46.

[6] Chou, T.-C., Chen, J.-R., and Pan, S.L. 2006. The impacts of social capital on information technology decisions: a case study of a Taiwanese high-tech firm. International Journal of Information Management 26, 3, 249-256.

[7] Chua, C.E.H., Lim, W.-K., Soh, C., and Sia, S.K. 2012. Enacting clan control in complex IT projects: a social capital perspective. MIS Quarterly 36, 2, 577–600.

[8] Corbin, J. and Strauss, A. 2008. Basics of Qualitative Research: Techniques and Procedures for Developing Grounded Theory. 3rd ed., Sage Publications, Thousand Oaks, CA.

[9] Cummings, J.N., Espinosa, J.A., and Pickering, C.K. 2009. Crossing spatial and temporal boundaries in globally distributed projects: a relational model of coordination delay. Information Systems Research 20, 3, 420-439.

[10] Dibbern, J., Winkler, J., and Heinzl, A. 2008. Explaining variations in client extra costs between software projects offshored to India. MIS Quarterly 32, 2, 333-366.

[11] Fiol, C.M. and O'Connor, E.J. 2005. Identification in face-to-face, hybrid, and pure virtual teams: untangling the contradictions. Organization Science 16, 1, 19-32.

[12] Furst, S.A., Reeves, M., Rosen, B., and Blackburn, R.S. 2004. Managing the life cycle of virtual teams. Academy ot Management Executive 18, 2, 6-20.

[13] Ghosh, B. and Scott, J.E. 2009. Relational alignment in offshore IS outsourcing. MIS Quarterly Executive 8, 1, 19-29.

[14] Govindarajan, V. and Gupta, A.K. 2001. Building an effective global business team. MIT Sloan Management Review 42, 2, 63-71.

[15] Heeks, R., Krishna, S., Nicholson, B., and Sahay, S. 2001. Synching or sinking: global software outsourcing relationships. IEEE Software 18, 2, 54-60.

[16] Holmström Olsson, H., Conchuir, E.O., Agerfalk, P.J., and Fitzgerald, P. 2008. Two-stage offshoring: an investigation of the Irish bridge. MIS Quarterly 32, 2, 257-279.

[17] Kern, T. and Willcocks, L. 2000. Exploring information technology outsourcing relationships: theory and practice. Journal of Strategic Information Systems 9, 4, 321-350.

[18] Kirsch, L.J. 1997. Portfolios of control modes and IS project management. Information Systems Research 8, 3, 215-239.

[19] Kirsch, L.J., Ko, D.-G., and Haney, M.H. 2010. Investigating the antecedents of team-based clan control: adding social capital as a predictor. Organization Science 21, 2, 469-489.

[20] Kotlarsky, J. and Oshri, I. 2005. Social ties, knowledge sharing and successful collaboration in globally distributed system development projects. European Journal of Information Systems 14, 1, 37-48.

[21] Krishna, S., Sahay, S., and Walsham, G. 2004. Managing cross-cultural issues in global software outsourcing. Communications of the ACM 47, 4, 62-66.

[22] Levina, N. and Vaast, E. 2008. Innovating or doing as told? Status differences and overlapping boundaries in offshore collaboration. MIS Quarterly 32, 2, 307-332.

[23] Markov, R., Wiener, M., and Amberg, M. 2011. Distance advantages in IS nearshoring: do they matter? In Proceedings of the 16th Americas Conference on Information Systems (Detroit, MI, 2011). Paper 329.

[24] Maznevski, M.L. and Chudoba, K.M. 2000. Bridging space over time: global virtual team dynamics and effectiveness. Organization Science 11, 5, 473-492.

[25] Nahapiet, J. and Ghoshal, S. 1998. Social, capital, intellectual capital and the organizational advantage. Academy of Management Review 23, 2, 242-266.

[26] Oshri, I., Kotlarsky, J., and Willcocks, L.P. 2007. Global software development: exploring socialization and face-to-face meetings in distributed strategic projects. Journal of Strategic Information Systems 16, 1, 25-49.

[27] Oshri, I., Kotlarsky, J., and Willcocks, L. 2008. Missing links: Building critical social ties for global collaborative teamwork. Communications of the ACM 51, 4, 76-81.

[28] Oshri, I., Kotlarsky, J., Rottman, J.W., and Willcocks, L. 2009. Global sourcing: recent trends and issues. Information Technology & People 22, 3, 192-200.

[29] Rai, A., Maruping, L.M., and Venkatesh, V. 2009. Offshore information systems project success: the role of social embeddedness and cultural characteristics. MIS Quarterly 33, 3, 617-642.

[30] Ranganathan, C. and Balaji, S. 2007. Critical capabilities for offshore outsourcing of information systems. MIS Quarterly Executive 6, 3, 147-164.

[31] Rao, M.T. 2004. Key issues for global IT sourcing: country and individual factors. Information Systems Management 21, 3, 16-21.

[32] Rottman, J. and Lacity, M. 2006. Offshoring IT work: 29 practices. In Global Sourcing of Business & IT Services, L.P. Willcocks and M.C. Lacity, Eds. Palgrave Macmillan, Basingstoke, UK and New York, NY, 223-255.

[33] Rottman, J.W. and Lacity, M.C. 2004. Twenty practices for offshore sourcing. MIS Quarterly Executive 3, 3, 117-130.

[34] Rottman, J.W. 2008. Successful knowledge transfer within offshore supplier networks: a case study exploring social capital in strategic alliances. Journal of Information Technology 23, 1, 31-43.

[35] Rottman, J.W. and Lacity, M.C. 2008. A US client's learning from outsourcing IT work offshore. Information Systems Frontiers 10, 2, 259-275.

[36] Sarker, S. and Sarker, S. 2009. Exploring agility in distributed information systems development teams: an interpretive study in an offshoring context. Information Systems Research 20, 3, 440-461.

[37] Scott, J.E. 2000. Facilitating interorganizational learning with information technology. Journal of Management Information Systems 17, 2, 81-113.

[38] Tiwana, A. 2004. Beyond the black box: knowledge overlaps in software outsourcing. IEEE Software 21, 5, 51-58.

[39] Willcocks, L.P. and Lacity, M. 2009. The Practice of Outsourcing: From ITO to BPO and Offshoring. Palgrave Macmillan, London, UK.

[40] Yin, R.K. 2009. Case Study Research: Design and Methods. 4th ed., Sage Publications, Thousand Oaks, CA.

Author Index

www.ingramcontent.com/pod-product-compliance
Lightning Source LLC
Chambersburg PA
CBHW081524220326
41598CB00036B/6322

* 9 7 8 1 4 5 0 3 3 0 8 0 0 *